My Very Best!

LEGENDARY CONVERSATIONS

with a Texas Disc Jockey

Tracy in 1988 at KNEL Radio.

By Tracy Pitcox

Legendary Conversations
By Tracy Pitcox

Copyright © 2007 By Tracy Pitcox

ISBN #978-1-4276-1799-6

FIRST EDITION

Heart of Texas Country
1701 South Bridge Street
Brady, Texas 76825
(325) 597-1895
www.heartoftexascountry.com

Branch Smith Printing
120 St. Louis
P.O. Box 1868
Fort Worth, Texas 76104
www.branchsmithprinting.com

Graphics, Design and Layout
Sandra Beddow, Robin Berryman Perez, Christy Blackwell,
Sharon Jackson & Charla Pitcox

For The Country Music Fan —
Thanks For Making It Possilble
For All of Us

LEGENDARY CONVERSATIONS
"The Beginning"

"Legendary Conversations" is a special compilation of interviews that I conducted throughout the last twenty years while working at KNEL radio in Brady, Texas.

My friend Billy Jackson had advised me to keep all of the interviews that I conducted with those artists that made Country Music great. He has encouraged me to put out a book for over ten years. These interviews have all been stored at the office and I decided it was time to go through them and transcribe some of my favorite ones.

I featured at least one artist each week on KNEL's Hillbilly Hits Radio Show for the first ten or fifteen years of the show. I was fortunate enough to interview some of the greatest entertainers in the Country Music business from George Jones and Tammy Wynette to Kitty Wells and Willie Nelson. It was an honor to visit with these incredible artists and learn more about their incredible careers. At the same time, I always enjoyed tracking down those artists who never achieved the major careers in the business. Their impact may not have been as large, but their contribution to the Country Music business was important. We have overlooked so many of these great artists.

I decided to compile these interviews in a book format just as they were heard live on the air. The artists and music industry individuals tell their story to you just as they did to my radio audience.

I tried to include as many dates that I could. I tagged the majority of the interviews with the date that we conducted them, but there were some that I missed along the way. We have done our very best to be as accurate as possible. I ask for early forgiveness if there is any incorrect information contained in the book. If there is, it is just simply from my mistake or the mistake of the artist being interviewed.

On the majority of the interviews, we have tried to keep them as close to the actual conversation as possible. There will be some speech flaws and problems with "proper English" from time to time, but remember we are all from the Country. We take great pride in that and also ask for your understanding while reading this book. When Loretta says "Ain't", don't get offended!

While choosing which interviews I would include, I listened to hundreds and hundreds of hours of old tapes from up to twenty years ago. Many of these artists have guested on the radio show on numerous occasions. They promoted their careers, latest recordings and even show dates while remembering the history of this business. I have tried to provide a good mixture of interviews just as they happened generally live on the air. We even added a couple on "new" artists including Garth Brooks, Mark Chestnut and Alan Jackson at the beginning of their careers.

Some of the interviews included in "Legendary Conversations" are more indepth than others. Many artists were very open and some did not want to discuss certain aspects of their life. As I have gotten to know many of these entertainers, I have learned what to discuss and what not to bring up. An artist is just like you and I, they have their good times and their bad times.

In the future, I plan to incorporate these interviews and the many others that I have been fortunate to conduct into another book about the industry itself. So many of these great acts are no longer with us and as time goes by we will lose many others. I am hoping that this book will help to promote not only their careers, but to serve as a bit of a history lesson for someone else at some other time in the future.

Since 1986, I have made a living from Country Music. The business has allowed me to enjoy a comfortable life in a small town in Central Texas. I have really enjoyed learning more in radio, music publishing, touring, managing entertainers, talent booking and promoting and now even in the recording end of the business through Heart of Texas Records. I have also learned that you do not need to live in Nashville or Austin to survive in the Country Music industry. I have visited many other states and even toured Ireland for ten days with Leona Williams. It has been a wonderful life and career.

My parents, Cecil and Evelyn Pitcox have been a very big part of my career. They took me to Nashville for the very first time. Dad even went backstage at the Opry with me and was a part of many of these interviews. Mom drove me to KNEL every evening at 7:00 PM and then picked me up at 10:00 PM because I was too young to drive when I started working at the radio station.

My high school friend Randall King actually talked Steve and Ellen Everett into hiring me back in 1986. Darrell Cowen was already working at the station at that time and was very instrumental in helping to establish the Hillbilly Hits radio show through radio station music director Josh Holstead.

I want to send a special thanks to Lynn and Luci Farris, the owners of KNEL radio, for allowing me to achieve what I have in the last several years. They have allowed me to pursue many different other interests while always maintaining my first love-KNEL. It has been a pleasure working for both of them since 1995.

Donna Jones has been very valuable to the "Legendary Conversations" project. She has transcribed all of the interviews for the book and did a great job. Donna even told me that she knew more about Country Music after transcribing these tapes than she ever cared to know! Michelle Young has been associated with KNEL for over ten years now and has helped to keep the commercials on the air so that we all get paid.

I would like to also remember one special lady, Snooks Black. Snooks worked with us at KNEL for over twenty years. At one time many years ago, I was trying to make a decision about leaving Brady and taking another radio station job offer. I talked to her about it and she gave me some great advice. She told me that I could be a "little fish in a big pond or a big fish in a little pond" and I had to make up my own mind. I am glad that I stayed. She was a very wise lady and we all still miss her.

There have been so many other employees at KNEL throughout the years and I feel that we have all learned something and grew together. Just putting up with me has been growth to some of them!

My darling wife Charla has been the greatest inspiration of my life. She has put up with so much during the last few years. On many occasions, I seem to devote more time and energy to the business when I should be spending more time with her. I can never thank her enough for what she means to my life.

Justin Trevino has helped me achieve so many of my goals in Country Music. His expert production ability and enormous talent has helped to make Heart of Texas

Records one of the most successful independent labels in Texas. He is one of the greatest vocalists in this business.

Branch Smith Publishing has done a great job putting it all together for us. I know absolutely nothing about the book business and excluding a few cookbooks, this is my first major book project. The Branch Smith publishing staff was incredible from the layout and design to completion and delivery.

We chose pictures from thousands and thousands in our collection at the Heart of Texas Country Music Museum. It would be impossible to list all of the photographers for the snapshots. We appreciate those individuals that contributed photos to this book. I finally narrowed it down to two hundred of my favorite photos before finding out that I had to eliminate half of those. I also added a few letters and notes from the past that you might find of interest.

I have a special appreciation to the many artists that are included in the project. They each gave up some of their time so they could be a part of the radio show and this book. There are many others that should have been included in this book. We simply ran out of room. Maybe if this one does well, we will consider doing a "Legendary Conversations" Volume II!

And most importantly, I would like to thank those many listeners and supporters of Traditional Country Music for keeping this industry thriving. Through rock and roll, the Nashville Sound, New Country and Country Rock, our form of music is still popular today because of those individuals who have kept the true form of Country Music alive and vibrant.

"Legendary Conversations" has been a year long gathering, editing and printing project. With each interview and chapter, I learned something new while revisiting these conversations. It is my hope that you will learn something as well about these artists and enjoy the history lesson that they each contribute to the book.

I will simply close this book the same way that I end the radio program.

May The Good Lord Bless And Keep You Until We Meet Again,

Tracy Pitcox
www.heartoftexascountry.com

TABLE OF CONTENTS

THE INTERVIEWS

Continued on next page

TABLE OF CONTENTS
Continued

FOREWORD

I have done lots of interviews through the years and I feel most comfortable talking to Tracy. He knows the right questions to ask and I feel that it is because he knows Real Country Music.

Tracy understands where the Heart of a Country Song comes from so he gets right to the entertainers soft spots and pulls out their true feelings. He gets a little more out of us than most people. Read "Legendary Conversations" and you will know what I mean. Tracy Pitcox, there is no doubt that you are the best.

I Love You,

Leona Williams

ACKNOWLEDGEMENTS

I am indebted to many people for allowing me to have a career in the Country Music industry. It is impossible to thank everyone, and I will apologize in advance for leaving anyone out. It was certainly not done intentionally. I wanted to recognize the following people for their special contributions:

Wylie Alexander, C.S. & Liz Anderson, Bill Anderson, Patti Allen, Ernie Ashworth, Donna Adams, Lonnie Atkinson, Grady & Joan Baker, Moe Bandy, James & Drucilla Banner, David & Pat Barbour, Donald Barley, Terry Beene, Kelsey & Frannie Behrens, Joe Bielinski, Grace Blackwell, Bill Bleckley, Ann Bolton, Tony Booth, Jerry & Maxine Bradford, George & Betty Brandenberger, David & Quita Bratton, Peggy Breshers, Boley & Ginger Brodnax, Denny & Sheila Brown, Donna Brown, Monroe & Valerie Buntyn, Frenchie Burke, Leta Mae Burton, Johnny & Lynda Bush, Hal Bynum, David Byrd, Tom Canfield, Bob Cannella, Henson Cargill, Leta Casey, Reggie & Ann Cason, R. W. & Ora Nell Cavin, Morgan Choat, Mildred Coker, Bob & Jeanette Conn, Wilma Lee Cooper, Carol Lee Cooper, Frank & Betty Corrollino, Darrell Cowen, Homer Dale Cox, Jerry & Cheryl Crabtree, Billy & Nan Crouch, Allison Crowson, Raymon & Bessie Curren, Betty Daugherty, Sonny Davenport, Bill Davenport, Clarence & Lydia Davis, Skeeter Davis, Al & Carol Dean, Cordell Dean, Billy Deaton, Glenace Denton, Jimmy & Mona Dickens, Amber Digby, Rosie Doss, Tony & Mim Douglas, Curtis & Sherry Doster, Shirley Dotson, Roy Drusky, Johnny & Connie Duncan, Dottsy Dwyer, Gail Dykes, Jimmy & Jenny Eaves, Bob & Connie Edmiston, George Edmondson, Don & Shirley Evers, Rua Ewing, Thomas & Frances Fain, Lynn & Luci Farris, Donna Fargo, Jimmie & Frances Fletcher, Bobby Flores, Joe & Pat Fortenberry, Tillman Franks, J.V. Friar, Clarence Friar, Marsha Garcia, Charles & Barbara Garner, Sammy & Raynette Geistweidt, Larry & Ila Geyer, Doyla & Mary Gilbert, Johnny Gimble, Roy & Laverne Goff, Adeline Goldman, Kinnan & Jacqueline Goleman, Norine Gotcher, Bob Grady, Claude Gray, Reverend C.L. Grimes, Bill & Jan Hagara, Chuck & Rosie Hamilton, J.E. & Shirley Hargrove, Smokey & Melba Harris, Violet Harris, Freddie Hart, Ima Harvison, Mrs. Jimmy Heap, Neva Ray Hector, Jerell & Peggy Hemphill, Tammy & Doug Hemphill, Martha Hemphill, Rick Henson, R.B. & Alice Herzog, Johnnie High, Rhome & Ginger Hill, Goldie Hill, Jason, Cindy & Makenzie Hines, Mirian Hinds, Bobby & Ann Hinds, Myrtle Holland, Ronnie & Kay Holloway, Cathy Holloway, Josh Holstead, Jake & Sheila Hooker, Ann Horne, Juanita Horton, Dan & Bea Houck, Jan Howard, Ron Huckaby, Doug & Rhonda Hull, Lois Hulsey, Bette Hunger, Vivian Hurd, Cornell & Debra Hurd, Ferlin Husky, Billy & Peggy Jackson, Margie Jackson, Sharon Jackson, Stonewall & Juanita Jackson, Wanda Jackson, Jake & Pud Jacobson, Goldie Jacobson, Norma Jean, Chuck & Pat Jennings, Peggy Johanson, Leah Johnson, Edward & Barbara Jones, Grandpa & Ramona Jones, George & Nancy Jones, Melba Jones, Rachel Jones, Ramona Kelso, Buford & Betty Kensing, Robert & Doris Kensing, Tommy & Francis Kent, Paul & Betty Keylich, John & Monki Kieffer, Merle & Judy Kilgore, Eddie Kilroy, Dave Kirby, Bill & Jan Kirkman, Marie Kiser, Delbert Kleen, Kevin & Sharon Klein, Danny Knowles, Elnora Koerner, Benny & Cordelia Kothmann, Joyce Lackey, Dave & Pam Lamm, Mabel Ruth Land, Buford & Velma

Lawrence, Cathy Lee, J.W. & Lou Lee, Mark & Leann Lee, Les Leverett, Bobby & Pat Lewis, Butch & Martha Liefeste, Warren Lightsey, Mary Lincoln, Johnnie Linn, Big Bill & Lila Lister, Shane, Tricia & Makaela Lively, A.J. Lockett, Jim & Connie Locklear, Ronnie Locklear, Margaret Locklear, Hank & Adam Locklin, Jim Loessberg, Charlie Louvin, Loretta Lynn, Al & Bobbye Machen, Bill & Cindy Mack, Hazel Maner, L.H. & Mary Manning, Barbara Martin, Lola Mask, Ronnie Mason, Billy Mata, Johnny & Frankie McGee, Darrell & Mona McCall, Jon McConal, David McCormick, Bernice McLaughlin, Elmer & Joanna McFadden, James Mensch, Zella Metzger, Betty Meyer, Frankie & Ann Miller, Matt & Murri Mills, Harry & Sue Mitchell, Pete & Paula Mitchell, John Morthland, Casey Monahan, Chester & Stella Moore, Johnny & Susie Moore, Scooter Morris, Oleta Moseley, Verelda Nelson, Joe Paul & Carolyn Nichols, Willie & Julie Nietz, Art & Opal Norton, Wanda Oglesby, James O'Gwynn, Jo-Anne Osbourn, Elgin & Ann Ott, Dicky Overby, Benton & Barbara Owens, Bonnie Owens, Robert & Graylene Owens, Carl & Bunny Palmer, Pauline Parker, Dolly Parton, Joe Nick Patoski, Elisabeth Peel, Virginia Peiser, Reva & Darrell Perkins, Sharon Pickett, Tony Pickens, Ray Pillow, Cecil & Evelyn Pitcox, Geraldean (Granny) Pitcox, Shane Pitcox, Dorman & Dixie Pitcox, Junior Pitcox, Alvin Pitcox, Henry & Dora Pitcox, Peggy Poovey, Curtis & Pat Potter, Charlene & Lois Powell, Norman & Marian Probst, Ronnie & GloryAnne Prophet, John Pronk, Jeanne Pruett, Ronnie Pugh, Leon Rausch, Elmer & Barbara Ray, Joe & Marcia Rebrovich, Del Reeves, Joy Reeves, Bobby G. Rice, Randy & Manuelita Richards, Don & Bonnie Ricketson, Jeannie C. Riley, Fred & Jackie Rinehart, Shirley Rinehart, Alton & Marilyn Roberts, Dorothy Roberts, Wiley & Virginia Robinson, Johnny Rodriguez, Bobby & Maudie Rountree, Ben & Angie Rubio, Mike Rutledge, Beth Schaffer, Jimmy, Loma and Steve Schooley, Glennetta Sanderson, Johnny & Cathy Sawyer, Clara Lou Sawyer, Bill Schneider, Larry & Gail Scott, Ray Sczepanik, Jeannie Seely, Marguerite Shackelford, Jean Shepard, Dottie Simpson, Tom Sims, Cal & Darlene Smith, Carl Smith, Ivell Smith, Morrison & Mary Smith, Sammi Smith, Terry Smith, Tommie Ritter Smith, Tumbleweed Smith, Weldon & Lindell Smith, Mollie Smith, Hank Snow, Beth Snowden, Kathy Snowden, Larry Sonka, Scott Spiller, Jay & Mary Spurlin, Oscar & Nora Stephenson, Carol Stevens, Logan & Gay Stevens, Jamie Stevens, Jim Stinson, Glendon & Bobbie Stokes, Eddie Stubbs, J.C. & Loma Surber, Reba Sutton, Stella Swenson, Rick & Melanie Tacker, Billy Talley, Jean Tally, Weldon & Nelda Talley, Chester (Papaw) and Dorothy (Maw) Tally, Carl & Janice Tally, Dale & Sherri Tally, Jean Tally, Jim Tarpley, Amanda Teague, Ewell Ray & Olee Teague, Leroy & Karen Tengwall, Alton & Gloria Thomasson, Hank & Ann Thompson, B.J. Thompson, Mel Tillis, John & Terri Tittle, Jym Tittle, Floyd Tillman, Shirley Todd, S.P. & Elaine Tomlinson, Frank & Carolyn Torres, Angelita & Lydia Torrez, Justin & Sissy Trevino, Erlene Tubb, Ernest Tubb Jr., Dean Tubb, Justin Tubb, Leon & Shirlene Tucker, Joel Turk, B.R. (Bert) Turner, Larry Turner, Mary Lou Turner, Boyd & Maxine Turner, Jimmie & Marie Vaughn, Bea Virdell, Robbie Wade, Betty & Eddie Waite, Darren & Mikey Waite, John & Shawna Waite, Billy & Bettie Walker, Cindy Walker, Gene & Mattie Watson, Ben Watson, Helvie Wertheimer, Buck White, Jan Wiggington, Brady & Tracey Williams, Ron & Amy Williams, Leona Williams, Gene Williams, Lawton Williams, Charles & Betty Winchester, Beverly Salter Wise, Robbie Wittkowski, Johnny Wright & Kitty Wells, Bobby Wright, Jim & Gail Wright, Otis Wycoff, Tammy Wynette, Gerald & Jewell Yarbrough, Royce & Patsy Zbranek, Harvey Zesch and Leona Ziriax.

Tracy at the board.

2000

Tracy: Why did you decide to record "Cotton Eyed Joe"?

Al: It was a song that I heard as a kid. No one had ever heard of the song. It had died. I had a cowboy from South Texas come up to me and ask if I knew "Cotton Eyed Joe". I said I did but I had not sung it in years. We sat down and taught the guys in my band, note for note, how I remembered the "Cotton Eyed Joe". The next time the guy came to a show and requested it, we said we would play it and he said he needed to go find someone to dance with. He found someone and we started playing and he started kicking around on the dance floor and the poor girl walked off in the middle of the dance. Every time we had a show he would ask us to play the song and he would drag a poor girl out on the dance floor and every time she would walk off. That is the way it started. We went to Nashville to record an album and my band and I recorded it. We recorded note for note how we had it. There was a lady at a music store in Kingsville, Texas. She suggested we put the song on a single. She also said that we should put "Jalisco" on the back of it because that was A&I Universities fight song so I did it. That was how the song got on the single. I took the single to a radio station in San Antonio. Gaylon Christy was the DJ there. He took the single. It was not on the play list but he played it. It became an instant hit and people started calling the station and requesting it. It started to spread from there and now everyone does the "Cotton Eyed Joe."

Tracy: Were you the first person to have a hit on the "Cotton Eyed Joe"?

Al: Well I did my version in 1967 and my version is the one that is played at ballgames whenever they want to excite the crowd.

Tracy: How does that make you feel?

Al: My oldest son and I were at a Spurs game and they started playing it over the PA system and he turned to me and told me that he was 16 years old when the original record was made. He said that who would have ever thought that after 30 years, they would still be playing that song and we would be listening to it. He actually played the drums when the original was made.

Tracy: There is not a dance hall in Texas that does not feature the "Cotton Eyed Joe".

Al: I got an award in 1987 from the Jukebox Dealers in Texas for having the most programmed record in the history of the jukebox. Every band I go see that has a fiddle player will come up to me and tell me that they learned to play the fiddle listening to my records. It is just like the song says, "If you're gonna play in Texas, you gotta have a fiddle in the band". For many years, there were not that many fiddles available. In fact, after the rock and roll era, we had trouble getting any kind of Country Music musicians. Everyone wanted to play rock and roll. It is good to see some of the Traditional Country coming back around.

Al Dean is on the the true legends of Texas dance hall music. Al and his family have been entertaining dance crowds for decades. He made some incredible instrumental recordings-even beyond the "Cotton Eyed Joe." I have to admit to spinning many of his songs not only on the radio, but while I DJ various events all over the state. His version of "Jole Blon" is one of my favorites.

I always admired Al for featuring his family in his performances. His true love is not only in Traditional Country, but in the many great Texas Dance Halls. It is a unique part of the industry and Al Dean is a unique part of the great music created in those halls.

Ribbon Cutting at the Heart of Texas Country Music Museum with Dave Kirby, Ron Williams, Leona Williams, David McCormick, Tracy, Justin Trevino, Johnny Moore, Al Dean and Frankie Miller (Big Bill Lister & Darrell McCall not pictured).

Alan Jackson

FEBRUARY 1, 1990

Tracy: Alan, where did you grow up?

Alan: I grew up in a town called Newnan, Georgia. It is about forty miles south of Atlanta. I lived there all my life until I moved to Nashville about four and a half years ago.

Tracy: Were you influenced by any musicians while growing up in Georgia?

Alan: I did not have a record player or radio growing up. Most of the music I heard was at church. Some of my sisters listened to R & B. I say that it is an influence on me just because it is soulful music as close to Country. George Jones is a soul singer to me. Later on, as a teenager, I got into the Traditional Country Music.

Tracy: You wrote a song about your home life in your first album and mentioned your mother. She must have been very influential in your life.

Alan: She is a real good woman. Her and my father are really good people. My father and her did the very best to raise us how they could with what means they had. I started writing the song when I moved to Nashville. It took me off and on about two years to finish the song. I thought that it was too personal to make it to an album but everybody liked it and I was real proud.

Tracy: When did you decide to pursue Country Music as a career?

Alan: It had always been Country. We listened to Buck Owens on Hee Haw every Saturday night. On Sunday, they would turn on the Gospel Jubilee and that was my early Country Music influences. My daddy played some Country records. As I got older, he got a stereo that was so long it looked like a bookcase. He would buy some honky-tonk instrumental records. I would listen to that. I started singing with a girl, we did a duet together and that later led to a band. I really got involved in Country Music in the late 70's when I was in high school.

Tracy: I know that you started recording demos in Nashville?

Alan: I have been recording on and off for about four and a half years. I would do some demos for other songwriters as well as some of the songs I have written. I did not record on a major record label until last summer. I got my record label with Arista Records in Nashville. We cut the album last September.

Tracy: Arista Records is now really promoting their Country division.

Alan: Actually, it is a label out of New York. Whitney Houston is on their label. In Country, they just opened an office in Nashville last summer and I was the first person they signed as a Country act. They have about ten acts and Exile is one of them. They are doing real well with their first single. They have also signed, Asleep At The Wheel.

Tracy: Arista has just released your first major project and your second single.

Alan: It is called "Here In The Real World" which is the title of the album. It is number twenty-nine and it is going real good.

Tracy: How does it make you feel?

Alan: It is real exciting having the record that you work so hard for, for so many years. It is really exciting but it is like it has not really hit me yet. I am just waiting for that moment. Merle Haggard one time said that the most exciting time of his career was getting there and once he got to the top, it was not exciting as the fight and struggle getting there.

Tracy: You are receiving a lot of great publicity from the project.

Alan: The first single was released last September. It did pretty well. It broke the ice for me as a new artist and new label. It opened a lot of doors for us. We are real proud of that. We released "Here In The Real World" in December of 1989 and it has been on the charts for about four weeks.

Tracy: You have a very Traditional Country Music sound. Do you want to keep that form of music?

Alan: That is all I could ever do. A lot of the Traditional Country acts in the past have been the southern dialects. With that kind of accent, it is hard to do something else. My heart is in traditional and always will be.

Tracy: Do you know what the next single will be?

Alan: No but there have been a lot of predictions. "Ace of Hearts" and "Short Sweet Ride" are ones that could be a single. Then there is, "Chasing That Neon Rainbow". Between those three I think there will be another single. It is hard for me to pick. I like them all.

Tracy: You are now on your first full tour to promote "Here In The Real World."

Alan: We started in December and have done a few dates. In January, we took some time off and I did some writing. We started the end of January and now we are into February.

Tracy: Do you have any major goals for the future?

Alan: One of the things that I would love to do is a duet with George Jones. I wrote a song a few years ago and I knew it was a duet and George Jones needed to do it. A lot of people are trying to get me to give the song to another act but even if it is costing me money, I am going to wait until I have the opportunity to do it with him. Maybe in the next few years, I can talk George into doing it with me.

Tracy: Have you met him yet?

Alan: I have been around him in Nashville but I have never met him.

Tracy: Are you concentrating on your own show now or working with other acts?

Alan: It is a combination of both. Right now we are doing shows on our own. We do have a few openings on the books. We have some things coming up with Ricky Skaggs and Clint Black coming up. I just want to keep singing for all the folks for many years to come.

I first met Alan Jackson in San Angelo, Texas, at a club named Texas The Club. Alan was traveling in his first tour bus and was so excited about his career. I remember how nervous he seemed and how humble. Of course, at that time he only had the two singles out and no one could imagine what his career would do in the next few years. His show was made up of primarily cover songs and he did a great job on the tunes of his heroes George Jones, Merle Haggard and George Strait.

Alan was later working a concert in Abilene, Texas. My mother had become a huge fan and we attended the performance. After the show, Alan was very kind to visit with my mom and few other people that attended the performance. He had added a few more singles and an award or two, but he was still the very humble and appreciative gentleman that I met on that cold February night in 1990.

Alan is one of the superstars that has stayed close to his Traditional Country roots. At a time when many have sold out to the pop and rock crowd, Alan has stayed the course. He has to be commercial-even recording with Jimmy Buffet-but Alan loves real Country Music and I feel that he will not waver too far from the tradition.

Andy Williams

Tracy: It is a thrill to be talking to one of the great music legends, Andy Williams. How are you Andy?

Andy: I am doing just great and it is wonderful to be talking to you as well.

Tracy: I am glad to be visiting about your new album, "We Need A Little Christmas".

Andy: It seems so long ago because we make Christmas albums in July.

Tracy: Is it hard to sing Christmas songs in July?

Andy: We put a Christmas tree in the studio and decorate it because we are in there for weeks so that helps a little bit.

Tracy: I am sure that everyone knows about your close association with Christmas because of your Christmas specials.

Andy: Most people only do one Christmas album. I have actually done six.

Tracy: When was your first Christmas Album?

Andy: My first one was about 1962.

Tracy: Is this a new collection of Christmas songs? Have you ever repeated any of your Christmas songs?

Andy: I did on this one but I recorded them in a different way. I wanted this album to sound more contemporary than the albums I had done previously. Part of that was because of the material I was doing. "Up On The House Top" is a lightweight Christmas song and I wanted to do it in a jazz way. I wanted to do "Away in a Manger" with a contemporary background as well. We hired young rock and roll writers in their twenties. They have a different sound to them. Then we had what I call adults with the strings and the horns.

Tracy: Do you select you own material when you make an album?

Andy: Yes. I always work with the producer. You sit down with the arrangers and go over every detail. They even do demos so I can hear what it is going to be like. I hear the rhythm tracks and they put on string synthesizers and horn synthesizers. It does not sound to good but I get an idea of what it is going to sound like. We do it this way mainly because I live in Branson. I was doing two shows a day and this album had to be done while I was working. Because we do not have the studios or the musicians to do the strings they were put on in Chicago and Nashville. I can put my voice on here but we cannot do the orchestra here.

Tracy: It sounds like a complicated way to do things but the sound is wonderful.

Andy: I think more and more albums are being done in pieces. Sometimes you may want to do the rhythm in Los Angeles but you want to use the strings from the Chicago Symphony.

Tracy: You are now living and working in Branson at your own theater.

Andy: It is a beautiful theater. When I first came here in 1991, there were only Country artists performing. I wanted my theater to be a representative of what I was and what I was doing so I made it a modern art gallery type theater. It is actually very pretty.

Tracy: Have you been pleased with you theater attendance?

Andy: During Christmas time, we are always sold out during November and December. During the summer times, we are not sold out. The weather is always nice and there is so much to do especially by the lake. It is really hard the fill the seats for the matinee during the summer.

Tracy: What does the future hold for Andy Williams?

Andy: I like it so much in Branson and I have a terrific wife, wonderful dogs and a new house on the water. I love my theater, I am very happy here. I do not see changing this life I have right away.

Andy Williams has a very impressive theater in Branson, Missouri. On one of our bus tours to Branson, we attended Andy's show and the production was outstanding. It still amazed me that at that time in his career, Andy still dressed up in the full "fruit headgear" and danced away with the other members of his team.

Andy's secretary called me one day and asked if I would help promote his new Christmas album "We Need A Little More Christmas" in Texas. I told her that I would be happy to and would like to interview the music icon. It was scheduled for the following day and she gave me a number to call. Andy answered his own phone and was very cordial. It was actually the only time that I have interviewed him and ironically it was to promote a Christmas project.

Big Bill Lister

MAY 26, 1989

Tracy: Bill, you actually started your career at KNEL in Brady, Texas.

Big Bill: Yes, I sure did in about 1938. That was in the days when Grady Burns had the radio station up above Rosenburg Clothing store on the east side of the square. There were several of us Country pickers who had radio shows then. It was usually just the singer and a guitar or two at that time. As a matter of fact, Cowboy Slim Rinehart also had a radio show on KNEL.

Tracy: You soon moved to San Antonio and had a tremendous radio career.

Big Bill: I did work for KABC radio in San Antonio. That was my launching pad before moving to Nashville and working for WSM and Hank Williams. While in San Antonio, I even cut some transcriptions for the border radio stations. Those stations were so popular all over the country. The Carter Family, Cowboy Slim, Patsy Montana and several others were on those border stations.

Tracy: "There's A Tear In My Beer" has brought resurgence to your career. Can you tell us the story of how you got to Music City from Texas?

Big Bill: Back in January of 1951, I moved to Nashville, Tennessee, and got a record contract with the Capital Record Company. I was also working on the Grand Ole Opry and I had gone to work as an opening act for Hank Williams Road Show out of the Grand Ole Opry. We were just traveling all over the country back in those days just entertaining the people. In October of 1951, we were in off the road for a week and Hank was doing some recording for MGM. I had a record session coming up with Capital during that same week. I had been having pretty good luck with doing a beer drinking song on each session.

Tracy: How many songs did you record at one time?

Big Bill: Back in those days, a record session consisted of four sides. Capital always wanted me to do one of the tunes as a beer-drinking tune. At that particular time, I just didn't have one. Hank and the Drifting Cowboys were recording at Castle Studios there in Nashville. I wasn't recording with them, but I was down at the studio. I told Hank that I had a session tomorrow night and I sure need a beer drinking song and I didn't have one. He said "Don't worry about it Bill, I'll have one ready for you." The next morning, he came by and left a record for me so that I could learn the tune. Apparently, after they got through with their session that night, he just sat there in the studio with his guitar and cut this thing for me called "There's A Tear In My

Beer." He cut it with just him and his guitar, but fortunately it was cut just like it would have been a master record in that day and time.

Tracy: Were you the only person to hear it at that time?

Big Bill: Yes, I played the tune three or four times to learn the words and get the tune in my head. I went into the studio the next night and recorded it for Capital. In those days, we did not have tape like we do now. You had to record right on to a disc. I put that disc into a box with other records, pictures, and song sheets and completely forgot it. When I left Nashville and moved back to Texas, I moved that box and stuff with me and it was stored in my garage in San Antonio for a number of years. In about '72 or '73, we moved up near Boerne and I stored it in my attic. I had completely forgot about even having that record.

Tracy: When you found this acetate, was it still in good shape throughout those years?

Big Bill: Nearly everything in that box was ruined except that record. That just convinces me more than ever that it was supposed to happen and happen now. When we found the record, my life Lila was up in the attic looking for something and came across this box. She asked what is this stuff and I said I don't know. I told her it was probably just a bunch of old junk and to throw it away. She said let's look at it and see what it is. The minute that we started playing that record, I realized that it was the only copy of Hank Williams singing, "There's A Tear In My Beer." Nobody except the engineer where he had cut it and him and me had ever heard it before. I knew immediately that if possible, I wanted Hank's old fans to be able to hear that record.

Tracy: How did Hank Williams Jr. become involved?

Big Bill: Hank Williams Jr. and I have stayed in touch with each other down through the years. He was soon to come to San Antonio, to play a show down there. Before he left Nashville, he called me. I had been out of the entertainment business for some time and messed around and got in the gun engraving business. I had engraved a number of guns for Hank. My son has now taken over the engraving business and Hank wanted him to do some guns for him. He called me from Nashville to see if Weldon had time to do some guns for him. I told him to bring them on. I didn't tell him that I found this record, because I wanted to wait and surprise him. After the show the next day, Hank and his manager Merle Kilgore came to the house. I've known Merle since our days on the Louisiana Hayride. When he, Hank and Weldon got through with their gun business, I told Hank that I had something that I wanted to give him. He asked what it was. I said, "It is something that you daddy gave me a long time ago and I just want to pass it back." I told him that I thought that it belonged with him.

Tracy: What kind of a reaction did Hank Jr. have to the acetate?

Big Bill: He was just really shocked with what I had there. They took it back to Nashville and the quality was good enough that he could do the duet with his daddy. The record that I handed Hank Jr. was just Hank Williams and his guitar. They added the band music and Jr. sings with his daddy. I am so pleased with the way that it turned out and the kind of music that they put behind it with his daddy's voice. I am so proud of what both of them are doing in the Country Music world today. There is no way I can describe the way it feels to be the bridge between two artists of the magnitude of Hank Williams and Hank Williams Jr.

Tracy: After Hank died, you went on to work with several other artists.

Big Bill: I worked some shows with Ernest Tubb, Jimmy Dickens, Hank Snow and Del Wood. Del's recording of "Down Yonder" was the first instrumental cut in Nashville to sell a million copies. Stringbean and I took a show out on the road for a while and played all over the Southeast. Then I left there and went to the Big D Jamboree in Dallas. I worked up there for a good while, before moving back to San Antonio. I then started concentrating on my other business. I have always enjoyed still picking a little throughout the years.

Tracy: How do you want to be remembered?

Big Bill: Somebody that stood tall for Traditional Country Music.

In 1989, I was giving a speech for the Future Farmers of America organization in Poth, Texas. On the way down to the banquet that day, I drove through Boerne, Texas. I had been familiar with Big Bill Lister's career and the recent articles written about him for finding the acetate of "There's A Tear In My Beer." I stopped at a service station just off the interstate and looked in a Boerne phone book. I found a Lister in the book and sure enough it was Big Bill. I told him about being a disc jockey and gave him my location. He told me that I was bout six or seven blocks away from his house and asked me to come over. We had a great visit that day and it would be the start of a long friendship.

Bill was actually the first Country Music entertainer to join me live on the radio later that year. He had many fans in Brady, especially since his career began at KNEL. His sister was still living here and he became one of the staunches supporters of our work in promoting Traditional Country Music.

"There's A Tear In My Beer" did much for the rise of our kind of Country Music. It did even more for Big Bill Lister. He had just about given up on the business. That recording and hundreds of interviews (including the popular "Nashville Now" television show) would give Bill something that he needed-a greater desire to create more music. The business was also showing him a better appreciation for his contributions to the industry.

Big Bill even returned to the studio to record "Take Me Back" for our Heart of Texas Country CD project. He then recorded a fantastic history filled project titled "Big Bill Lister Remembers Hank Williams Through Story and Song." He told his story and the relationship that he enjoyed with Hank Williams. Hank Jr. and Jett even wrote the liner notes.

Big Bill is a very tall man in stature. In my book, he is even taller in real life and a true friend not only to Country Music but to me as well.

Bill Anderson

Tracy: It has been a while since you have had an album on a major label. Tell us about "No Fair Falling In Love".

Bill: Gary Nicholson and I wrote that song and about four days after we wrote it, a new group came to town called, Lonestar and they were suppose to record it. I thought that they were really good but I did not know they were going to be as big as they are. Their first album was terrific and that song was suppose to have been in their first album. When they did not put it out, Tracy Byrd was going to but it did not make his album so by george I said I would cut it and it would make my album!

Tracy: It is great to hear you on a new album. How did this project come about?

Bill: Jim Ed Norman, who is the president of Warner Brothers in Nashville, approached Steve Wariner about it when Steve was at Warner Brothers doing a duet with Anita Cochran that turned into such a big hit. Steve told Jim Ed Norman that we wanted to get into record production. Jim Ed admitted that he listened to the Grand Ole Opry a lot and he knew that I was pretty visible at the Opry. He asked Steve, if Steve and I were pretty good friends and Steve said we were. Jim Ed told him to produce an album of mine. It was totally out of the blue. It was a great pleasure to work with Steve on this project. He is such a talented guy. He brought so much to this project.

Tracy: You have been fortunate to get several of your songs cut by many of the new artists in Country Music. Steve Wariner is no exception. He cut, "Tips of my Fingers". A special version is included on this album.

Bill: The version on this album is the version that Steve and I decided to go after with all five of us who had hit records of the song, Roy Clark, Eddy Arnold, Jean Shepard, Steve Wariner and myself. I am particularly proud of this version. I would go to the store and buy Eddy Arnold's records when I was a kid. It is hard to believe that we are together on the same record. Jean Shepard was the first Grand Ole Opry star that I interviewed when I was a disc jockey.

Tracy: She may not admit to that.

Bill: She will admit it. I was one of those kid disc jockeys that did not know when to quit talking and I kept asking her questions until I nearly drove her crazy. Finally she said, "Well Bill, I don't want to take up anymore of your time". That is about the nicest anyone has ever cut me off.

Tracy: You are staying very busy with the Opry and touring.

Bill: I enjoy it. If I did not enjoy it I would quit doing it. As long as the good Lord blesses me with good health and with the fire, I will continue doing what I love to do. I consider myself lucky to be able to do it.

Tracy: Sara Evans recently recorded "Walk Out Backwards" on her first album.

Bill: Sara had a great record. I was glad that she included that song on the album. There are some things out there that I am excited about. Collin Raye has a song that Steve and I wrote called, "Make Sure You Got It All". We are really excited about it. Mark Wills has a song, "Wish You Were Here", that Skip Ewing, Debbie Moore and I wrote. There are several new artists that are recording my songs.

Tracy: Tell us about the song "Twenty Years".

Bill: That is a very special song to me. I have been back to my hometown. I was not gone for twenty years but there is some truth to the song, including my girlfriends name from high school. It is always great to write from experience.

Tracy: What are you plans for the future?

Bill: I am taking it one day at a time. I never thought or dreamed that I would be doing a new album. I sit back and take it one day at a time.

Bill Anderson has enjoyed several successful careers-disc jockey, songwriter, artist and businessman. Ironically, Bill has done them all very well. There are few songwriters that are still actively getting as many new songs cut as Bill. Just in the last few years, his songs have been recorded by Joe Nichols, Brad Paisley, Allison Krause, George Strait, Mark Wills and Steve Wariner.

Bill was working in Corsicana, Texas, at the Lefty Frizzell Festival. I took a group to see the show. His road manager asked me to pick Bill up at his hotel room and bring him to the venue. Frankie Miller and I drove over and got Bill and drove to the outdoor venue. We were in our little 15 passenger van and drove over to Bill's bus. As I was letting Bill out, he told me to just park beside his bus. Bill's bus was on one side and Connie Smith's bus was on the other side with our little van in the middle. I have a great picture of the three vehicles together!

Bill has one of the most organized fan clubs in the history of Country Music. His workers are some of the most loyal and dedicated fans. I got in the Bill Anderson Fan Club line at Fan Fair one year by mistake and by the time I got out, I had purchased a Bill Anderson T-shirt, three fans, two bandanas, a life size poster and a sponge in the shape of Bill. They love him and he returns that love right back to them as well

In this interview, Bill was promoting his latest album. It was his first project on a major label for several years. He was excited about it and so was I!

He was inducted into the Country Music Hall of Fame in 2001. It was a well deserved honor for a true Hall of Famer.

FEBRUARY 1989

This portion of "Legendary Conversations" is a little different than the other interview segments. This was taken on my first radio appearance with Country Music Disc Jockey Hall of Famer Bill Mack at the WBAP studios in Ft. Worth. I was a senior at Brady High School and we were in Ft. Worth for the Fort Worth Livestock Show with a large group of Brady FFA Members in February of 1989. I think there were four or five of us in each room and one night after we got back to the hotel, I decided to call Bill Mack.

I had talked to Bill on several occasions and thought that I would just phone him after he started his show at midnight to say hello. After telling him that I was in Ft. Worth, he invited me to come by One Broadcast Hill and hang out at the station. I was not about to miss that opportunity! I had been in radio for a couple of years and sitting in with the Legendary Bill Mack was a dream come true.

The only problem was getting to the studio. The school had a policy of not allowing anyone to leave the premises without supervision. It was midnight and I hated to ask permission, so my friend and I snuck out of the hotel and caught a cab to WBAP. Bill let us inside the building and it was such an incredible night. His calls came in from all over the Country and I believe that Tanya Tucker called him that night just to "check up on him." I was so excited about being with him at WBAP.

After being there for three or four hours, we decided that we needed to go back to the hotel. A huge ice storm had hit Ft. Worth while we were there and all the interstates and roads were covered over with a thick layer of ice. We started calling cabs and everyone turned us down. I swear that we called over twenty cab companies and no one would pick us up. It was close to 5:00 AM and we only had about an hour and a half before our ag teacher, Ronnie McAnally was to give us our wake up call so we could feed animals at the show.

We were sweating an expelling!

Bill Mack got on the air and appealed for a cab to take us back to the hotel and the lines started lighting up at WBAP! Every cab driver in Ft. Worth called and offered us a ride. The operators might have refused to help out a couple of Country boys, but they would do anything for Bill Mack!

We made it just in time for the wake up call and were iced in for an extra three or four days. It took some time before I told Mr. McAnally what happened that night.

Since that time, I have had a chance to join Bill on the air on both WBAP, XM Satellite Ranch and of course over KNEL in Brady. I also MC'd a show that he was a part of with Tony Douglas in Canton. He has always been very kind to me throughout the years.

Bill taped the following for me that night. I thought I would include it in "Legendary Conversations."

Bill: I have some guys out here that have been visiting my show. What is your name darling?

Margaret: This is Margaret with American Cab Company.

Bill: I want to thank you very, very much. One of your whiz jobs is on the way is it?

Margaret: Yes it certainly is Bill.

Bill: Do you know where we are located?

Margaret: I sure do.

Bill: Margaret, I want to thank you and let me ring the cowbell for you and your fine company. The guys will be waiting for you.

Bill: Speaking of the guys, I got to put him on. He came by to visit my show tonight. He is in broadcasting and I like it because he is starting out just about the same age that I was. I started broadcasting when I was sixteen years old. Here is my pal, Tracy Pitcox. How are you doing Trace?

Tracy: Just fine Bill and we have to thank you for allowing us to come on with you.

Bill: You heard the cab company is coming. We found you a cab.

Tracy: Thank goodness. Bill, you are a remarkable man. We tried every cab company in the book and no one would get out in this weather for us.

Bill: You know that you could stay here until Monday. I certainly wouldn't mind.

Tracy: I would be honored, but I guess that I need to get back to our radio station in Brady.

Bill: You are a friend of Joe Holstead's son.

Tracy: That is right. Joe's son, Josh Holstead works with us at KNEL in Brady.

Bill: Josh is a good pal of mine too. I have to tell you that I listened to his show being broadcast at a truck stop on Interstate 20 not too long ago. I was listening to Josh coming in and he is a good disc jockey. Joe Holstead is known to do some good stuff for us here at WBAP 820. Tracy, I am so glad that you could come by and see me. Do you ever have anybody come out to Brady and go deer hunting?

Tracy: We are known as part of the Deer Hunting Capital of Texas.

Bill: I used to work in San Antonio and I would go to Brady a lot. I truly love that part of the country and I want to wish you nothing but the very best in your radio career. You told me a while ago that one of your favorite Country singers is Ernest Tubb.

Tracy: Yes, he is my all time favorite singer and a great inspiration.

Bill: He gave a great helping hand to me and that puts you in good company. What is your pal's name there.

Tracy: His name is James Roberts and he is with our FFA group in town for the Ft. Worth Stock Show.

Bill: I want to mention that you are the Area VII President for the Future Farmers of America.

Tracy: That is right and I will be running for state president next year.

Bill: My boy, my boy. Let me ring the cowbell for you.

Tracy: Bill, I want to thank you so much for allowing me to come on the air with you. Most disc jockeys, especially those with your status, would not allow me to bust in on their program. That means a whole lot to me and I really do appreciate it.

Bill: You are welcome here any time. You don't have to call ahead of time, just make sure that I am here.

Tracy: I really appreciate that invitation. You are one of my heroes and I have enjoyed listening to you all of my life.

Bill: Like I said, I started out when I was sixteen. I know that you started at just about that age three years ago. I wish you nothing but the best there in Brady, and if you move around let me know where you go. When you come back, I will expect you to keep doing what you are doing and maybe you can take over the show. With your excitement in this business, I know that you are going to go a long way.

P.S. The American Cab Company refused to take any money from us that night. The driver said that he was doing it for his friend Bill Mack-who he never had the chance to meet. That once again proved to me the power of the airwaves.

Billy Grammer

JUNE 16, 1990

Tracy: How did you get started in the Country Music business?

Billy: I went into the Army for a short while and was discharged because of an eye injury, which I still have today. I went to Washington, D.C. and spent my apprenticeship as a machinist toolmaker at the Washington Naval Gun Factory. This was in the latter part of the war era. At the end of the war, I found myself on the streets along with others. The war effort was over, jobs were not available and I found myself going back home. I received a letter from a guy who had heard me play and sing. He knew I had some talent. He invited me to go to Arlington, Virginia, to audition. The guys name was Connie B. Gay who was one of the founders on the Country Music Association. Connie was my boss at WARL in Arlington, Virginia. You know the old saying, I went and auditioned, got the job but yesterday I couldn't spell entertainer, today I are one. It just developed. I was a singer and all at once, I was kicking off the program by sticking the electric guitar up to the microphone. All at once, I found myself being asked to front for the bigger artists like Clyde Moody, Grandpa Jones and many others. That was my start. This was in the late 1940's. I worked with King Record Company. In just a short time, they were flying me to Cincinnati and I was doing some guitar work.

Tracy: In 1959, your hit "Gotta Travel On" debuted on the charts.

Billy: I just came off the Jimmy Dean CBS Network Show. I was with him almost four years. I met Jimmy prior to him being a big star. In fact, I was instrumental in putting Jimmy on the first professional tour that he was on. I introduced him to Connie B. Gay in 1951. When Jimmy went to New York, I was invited to go up there but I did not want to go to the big city. I recorded "Gotta Travel On" for Monument Records, which was their first record. Fred Foster came to me and told me that he wanted me to record for him. I jokingly asked him if we were going to record "Star Spangled Banner" or "You Are My Sunshine". He said he found a song in the Library of Congress called "Gotta Travel On". I worked on it for about three weeks. I put the rhythm and modulations in the song and then I went to Nashville. I needed an intro but I could not figure it out. Chet Atkins was playing guitar on sessions at that time. He was bored with us trying to decide on an introduction so he started strumming on his guitar and I knew what he was playing was it. We had a lot of good help, a lot of fortune and the Lord has been with me.

Tracy: How high did "Gotta Travel On" go on the charts?

Billy: It went to number one in the pop field. It never did make number one in the Country field however; it was one of the biggest Country records of it day. At that time, there was a fight going on between Country and pop. When you crossed over, the Country boys were offended. It was being played and people were buying it and that is what they knew me for. I never did receive an award from the Country Music industry except for the Music Reporter Magazine. They did recognize me for the song. Those were the days when things changed. In later years they saw they were wrong but I suffered because of it. I talked to Moon Mullican and different people about it and they said they went through the same things. Moon had "Jole Blon" that went from Country to the pop charts. People were offended. It sounds funny today.

Tracy: Having a song on both the Country and pop charts would guarantee great sales.

Billy: "Gotta Travel On" sold 1.3 million. I have never had another hit sell a million. "I Wanna Go Home" sold almost 300,000. It should have gone on to sell a million but my company missed the boat. Bobby Bare called me from California and told me that I had a hit that they were not doing anything with. I told him to jump on it and he had a pop hit in just three weeks.

Tracy: Bobby had tremendous success with that song.

Billy: He had a number one pop and Country hit. My company missed it. They were not on the ball.

Tracy: When did you join the Grand Ole Opry?

Billy: As a result of the success, I was invited as a guest on the Prince Albert portion of the WSM Grand Ole Opry in 1958. On February 20, 1959, I was invited to join the Grand Ole Opry. I was a guest three times prior to signing. The song was so popular. I encored three times on the Prince Albert Show. There is not time set aside on the Prince Albert Show. They had to cut something. The show is timed out to the minute and when the NBC chimes come in, whether you are done or not, you are done. They recognized that I had just come off of the Jimmy Dean Show and I have worked with a lot of Country artists and had a Traditional background so they invited me. The only way to get to the Opry is if you are invited. Stonewall Jackson was the only one that I am aware of that was not invited at the time.

Tracy: Stonewall came to Nashville without a major recording deal.

Billy: No, he did not have a big hit but he had such a great voice they invited him to be a guest and people loved him.

Tracy: That does not happen very often.

Billy: No because there is just not enough room. There are so many out there that could be an Opry member and they have big hits but there is just not enough room to program them. When you have 65 artists and 32 show up on a Saturday night, where do you put them?

Tracy: Do you still play the Opry?

Billy: Yes but I am semi-retired. I am still tied to the Opry. They have really been gracious to me so why quit.

Tracy: Tell me about the Grammar Guitar Company.

Billy: I started in 1965 and built the first one. A guy by the name of Clyde Reed, J.W. Garr and myself started. I was the designer and had ideas with the guitar. J.W. was the craftsman and I told him exactly what to build. I called the shots on it and I sawed eighteen guitars up before we accepted the first one. These guys thought I was crazy. I told them that I was the guitar player and if they did what I told them, we would have a good instrument. I ran it until 1970 and R.G. & G Musical Instrument Company people took it just so that it could go on. I took it with a royalty figure and a contract. They had trouble in the beginning. They had the excitement but they just could not do the right things and they went bankrupt. I took the name back but I lost my passion in building. Those original instruments are becoming collector items and I have people asking me about them all over the country.

Tracy: Are there any Grammer Guitars still around?

Billy: Yes, if you can find them. There are none in production. We had five a day going for three years. I had a workforce of eighteen people. My wife was in Dallas and walked up to the American Airlines guy and he had his head down doing something and never looked up. My wife told him she was Mrs. Grammer and she told him she had reservations. He never looked up and he said like Billy Grammer, the Grand Ole Opry, Grammer guitar and she said that is my husband and he looked up startled and got so interested that he had someone take over his worked and talked to her for about twenty minutes. I have always been proud of our guitars and my career.

I had visited with Billy Grammer on several occasions on the telephone, but I first met him on the General Jackson Showboat in Nashville. We were at the Golden Voice Awards and Billy and his wife were seated near our table. I went over to him and introduced myself. At that time, Billy was already nearly blind, but was very sharp. We talked about songs and guitars of course and I really enjoyed out thirty minute conversation.

In June of 2005, I attended the Skeeter Davis Estate sale in Nashville. I was going through several large stacks of photos and was "ease dropping" on a couple of ladies. One was talking about attending the sale because her dad had worked many shows with Skeeter throughout the years. I could not help asking who her father was and she told me that I had probably never heard of him, but his name was Billy Grammar. I replied that not only had I heard of him, but I was a big fan as well.

It bothers me that many of the legendary acts that I grew up listening to are too often forgotten by the industry. Billy was never a superstar, but he certainly made his mark on the business in several very innovative ways.

Billy Parker

JULY 21, 1989

Tracy: Billy Parker is one of the greatest names in Country Radio. Billy, you actually spent a lot of time on the road before entering radio.

Billy: I had a friend named Cal Smith who was fronting the Ernest Tubb Band and in 1968, Cal called me. Cal had a record that was going really well for him called, "Drinking Champagne". He had some other records out and Ernest and Cal decided that it was time that Cal goes out on his own as an entertainer. They were thinking about who could replace him as a Texas Troubadour front man so I got a phone call one afternoon and Cal asked me if I was interested. Of course I was interested but that was a big move from Tulsa to Nashville. I thought about it and that same day my wife and I made a decision. We always wanted to be on the Grand Ole Opry and we always wanted to record for Decca Records. We were already recording for Decca at the time but it substantiated the deal. I made the decision and we made the move and in June 1968, I went to work fronting the Texas Troubadour Band. The way that I met Ernest was through a song that I recorded in 1959 called "Thanks A lot". Ernest as well as Brenda Lee recorded that song. Ernest and I had a pretty good repor.

Tracy: One of my favorite Billy Parker stories is about the Troubadour Hats.

Billy: Being the front man of the Texas Troubadours I felt like the spokesman for the band. I never was a hat wearer. I do now, but I did not then. Most of the other band members did not like to wear hats either. One night we were on the bus leaving an engagement and we would always go to the icebox and Ernest always kept crackers, peanut butter, Vienna sausage and other stuff like that. I told one of the other guys that I wanted to talk to Ernest about us not wearing the hats anymore. I got me some crackers, peanut butter and a Coke and I went to Ernest and I told him that I wanted to talk to him about something. I told him that the guys and I have been talking it over and we have been wearing the hats and the Troubadours uniform, which I loved, but the hats were hot and uncomfortable and I told him that we wanted to discontinue wearing them. He said son, that is no problem you don't have to wear the hats at all and you also don't have to be a Texas Troubadour. I got my crackers, peanut butter and my Coke and went back to my seat to sit down and I never mentioned hats again. He always believed in them and they looked good but it did not take me long to get put in my place.

Tracy: What is the title of your new album?

Billy: The album is called "Always Country". Speaking of E.T., I have a song on the album in tribute to him. It is titled "Thanks E.T., Thanks A Lot". I did not write that song. A boy named Tommy Williamson wrote it. He is from Texas. He met the General who is a producer of mine on the record label. He sent the song to the General for me to record and I took a liking to the song and it said what I wanted to say. The first song that I recorded was called "Thanks A lot", and he covered me on it so I thought that it was a way to pay him back.

Tracy: Are there any other songs on the album that you are fond of?

Billy: There is a song that was re-released that I am proud of called "Lord If I Make It To Heaven Can I Bring My Own Angel Along". This song will probably be the best song that I have ever recorded as well as the most requested. There are some very positive songs like "She's Sitting Pretty", "You Are My Angel" and "I Found A Miracle In You". I like positive songs. I like cheating songs too but I really like positive songs.

Tracy: How long have you been associated with KVOO radio in Tulsa?

Billy: Nearly 18 years. It is hard to believe.

Tracy: Is it difficult to be a disc jockey and a recording star?

Billy: I think that it is the best thing that has ever happened to me because of the fact that the combination keeps me busy all the time. It has really worked out well for me. I am now with RCA Records in Canada and have had some top ten records. I have been in love with Country Music all of my life. Being a disc jockey and a recording artist as well has enabled me to live out my dreams in this business.

I grew up listening to and loving radio. My favorite disc jockeys were Larry Scott, Bill Mack, Barney Cannon, Dave Nemo and Billy Parker. The music coming from KWKH, KVOO, WSM and WBAP was my kind of music. I would call those great "toll free request lines" and request the music of Ernest Tubb, Kitty Wells and Loretta Lynn while I was in my early teens. It was so special listening to the all night trucking shows belting out solid Classic Country Music.

Billy Parker was always so kind on the phone. As a kid, I was like so many other listeners. I had to be a pest in calling too often requesting music. Billy never seemed to be agitated. He was always gracious. I aspired to be just like those guys. I will never reach their fame or notoriety, but I hope that my futile attempt to follow in their footsteps might bring them a little joy from time to time. They were and still are my heroes.

My Family Photos

The Pitcox Family

Charla & Tracy Pitcox

The Tally Family

The Garner and
Brandenberger Family

Minnie Pearl's
MUSEUM
1500 Division Street
Nashville, Tennessee 37203

POST CARD

Thank you so much for your sweet letter! You stay a true country music fan! Study hard!

Minnie

SPC46
© 1985 Southern Post Card Co., Box 306, Goodlettsville, Tenn.

Postcard from Minnie Pearl in 1986.

Brady, Texas Mayor Bud Gober presenting my first community award in 1989.

Roy Acuff signing a poster for me at the Grand Ole Opry.

A large group of volunteers and listeners gather at KNEL in 1990.

The 1956 Flxible Jim Reeves Tour Bus as it arrived in Brady.

Conway Twitty at the San Antonio Stock Show.

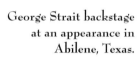

George Strait backstage at an appearance in Abilene, Texas.

Billy Walker backstage at the Grand Ole Opry.

When *Country America Magazine* named me an 'Everyday Hero', Norman Motors and Norwood Advertising erected this billboard in Brady.

George Jones told me that he should kill me for bringing so many people backstage to his show in Abilene, Texas.

Porter Wagoner wearing his "Fiesta Texas" shirt at Opryland.

Justin Tubb talks about his history in Country Music in our first office.

Photos – D

The Singing Ranger Hank Snow
on his way to dinner.

Leona Williams and Dave Kirby pose in front
of the "Dave Kirby Marker" which is now a the
Heart of Texas Country Music Museum.

One of our
bus tours to
Carthage,
Texas, and
the Jim
Reeves
memorial.

Johnny Lee tells me a delightful story
in Branson.

Barbara Mandrell backstage at
the Grand Ole Opry.

My pride and joy, the
Heart of Texas Country
Music Museum in
Brady, Texas.

Barbara Fairchild
and I on the dance
floor. She wrote "I
enjoyed our dance."
I did too.

The Whites at the Grand Ole Opry.

Goober is still one of my heroes.

Mel Tillis gives me a pair of boots for our museum.

We are all a "little cowboy" inside thanks to Gene.

Mildred Keith took the last photo of Patsy Cline before her death in 1963. She brought me a copy in Kansas City at a show.

Kitty Wells, Justin Trevino, Johnny Wright and I on the "Kittyhawk" tour bus somewhere on the road.

In spite of being such a superstar, Loretta has always treated me like one of the family.

FREDERICTON — MONCTON — SAINT JOHN

Handlyn MOTELS

ROUTE TWO   NEW BRUNSWICK   CANADA

We have an extensive collection of Jim Reeves artifacts at The Heart of Texas Country Music Museum. This is a Letter from Jim Reeves writing to his wife Mary.

5-13-59

Hello Darling;

while the boys are finishing packing for our drive to Chatham today I'll write you a note. We are having fair crowds, not fantastic, but we'll make a few _skins_. All of us are feeling fine. The weather here is simply beautiful, the lakes are so pretty — makes me wanna "drown a minner". The people here in New Brunswick are more backward and crude than in any province we've been. They are friendly though, maybe our situation will improve generally when we get to Nova Scotia & the Maritimes —

There are so many things I would like to say, but they'll wait — I'll just say that I love you, think about you constantly, and need you all the time. I'll see you in a few days.

All my love,
Jim —

One of our group trips to catch up with Moe Bandy in 1998.

One of Country's wealthiest entertainers,
thanks to "Big Bad John" and sausage,
Jimmy Dean and I at the Golden
Voice Awards.

Wilma Lee Cooper and her daughter
Carol Lee at a Nashville banquet.

MCing a show with
Texas Legend Johnny
Bush. Benny Fred
Kothmann and Sammy
Gerstwerdt are tuning
up the steel and fiddle.

Darrell McCall, Tony
Booth and Curtis Potter
working the Llano
Country Opry show in
Llano, Texas.

MCing a show with Country Music Hall of Famer Floyd Tillman.

An early shot of Dave Kirby looking up to his hero Big Bill Lister.

When Cal Smith visited us in Texas, I could not resist holding the great Ernest Tubb's guitar.

Lynn, Casey and Liz Anderson doing a great job keeping music in the family.

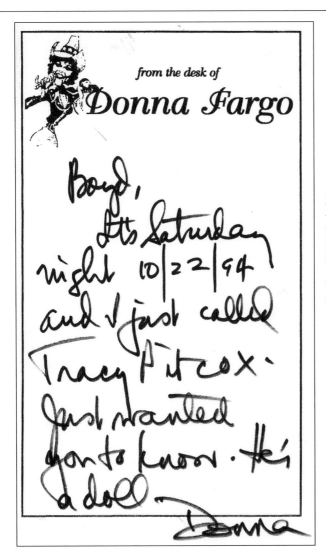

from the desk of
Donna Fargo

Boyd,
It's Saturday
night 10/22/94
and I just called
Tracy Pitcox.
Just wanted
you to know. He's
a doll.
Donna

Member Boyd Turner was a huge Donna Fargo fan. Boyd asked Donna to give me a "surprise call" on the air and then sent this note to him.

Leona Williams, Pepper Saucier, our driver and my darling wife Charla while on tour in Ireland.

Photos – L

1998

Tracy: How did you get started in the music business?

Billy: I was living in White Face, Texas. I had picked 329 lbs of cotton that day and my dad gave me twenty-five cents to see a Gene Autry movie and I said I was going to do what that guy did. I picked turkeys that Christmas to buy me a cheap guitar. I paid $6.25 and $.25 for an instruction book and I taught myself to play. When I was 15, I entered a contest in Clovis, New Mexico. I won it so they gave me a fifteen-minute radio program every Saturday with my guitar and me.

Tracy: You had a tough childhood and even spent some time in an orphan home.

Billy: My mom died when I was four. My two brothers and I were put in an orphanage in Waco. We were there for about five years. When I was about eleven, my dad remarried and we moved to Portales, New Mexico. Later on we moved to Clovis, New Mexico and then to Whiteface, Texas.

Tracy: At that time you were working on the radio.

Billy: Lubbock had a Jamboree at the arena and I was playing anywhere someone would pay to hear me sing.

Tracy: It's a long way from there to the Grand Ole Opry.

Billy: I started out on the Big D Jamboree after I got out of high school.

Tracy: You were there in the height of the popularity of the Big D Jamboree. Many of Country Music's biggest stars used it as a stepping stone.

Billy: Yes, I was. In fact, I pulled a mask gig on the Big D Jamboree called the Traveling Texan, The Mask Singer of Folk Songs. I was a folksinger back then. It was really popular. We had a great big unveiling. They came on and said the Traveling Texan is none other than Billy Walker and everyone went Billy Who? It helped me get a record contract with Capitol Records. I was very grateful. I stayed with Capitol and the Big D Jamboree for about a year and then I got a contract with Hadacol. Hadacol is a product that was very popular back in the early 50's. I got a 16-station radio hook-up for Hadacol and we did it out of Wichita Falls. I moved to Wichita Falls and I was doing local radio and then I would do the network show. That lasted for about a year and a half. By that time I had switched to Columbia Records and the first hit I had was "Anything Your Heart Desires". Then my Hadacol played out. Then the government came in and said it had too much alcohol in this so it shut Hadacol and my program down. Dudley J Le Blanc had to shut it down. I was in Nashville recording and Webb Pierce, Faron Young, and I were over at a downtown Nashville hotel, and Webb asked when I was going to go be on the Louisiana Hayride. I told him that my deal with Hadacol just ended so I asked when I could go. He picked up the phone and called Horace Logan and told him that they needed Billy Walker on the Louisiana Hayride and Horace asked when I wanted to start. They wanted me to start July 15 so I did and was on there for three years.

Tracy: The Hayride was a great launching pad in the 1950's and 1960's.

Billy: It was a great show. We had a lot of acts that came on that were network figures in the Country Music industry.

Tracy: You were on many shows with Elvis at this time.

Billy: I already had a couple of records that did really well. In 1954, Slim Whitman and I played the Overton Band Shell in Memphis and Bob Neil who promoted the show for us asked if he could put this kid, which was Elvis, on for a couple of songs. I told him if he was good enough for him, he was good enough for me. I watched him and he really knocked the crowd out. I went back to the Hayride and told Horace that I did not know what that kids got but he has something different. Slim went into Horace's office about that time and Slim, who really stuttered, said that he had a funny name. I said yeah, his name is Elvis Presley. In the write up that night, they called him Elvin Presley. I got Elvis' phone number from his mother so I gave it to Horace. Back in those days if you saw talent, you tried to help them just like some-one helped me.

Tracy: How many years have you been with the Grand Ole Opry?

Billy: I joined on January 1, 1960.

Tracy: That must have been one the high points of your career.

Billy: The Grand Ole Opry was the epitome of success as far as Country Music was concerned. I had already been at the Louisiana Hayride. In the mid 50's, after the Hayride, I joined Red Foley on the Ozark Jubilee, the very first Country Music television show, out of Springfield, Missouri. I spent almost four years there. I have been here almost 38 years.

Tracy: You are one of the elder statesmen of the Grand Ole Opry.

Billy: There are about half a dozen people who have been there longer than me. When I was working the Louisiana Hayride, one of the first jobs I took was playing a weeklong gig with the house band at the Moulin Rouge Night Club in Lake Charles,

Louisiana. Jimmy Newman was the house band down there. I know Charlie Louvin has been here at least three years longer than me and Porter Wagoner was also here a few years before I was. Jean Shepard has also been here longer than me.

Tracy: You have enjoyed over 30 years of recording contracts in this industry.

Billy: I have recorded with a lot of different labels. I was with Capitol for a couple of years and with Columbia for 15 years. I never lost a contract because I could not sell records; I lost a contract because of politics. I was never much of a politician. You earn your respect by the talent you have and your ability to find songs that will sell. Greed gets into every company. It is not you and the company, it is the people associated around you that want part of your songs, they want part of your money for the recording contract and they have nothing to do with it. I was with Monument for four years when it was a major label with Roy Orbison, Boots Randolph, Jeannie Seely and Ray Stevens. I was with MGM for five years and politics got into that deal. My last major label was RCA. You add all that up and it is 30 years.

Tracy: You were scheduled to be on the plane with Patsy Cline, Cowboy Copas and Randy Hughes when it crashed in 1963.

Billy: That is right. We had worked a benefit show for a disc jockey. I had some problems back home and needed to get back to Nashville as soon as possible. Hawkshaw had a commercial airline ticket. He heard about my predicament. He came over to me and said you be Hawkshaw Hawkins on that flight and handed me his ticket. There were several people that actually thought that I was with Patsy, Cowboy and Randy on that flight when it went down since I was supposed to be with them. I admit that I had some major problems after that plane went down. It was certainly a close call and I really don't understand why I was spared and the others weren't.

Tracy: Your First Generation Records project was very special to you.

Billy: Sometime in 1979, Pete Drake, who had been a friend of mine for many years and who also worked on the road with me in 1960, started putting the project together and asked if I would do some of it. I was happy to work with Pete because of what he meant to me and we had a really good sound together. I thought we had a really good product. It still sounds good today. It is just as fresh today and when we cut it.

Tracy: You re-recorded some of your songs.

Billy: "Charlie's Shoes", "Across the Brazos at Waco" and "Funny How Time Slips Away" were the three songs that I re-cut for the album.

Tracy: What about the song "Till I Drink Milwaukee Dry"?

Billy: John Riggs and I wrote that song. I do not know where we were. John was Ralph Emery's sidekick on the midnight show that Ralph did on WSM. John wrote many good hits. He used to get on my bus and ride to show dates with me. We would pick up the guitar and write a song here and there. Pretty soon you have quite a few songs written together and this was one of them. There are two or three songs on this project that we wrote together. I had a song back in 1978 that created a lot of controversy. It was the theme song for a CBS television special. The CBS special was "See You In Court". It was lawyers suing lawyers. The song was called "Lawyers". John and I wrote the song from first hand experience.

Tracy: What would you like to be doing in the future?

Billy: I would like to keep doing what I am doing. I am always looking for a fresh song. I want to keep writing songs and keep performing as long as my health lasts.

Tracy: In the years to come, how would you like the Country Music fans to remember Billy Walker.

Billy: Just simply as a good singer.

Billy Walker and I shared the same birthday-January 14. He was one of the first artists that I became acquainted with on my Nashville trips. He and his wife Bettie were always great with sending product, granting interviews and visiting with my bus tours in Nashville.

Billy was known as the "Tall Texan." He started life out on a very hard road and achieved a substantial amount of fame and honors. I always enjoyed Billy's openness and his deep knowledge of Country Music's rich history.

I was MCing a show in Missouri with Ferlin Husky, Leona Williams, Leon Rausch, Stan Hitchcock and several others when I got the call about Billy and Bettie's passing. They were driving back to Nashville after performing near Gulf Shores. Billy was driving the van and it overturned south of Montgomery on Interstate 65. Alabama state troopers found 77 year old Billy, 61 year old Bettie, 44 year old Charles Lilly and 40 year old Daniel Patton Senior at the scene. All four were dead. The only survivor was the Walker's grandson Joshua Brooks and he was critically injured.

There is still some confusion about what happened. At first, it was speculated that Billy fell asleep while driving. After Joshua's memory started coming back, he remembered a loud explosion (like a tire blowing) and then Billy warning everyone to hold on.

Whatever the cause, it was a sad day for Country Music. At the conclusion of our Missouri show, I told the shocked audience about the loss. They joined the entire cast in singing "Wings Of A Dove" especially for Billy and Bettie. There were several tears in that audience and in the hearts of Country fans all over the world.

OCTOBER 16, 1999

Tracy: How did you become involved in the Country Music business?

Bobby: I was raised into it. I really did not have a choice. I hope my choice would have been to do music. My family was in it. There were six of us kids and my parents. I lived in Wisconsin and then moved to Tennessee in the 1971. I was on my fourth national chart record. It is when I had "Mountain of Love".

Tracy: You had the first hit on that song.

Bobby: Yes, I believe I was one of the first ones to start re-recording some of the rockabilly songs and making them Country. "Sugar Shack" was also one of the songs that was re-recorded. That was a trend that worked for me real well. My first seven songs were oldies that were recorded as Country. Another song was "Suspicion". That is the song that got Eddie Rabbit's career going. I was writing with two other writers and decided to put out a song of our own that had never been out before but we did not know how radio would accept it. The song was "You Lay So Easy On My Mind".

Tracy: When you were writing it, did you think that it would become as popular as it did?

Bobby: I thought maybe we had something unique but we did not know how well it would do.

Tracy: Although you had other chart hits, "You Lay So Easy On My Mind" has become your biggest.

Bobby: Yes, it was definitely a signature song for me. It was by far the biggest song of my career. Texas has been really good to me with his song.

Tracy: It has also been covered by some major artists.

Bobby: I have been honored. Some of my heroes and people that I have followed because of their talent recorded it. Loretta Lynn and Conway Twitty did a duet on it. Roy Orbison, Pat Boone and Andy Williams have all recorded it. Andy actually titled his album after it. David Houston also had it on an album.

Tracy: You are still active in the music business. You are still recording and producing.

Bobby: I spend a lot of time in the studio doing production and working with other artists and putting things together for them. We have our own label to put out products overseas. At the same time, I try to keep my own career going. I like to do shows and meet the people. I have a new single out right now. It is called "I Don't Want To Think About It". It is written by a guy in Arkansas. I enjoy all aspects of the music business.

Bobby G. Rice is a very versatile entertainer. He is one of the performers who branched out into the production and promotions division of the industry. He still produces a compilation cd on a quarterly basis of new and upcoming talent for radio stations throughout the country.

Bobby has also been a part of several of the shows that we have produced in Nashville especially the Leona Williams Fan Appreciation Show.

Bobby headlined our Mason Country Opry show several years ago. My friend Monroe Buntyn and I went to San Antonio, Texas, to pick him up at the airport. On the way, the alternator went out in our van in Fredericksburg. After a very quick repair job, we were about two hours late in picking up Bobby. The majority of stars (and even I) would have been upset about the situation, but he was very understanding. A packed house later, all was well and the van is still running on that alternator!

1994

Tracy: You appeared on the Grand Ole Opry at quite an early age.

Bobby: I was 20. I sang "Fraulein". I stayed on there for about two years.

Tracy: "Fraulein" was one of the greatest songs in the history of Country Music. How did you find that song?

Bobby: Lawton Williams, a man from Dallas wrote the song. It was something that just happened. I recorded the song in 1957. It became a huge hit almost immediately.

Tracy: That is a signature song that you will be remembered by forever. Did you think that it was going to be a big hit when you first recorded it?

Bobby: No, I didn't know anything about recording. I was just getting started and had very little knowledge about the industry. I knew that I enjoyed performing, but I never knew that "Fraulein" would become a standard.

Tracy: That was the start of your career in Country Music

Bobby: I had been doing it locally since I was nine. I had done two radio shows a day and I had done a radio show once a week.

Tracy: Soon after that, you recorded a song that has been a seasonal classic "Jingle Bell Rock".

Bobby: In fact, I just finished recording it again. I have done a brand new Christmas album that I am very proud of.

Tracy: Do you know how many copies of "Jingle Bell Rock" have been sold?

Bobby: It is over 100 million.

Tracy: Tell us the history of "Jingle Bell Rock".

Bobby: When they sent me the song from New York, it had a guy trying to sing it with an organ. It did not have a bridge to the song so I put the bridge and changed the music to it. We went in and in fifteen minutes, we cut a tape. I asked them what was this rock stuff in Christmas.

Tracy: You had no idea in 1994 they would still be playing that song.

Bobby: It has been featured in over twenty movies and I do not know what all. At Christmas, you hear the song everywhere that you go from Christmas trees to stuffed animals. "Jingle Bell Rock" really helped my career. If you ever get a Christmas hit, you will always be remembered.

Tracy: Tell us about your latest project featuring the song.

Bobby: I recorded it, "Little Drummer Boy", "Silent Night" and we recorded "Rudolph". We recorded these with strings and horns. It really sounds good.

Tracy: I remember reading that Ernest Tubb was really impressed with you and helped you early in your career.

Bobby: Ernest is the one who got me on Decca Records. I was down there to do the Midnight Jamboree and he liked my singing and so he had me send him a tape so I sent him a demo. About three weeks later, Paul Cohen, which was with Decca Records, called me and wanted me to meet him in Nashville. I went down there and sang about eighteen songs and signed a contract. I traveled with Ernest for about a year. He was a fine man.

Tracy: What was traveling days like back then?

Bobby: Everything was by limousine and nothing but two lane roads. It is nothing like it is now. We did not have the big buses or the luxury of flying from date to date. It was a lot of work compared to touring today.

Tracy: Are you still performing on a regular basis?

Bobby: I just finished 180 days in Branson last year. I worked over 200 days last year. I worked in Branson for two months. I will be off a month and then I will do a few more months and then start working November and December here. I have a tour that Ferlin Husky and I will start on in the end of November.

Tracy: Where do you work at when you are in Branson?

Bobby: I work at the Christy Lane Theater with Ferlin Husky.

Tracy: You have a new Country recording project coming out.

Bobby: I am getting ready to do two Country albums of songs that I wrote.

Tracy: You have had many other hits besides "Fraulein" and "Jingle Bell Rock". Another classic in both the Country and pop field is "My Special Angel".

Bobby: "Special Angel" has sold about fifty million. It was a big song and still is.

Tracy: What is your favorite song that you have recorded?

Bobby: It was one that was not that big of a hit. It was "Miss Memory". It is on Bear

Records who has a 62 song CD out on me right now. They released it in Germany. It is one of my favorite songs. I recorded over seventy five albums.

Tracy: One of my favorite songs is "I'm The Man". What can you tell us about that song?

Bobby: I got that from the Wilburn Brothers. I was working for Sure Fire Music at the time and Doyle brought it to me and said that we should cut it so we did. Instead of doing "Life Turned Her That Way" I did "I'm The Man". I got "Life Turned Her That Way" from a man in Germany and gave it to Mel Tillis.

Tracy: Is it hard to pick out which songs are going to be hits?

Bobby: Yes! I cannot do it. If I were a song picker, I would be in bad shape.

Tracy: What are your plans in the future for Country Music?

Bobby: I am going to keep working and plugging away. One of these days I want to retire.

Tracy: When you think about it, what do you want the fans to remember you by?

Bobby: The fans are what make you. Some people say that they do not like to sign autographs but you better worry when they don't want you to sign one. I sign them even if it takes all day. When we are on a Legend's Tour, we usually have about 20,000 people and we sign until everybody is gone. It is one of those things that if they quit wanting autographs then you are in bad shape. When they are dancing to my music, I want them to remember the guy who made it.

I have played Bobby Helms' music throughout my entire career. Bobby was very fortunate to have several major hits including "Fraulein" "My Special Angel" and of course "Jingle Bell Rock." Bobby was also one of the first artists to enjoy a very large pop music following especially after "My Special Angel."

Justin Tubb gave me Bobby's number and I began corresponding with him. He and Justin worked many tours together and Ernest (Tubb) was instrumental in his early career. At the time of this interview, Bobby had just signed on to work another season of the "Shower of Stars" at the Christy Lane Theater in Branson. The show featured many great legends with Ferlin Husky as the primary host and various other artists rounding out the showcase including George Hamilton IV, Dick Curless, Melba Montgomery and Tommy Cash.

In my opinion, it was a great winning combination. You could be entertained and see several great artists on one package. At that time, Branson featured many great names from the Country Music business. Today, there are only a few name entertainers working there. I hope that changes in the future. As they say, every show must have an end and the "Shower of Stars" would only last through one more season. Bobby continued to work the road some before his death.

One of my favorite Boxcar Willie photos taken by Shirley Hargrove in Branson Missouri.

Boxcar Willie

June 1998

Tracy: How did Lecil Martin become Boxcar Willie?

Boxcar Willie: I saw a hobo in a boxcar and he looked like a friend of mine, Willie Wilson. I said, "there's Willie in a boxcar". It was not my friend; it just looked like him. I wrote a song called "Boxcar Willie" back in 1958. In 1976 I started performing as Boxcar Willie. I was forty-four years old. I am sixty-six now.

Tracy: Are you amazed at what you have become?

Boxcar Willie: My wife and I were talking about that the other night. You always imagine that you will have success but not even in my wildest dreams did I think it would reach so far. When I was sick I got over 7,000 get well cards. Everyone took time to write a message or a note. They would send me a note telling me about their friend's situation or a relative's situation. The cards came from all over the world. It made me stop and realize that there were a few people who thought a little bit about me.

Tracy: The first time I heard of Boxcar Willie was on a mail order TV album.

Boxcar Willie: That first came out in England as a mail order album. The postal company went on strike so it was put in the retail stores and received a platinum. The same company wanted to know if I had rights in the USA and Canada, which I did, so they released it there as well. The same thing happened in Canada with the postal service. It could not be delivered so it was put in the stores. It received double platinum, one for retail and one for mail order. All total we have a little over 3.2 million copies of that album.

Tracy: In general, most artists need a single off of an album in order for it to do well, however, you have never had a hit single.

Boxcar Willie: Not according to the charts. "Bad News" got up to twenty-eight and "We Made Memories" was seventeen or eighteen. But I have never had an airplay single.

Tracy: The Grand Ole Opry has been a very important part of your life

Boxcar Willie: I have been there nineteen years now.

Tracy: Roy Acuff has been very instrumental in your career.

Boxcar Willie: He is the one who brought me to the Grand Ole Opry. He asked if I wanted to join the Opry and I told him it was something that people dreamed of. The following Saturday night he made me a member of the Opry.

Tracy: You made a promise to Mr. Acuff.

Boxcar Willie: I was fixing to go out on stage; they were introducing me. He grabbed me by the coat sleeve and told me to make him a promise. He made me promise to keep the "Cannon Ball" alive after he was gone. I told him that he did not have to worry, I had planned on doing it anyway and that is what I have done. We close our show with it.

Tracy: You were one of the first artists to move to Branson.

Boxcar Willie: I was the first major artist to buy a theater in Branson. Everyone else was using somebody else's name but I was the first to use my own money.

Tracy: Were you afraid of the gamble?

Boxcar Willie: It was like rolling the dice. Boxcar Willie was a gamble. I was afraid. Roy told me that it was a gamble for him to leave the Opry and go perform. He had a place called Dunbar Cave in Clarksville, Tennessee. He understood what I was going thorough.

Tracy: Do you think that Branson is going to continue to thrive like it has been?

Boxcar Willie: Oh yes. There will be some shows that come and some shows that go. The mainstay of Branson will always be here. We have some big names here and they are doing really well.

Tracy: You have been fighting a tough battle.

Boxcar Willie: I have been fighting for my life. I have been fighting the charts for monetary survival but I have been fighting for my life with mantle cell lymphoma. It is a fast acting form of leukemia. I saw the doctor today and he gave me a 100%. I have to do some more chemotherapy but I am doing great.

Tracy: Has your illness been a hindrance to you performing?

Boxcar Willie: I cannot go out on the road. I get really tired. It takes all I have to do a two- hour show.

Tracy: What is the fan reaction as you are performing?

Boxcar Willie: It is amazing. Sometimes I get a standing ovation just by walking out on the stage. This time last year I was only given three months to live. At the end of three months I could not pay my bill so they gave me another three months. I have been living on three months at a time. When you don't pay the doctors, they will let you live!

Tracy: Is your son still performing with you?

Boxcar Willie: He was but he went back to laying bricks. He will probably be back in a week or two! A few weeks in the hot sun and he will be back in the air conditioner.

Tracy: What does the future hold for you?

Boxcar Willie: Whatever the Good Lord has in mind. I plan on being at the Boxcar Willie Theater for another five or six years and then it will be time to sit back and do what I want to do.

I caught the Boxcar Willie show at least twenty times throughout the years-the majority of those shows at his theater in Branson. Our Branson tours would always stop at his theater and his show was always one of the highest rated on our tours. Boxcar even built his own museum next to his theater and it was a highlight of a trip to Branson. I never imagined that many of the items in his museum would someday get a new home at the Heart of Texas Country Music Museum.

I always admired Boxcar for his incredible band-many of them originally members of Tony Douglas' Shrimpers. Chuck Jennings became a "right hand man" for Boxcar and could sell ice to Eskimos. One year, he was selling Boxcar Willie stuffed dolls that were about the ugliest doll that I ever saw! I ended up buying two because Chuck told me what a limited supply he had left. He still had part of that limited supply six months later when we returned!

Boxcar started his career in Texas and always had a love for the state. He would always ask questions about Texas and the music scene in our area.

It was very unfortunate that Boxcar did not get to sit back and do what he wanted to do. I only saw Boxcar one other time after this interview and I wish that I hadn't. The cancer that he was fighting was gaining strength and took virtually all of his ability to entertain. I even brought my recorder that night to get a "Boxcar update" for my listeners, but I never took it out of my bag. I could tell that it was over and instead of more questions and taking his time, I simply went backstage and shook his feeble hand for one last time.

After his death, his widow sold everything-the theater, motels and even his beloved museum and its contents was on the auction block. Priceless items went for pennies on the dollar. Thanks to the generosity of Sally and Carl, our Heart of Texas Country Music Museum preserved several of his paintings, letters and photos from President George Bush and items from many artists including Jean Shepard, Johnny Wright, Margo Smith and others that were housed at the museum.

I have a hard time believing that a Boxcar Willie Museum in Branson would not draw enough people to make a financial profit for generations to come. His legacy was dimmed with the decision to liquidate and scatter his memory to the wind.

Buck White

APRIL 26, 2002

Tracy: Were you always musically inclined?

Buck: I started playing music when I was 12 or 13 years of age. I played piano good enough to play in honky-tonks when I was 16. I got interested in playing the mandolin and guitar when I was 18 and then I formed a band and went to Abilene and then I got on the radio in 1950. I played on the show that Slim Willet was the emcee on. He sang the song "Don't Let The Stars Get In Your Eyes". I played the piano on that song when I was about 19. I then went back to Wichita Falls and played dances all through the fifties and then my wife got tired of me playing in dance halls so we decided to move to the country. That is when my family and kids and I started performing. During the 1960's we played for whoever would listen to us. Around the late 60's, my girls wanted to play all time and wanted to move to Nashville so they talked me into it.

Tracy: Was it a hard move for you?

Buck: I only knew one person. The first night we were there I took the kids to the Grand Ole Opry. I know they got tired of seeing me down there. We finally got invited as a guest. We did that for about twelve years and then in 1984, they made us members.

Tracy: That must be a highlight in your career.

Buck: It really was. It was the greatest thing. I had always dreamed about it. I really enjoyed playing dances but I love playing for people that will sit there and watch you.

Tracy: You have had a lot of great hits throughout the years.

Buck: That started in 1982. We signed with Capital Records and put out a record that was too Country to get any interest. We then moved over to another major label. Our first record with the new label was a top ten hit. We had four more that were top tens and the other three were top fifteen. That is what got us started and invited to the Grand Ole Opry and traveling all the time.

Tracy: You were able to keep your family together that way.

Buck: My wife decided to get out of the business because of having younger daughters at home as she did not want to leave them. The two oldest Cheryl and Sharon kept playing.

Tracy: Where did you gain your son-in-law Ricky Skaggs?

Buck: We played in Kilgore, Texas and Ralph Stanley was there with Ricky and Keith Whitley. They asked my girls if they could have the words to one of the songs that we sang. I think they already knew the words they just wanted to come over! They became friends and later in years they got together and settled down.

Tracy: The resurface of bluegrass has been great for your career.

Buck: It has stirred up a lot of interest in old time music. The first tour we did was 19 dates and all the shows were sold out, some within hours. It is a very exciting time for our music.

Some of the first 45rpm records that I played as a disc jockey were by The Whites. They were releasing some great Traditional Country records in the late 1980's. Unfortunately, at that time the Traditional Country sounds were not very strong. There were some including Gene Watson, George Strait and Ricky Skaggs that were doing their part, but it was a tough battle.

The great family harmony of The Whites was a great fresh sound to Country Radio. I would see them on television and hear them on the Grand Ole Opry, but really did not know The Whites. After corresponding and doing a few interviews, Buck White and I became better acquainted.

I was surprised by his visit at KNEL a few years ago. He and his wife had been in San Antonio and decided to come to Brady. Buck joined me on the air and our listeners really enjoyed hearing about his journey from Texas to Nashville.

APRIL 30, 1998

Tracy: Cal the last time I talked to you, you told me that you were not going back out on the road.

Cal: I wasn't. But every time I would do the TNN show I would get letters from people wanting me play some shows. My wife and I decided that we would go back out on the road. I just completed a tour of Florida. We had some good crowds. It is amazing that after all the years of being off the road I have been playing for sell out crowds.

Tracy: You had the greatest song of your career in 1974, "Country Bumpkin"? I am sure you get tired of talking about it.

Cal: No, when you get a song like "Country Bumpkin" and it becomes a Country Classic, you feel blessed. "The Lord Knows I Am Drinking" is another song that has supported me for a lot of years.

Tracy: Did you know at the beginning what kind of impact those songs would have for the business?

Cal: I knew that "Country Bumpkin" would be a number one record but I did not realize just how big it would be. I felt the same way about "The Lord Knows I'm Drinking". At that time, I had some doubts that maybe they would take it wrong. It was a big record and I am thankful that it was as successful as it was. I was afraid that some Christian people would take it the wrong way. But, it sold more with the Christians than anyone else. In fact, Billy Graham said something about it on one of his shows. I played a show once and a preacher came out and wanted to introduce me on stage. He had a big congregation in his town and he said that I have made a song that really fits the town. I have had a lot of preachers tell me that I can record a song that really hits. Bill Anderson wrote the song and it was a great song. The song put me in the spotlight. I found some songs on my own and recorded them in the same session and put them on the same album. I think that the Lord has really been looking over me.

Tracy: I had a request recently for your song "Jason's Farm".

Cal: Every show that I have done, I did not have that on my list of songs to do but I would get a lot of requests for that song and, "I Can Feel The Leaving Coming On". I had forgot all about that song. I was going through some of my albums the other day and I did not even remember cutting that song. I want to say hi to all my Texas fans. I want to thank them for their support through out the years.

Tracy: You were a part of Ernest Tubb's Texas Troubadours for a few years.

Cal: Those were the best years of my life. I had idolized Ernest every since I was a small boy. My most prized possession is his guitar. He gave me his guitar about a year before he passed away. He said it needed to be played and I told him that at every show I would play it and I have. It makes me feel really good. I have people come up to me and ask if they can have their picture taken with Ernest's guitar and myself. I had a lady who just wanted to touch his guitar. The world loved Ernest so much that the people want a picture with his guitar any way they can get it. It makes me feel good knowing that I had the pleasure of working with a man that the world thinks a lot of. Ernest and I became like family. I could not have loved him any more if he was my own flesh and blood. He left such an impact on the business. Ernest loved his fans and they were loyal to him. It was a great loss losing him.

Tracy: I saw a picture of one of your fans with you and the Ernest guitar. He said you allowed him to play the guitar.

Cal: I remember that. I was playing at the North Town Opry in Kansas and this man came out and wanted to have a picture taken with the guitar and myself. I did better than that, I let him strap it on and we took pictures. It makes me feel good that people loved Ernest so much because I did.

Tracy: Are you still touring?

Cal: Yes. I would love to come to Texas because I really love the fans down there. Ernest always called me his Oklahoma Troubadour because I am from Oklahoma but as far as I am concerned, Oklahoma and Texas are about the same. The fans are great and they treat you kind.

Tracy: I want to thank you for giving us a uniform for The Heart of Texas Country Music Museum.

Cal: It was my pleasure. Regardless if I have won awards, it is the people who are responsible for your success. They are the ones who make my living for me. It is always great to give a little something back to the people who have given so much to me.

It is no secret that one of my favorite singers is the late Ernest Tubb. The first cassette tape that I ever bought was E.T.'s "Thanks A lot." I remember first really listening to Cal on a couple of Texas Troubadour albums. His voice was so unique and so hard Country.

Cal co-hosted my radio show in 2005. He spent the evening with me taking calls from the listeners and relating stories about his incredible career. He was having some severe back pains and memories of losing a son were still heavy on his mind. Even through all of that, he was still telling the listeners how lucky and thankful he was for his career.

I also remember watching the Nashville Network's Music City Tonight Show back in 1994. Garth Brooks and Cal were both on the show. Cal had heard that "Country Bumpkin" was one of Garth's favorite songs. Cal gave Garth his CMA award for the classic song. Not many artists would even consider such a gift. That is Cal Smith.

"Country Bumpkin" Cal Smith visits KNEL radio.

Carl Smith

1989

Tracy: On the telephone with me right now I have one of the legends of Country Music, Mr. Carl Smith. How are you Carl?

Carl: I am fine, how are you Tracy?

Tracy: I am doing just fine. I wanted to ask how you got involved in this world of Country Music?

Carl: I got involved at a very early age. As far back as I can remember. I started playing on the radio when I was 16; back in 1944

Tracy: You are going to give your age away.

Carl: Oh its no secret, March 15, 1927. It's on everything that was ever written. I am proud of it. I have been in the Country Music business ever since.

Tracy: One of your first big hits occurred in 1951 with "If Teardrops Were Pennies".

Carl: Yeah, I started recording in 1950 and the first record I had was "I Over Looked An Orchid". And then after that came "Lets Live A Little", "If Teardrops Were Pennies", " Mr. Moon", "Don't Just Stand There" and "Old Mother Nature". It just went along from there.

Tracy: "I Overlooked An Orchid" has become one of the standards in the business.

Carl: That song was written by a guy in Knoxville, Tennessee. That is where I was working at the time. My name is on it but I did not write it. I changed things in it and it was one of them songs that was floating around and when I started recording. The guy who was responsible for me going to Columbia Records was a song plugger named Troy Martin with Peer International Southern Music. I recorded many of their songs in the beginning. In fact, all the songs I recorded was theirs. He was my main scout for finding me songs, and that was one that he found.

Tracy: It is still featured on many of your greatest hits packages.

Carl: It was one of the most popular songs I ever had because all the time I was in the music business. It was probably the most requested songs I had steadily through the years. It wasn't a big selling record when it was first out.

Tracy: You were just getting into the Country Music industry, right?

Carl: Yes

Tracy: What was your biggest selling record?

Carl: I don't know. Some songs in the music business, your money usually comes from your dates on the road. You can have a record that sells 150,000 and it might draw you more people than some records you had that sold 7 or 800,000. The biggest selling I had was "Let Good Ol' Mother Nature Have Her Way". It sold 947,000. That is the closest I ever came to selling a million records. This was in 1953.

Tracy: Your recording of "This Orchid Means Goodbye" resembled "I Over Looked An Orchid". Were you specifically looking for an answer song?

Carl: I was looking for certain things and if I had not done " I Over Looked An Orchid", I would have done "This Orchid Means Goodbye". It came along about 4 or 5 years later. I lose a little track of time. When you are 62 you get a little senile about what happened 30 years ago.

Tracy: How many albums do you have with your name on them?

Carl: There are about 40 or 42. Some are greatest hits and some are albums with other people. I remember Billboard put up something like a discography and I had 90 something chart songs and 40 something top tens. I am not sure, I am taking her (the Billboard) word for it.

Tracy: You had so many hit records, so why did you leave the music business?

Carl: I stayed in it until 1978 and I just got tired of it. I got tired of being on the road and I had teenage kids at home and I was not spending enough time at home with them and just decided I wanted to do something else.

Tracy: You were big in horse raising right?

Carl: Yeah, I raised a lot of horses. I still show them every weekend but I do not raise them anymore. I stopped about 4 years ago.

Tracy: Tell us about the Grand Ole Opry. How did you get you first appearance?

Carl: My first came from the same guy who got me on the record. He took a couple of dubs, that is what we called them back in those days and he took them to Jack Stapp who was program director at WSM, the Grand Ole Opry, at that time and he also took them to Don Law who was PR manager at Columbia Records and both agreed to give me a trial. I came to Nashville and done live early morning radio shows six mornings a week for about a year or two and during that time they would put me on the Opry and records started to happen so they made me member.

Tracy: How long were you a member?

Carl: About six years.

Tracy: One of my favorite songs that I would like you to comment on is "Airmail to Heaven". You remember that don't you?

Carl: Yeah, It was one of those songs that struck me. It was one of those message songs. I thought it was kind of a sad but true message and I enjoyed singing it. So I recorded it and it was a very good selling record.

Tracy: How many days were you on the road per year?

Carl: During the 50's it was about 90% of the time. I done a show with Phillip Morris for 18 months. We worked 6 weeks straight and then off a week. Before that, it was just tours. In the 1960's I cut down to working 4-5 days a month only on the weekend. I did a TV show from 1964-1969 I guess.

Tracy: Were there any artists or fellow musicians that helped get you in the industry? Who were your heroes?

Carl: Ernest Tubb and Roy Acuff, people who were on the Opry. Ernest Tubb and Hank Williams probably helped me more than anyone else. Hank wrote a couple of songs to help get me started. I worked on the road with Ernest and he helped me a whole lot. He was a very nice person to help people and advise them on their appearance on stage and he would tell you about little things that you were doing that you should not have been doing.

Tracy: You recorded a duet with Ernest on the Legend and Legacy album "Don't Just Stand There."

Carl: Yeah, he gave me that song. One night we left the Opry about 3:00 in the morning and we were driving down the highway and he was telling me about it. He had it to record himself but he decided that I would have it.

Tracy: Whenever they write the history book of Country Music and they come to that page that has Carl Smith on it, what do you want your fans to remember as or by?

Carl: I don't know (laughing). I never thought about it. I guess just whatever their opinion of me is. Whatever they think is what I want them to remember me by.

Tracy: Would you like to say anything to all our Brady, Texas listeners before I let you go tonight?

Carl: Yeah. What do you say to Texas? They always know everything! I married a Texan. I know they know everything!

Tracy: We need to mention that you are married to the great Goldie Hill. She is retired from the business as well.

Carl: She retired when we got married.......but if I ever think of what I want to tell them (Texans), I will call you back.

I met Carl Smith for the first in Nashville at the Ed Gregory bankruptcy auction. Gregory had bought a large amount of memorabilia from several artists including Jim Reeves, Faron Young and Carl and Goldie.

I immediately recognized Carl and Goldie. I had corresponded with Goldie by email many times and had conducted this one interview with Carl. I really did not expect Carl to be very nice. I realized that he was away from the business and really did not enjoy talking about it very much. Of course, I live eat and breathe the business. I approached Carl and introduced myself to he and Goldie. Goldie hugged me and Carl was very kind.

My friend Mike Rutledge and I were there to buy Jim Reeves' 1956 GMC Flxible tour bus. After winning the bus, Carl immediately walked over to me and shook my hand to congratulate us on winning the bus. That meant so much to me. He then pointed out a couple of items (two pairs of boots and two hats) that belonged to him that was also in the auction. I ended up going home with them as well!

Charlie Louvin

APRIL 13, 1990

Tracy: How did you get started in the Country Music business?

Charlie: My dad picked the banjo for his own enjoyment and my mom played the banjo for her own enjoyment as well. We had the craving from one side of the family and knowledge from the other side of the family. Ira and I entered an amateur contest and we won three weeks in a row. First prize was a fifteen- minute radio show at 4:00 in the morning on a 250- watt radio station. That is what we wanted and we won it.

Tracy: How did you get a recording contract?

Charlie: That came much later. Our first recording was in 1947 but we did not have a contract at the time. We recorded on Eddie Hill's record contract. We were working for him in Memphis and he was working for Apollo Records. Apollo is a subsidiary of Mercury Records. We got to meet Fred Rose and he liked our songs and liked our singing so he got us a record deal with MGM Records in 1949. We only recorded twelve songs with MGM because Mr. Rose did not feel we were getting a fair deal so he got a contract with Capitol Records.

Tracy: Were most of your hits on Capitol Records?

Charlie: Yes. We were with Capitol for many years and had a lot of success on that label.

Tracy: Around 1955 you recorded the hit song "When I Stop Dreaming".

Charlie: That was our first secular song. We had been a gospel duet up to that point. gospel music was an important part of our career, but "When I Stop Dreaming" opened a lot of doors for us.

Tracy: Where did you find that song?

Charlie: That is an easy song, especially when you are a dreamer. A dreamer is a very important person because we dream the ideas and other people make the money. We are not interested in making the products, we just dream the dreams. It was the first time that Country Music lovers heard of the Louvin Brothers. We had quite a few gospel albums out at the time but that is different from Country.

Tracy: You followed that with "Cash on the Barrel Head' and "I Don't Believe You

Met My Baby" among many other hits. Those songs gave you the opportunity to work the Grand Ole Opry.

Charlie: We started out on the Opry in 1955 and from that point on, the business was ours. We won a couple of awards in 1960 but from 1955-1959 we won all the awards that a small vocal group could win. There use to be jukebox awards and then the disc jockey's most played award and the best selling awards. We won about everything that could be won.

Tracy: The album with "My Baby's Gone" has been re-released.

Charlie: Yes it has. It is on the Stetson Label out of England. They have put out several gospel as well as secular albums. One of the albums was "I Forgot To Cry" which is one of mine. The records did well.

Tracy: Ira's death really changed your career perspective.

Charlie: He was killed in an automobile accident on Father's Day in 1965. Ira and I were not singing as a duet at the time. In 1963, we dissolved the duet partnership. In early 1964, I came out with "I Don't Love You Anymore", which was my first solo record. We were fortunate to have "I Think I Will Go Cry Myself To Sleep". A little later we had "Will You Visit Me On Sunday", we had success which is something that is normally not done after you are a part of a duet for twenty years. It is not easy to go separate ways and have success. Ira and I had to dissolve our partnership to keep from killing each other.

Tracy: Was it hard for the industry to accept you as a solo artist?

Charlie: I do not know. I suppose it was. It is not done too often. It was something that was not lightly thought of. It was a necessity. Singing was the only thing that I knew how to do so I continued with what I knew.

Tracy: In 1970, you teamed with Melba Montgomery for a series of duets.

Charlie: We had two albums and several singles. We won a Grammy together with "Something To Brag About". We also had "Did You Ever?" We have some serious songs on the album but the label would only release the humorous songs.

Tracy: How long have you been with the Grand Ole Opry?

Charlie: I just celebrated my 35th anniversary.

Tracy: What do you think that the Grand Ole Opry means to Country Music?

Charlie: None of it would be here if it was not for the Grand Ole Opry. The Opry needs old timers like myself. The acts that command $50,000-$75,000 a night don't

come in but once a year so that makes traditionalists like myself a little more important to the Grand Ole Opry because they have to do shows once a week.

Tracy: I found a video recently from the Grand Ole Opry and the featured song was
"Ten Years Three Kids Two Loves Too Late". It was one of the prettiest songs I have
ever heard. I am surprised that it was not a top ten record for you.

Charlie: It was a gorgeous song and it should have been. I recorded that for First
Generation Records. Pete Drake produced it. As if often the case, the songs that
should have been hits are often left hidden in the albums. It is hard to determine what
will be a hit record and what will be a flop.

Tracy: What are you doing now?

Charlie: I live in Alabama and we have a Bluegrass Festival and we mix a little
Country with it. This year, 1990, marks our 8th year here. We have a lot of people
from Texas come to the Festival. My group and I work on Saturday nights the other
three nights I am working with Charles, part of the Whitson Brothers team. I also
worked with Charles in England. The Louvin Brothers music is extremely popular in
England. We have a new record coming out titled "Everytime You Leave".

Tracy: Was your "Precious Jewel" video recorded live at the Opry?

Charlie: The introduction was. I asked Roy Acuff if he would allow us to sing his song
"Precious Jewel". He said that he would be honored so my group and I did an arrangement and Roy did an introduction for us, which was longer than the song. Many people told us that we should record the song exactly like we did it with Roy doing the
introduction.

Tracy: What are your future plans?

Charlie: I want to continue to work the Grand Ole Opry and travel to see all of our
friends. The music business is really the only life that I know. It is a very hard business, but one that can be rewarding. I hope to continue to perform as long as the fans
want to hear me.

*It is exciting to know that Charlie is still working to entertain his many fans. Fifteen years
after this interview, the Country Music Hall of Fame finally recognized the Louvin Brothers
by inducting them into their Hall of Fame.*
*Justin Tubb was staying with us for a couple of weeks in Texas while working a few road
dates back in 1997. Charlie called Justin one night. Charlie was in Austin doing a promotion for a new album that he recorded for the Watermelon label. Justin told Charlie that he
should drive to Brady (about two and a half hours) and co-host our Hillbilly Hits Radio
show. Charlie agreed. I had booked Justin that night in Junction, Texas, on a package show
with Johnny Duncan, Johnny Bush, Justin Trevino and Bill Mack. Charlie did a great job*

on the radio show and we featured much of his catalog throughout the night. We wrapped the radio show up and I rode to Junction with Charlie to join Justin and the other entertainers. Charlie was driving and I will never forget an incident that happened that night. A drunk jumped right out in front of Charlie's pickup. He slammed on the breaks and barely missed running over the guy. I was just thinking of the headlines - "Country Music Legends Runs Over Drunk". Thank goodness that it did not become a reality.

After we arrived at the venue, I checked in with the promoter to get the money. Charlie was with me and after meeting the guy, he told me that I was going to have some trouble. He sensed it from just meeting the guy! At that time in my life, I was young and naive and trusted absolutely everyone. I brushed Charlie's comments off and bought the guys excuse for not paying right now-hook, line and sinker!

To make a long night longer, we never got our money. I think that Bill Mack and Johnny Duncan might have gotten some of their money, but the rest of us didn't get a dime. The guy was a crook that wanted to be a star himself. He thought that a big show in Junction, Texas, would draw people from all over Texas. It would be the launching pad for his career to work with such legends. I think the only ones that showed up were from our area. They stayed away in droves.

I learned a valuable lesson. Don't trust anyone without cash up front when dealing with promoters. Charlie, Justin Tubb and I had a late night breakfast at the Segovia, Texas truck stop before heading back to Brady. It was a long night.

I still see Charlie on my trips to Nashville. I always enjoy my time with the great Country Music legend. He can be found at the Louvin Brothers Museum on Music Valley Drive much of the time visiting with his many fans.

∿∿

1995

Tracy: Charley Pride has enjoyed an incredible career in this business. How did it begin?

Charley: When I was growing up, I listened to the Grand Ole Opry and Bill Monroe, Roy Acuff and Ernest Tubb. That was the kind of music that we liked. We had a big family. I was one of eleven children. I actually wanted to go into the major leagues in baseball and break new records. An injury kind of sidelined my career. I had different people tell me about how they enjoyed my singing. Then Red Sovine and Red Foley made an appearance in Helena, Montana. I made some demos for RCA. Chet Atkins heard them and then signed me to the label.

Tracy: You are recognized as the first major Black Country Music singer.

Charley: I never really thought about it at first. I just loved to sing and I loved Country Music. After I got to Nashville and started having some success, people started asking me how I felt to break the barriers in Country Music. I did not know what they were talking about at first. I just wanted to sing Country Music and for people to like me.

Tracy: Your big break came with "The Snakes Crawl At Night."

Charley: The single was released in 1965. I was so nervous going into that studio. It was the first time and I was nervous about the session and about how people would like the song.

Tracy: You have had so many good records throughout your career; do you have any idea how many albums you have had?

Charley: I think that I have had about sixty.

Tracy: Do you know how many top tens and number ones you have had?

Charley: Some say thirty-one and some say thirty-six. At least half of the singles that I have released are number one or in the top five. I was lucky enough to win three Grammy Awards and they say that I sold over 70 million records.

Tracy: You were also named Entertainer of the Year in 1971.

Charley: That was a nice award. I have always tried to be a good entertainer. Anyone can be a good singer, but our main goal on that stage is to entertain. Many people have to save their money to come to a show and I want to make sure that they get their monies worth every night.

Tracy: You recorded a great song called "Does My Ring Hurt You Finger".

Charley: Jack Clement, who was my producer, wrote that song. That song is still popular and has been in my shows since it first came out. Jack actually produced most of the big hits I have had. Jack produced just about everything from '69 to the middle '80's.

Tracy: Your biography has recently been released.

Charley: We are very pleased by the way it turned out. Jim Henderson was the co-writer of the book and put it all together. He made sure that everything was correct. If there is anything you want to know about Charley Pride I encourage you to read the book and I also want to encourage everyone to visit the Charley Pride Theater in Branson.

Tracy: "Crystal Chandelier" is a song that was very popular for you. Do you have any special memories of that song?

Charley: I remember Jerry Reed was playing guitar on that song and Junior Husky was on bass. There were so many guys that I have worked with that sometimes I have to look at the album to see who I worked with. The song was never a single for me in the United States or Canada but it was released in Scotland, Ireland, England and about three times in Australia and New Zealand. They wanted to release it but it just never happened. I have been doing it on my show for over thirty years. It has become one of our most requested songs.

Tracy: What does the future hold for you?

Charley: I keep telling myself that I am going to cut back. I have a lot of business interests and between those and the music, I stay very busy. I want to cut back and enjoy a little bit of that hard work that I have put in for the last thirty years.

I interviewed Charley Pride at his apartment area backstage at the Charley Pride Theater in Branson. Charley and Rozene were spending a lot of time at the theater and the crowds were packing into those theater seats. The theater was not owned by Charley, but his name was on the building and he was the star. Many of the theaters in Branson are not owned by the star. In most cases, it is in the best interest of the artist not to own the theater.

Charley was actually watching some sports game as I went backstage. I will never forget how Rozene continued to call him "Pride" instead of Charley. It was easy to see that

Rozene was definitely the one that took care of the business and let Charley take care of the entertaining.

A few years later, I was at the Opryland Hotel in Nashville. Big Bill Lister had gone to Nashville with me and we were promoting his album "Big Bill Lister Remembers Hank Williams Through Story and Song." I was actually standing at a urinal in the bathroom when I looked over and Charley Pride was standing next to me. I reintroduced myself to him as we were standing there. I mentioned that Brady, Texas, was the hometown of Dave Kirby, the writer of "Is Anybody Going To San Antone?" He remembered and then exclaimed, "You will never guess who I just met. Big Bill Lister, Dave's uncle and he played with Hank Williams!"

I thought then that even being famous does not keep you from being a fan as well.

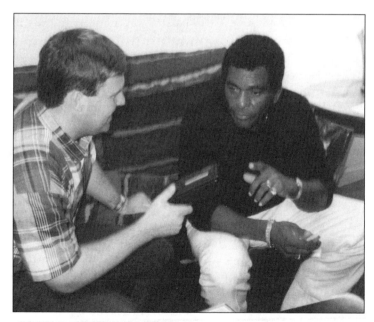

Charley Pride being interviewed backstage at the Charley Pride Theater.

Charlie Walker

SEPTEMBER 30, 1989

Tracy: Charlie Walker is a great legend in Central Texas and we are proud that he is our special guest. How are you Charlie?

Charlie: How is everybody out there in Central Texas, KNEL territory?

Tracy: How you got involved with this business we call Country Music?

Charlie: It is a long story and it will take a long time to tell it but I grew up in a cotton farm north of Dallas. I had always loved Country Music from listening to the records of Jimmie Rogers, America's Blue Yodeler, Gene Autry, Roy Acuff and Ernest Tubb. We started listening to the Grand Ole Opry back about that time. I did not know how to get into the business but I knew that I wanted to do it. There were several programs out of Dallas that we use to listen to on the radio all the time like Blue Sky Boys and several others and I ended up going down when I was about 15, auditioning for one of these programs well, they put me on the radio and let me sing. That was big time stuff then, singing on the radio.

Tracy: I am sure that it was a very exciting time in your career.

Charlie: It certainly was and then one thing led to another and I ended up getting a job at one of the big honkytonks there in the Dallas area and then from there I got into radio, one thing just kept leading to something else. After I served a couple of years in the military I ended up in San Antonio and I was a broadcaster there for many years

Tracy: You were one of the most popular disc jockeys in Texas.

Charlie: In fact, I was voted into the Disc Jockey Hall of Fame in 1981 here in Nashville. That is kind of what I did there but I started making records back in the early '50's and I had two or three that had done pretty good. I had one song "Telling Her Lies And Feed Her Candy." It had done pretty good all over that country. But in 1958, we hit real big with "Pick Me Up on Your Way Down". I know that it was in the charts almost all of 1959, nearly a whole year. They don't do that anymore. They do not stay on charts that long. Back then if you had a song that was a big seller it was likely to stay on the charts for a whole year. That is what happened and then I finally gave up my broadcasting job and moved up here to the Grand Ole Opry and I have been here ever since. But I do still get out to Texas a lot, in fact, I remember going to Brady way back yonder. I remember I got a job as a vocalist with

62

Bill Boyd and his Cowboy Ramblers out of Dallas, they were on the radio everyday and they had a big western swing band and I became his vocalist and we played a show in your city park. We did a show there way back in the 1940's and it seems to me we had a feed company out of Fort Worth sponsor us. We had to go in there and do a show for the local citizens. I had heard of Brady a long time… there are a lot of guys that became very big in Country Music that were from Brady; I do not know if you knew that or not but the Farr Brothers, you know the Sons of the Pioneers. They were raised around there as boys.

Tracy: They were born near Rochelle and Llano.

Charlie: I do not know how long they lived there and of course they ended up in California and went with Roy Rogers and formed the Sons of the Pioneers. But I had always heard they were from Brady

Tracy: Texas did produce a lot of great entertainers.

Charlie: I know that a lot of people go deer hunting in your part of the country. When I was in San Antonio, the Central Texas area was always popular with the deer hunters. I love that deer hunting. I love venison. It is one of my favorite foods. I am a hunter and a golfer and when the fall weather gets here, that is when it is the best season for both of them. Of course I am a fisher too but I am more into hunting and golfing. I love the fall of the year.

Tracy: After you did "Pick Me Up on Your Way Down", you had a hit with the song that was nearly an answer in "I'll Catch You When You Fall".

Charlie: Yes I did. That was written by the same guy who wrote "Pick Me Up on Your Way Down". That was Harlan Howard. "Pick Me Up" was his first hit and gosh he is one of the greatest in the business. He was working in a print shop in Los Angeles when it hit real big and I called him up and told him to write me another song and that is the song he wrote "I'll Catch you When You Fall". I've recorded a number of other songs that he wrote.

Tracy: Did he write "Close all the Honkytonks" for you?

Charlie: No, no, that was written by a guy in California, Red something. He was writing for Buck Owens publishing company at that time and he pitched me this song and I recorded it. It did real well for me back in 1964. It was a real big hit.

Tracy: "Don't Squeeze My Charmin" was another song that brought a lot of attention to your career.

Charlie: "Don't Squeeze My Charmin" it was a really big record. It was one of those things that, well as you know it was a TV commercial. A couple of songwriters thought it would be a good song to write for someone like Charlie Walker. I had done all those up tempo, honkytonk, waltz type things. Yeah, that was a big record. It was on the jukeboxes all across the country.

Tracy: So they picked you for that song; is that right?

Charlie: Yeah, they sure did and that is how that came about. It is still a big record when I am touring. I still get a lot of requests for it.

Tracy: Those two could be considered standards and even "career songs."

Charlie: Well, "Pick Me Up on Your Way Down" is a standard. It was sold several million records. You can still buy it in the Hall of Fame Series, so it is the biggest record that I have ever made. In fact, CBS Records just re-issued on compact disc. Also, they put out an album last year, or the year before on the 60 biggest songs in the history of Country Music and "Pick Me Up" was one of them. It sure is nice to be included with songs like "Silver Haired Daddy of Mine" and "Wabash Cannonball", and all of them.

Tracy: What is Charlie Walker doing now?

Charlie: I am on the Opry and I am touring a lot. I am going to Canada this weekend. I was just over in Sweden and Norway back in April and we had a real successful tour over there. We will be going back probably next. They love Texas music over there. They don't care much about that modern pop culture but they love that Texas swing and honkytonk stuff just like I do. I will be going back at least once a year I imagine.

Tracy: When they write the book of Country Music and they come to that page that has "Charlie Walker" on it, what do you want your fans to read on that page and remember you as?

Charlie: Gosh I would like them to remember me as a guy that recorded good songs. Songs that were not just a flash in the past but songs that carry on and are sung by other people. Being from Texas, I have a Texas sound to my music so I hope that they will remember me from that sound.

Tracy: Charlie is there anything you want to tell our listeners tonight?

Charlie: I just would like to say to all the listeners at KNEL, there in the Brady area, they have all been nice to me and I hope they will keep requesting my songs and I really appreciate you having me on as your guest of the night . Anytime you come up this way you give me a call and we will sit down and you can fill me in on how everything is going on in Central Texas. Tracy, I do appreciate you calling and you give all my friends in Texas my best. I really miss them. My heart is there. I do get to see them from time to time. I was out in Houston recently so one of these day I might get to come out to that good ol Brady area and if I do we will get on with Tracy there at KNEL and visit with the folks.

This was my first interview with Charlie Walker. I love his music and my radio listeners have always enjoyed that special Texas Swing style that Charlie has stayed true to throughout the years.

Backstage at the Grand Ole Opry one night, Charlie told me one of the funniest stories that I have ever heard. He was there and Garth Brooks was on the show that night. There were about twenty young girls crowded around Garth's dressing room waiting to get a glimpse of the hottest act in Country Music.

Charlie opened up his dressing room door and said "Excuse me ladies, but I have a very important announcement to make." The Garth fans were listening intensely hoping to get some kind of announcement about their star. Charlie said, "Forty years ago, your grandmothers were crowded around MY dressing room." He then closed the door and chuckled. I did too.

JULY 19, 1996

Tracy: I am very excited to be talking to Chris Le Doux. Chris how are you doing?

Chris: Hi Tracy, I am doing good

Tracy: How did you get involved in the music industry?

Chris: When I was in high school, I had a guitar and I started learning a few Country songs. Eventually, I started doing rodeos and I started writing songs about that lifestyle. I made my first album in 1972 with the push of my mom and dad.

Tracy: You sold those albums in the back of your pick-up truck

Chris: That story is blown out of proportion. I had a few in the back of my truck. I gave away about eighty percent of them to my friends. If someone wanted one really bad I would dig one out of the back of my truck and sell it. It was my parents that set up a mail order business. My brother went out on the road and he sold some tapes to the rodeos. I was too busy riding bucking horses.

Tracy: I remember your dad promoting your independent projects. 1976 was a big year for you.

Chris: Yes it was. I won the gold buckle in the bare back riding, I had been trying to do that for several years.

Tracy: Do you owe a little of your success to Garth Brooks?

Chris: Yes, an awful lot. I owe more to my folks and my early fans but it was Garth who gave me that one mention and that song that gave me credibility through out the Country Music industry. Most of them down in Nashville did not know who Chris Le Doux was. I was living in Wyoming at the time.

Tracy: "Whatcha Gonna Do With A Cowboy" was a great duet with Garth for you. Why did you decide to record the song?

Chris: Garth and another guy wrote the song. Garth did not record the song because he said that he was not a real cowboy so he couldn't pull it off. The real cowboys might take it as a slap in the face.

Tracy: Tell me a little bit about your road shows.

Chris: I leave it as a surprise. I hate to give anything away.

Tracy: You just really like to have a good time and I know that entertaining and rodeo must have a lot in common. Do you enjoy performing?

Chris: We do. I am enjoying this. It is almost like the rodeo, except I do not have to worry about getting hurt.

Tracy: Tell us a little bit about your family.

Chris: I am married with five kids. All the kids are into sports and they are dabbling in music a little bit. They are all on the road with me right now.

Tracy: We have been getting a lot of requests for the song "Gravitational Pull".

Chris: That is a crazy song. It came to me through Capitol Records. They sent me a bunch of songs on a tape and the first time that I heard it, I thought that the song was terrible. It was a guy just rambling but I did like the chorus. I took the song and I took out some of the verses until it sounded like it had a rhyme and a flow to it. I am always looking for things that are different. Not the same memory, misery, burning bridges songs. This song describes love in a totally different way. It is more up my alley.

Tracy: It is a great song and your entire CD is great as well.

Chris: We just did it. You get so close to the project that you cannot be objective. You think that it is good but you have to let it go out and see if the people like it, if radio likes it and the critics and just hope for the best.

Darrell Cowen was the first person to bring Chris LeDoux to my attention. Darrell knew Chris from following the rodeo circuit. Chris' dad Al LeDoux made sure that KNEL was serviced with every Chris LeDoux project. At that time, he primarily just released albums and would sell them on the road.

Al would mail them out to stations that he thought would play his son's records. That included many of the smaller stations throughout the country. The larger conglomerate owned radio stations would not touch a Chris LeDoux album at that time.

After Garth brought attention to Chris and his music, everyone joined the bandwagon. Chris' older projects were re-released and he had a very successful career in the business. His music changed a little after signing with Capitol Records. He broadened his horizons from the rodeo themes to appeal to a bigger audience. Chris never forgot or left his true love and his induction into the Cowboy Hall of Fame was well deserved.

Chris is one of the few entertainers that I never had an opportunity to meet. He passed from this life all too soon, but he lived his life to the fullest and left a lasting legacy for others to follow.

Chubby Checker

DECEMBER 13, 1999

Tracy: I am excited to be talking to one of the icons of the entire music business, Mr. Chubby Checker. How are you Chubby?

Chubby: Tracy is my brother's name so I am use to talking to Tracy's all the time.

Tracy: How did you get involved in the music business?

Chubby: I saw Ernest Tubb perform at the Paper Mill in South Carolina, when I was four years old and that is when I decided that I wanted to be on stage like Ernest Tubb. We are celebrating the 40th anniversary of Chubby Checker dancing apart to the beat. Before Alexander Graham Bell-no telephone; before Thomas Edison- no light bulb; before George Washington Carver-no oil from seeds and cloning from plants; before Henry Ford-no engine; before Walt Disney-no animated cartoons; before Chubby Checker, no dancing apart to the beat. What is dancing apart to the beat? It is a dance that we do while looking at each other while we dance to the beat of anybody's music. Before Chubby Checker, it did not exist.

Tracy: It is amazing that it has been 40 years!

Chubby: For 40 years, people have been looking at each other doing what they want to do on the dance floor to music with a beat. Before Chubby Checker, it did not happen so we are celebrating that. You are going to start seeing Chubby Checker in the airports, gift shops, you are going to see an exercising machine called the Twistersizer. You should start seeing that this January on infomercials. It is a machine and you put on your favorite music, you move on this machine and it gives you a great workout.

Tracy: I understand "The Twist" is a song that has re-entered the charts and has made it to number one again.

Chubby: "The Twist", is the first platinum given to anyone. "The Twist", is the only song that has gone number one twice with in a period of 18 months, it has never happened in the history of music. I am hoping that "The Twist" will be the song of the century because it has really supported the music business for years. Dancing apart to the beat is like the creation of the telephone; everybody uses it since it came out. Dancing apart to the beat was the biggest thing that happened in the music business and it is still the biggest thing that has happened.

Tracy: You were still in high school when "The Twist" came out.

Chubby: Yes I was, in fact I recorded "The Twist" last month, forty years ago. When I graduated from high school in February 1960, the record was already out. We were out going to little places promoting the music and the dance. By October of the next year, "The Twist" went to number one; it was on my birthday, I was only 19.

Tracy: It is phenomenal for somebody so young to get so much recognition.

Chubby: I was 19 on Oct 3, 1941. By the time it came out the second time, we were doing "The Pony". "The Pony" is a dance that everybody does. It is the dance that was real fast when it came out but we have slowed it down and is a dance where you go 1-1-2 1-2. We also had "The Fly" and "The Shake". The dance as we know it started to evolve along with the different beats that came out in the 1970's, 1980's, and 1990's. But before Chubby Checker, and I keep stressing this because I want everyone to know, especially all you young people out there that think that they are so cool. All the rappers out there are doing "The Pony" and that is my dance. And all you guys out there getting funky with your beat, all you kids, black, white, brown, yellow, clear as water, you are all doing "The Chubby".

Tracy: You really changed music forever.

Chubby: I am just so happy that I am the only person on the planet that can make such a claim. Nobody else can. I do not think that people realize that Chubby Checker has fronted the music business for 40 years. It is hard to believe that such a thing can happen by any one person. I do thank Hank Ballard for writing "The Twist". Without Hank writing the song, I know I would not be here. His version just died but the kids in the inner city made up the dance to it. I took the song and made up the dance and put it together, added a few things to it, told people what it was and when I went on TV with it, the world changed forever, nothing will ever be the same because of that song. By 1979-1980, I looked around and realized what I did. I would see all these kids dancing in China and Philippines, England, Puerto Rico, South America, all over the world, they are doing what I started. I know that there are a lot of engines in other cars but Henry Ford is the one that started it. Just like Alexander Graham Bell and Thomas Edison, there are other variations, but they are the ones that did it.

Tracy: It is pretty good for a guy from Philadelphia to do something so incredible.

Chubby: I came to Philadelphia when I was 8 years old but when I saw Ernest Tubb I was in South Carolina where I was born on a little farm, population 52. By the way Tracy, I want everyone out there to be on the look out for Chubby Checker's new album called "The Texas Twist". We recorded it in 1994 but we will be releasing it through Sony Music. We took "The Twist" for the entire boot scooters and we made it into a two-step. There are 18 Country songs on that one tape. I will not be making another one though. I did my one Country release of my lifetime. I was born in South Carolina in 1941 and there was no rock 'n roll around then so when I sing Country Music, it is for my soul. It is fantastic and really enjoyed doing it and you will not even know that it was me doing it.

A gentleman from Menard set this interview up for me. He was a friend of my longtime friend Sonny Davenport. He stopped by the radio station one day and was talking about being friends with Chubby Checker.

I have to admit that I have listened to so many stories from so many people, that many of them are forgotten about as quickly as I hear them. Everybody is friends with George Strait and had a cousin that played for Bob Wills.

He was telling me about Chubby recording a Country project and that I should interview him about it. I told him to set it up and I would be happy to talk to the great Chubby Checker-never thinking that I would hear about it again. A week later, I was interviewing Chubby Checker!

Chubby was very charismatic during the interview. He seemed as delighted to be talking to me as he would have been visiting with Dick Clark. Chubby was in no hurry and we visited for several minutes after the interview about his love of Texas and desire to work more in the state.

He also spoke of his love and affection of Ernest Tubb. That was a big shock to me, but he mentioned several of E.T.'s classic songs that he recited by heart. The creator of "The Twist" remembering "It's Been So Long Darlin'" impressed me.

I believe that you can tell in the interview that he is very secure in himself and his career. He knows what he means to the music business and wants to make sure that everyone else does as well. I have no problem with that because he has certainly made a significant mark maybe not in Country Music, but in the industry as a whole.

Chubby's Country project did not do what he wanted and he returned to the music that made him famous.

Connie Smith

MAY 17, 1999

Tracy: I am visiting with one of the greatest singers in Country Music, Connie Smith. How are you Connie?

Connie: I am doing just fine and thank you for that compliment.

Tracy: What part did Bill Anderson have in your career?

Connie: He heard me sing in a talent contest in Ohio and offered to bring me to Nashville to sing on the Ernest Tubb Record Shop and later I did a demo session with him. When RCA contracted me, Bill wrote about 33 songs that I recorded. He was very influential.

Tracy: Your first session with RCA resulted in your biggest hit.

Connie: On the very first session, we recorded three songs and one was "Once A Day". It was released and was number one for two months.

Tracy: "Once A Day" is one of those songs that has lived on forever, it is one of those "career" songs.

Connie: It really is. Bill told me years ago that over fifty people have recorded that song since I recorded it. It is a hit song that does not care who sings it.

Tracy: Female vocalists were not as recognized as men in Country Music at that time. Was it difficult to get started in the business?

Connie: Not really, it kind of pulled me along because I was not really career oriented. I just wanted to grow up, get married and have a bunch of kids and I just happen to love to sing. I never felt any resistance being a girl. I just did my thing and helped raise my family. I quit for a while when the kids were small. But when I first came here, "Once A Day" hit so fast and so hard, it had a life of its own.

Tracy: I have heard you say so many times that you did not really want a career in the music business.

Connie: I just loved to sing. I loved to record, I love to sing and I love the people, it was just a natural thing that happened but if I am around the house, I am going to sing as well.

71

Tracy: You have had so many songs that so many other singers would loved to have had. Do you feel lucky about the material you have been fortunate enough to find?

Connie: I think that is a major factor in my success; I was so fortunate to have such great songs. I recorded 33 Bill Anderson songs but I also recorded 68 Dallas Frazier songs. That was just a natural thing. When Dallas would write, it would fit me. A couple of songs that he wrote for me was actually about me. "Where's My Castle" and "Just For What I Am". I do believe that I was very fortunate to have those songs. Actually, a couple of songs that I cut on my first album, Bill wrote for other people. "Once A Day" was actually going to be pitched to Kitty Wells and "Tiny Blue Transistor Radio" was going to be pitched to Skeeter Davis.

Tracy: You were also featured in a memorable movie.

Connie: "Road to Nashville"- I taped it with Marty Robbins and Doodles Weaver. I was a co-star. I really did not know what I was doing. The movie starts out with me driving into the airport in Nashville in a Lincoln Continental convertible and at that point I did not even have a drivers licenses. In that movie, I sang one of the first songs that I ever wrote "Never Get Over Loving You". I wrote it before I ever came to Nashville.

Tracy: Even though you took a short leave of absence to raise your family, you stayed true to the Grand Ole Opry.

Connie: I love the Grand Ole Opry; it is home base for me. I have really missed it lately, I have only been there once in the past year because I have been so busy in one way or another. I got married about a year and a half ago so trying to get everything in order here took a lot of my time. I moved and sold my home and I still have five kids that take momma's time even though they are grown-ups. Between all of that, being on the road and having a new album out and supporting Marty (Stuart) in all he does, it keeps me pretty busy.

Tracy: You have a son that lives over seas.

Connie: Yes, he lives in Norway. I also have a son in Taiwan. My son in Taiwan teaches English and is studying Chinese. He will be there for a couple of years. My oldest son Darren, who is in Norway, has been there for several years. He is married to a Norwiegn and my three grandchildren are also in Norway. I have a trip planned over there this year. When I am offered something in Norway, it is a great excuse to see my kids and grandkids.

Tracy: Darren inherited some of your talent.

Connie: The great thing about Darren is that he can play any instrument that he picks up and he is a very fine songwriter. He went overseas in 1984 with "Youth With A Mission". He went with the mission musicians because he sings and writes and uses that a lot in the ministry. He is going to college now and studying to be a psychologist. He is currently working in a mental institution plus taking care of the kids because his wife is a stewardess. He tries to pick on the weekends.

Tracy: You have done a great job raising you children and maintaining a career.

Connie: I have wonderful kids, in spite of me. My three daughters are in town with me. My youngest daughter graduated from college this past year. I am confident that she will sing- probably contemporary gospel. She loves to sing and loves gospel music My second daughter Jeanie, when she was young she wanted to be a rock and roll guitarist. Knowing her, she will end up as president. My oldest daughter Julie is 25 and she got married recently so she is married and working all week and then going to college on the weekend.

Tracy: You were working with Marty and then feel in love with him. That must have been a great experience for you.

Connie: It was. I met Marty when he was 12 years old, and he came to one of my shows. He had his mom buy him a new yellow shirt so I would notice him. He told his mom on the way home that night that he was going to marry me. It took him awhile but he finally got around to it. When all my kids left home, I knew that I had to do something. I thought that I could get in the business because I never really did that full force before, but if I did, who would I want to work with. I wanted to make records again because I had not done that in 20 years so I wanted someone who would respect who I am and where I have come from but also someone who would have a sense of what is going on today. I thought of everybody that I knew and the only person that I could think of was Marty Stuart. I saw him at the Opry one night and asked him if he would be interested in working with me and he said yes. When we started working together, he knew what was going on but I had no idea. Every time I tried to run, he came after me so he won.

Tracy: Marty was also instrumental in your new album.

Connie: He co-produced the album and he and I co-wrote most of the songs. Marty played the guitar and the mandolin, so his tracks are all over the new album.

Tracy: How does it feel to have a new album out after such a longtime, on a major label at that?

Connie: It feels wonderful. I had so many loyal fans that have been so good and have followed me around the country. Although I was out of the business for a while, what they do not realize is that once my youngest daughter started kindergarten, I went back to work. Even though I was not recording, I was on the road supporting my family. I have fans that waited a long time; they have been so loyal. I am glad to be able to offer them some new material. When I got in the studio, it had been so long that I had to learn all over again because everything had changed.

Tracy: You have given us a lifetime of music and I think that you have one of the greatest Country voices that God gave anybody. Are you still touring?

Connie: Thank you very much. I have dates in Ohio, Norway, Japan, Texas, all over the country. You name it and I will be there before the year is through just as long as the fans want to listen to Connie Smith.

Connie Smith is still one of the finest vocalists in the industry. I truly cannot remember the first time that I met Connie. It seems that she has always been a part of my Nashville trips. She has always made time out of her busy schedule to say hello.

Connie was coming to Texas to work a show that Floyd Tillman was featured on in Austin. She told Dickey Overbey about the show and about looking forward to meeting Floyd for the first time. Floyd was in his latter years and I had been close enough to him to realize that I need to put a "bug in his ear" about Connie. Of course, Floyd was well versed with those in his generation, but he some times needed help with those artists he referred to as the "younger generation". I could not make the gig, so I called Floyd and told him about Connie and about how she was looking forward to meeting him. Connie later recalled going up to Floyd and him saying something like "and I bet your name is Connie" as he smiled that big famous grin.

Justin Trevino is one of Connie's biggest fans. When we were working on the Floyd Tillman duet album, Justin and I talked about asking Connie to join the historic album. Connie has not recorded many duets in her career, so we were not sure that she would agree to do it. We were certainly pleased when she added her beautiful vocals to "I Love You So Much It Hurts Me."

One of my favorite Connie Smith stories actually deals with my friend Sonny Davenport. Sonny has always been a fan of Connie's singing-and her looks! We were in Carthage, Texas, for the Texas Country Music Hall of Fame ceremonies about six years ago. Connie was one of the entertainers and I asked her about meeting Sonny. I went and asked Sonny to go with me backstage. When I introduced him to Connie, he was in a state of shock. He looked up and said "I have been listening to you all of my life." That is a great compliment, except for the fact that Sonny is fifteen years older than Connie! She enjoyed the irony and I remind Sonny of it as well.

2004

Tracy: It is always great to see Curtis Potter. Curtis, you were raised around our area of Texas.

Curtis: That is right. I was born in Cross Plains, Texas and raised in the Abilene, Texas area. As a matter of fact, I still live in Abilene today. I always enjoyed singing while growing up. I started working for KRBC television in Abilene on the Bill Fox Show when I was just a kid. It was a show that featured local and regional talent. They gave me my own show when I was 16, and I also was a frequent guest on the Slim Willet show. That early television experience kind of gave me the entertainment bug.

Tracy: You were also working the honkytonks at this time.

Curtis: Oh yes, that was the only place to make a living back them. There were several clubs within a couple hundred miles that we played. At that time, you could make a living-maybe not a real good one-by playing the honkytonks.

Tracy: Hank Thompson has played a very vital role in your career. When did you meet Hank?

Curtis: It was the later part of 1958. He played Abilene, Texas. Billy Gray invited me up on the stage to sing a song. At that time, Hank was getting ready to disband. I actually started working for Billy Gray at that time. After two or three months, Hank hired the whole band and we all became the Brazos Valley Boys. He disbanded the group originally because it had gotten too large. I think he was carrying twelve or thirteen pieces at that time. It was just too much. When we went back to work for him, we were using eight pieces-which was still a good sized band at that time.

Tracy: The years when you traveled with Hank were some of the best band years for the Brazos Valley Boys.

Curtis: We were the number one band for thirteen years in a row. We had Bobby Garrett and Bert Rivera on steel guitar. Curley Lewis and Keith Coleman on fiddles, Junior Nickles on drums. There were quite a few different ones coming and going at that time. I played bass and opened the show for Hank.

Tracy: Did you learn much from Hank?

Curtis: I watched that man and appreciated how he carried himself and how he presented himself to the public. You can learn a lot from folks like that. We were working some of the biggest concert halls in the country at that time and even some of the smaller dance halls. Hank always knew how to handle any audience that he appeared before. He is truly a star and I admire him very much.

Tracy: You started having some recording success.

Curtis: I did. The first song that got me some attention was "You Comb Her Hair Every Morning." That song did some great things for my career. I also had "Walkin' Talkin' Breathin' Case of Sorrow" around 1973, and then I recorded the "Texas Dance Hall" album with Darrell McCall and Ray Sanders soon after that. I also had some stuff with Hillside records.

Tracy: You helped to start Step One Records.

Curtis: I enjoyed working for Step One. It was in the middle '80's and Step One allowed me to focus some on the business end of the industry. We had some success with a lot of artists including Gene Watson, Clinton Gregory, Ray Price and even Kitty Wells.

Tracy: You had some success as well especially with the duet album with Willie.

Curtis: We actually had a number one video back in '95, with "Turn Me Loose And Let Me Swing." It was from our album "Six Hours At The Pedernales. We named it that because it just took us that long to record the album.

Tracy: You are now enjoying the release of another new album.

Curtis: Jim Loessberg produced my new album, "Walking On New Grass." We got together a while back and he said, "Let's do an album." I was excited about it. Jim played steel on it and does a great job. It is definitely Country and I wouldn't do it if it wasn't.

Tracy: Did you have trouble picking material for the project.

Curtis: Well, there is so much good Country out there. Jim helped me a lot to find some of the stuff. There are some good old songs that people haven't heard in a while. We titled the album "Walking On New Grass." Of course, Kenny Price had such a great record with that. They called him "the round man of sound".

Tracy: I guess that my favorite is "Someday, I'll Sober Up."

Curtis: Actually, that is also my wife's favorite on the project. Johnny Russell wrote it and had a great record on it, but it wasn't a big hit for him. Jim found that song and I actually hadn't heard it. After listening to it, I said that we had to cut it. It is just a good old Country drinking song.

Tracy: What is your favorite on the album?

Curtis: "Mama Was The Rose" is my favorite song on "Walking On New Grass."

Clinton Gregory recorded that on Step One Records quite a few years ago and so I told Jim that I wanted to do it for this album.

Tracy: You are known for that great Texas style of music.

Curtis: That is true. I am known for the Honky Tonk style of music and of course, I enjoy doing that music. I also love the pretty stuff like the Ray Price sounds. As a matter of fact, you played a Price song the other day that I just fell in love with. It is called "You Just Don't Love Me Anymore." He has still got it.

Tracy: You have a connection to Ray.

Curtis: I have worked several shows with Ray and I have known him for it seems like a hundred years. That guy has influenced more Country singers than anybody in the world. I met him just before I started working for Hank Thompson. We did a lot of dates together while I was with Hank.

Tracy: I know that you are still on the road. Where are you heading next?

Curtis: I am going up to Wisconsin and work a week with the Texas Playboys. Sometimes when the great Leon Rausch decides not to travel with the group, they call me and ask me about singing some of that great Bob Wills music.

Tracy: How does Curtis Potter want to be remembered?

Curtis: I would like to be remembered as someone who enjoyed Country Music and the people who enjoyed listening to it.

I was trying to remember the first time that I ever met Curtis Potter. It just seems that Curtis has always been around and a part of what we have been doing. I became a fan of Curtis at a very early age. His sound resembled some of my favorite singers including Ray Price, Hank Thompson, Johnny Bush and Darrell McCall. He has always been unapologitacally Country.

Curtis only lives a couple of hours away from my hometown. While working with Step One Records, he would make several radio tours with many of the artists that Step One was promoting including Gene Watson, Clinton Gregory and even his former boss man Hank Thompson. Curtis made several stops at KNEL to visit with us, and I always included him in any interview. I have forever felt that Curtis' career was never properly promoted.

A few years ago, Curtis was having some difficulty after heart surgery. Many of his friends got together and hosted a special benefit for him in Priddy, Texas. I have MC'd and helped to organize dozens of benefits, but this was one of the ultimate. Johnny Bush, Darrell McCall, Frenchie Burke, Billy Mata, Jake Hooker, Johnny Lyon, Justin Trevino, Kelly Spinks, Frankie Miller and a host of others donated their time and talents to help one of their own. The love that was shown that day was evident to me that Curtis Potter was loved by this industry. He has always loved this industry as much, or maybe even a little more.

Darrell McCall

JANUARY 21, 2007

Tracy: Darrell, how did your career begin in the music business? I know that you had some early success with "The Little Dippers."

Darrell: Actually, when I first got to Nashville, there a couple of things that I did do in the Country field. I recorded a thing with Bill Anderson and went out on the road with Bill for the first month or so. Bill needed someone to sing harmony and I was in the studio to just watch. I think the song was called "99 Years". I always wanted to record Country because I was raised that way. The Little Dippers spot came open and I jumped right in the middle of it, because I needed to make a dollar and eat. Buddy Killen with Tree Publishing put that group together. Johnny Paycheck introduced me to Buddy when we first got to town. He wrote "Forever" and was looking for a male soprano voice in the group. I just happened to be painting his offices that night. He was interviewing people and I told him that I could do that part. I got down off the ladder and went over to the piano and sang the part. Buddy told me to go down and get fitted for a new suit and we headed to the Dick Clark show in New York.

Tracy: Meeting Dick Clark had to be something special for a Country boy.

Darrell: It really was. That was the main thing on TV when I left home. I never thought that I would ever be a part of American Bandstand. That was one of the first major things that I did out of Nashville. Dick was very nice and a true gentleman. He made you feel so right at home on the set. I was scared to death, but it was still fun.

Tracy: You had some experience as a disc jockey growing up.

Darrell: They had opened a little radio station in Hillsboro, Ohio, and I was still in high school. I was picking around with this friend of mine in high school. He played lead guitar and so did I. We did some Louvin Brothers and Everly Brothers stuff. There was no one with any experience with a microphone in town when they decided to open up that radio station. They asked the Chief of Police Willard Parr if he would do it since he had experience with a microphone talking to the cars at night. Willard called myself and Darrell Mullins in and we started doing a little show on a Saturday morning. It was an hour show and we did not know what we were doing, but we were having fun.

Tracy: You soon signed with Phillips Records.

Darrell: I actually first signed with Capital and had a song called "Beyond

Imagination." Roy Drusky wrote that. He and I also did a Sesac album together. I was on Capitol for about a year and then Shelby Singleton signed me on with Phillips. He let me cut Country. I cut a song called "A Stranger Was Here." I was begging them to put a steel guitar on there because I loved steel so much. They said, "We'll let a guitar play like a steel guitar." That was in 1960 or 1961. If you were 18 or 19 years old, they didn't want you to put a steel guitar on your stuff especially if you just got back from American Bandstand. They wanted you to cross over into that other area and sell more records. In my heart, I have been Country all of my life.

Tracy: You were also featuring in the movie "HUD" around that time.

Darrell: That was a year or two later. I was out hunting at the time and had gotten into that fast draw thing. I had my old 45 and my old rig on and I had been out in the woods hunting and fast drawing when Hubert Long called me. He said that he wanted me in the studio right away. Of course, I had my old boots and my hat on and I told him that I was going to have to come in just that way I was. He told me to come on in because they needed me right away. I ran in and all these guys from New York were in the studio. I walked in and they said I was exactly what they were looking for. I walked in and they filled me in on the Paul Newman movie and wanted me to do a song in the studio.

Tracy: You embarked on a little acting career at that time.

Darrell: I'd do anything to eat a sandwich. I never did claim to be an actor. I was in "Road To Nashville" and "Nashville Rebel" and "What Am I Bid" with Leroy Van Dyke. I never did pursue acting. They would just call me and I would try to do anything that I could to keep my head above water.

Tracy: You would soon return to the studio and work on your first album.

Darrell: Little Richie Johnson signed me with Wayside. The owners were in Massachusetts and they wanted me to fly up there and shoot the album cover. I flew up there and they picked me up in the airport in a Pierce Arrow and took me to the old mill with a waterwheel on it that Henry Wadsworth Longfellow wrote all of his stuff at. They had the pictures taken there for my first album "Meet Darrell McCall". I was tickled to death. They let me have Lloyd Green on steel and Pig Robbins and all the main pickers in Nashville.

Tracy: Your song "Eleven Roses" came about shortly after the "Meet Darrell McCall" album.

Darrell: I was working for Hank Williams Jr. at the time. It was a thing that I had pondered in my mind for a long time. I had never been away from home too much and our mother raised us five kids practically by herself because our dad was always gone. I got to missing her real bad because I hadn't been home in about three years. This was probably '61 and I sent her eleven roses with a little note saying that she was the missing rose and that inspired that song idea. In the later 60's, I put it together one night and Lamar Morris told me to sing if for Hank. Hank listened to it and asked me to sing it again and again. He told me that he really liked the song and I told him that I needed to add another verse to it. He kept wanting me to sing it. We got off of the road and about three days later, Hank called me at about ten or eleven at night and told me that he just cut my song. I told him that I wasn't through writing it yet. He said, "believe me your finished with it and MGM has heard it and has flipped over it."

Tracy: Were you hoping to save it for one of your sessions?

Darrell: I really don't know. All through the 60's, I was just trying to do something to fit in-to sing, act or write or whatever. Just hoping that if I threw enough stuff against the wall that something would stick.

Tracy: You were a part of some of the great bands in the business as well.

Darrell: I was playing bass and singing on the road with Hank Jr. when "Eleven Roses" came into being. I also worked in the early days with Ray Price and the Cherokee Cowboys for two or three years singing harmony and playing bass. I worked with Faron for quite a while. I even worked with Charley Louvin for a little bit. One of the guys that I really admired and still admire today is the great Carl Smith. I tried to take a little bit of each one of them and put it in myself.

Tracy: "There's Still A Lot of Love In San Antone" helped to turn your solo career around in the early 1970's.

Darrell: Doodle Owens and Lou Rochelle came to San Antonio. They told me that they wanted to write me a song. They were staying out at our house. So they went to town one night and they came in the next morning looking really bad. They had this song wrapped around the neck of this little guitar and they gave me the song and the guitar. It was "Still A Lot of Love In San Antone". Of course, I feel in love with it and went right to Nashville and cut it. I think that was right at the time that Country Music was trying to come back. That was when Johnny Rodriguez hit real big with "Pass Me By" and Willie with "Blue Eyes Crying In The Rain." It was time for the Country stuff to come back.

Tracy: Speaking of Willie, "Lily Dale" was the first duet that the two of you recorded.

Darrell: Willie had known that I had been on a few different labels. If you don't have the money people behind you, you can be a tax write off real quick. The times that I have been on the other labels, my records were always in the charts but I never had the big hits. The hits were controlled by how much add space that you bought in the trade magazines. When I signed with CBS Lonestar, Willie said "I want you on the label and I want you to choose the material that you want to cut and use the musicians that you want as well." He told me that he only wanted to hear the finished product. I called Buddy Emmons and a few others and I always wanted to cut a Bob

Wills tune. I always did "Lily Dale" on our shows with Ray and Faron and Carl. I was in the studio that morning just kind of running through it so the boys could get the charts down when Willie walked in. He came up to the mike and was talking to me. I started singing it and he started singing harmony with me. The engineer said that it was sounding great as a duet. He asked if we wanted to do it as a duet. Willie said it was fine with him as long as I didn't mind. I was tickled that he wanted to do it because he had just had "Blue Eyes Crying In The Rain." We went through it one time and the rest was history.

Tracy: You also recorded another duet with Waylon Jennings some time later.

Darrell: That was on Indigo Records. It was a killer duet. I did a complete album for them and it was never released. They did release "Memphis In May" but the full project never saw the light of day. Curtis Potter and I recorded a couple of things for Hillside. I was never actually signed with them. He just called me one day when I was mowing the grass and asked if I wanted to come to his session. I went over there and the first thing that Curtis asked me was "What are we going to do?" We wound up cutting "San Antone Medley" and some other stuff.

Tracy: Step One Records put you and Johnny Bush together for a project.

Darrell: We actually recorded that album together and then shopped it around. Step One picked it up and decided to release it. It was a fun project to do. We got some stuff together and went up to Willie's studio. John played drums and I played bass and then we added our voices and flew Buddy Emmons down from Nashville. We would record a song or two and then go out and hit a round or two of golf and come back and do some more. It was fun doing that with John.

Tracy: The road has changed so much from when you started in your career.

Darrell: It has changed so much. Those are the times that I really cherish. Those are the people that I grew up with. I was just a little ole kid when I came to Nashville and didn't know anyone. Johnny Paycheck and I came to town together. Those people like Porter Wagoner, Charlie and Ira Louvin, the Wilburn Brothers, Don Gibson and so many more all hung together. We all shared the same bowl of chili just to stay alive. When I first went to the Grand Ole Opry, it was a dream to me just to be there. There were two dressing rooms on one side of the stage and one on the other. All of us from the biggest star to the least musician changed clothes together, rehearsed together in the same dressing rooms. We knew whose bus or car broke down. We knew whose wife was sick or who got drunk and missed their show date. We all visited and it was so family. The closeness was there. When we left the Ryman and everyone got their own dressing room, people didn't visit. Patsy (Cline) was a dear friend. When Dottie and Bill West first came to town, I would sneak them in the back door with me. We all helped each other out.

Tracy: How do you want to be remembered?

Darrell: I just want them to know that I am what I am. I am not someone to be looked up to or idolized. I am just the same as everybody else. I feel like we are all God's people and we have all been given gifts. He just happened to give me the gift of singing. I am supposed to give it to everybody else. I don't sit here and sing to me at the house by myself. He gave me that gift and He told me that as long as I do it that he would take care of me. I am going to do it as long as He will let me sing and as long as people will come out and support our music. It is one of those gifts that took me all over the world. I have had dinners with kings and queens. I guess that legacy that we want to leave is that we are all the same people and no better than each other. Some might have more than others, but basically down in the heart we are all exactly the same.

I have listened to Darrell McCall music all of my life. I thought for years that he was from Texas. He is as much a Texan and I am. He was actually born in Ohio, but he got to Texas as soon as he could. He loves working in Texas and is one of the constant dance hall draws all over our great state.

I met him the first time at London Dance Hall. I have probably interviewed him fifty times throughout the years and he always shares something new and enlightening at each interview.

Darrell called me a few years ago while still living just outside of Nashville. He was driving back and forth to Texas nearly every weekend. He told me that he would love to move back to Texas and if I found a little place around Brady or San Saba in Central Texas to let him know. I took him serious and called my friends Logan and Gay Stevens in Fredonia, Texas. The Stevens are successful farmers and ranchers and have several places around Brady. I told Gay about Darrell's desire to move back to Texas and asked her to call them sometime. It took a couple of years, but we are proud to say that the McCalls are now residents of our small Central Texas area. They absolutely love it here and told me that they never want to leave.

Darrell and his wife Mona both record for our Heart of Texas Records label. Darrell is doing just what he wants to be doing. Living his life while playing and recording some great Country Music.

DECEMBER 5, 2001

Tracy: I know that Baseball was your first love, even before music.

Dave: Maybe it is fate that you are calling me from Texas because that is where my arm went bad. It was in Gainesville, Texas.

Tracy: What happen to your arm?

Dave: I was with the White Sox chain and they sent me to Gainesville for the state league and I was doing the fastball stuff and it all went to pieces. Back in those days, you did not have the chance to fix your arm and it would be better. My baseball career ended in Texas. When I left there, I went back to the Midwest and worked on trucks.

Tracy: Were you singing at the time?

Dave: No. A friend of mine was a DJ in Wisconsin. He went to work at a station in Stephens Point, Wisconsin. At that time I was working on the railroad so I went to see him one morning after work and while I was sitting there waiting for him to finish up, I saw a guitar sitting in the corner so I picked it up and was playing the few songs that I knew which were Hank Thompson and Eddy Arnold. The program director came around the corner and told me that I sounded pretty good and for me to come back after my shift at the railroad and do about fifteen minutes of Country Music after the news. I thought that he was kidding so the next day after my shift at the railroad, I went home and went to bed. My mom woke me up and told me that there is a guy at the radio station that is very upset with me. I didn't realize he was serious so I went and apologized to him. I told him that I would do a few songs for him. I had never sung on the radio before so I went and sang a few songs and we even got some mail. They were trying to build me into something special so they offered me $5 a show Monday, Wednesday and Friday. I learned a few more songs and stuck with it. That is how it all got stated.

Tracy: You had an accident involving a hit and run.

Dave: I was a bandleader in Minnesota and I had a day off but a friend of mine got sick and asked me to help out so I did. After I got through with the job, I was going over to a chicken place so I parked my car, opened the door, luckily for me I shut the door. They considered me a guy headed for the cemetery. For about a year I was out of the business but all the guys that I knew like Jimmy C. Newman and Hank

Thompson told me that I was not going to quit. That was when "Six Days On The Road" came to be. This was in 1963.

Tracy: What a huge hit. That song did so much for the music business and became the trucker's anthem.

Dave: I never expected that. I was a truck driver but not like some of these guys that go out on the road. They are gone all night long and I use to do day jobs. That really had no bearing on the song. Jimmy C. Newman and I were really good friend through the years and he used to work with my band in the Midwest. Finally, he told me I was not going to quit the business and he had heard that I was going to do some records. He threw a tape in my guitar case and said if I had time to record the song that was on the tape it would be a hit. He said it was not his type of song. I got a settlement from the company who hit me so I took that money and I used it to record the session. That is what you call true show biz! Take the money and run to the studio. We had done three songs and I had a half an hour left so I thought about that tape and I brought it out and while the girl was typing it up, the band was learning it in the studio. We took one shot at it and it did not turn out, the second time, we just went through it and the third time I knew that we could handle it. We got it on the third take.

Tracy: A few years ago Sawyer Brown recorded, "Six Days on the Road". What did you think about that?

Dave: It threw me a little but I expected it to happen sooner or later. You could take the song and move it into any tempo that you want. It just happened that Sawyer Brown did it with what I call rockabilly. They got the rhythm for the modern day teenager and it worked.

Tracy: You have a new album out and it is great. I have already been using the single "You Ain't Gonna Truck With Us".

Dave: That is a nice story. The reason that came up is because all the boys over at Southern Artist thought that they should do something for the effort to make sure what we are up against. They thought of me and that the truckers never got covered and given any credit and to warn them that things could happen to them also. They chose me and asked if I would be interested in telling a story. I was interested only if it was a story that would tell them guys to be careful. They said they had one and I said I had one too. I was working on a song just to be working. Mine was a little more hardball. They did not want to use it because some of the disc jockeys may not be familiar with me and how I am. I tell it like it is. "Don't Come Messing Around With US Truckers" is one of the songs. Tom Stewart did a wonderful job with it. The main thing that I wanted to get across was what the song was about that. These guys have been with me for so long and when they are driving they can be careless every once in a while but they need to remember who is around them and what they are trying to do.

Tracy: Are you still working the road?

Dave: Oh yes! If you have wondered where I have been, and this is a funny story, in 1979, things were getting a little hard and dates were hard to come by. I got a call from Germany and I was asked if I would be interested in going to Germany to do a TV special. I thought it was Bobby Bare pulling a trick on me. This guy was really serious. There was a group over there called "Truck Stop" and they did not sing any English. They did not know what a truck stop was, they just liked the name. They recorded a song that means I want to hear more Dave Dudley. It went to number one and they had a number one TV show and I was on it. It really went over well so I was over in Germany for twenty years. So if you were wondering where I have been, that is where. I have toured Yugoslavia, Austria, Switzerland and Norway. When I got here, I did a movie or two and just lost track of time. But I am back now. I came back in 2000. This project is the first one since I got back. We are doing some concerts. We were in Canada with the Grand Ole Opry and we have done some state fairs. We are doing some really good things. My trucking buddies and I are still hanging out. It is good that they still remember me.

It is amazing that one song can give an artist a career's worth of work. "Six Days On The Road" took Dave all over the world. He had several other good songs, but none as big as the trucker's anthem.

It took several years to catch up with Dave, because I simply did not know where he was living. I really enjoyed this interview. Dave's real name is David Pedruska. He changed his name to fit in more with the Country Music audience.

His last chart record was "Rolaids, Doan's Pills and Preparation H" back in 1980. The title should have one some kind of an award. It was great that he released a new project (and did this interview) just a couple of years before his death.

David McCormick

1998

Tracy: You are the president of the Ernest Tubb Record Shop. How did you become acquainted with Ernest Tubb?

David: I came to Nashville to go to school. I began working for an insurance company. All I had was five shirts and five pairs of pants, a card table with four chairs and a bed in a one-bedroom apartment. I was barely making it. I was looking for part-time work and I had a friend who worked full-time at the Ernest Tubb Record Shop. She told me that there were some openings at the shop and she suggested that I go down there and work. I told her that I did not know if I could handle listening to Country Music all day long. I was fan of Country Music but I did not love it the way I learned to later on. I went down and talked to the manager and later was able to meet Mr. Tubb and I began working evenings and weekends. I worked in mail order, sweep and mop the floors, what ever need to be done. It started from there and later on, the manager's position became available. Mrs. Tubb was involved with the Midnight Jamboree at that time and I told her I might be interested in the job. She said she would love to have me. She would come down to the record shop a lot and she would talk to Mr. Tubb about me and he said that Mrs. Tubb had given me a really good recommendation. He said that he never hired anyone for that position that was as young as I was but because she had really bragged on me a whole lot and the times he had seen me, it seemed as if I was a pretty good guy that would do the kind of job I expect that he would bring me in for ninety days to see how it would go. I was twenty-one when I became manager.

Tracy: At that time there was only one Ernest Tubb Record Shop in Nashville.

David: Yes, the Broadway store.

Tracy: Was mail order predominantly your business?

David: No, it was about 40-50 percent. At that time radio was the median for mail order. We did not have the Nashville Network or other TV programs that did Country that offered mail orders. Mail order is still a very big part of this business.

Tracy: How many employees did you have when you started as manager?

David: Six full-time employees and about five part-time employees

Tracy: How does that compare to today?

David: We have a little over 100 employees involved in the Ernest Tubb Organization. That includes mail order and the Midnight Jamboree and the Texas Troubadours Theater.

Tracy: Was Ernest very active in the record shop business?

David: No, because he was never here. We did not get to have him on the Midnight Jamboree but maybe five nights a year. He worked the road about 250-300 days a year. We did not get to see him very much but it was a great thrill when he was here. I do recall one time he was here to pick up some mail and I told him we were mailing some catalogs out and he said to put him to work. I have picture somewhere of him putting labels on catalogs. He helped us out one night and it was a real thrill for everyone to have him help out. I will never forget that, but he was on the road a lot. I never did have the pleasure of having him here enough.

Tracy: When he was not there, who took over the Midnight Jamboree?

David: We had a different Opry act each week. Back in the early years, Bobby Lewis was one of them. Mr. Tubb took him under his wing when he was on the United Artist label.

Tracy: He also favored the Wilburn Brothers

David: When I came to the record shop, The Wilburn Brothers and Loretta Lynn were regular hosts of the Midnight Jamboree.

Tracy: What impact do you feel the Midnight Jamboree had throughout the years?

David: It built the record shops into what they are today. It is the right arm of the record shop. We have had a wonderful on going relationship with WSM for over fifty years. It continues to be that today.

Tracy: It is also a good springboard for young talent.

David: We still do it the way he started it in 1957. We have a new artist each week.

Tracy: The very first time I heard Garth Brooks and Randy Travis on the radio was on the Midnight Jamboree.

David: Just about everyone has done the Midnight Jamboree at one time or another.

Tracy: How did you go from becoming manager to a partner in the record shops?

David: It was complete surprise to me. In 1975, Mr. Tubb called me to his attorney's office and I thought I was going to get fired so I was a little concerned. He told me that he appreciated all the things that I have done and he said he wanted me to come in as a partner. He brought Justin Tubb in at the same time along with Mr. Mosley who is now deceased. It was a thrill and a big surprise. It was the last thing that I would have expected but that is just the type of person he was.

Tracy: How many shops did you have at this time?

David: We had opened our second shop in 1975. Around 1978, we opened our third shop. The Midnight Jamboree left the location of the first record shop and moved to a new location on Demombreum Street. We moved it from Demombreum Street to Music Valley. We built a mini-theater on the side of the record shop. We built it in an old log building that had been here for many years. The theater would sit about 125 people. There was standing room for about another 50-75. We built the Texas Troubadour Theater when the new complex came.

Tracy: On Music Valley, The Midnight Jamboree was very hot during the summer and very cold in the winter but it was always packed.

David: When it was on Broadway, we had a thermometer and it would get to 106 degrees with everyone packed in. We sweated through those days. Now we have 500 padded seats in a beautiful theater. It has came a long way but I have always thought that each time we have moved the Midnight Jamboree, it has lost a little bit of the atmosphere of what it was when people came and stood up. Every once in a while we will go back to Broadway and hold a Midnight Jamboree Special.

Tracy: A lot of the larger artists like Alan Jackson and Tracy Byrd want to do the Midnight Jamboree at the original location.

David: Yes they do. Alan just had a fantastic time doing the Midnight Jamboree. It turned into two hours and forty minutes the night he did it.

Tracy: In the late 1970's or early 1980's you became more than just a manager of the Ernest Tubb Record Shop. You became manager of a lot of Ernest's personal life.

David: I had the honor and privilege of doing anything that he needed done. Whether it was to check his mail or go to the grocery store for him. During the last years of his life, we grew a lot closer.

Tracy: When did his health begin to fail him?

David: In about 1981-1982. He was pretty sick in the late 70's; he carried oxygen on the bus with him. He stayed out on the road as long as he could.

Tracy: Do you think that he had concerns for the future of the record shop?

David: I think he did. I have an interview where he talked about the record shop and how they exceeded his expectations.

Tracy: You also have a shop in Pigeon Forge.

David: I opened that one and then one in Branson and Fort Worth Stockyards.

Tracy: Ernest passed away in 1984 and since then you have really created an empire.

David: It has been a wonderful experience and a great ride for me. As long as I am here, I am going to give the people of Country Music what they want to hear.

Tracy: From the time Ernest hired you until now, what are you most proud of?

David: There are so many things that I am proud of, but what I am most proud of is that I was able to work for him for sixteen years and continue what he started with his high standard of excellence in treating people the way they needed to be treated. The highlight of my career has been his legacy. Keeping him out there and doing what he wanted.

I owe a lot of my success to David McCormick. David helped me so much in the early part of my career. David always considered me on the same level of many of the "really great disc jockeys." He set up several interviews and introduced me to many people that became my friends throughout the years.

David always made sure that I had any product that I wanted or needed and even gave me every one of the Ernest Tubb boxed sets (which range in the $150 range) as they came out. He was always very caring toward anyone in the Traditional Country Music business.

I first met David at the Ernest Tubb Record Shop when I was nineteen. It was my first trip to Nashville and we were at the Ernest Tubb Midnight Jamboree. I wanted to interview Justin Tubb and had corresponded with Justin and David on many occasions. David prepared reserved seats for my family at the Jamboree and even set up an interview with Justin Tubb for me at 2:00 AM after the show!

One of the greatest thrills of my life was actually reading the "Ernest Tubb commercial" on the Midnight Jamboree for the first time. Carol Lee Cooper was MCing that night and David asked if I wanted to do the commercial spot live. I was thrilled and scared to death at the same time. David invited me to MC on several occasions since that time and it is always a great honor. I will never get the chance to MC a Grand Ole Opry spot, but the Midnight Jamboree is just as important to me!

David and I spent one day on a "cemetery tour" in Nashville. He was kind enough to take me to all of the area cemeteries pointing out the final resting places of great like Roy Acuff, Tammy Wynette, Bill Monroe, Doyle Wilburn, Minnie Pearl, Hank Snow, Ernest Tubb and so many more. That is not the first tour that most people take in Nashville, but it was definitely a highlight for me.

When we opened the Heart of Texas Country Music Museum in 2000, David and some of his staff flew down to be a part of the celebration in Brady, Texas. He even presented us with a special plaque commemorating the event.

Since Ernest Tubb's death in 1984, David has single handedly created a great empire honoring E.T. The Ernest Tubb Record Shops continue to be the place to purchase the finest in traditional Country Music. I am happy to say that the Ernest Tubb Record Shops carry all of our Heart of Texas Records. We are a frequent advertiser on the Midnight Jamboree and appreciate the relationship that we have with this institution of Country Music.

That relationship has been possible because of the kindness and friendship of David McCormick and his wonderful staff at the Ernest Tubb Record Shops.

Bobby Lewis, Leona Williams, David McCormick, Martha Carson and I working a show at the Texas Troubadour Theater in Nashville.

MARCH 16, 1990

Tracy: How did Del Reeves get started in the Country Music business?

Del: It all happened when I was very young. I had my own band when I was twelve and living in North Carolina. I went in the Air Force and I started playing clubs in California. I met Chester Smith who introduced me to Capitol Records. Ken Nelson started recording me. My first records were with Capitol Records. That was the start of everything. We moved to Nashville in 1962.

Tracy: You recorded "He Stands Real Tall" and "Be Quiet Mind" in 1961.

Del: I moved to Nashville on account of a top ten record that we had, "The Only Girl I Can't Forget". I called my friend Hank Cochran and he told me that if I was going to make the move I needed to do it now because everybody was talking about the song. I had "He Stands Real Tall" and "Be Quiet Mind" on Decca but I was still living in California.

Tracy: Who introduced you to Decca Records?

Del: Slim Williamson. I first cut a song with him that received some chart action on Peach Records. We were cutting in the old Bradley Studios in Nashville and Owen Bradley walked through and heard me sing. He told Slim that he wanted me on Decca. That is how I got on Decca.

Tracy: When did you make your first Grand Ole Opry debut?

Del: October 1966 and I have been there ever since. Porter Wagoner introduced me that night. I was crying so hard and Porter started crying. We just stood there hugging each other and crying.

Tracy: What do you think the Grand Ole Opry means?

Del: I have got to say the same thing that Roy Acuff said and I am using his words. I think to a young kid who listened to it in the 1950's and always wanted to be on the Opry, it is a mother church of Country Music.

Tracy: Was "A Girl On A Billboard" your biggest hit?

Del: That one and "The Belles of the Southern Bell". "A Girl On A Billboard" crossed over and went pop. In those days you could not go pop with an eye full of fire-crackers. Everybody was so excited. They could not believe a Country song would go in the top forty pop charts. Whether it was the biggest or not, I don't know but it was one that got us known across the nation.

Tracy: The business really opened up for you right after "Girl On The Billboard."

Del: We had nine number ones and about thirty-five top tens. We were on United Artists Records and I was with them for about fifteen years. It was a great run.

Tracy: How many albums have you had out?

Del: I believe about 40 albums. Back in those days we would put out about four albums a year. Today you put out one or two albums and pick out five or six singles from it. Those days you had out three or four singles a year so you put out an album with each single.

Tracy: You have been in Country Music for over twenty years. How has it changed since you got in the business?

Del: I was talking with Ricky Van Shelton and he said that young people are making Ricky Van Shelton and it was the same people then that made me. I grew up with the forty and fifty year olds and I stayed with Country Music and so has Ricky Van Shelton. Ricky, Randy Travis, and George Strait are all doing purely Country Music and it is happening for them. That should tell you something. I think that from 1975 to 1985, we went through a heck of a time going through the pop charts. Today we can sell platinum by going Country.

Tracy: You and I were talking earlier about the resurfacing of Traditional Country Music. Do you think that it is going to keep going?

Del: It is unbelievable. From Portland, all the way to Orlando, Florida, they have six stations that started the Traditional Country Music. I have interviews with all of them and I am very happy to be doing it. Nothing in this world makes me happier. It is really on its way back. Willie Nelson is starting the Cowboy Network and my old Country Carnival television show is going to be shown on there. He bought all of them. Those were some of the greatest shows with the stars that we had.

Tracy: You had about everybody in Country Music on there.

Del: We surely did have all the greats from Lefty Frizzell all the way to Ernest Tubb. We had a lot of pop musicians as well as movie stars.

Tracy: How long did you do the show?

Del: We did it for three years and four months. We did seventy-eight shows that will now be shown on the Cowboy Network with Willie Nelson.

Tracy: The Nashville Network has brought back a lot of classic Country Music shows. It is good to see those again.

Del: It sure is. It is nostalgia. You have the younger generation to see that their mom and dad listened to them and they can see for their self why their parents liked them.

Tracy: What do you have planned for the future?

Del: I am going into Gatlinburg, Tennessee, which is a resort area, starting June 11. We will be there six nights a week until September 4, and then we will take a three-week break and do the television shows and then come back and do the Grand Ole Opry. I am always looking forward to sitting down and entertaining the folks.

I have always been impressed with Del Reeves' ability to entertain. He has that God given talent that few others possess. His song material is great, but his true genius is his stage charisma. His impressions and ability to connect to the audience has given him a very successful career.

I have been with Del many times throughout the years and always enjoyed his many stories. The last time that I saw him was backstage at the Grand Ole Opry, he was outside under the entrance canopy waiting for a limo to pick him up and take him to Tootsie's Orchid Lounge in downtown Nashville. Tootsie's is actually behind the Ryman Auditorium (the old home of the Grand Ole Opry) and gave the opry members a place to knock down a few cold ones between shows. I thought how ironic it was that even though the new Grand Ole Opry house had all the great conveniences of home, it (and Del) was still missing Tootsie's.

My friend Sharon Jackson relays a great Del Reeves story. She was to pick Del up at DFW airport for a show with Joe Paul Nichols in the 1980's. Joe Paul is very business like and always expected the finest from any entertainer that he booked throughout the years-and rightfully so. The last thing that he told Sharon was to get Del to the auditorium and not to stop at any liquor stores on the way. Sharon and Joe Paul have a very special relationship. She would do anything to help further the cause of Joe Paul and Country Music. She picked Del up and he asked her to make a stop. Sharon ignored the Grand Ole Opry legend. Del was telling Sharon about how thirsty he was and about the long flight. She told him they had to go straight to the venue. He kept mentioning liquor stores that they were passing, but Sharon kept right on passing them up-one right after another. Finally, they arrived at the venue and Sharon let an irritated (and thirsty) Del Reeves out to work his show. I think that the next time Del worked in the DFW area, he made other pick up arrangements. Sharon kept her word to Joe Paul and the show went on!

Del Reeves was actually the first Country Music artist to pass away in 2007, on January 1, after a long battle with emphysema.

Tracy: Dolly, you had the perfect rags to riches story.

Dolly: We were very poor growing up, but we didn't know it. There were twelve of us kids. Those times gave me some great inspiration for future songs. I was taught to count my blessings while growing up. We may have been short on money, but were never short on love.

Tracy: When did you begin singing?

Dolly: I have been singing since I was a kid. My uncle Bill Owens actually was the first to recognize that I had a little talent. He took me to a lot of the people who were involved in the business in Nashville. We made several trips to Nashville trying to find someone to help me. I was actually on the "Cass Walker Show" in Knoxville, Tennessee when I was about ten years old.

Tracy: When did you make the big move to Music City USA?

Dolly: I moved to Nashville right after I graduated from high school. I started knocking on doors and trying to get people to listen to me. My first big break came in 1966 when I joined the "Porter Wagoner Show." At that time, it was the biggest syndicated show out of Nashville.

Tracy: You and I were talking about that time in your life earlier. You actually replaced Pretty Miss Norma Jean on that show. Many of the fans had a hard time accepting you.

Dolly: It was very difficult. I was so excited to be working with Porter and be on television. At this time, we also worked the road all over the country. When I first joined the cast, I would go out on stage after being introduced and the reaction was not that great. As a matter of fact, people would shout "Where's Norma Jean?" They were so used to seeing Norma and she was such a big part of that show. It took a while for the fans to accept me, but I am sure glad that they did!

Tracy: You recorded some great duets with Porter and he helped you pick material for your solo projects as well.

Dolly: I will always be grateful to Porter for what he did for me. We had a lot of success. I told Porter when I joined him that I did not want to be someone's girl singer forever and I wanted to have a solo career. So after five or six years, I decided it was time to move on.

Tracy: Porter was not very happy about that.

Dolly: He wasn't, but I knew that I had to make the break and work on my solo career. As long as I was there, it would always be the Porter Wagoner Show with his girl singer Dolly Parton. It was time to make it on my own or die trying. It was like a divorce during that time, but I am happy to say that we patched all of that up and Porter and I are close friends today.

Tracy: You even wrote "I'll Always Love You" for him. That song brought you a lot of acclaim and financial success.

Dolly: I was trying to leave the show. We had talked some about it, but Porter was having such a hard time with it and so was I. I knew that the only way that I could express my feelings were by writing a song. My songs can express certain emotions and feelings that are so hard for me to talk about. I knew that as long as I was with Porter that I was going to be in his way, so I wrote that I had to go but I hoped that life treated him kind and hoped that he had everything that he ever dreamed of. And that I'd always love him.

Tracy: I was told that Elvis wanted to record the song in 1974, but his manager Colonel Parker demanded half of the publishing rights.

Dolly: It broke my heart because I thought that Elvis would do a great job on the song. I just didn't think it was right to give half of it up. In the end it paid off, because Whitney Houston recorded the song in 1992 and it sold several million. I didn't even know that she recorded the song until I heard it on the radio one day. I was riding in the car and turned on the radio and nearly had a heart attack when I heard Whitney singing "I'll Always Love You."

Tracy: Today you are doing a duet with Floyd Tillman. You told me that you were a fan of his songwriting. Is writing an important part of your career?

Dolly: Writing is my favorite part of the business and I admire other writers like Floyd. I enjoy writing more than performing or singing. I write every day. I love the creative side of the business and creating songs is something that is very rewarding for me.

Tracy: You are truly a beautiful lady and I have always enjoyed the positive chemistry that you seem to produce.

Dolly: Thank you. I have told many times that I patterned my look after our town tramp. I thought that she was beautiful when I was a little girl. She had more and bigger hair, more color and dressed in a different way. I think of it as a Country girl's idea of glamour.

Tracy: Dollywood is another very important aspect of your career. It has enabled you to help so many others.

Dolly: It is another part of my life that has exceeded my expectations. We are very devoted to helping children. The Imagination Library, through the Dollywood Foundation, gives a book a month from the time a child is born until they start kindergarten. The idea is that they will start to love reading books. We started this in my home county of Sevier County and now it is spreading all over the country.

Tracy: Did the idea come from your love of reading?

Dolly: I do love to read. I have always wanted to educate myself with reading and I enjoy positive thinking books, books on religions and of course those from the best seller lists.

Tracy: You opened several doors for Country Music during the 1980's, but also alienated many of your more Traditional Country Music fans.

Dolly: I wanted to appeal to as many people as I could. The industry was in a big transition at the time. Many of the hard core Country fans were afraid that I was going to leave them, but that was not true. I love all kinds of music. I never lost any of my Country ways or even my Tennessee accent! I wasn't trying to offend anybody, but I just love doing all kinds of music. I have gone back to my roots in recent years while recording Bluegrass and more Traditional Country sounds. The sounds that I heard in the Tennessee Mountains while growing up.

Tracy: You have accomplished more than virtually any other female in Country Music. Are you content with your career and life?

Dolly: I am very content and happy with my life. I have done so much in my career and accomplished more than I ever thought imaginable. I love the business and I love being involved in so many different aspects of it. I have a good family and good friends. I don't ever want to retire.

I had always wanted to meet Dolly Parton. There are few icons in the business and Dolly is certainly one. While working on guests to be on our Floyd Tillman duet album, I had already lined up Willie, Merle Haggard, Leona Williams, Hank Thompson, Ray Price, Johnny Bush, Darrell McCall, Frankie Miller and Lawton Williams. I was needing a female artist to sing "Slippin' Around" with Floyd. I contact Kitty Wells at first about going into the studio. She was having some problems at that time and was under doctor's care for some vocal rest. I then thought about Loretta Lynn, but Loretta was in contract negotiations with a couple of different labels and was unable to be a part of the album.

One day, I started thinking about Dolly. I thought that she would be a great person to be a part of the project. The only problem was that I had never met or talked to Dolly. I decided to write a letter to Dolly and explain the concept of the album and asked if she wanted to do a duet with Floyd. Four days later, I received a call from Dolly's assistant stating that she received the letter. I was expecting the "but, Dolly is too busy…" Instead, it was "Dolly would be honored to be a part of the Floyd Tillman album. She has been a fan of his writing all of her life."

The session was incredible. My friend Gay Stevens and I flew to Nashville and Darrell and Mona McCall joined us at the session. Dolly actually arrived before we did. She went through McDonalds with her friend Judy Ogle and picked up coffee. I remember telling Judy that it must be a problem for Dolly to go to McDonalds or Walmart. She replied that it was impossible for her to do tasks like that due to being so easily recognized.

Dolly worked for several minutes with Floyd's vocals deciding what she wanted to put on the track. It was a magical moment seeing Dolly become so creative. I will never forget the last words that she said as she was leaving the studio that day. Dolly said "If you get back home and my vocals are not good enough, let me know and I will do them over again."

This lady, worth 100 million dollars, was doing a favor for an 85 year old Country Music singer and a 33 year old Texas disc jockey for free and wanted to make sure that we were pleased with her performance. She refused to take any money for her trouble and even wanted to help promote the project through her fan websites.

I became a much bigger Dolly Parton fan after spending that day with her in Nashville. She is an icon for many reasons and I learned a few more on that day.

Dolly Parton recording "Slippin Around" for Heart of Texas Records. She told me that she needed her "granny glasses" for the session.

Tracy: How did you get started in the Country Music business?

Doug: I was born in the swamps of Louisiana on a houseboat. I grew up around Jennings, Louisiana, and started in the Country Music business professionally when I was nine years old. I actually started in a club called, The Bucket of Blood.

Tracy: You developed your own very unique form of music. How did you come up with that winning style of Doug Kershaw?

Doug: I just started working at it. I started with the French Cajun Music and my brother and I started playing Country Music. I wanted to take my roots with me but I also wanted to be universal. I borrowed from Fats Domino and from this person and that person and then I realized that I could develop a style of my own and I did. My music is actually a big mixture of a lot of other music.

Tracy: Who were your influences growing up?

Doug: People like Hank Thompson, Lefty Frizzell, and Fats Domino.

Tracy: When did you start recording?

Doug: In 1954. That was on a small label and then in 1955, I had my first major record titled "So Love Me Baby". It was not the best song in the world, but it did get me started.

Tracy: That was during the early days of Country Music. How were you accepted?

Doug: We were accepted great. It was amazing but by 1957, we were members of the Grand Ole Opry. At that time, it was nearly unheard of to become members of the Opry in such a short amount of time. It was fantastic. At that time, my brother and I were the youngest members. I still get a thrill playing the Grand Ole Opry. It is a great feeling even today.

Tracy: I know that you are still making personal appearances all over the country.

Doug: I am still doing concert dates and I am planning a new album with Barry Becket, he produces for Alabama, Hank Jr., and Eddie Raven. We have also wanted to do a trio album with Eddie Raven, Jo El Sonnier and myself. I think that would be a great project for those people that enjoy real Louisiana music.

Tracy: Do you still write?

Doug: Not as much as I use to. I really do not take the time like I should. It was important in the early part of my career. Writing takes a lot of time and I should devote more time to it.

Tracy: You and your brother Rusty had some big hits. What are some of your favorites?

Doug: "Louisiana Man" is my favorite. It is the first song that was broadcasted from space and transmitted back to earth. It brought a lot of attention to us throughout the years. It is still considered a standard in the business. I would not think of doing a show without "Louisiana Man."

Tracy: Didn't you re-record, "Louisiana Man" on a recent session?

Doug: I re-recorded it many times. It is on my new album "Hot Diggidy Doug".

Tracy: "Louisiana Man" was your biggest single record. Do you have any idea how much that single made?

Doug: I have no idea. I have recorded it numerous times but I only had it as a single once. I recorded it in 1961. It went to number 2. It was one of the first songs to play pop and Country. It was one of the first songs to crossover.

Tracy: You also went into the studio recently with Hank Williams, Jr.

Doug: Yes, I did. In that album I also have a song with Fats Domino.

Tracy: That must make you feel great to be able to record with some of those great legends.

Doug: It really does. I want to keep doing that. These people have been friends and heroes of mine for years.

Tracy: You appeal to both younger and older audiences.

Doug: I just played for more than 5,000 people and half of them were teenagers. I have fans of all ages. I really do not understand why I appeal to the younger folks. I do not know. I think that maybe I am exciting to them and I am sure that their parents have heard of me. I do not really know.

Tracy: Do you ever have the opportunity to go back to Louisiana?

Doug: Yes, I go all the time. My family is still there. I played the Super Bowl and I played the Jazzfest. We also did a TV special in Lafayette.

Tracy: Is there anything that you would like to do that you have not done?

Doug: I want to act. I have never done it but I really want to. I want to do some serious stuff. I love being in front of the camera and would love to do more of that.

Tracy: How many albums have you done?

Doug: I believe that I have done twenty-four albums throughout the years.

Tracy: Your fiddle playing has been very important to you.

Doug: Yes, it has been. I grew up playing the fiddle. It was a hillbilly instrument. People kept telling me that if I was going to play Country that I could not play the fiddle. I argued why because I was good. It is such a part of me. I do not think that I was the first to electrify the fiddle, but I was the first to make a hit playing the fiddle.

Tracy: You have also played your instrument on other sessions.

Doug: I play the fiddle on all my albums and have played it on albums for other people including Bob Dylan.

I do not know Doug Kershaw very well. I have always enjoyed his shows. He worked one season in Branson with Leona Williams, and that was actually the first time that I caught his entire performance. He is a master entertainer. I have always enjoyed the Cajun music and book Fiddlin' Frenchie Burke a few times a year. I was amazed at how their shows resembled. The Cajun aspect of the music is filled with so much high energy. There are very few "slow moments" during the show. They both make sure that the audience is part of the performance and that is a true gift.

The Doug Kershaw show is a must see for all Country Music fans.

MARCH 1996

Tracy: How long have you been in the Country Music business?

Ernie: I just celebrated 32 years with the Grand Ole Opry.

Tracy: How did you feel the first time that you appeared on the Grand Ole Opry?

Ernie: I felt scared to death. I was shaking like a leaf. I was there when Ernest Tubb was there and he saw that I was scared to death and came over and said, "what's the matter son". I told him it was my first time on the Grand Ole Opry and I was scared to death, and he said, "son, we are all afraid". He got me calmed down and I went out and did my job.

Tracy: What was the first song that you sang on the Grand Ole Opry?

Ernie: The first song was, "Because I Care". I was recording for MGM in the 1950's. That was the record that I had out. When I joined Hickory Records I re-recorded the song and I also did a video with Becky Hobbs of "Talk Back Trembling Lips" and Curb Records re-released some of the top ten songs that I had. They must have really liked it.

Tracy: Did you leave the Country Music business for a while?

Ernie: Yes. I was trying Country in 1955 and then Elvis came out and everything went rock and roll. I was not doing any good so I went back to my hometown in Alabama and worked in guided missles. In 1960, Wesley Rose, he was the one who guided and led my career and was president of Acuff-Rose Publishing Company. He called me in and recorded me on Decca Records. I did a song called "Each Moment Spent With You" which was a top ten record. I also did "You Can't Pick A Rose In December", which was written by a great Texan Leon Payne, it was also a top ten record. I then changed over to Hickory Records. I recorded a song called "Everybody But Me" that went to number three. And then, "I'll Take The Chance" went number two. My third album was "Talk Back Trembling Lips", it went number one and was the song that took me to the Grand Ole Opry.

Tracy: I am sure that song has been your biggest hit.

Ernie: I have had twelve top ten records during my career. I was on TNN with Porter Wagoner one night and I told him I had twelve top ten records. From 1960-1970, every record that I recorded was a top forty or better. I mentioned, "Talk Back Trembling Lips" and if no one has heard that song, I might as well not even mention the other songs.

Tracy: I understand you own your own radio stations?

Ernie: That is where I am now. I am in Nashville. I figured I better go a head and buy my own radio station in order to get my records played! We have a station in Gallatin, Tennessee, and we play classic Country Music. We also have a five hour a week show of Bluegrass. In Ardmore, Tennessee, I have another radio station that my daughter runs. The format there is positive Country. It is Country gospel. There are not any drinking or cheating songs.

Tracy: How would you like to be remembered?

Ernie: I would like to be remembered as someone who loved the industry and our Country Music fans and tried to help further the music business.

I have always enjoyed the great costumes that Country Music entertainers have adorned. Ernie Ashworth took his biggest hit "Talk Back Trembling Lips" and created not only a signature sound, but a look as well. His "lip suits" were nearly as popular as his entertaining.

Ernie actually donated a great suit to our museum several years ago. It was designed by Harvey Krantz and featured several pennies throughout the suit. It was actually given to him one night at the opry by Hank Snow. Ernie then passed it on to us.

Ernie worked for our organization on a couple of occasions and was always a professional and I enjoyed listening to him talk about the golden days in Country Music.

JUNE 1998

Tracy: I am visiting in Branson, Missouri, with Ferlin Husky. Ferlin, how are you?

Ferlin: I am doing fine, Tracy. It is good to see you buddy.

Tracy: You started out in the County Music at a very early age. You even entertained while you were in the service.

Ferlin: My uncle Clyde Lewis was one of my early inspirations. He taught me to play the guitar. I was in the business a while and started working some of the honkytonks with my uncle in the St. Louis area before I went to the service. I snuck into the service when I was just a kid. I started doing some entertaining on the ship. I had my guitar with me and we were transporting troops. There were some scary times over there and whenever we would have an alert, I would calm the boys down with stories. Our neighbor back home was named Simon Crump. I would tell stories about him out there in the country. The guys would say, "Come on Country and tell some more of those Simon stories." Then when I got out of the service in 1946, I came back home. I went to California in 1947. I worked in the St. Louis area and worked my way out to California.

Tracy: When you came back, you started using the name Tex Terry.

Ferlin: I was using Tex Terry in St. Louis. My parents really didn't want me to go into the entertainment business, so I used Tex Terry so people really wouldn't know who I was. After I got to California, Tex Ritter and Tex Williams were both on Capitol Records and Smiley Burnette encouraged me to change my name. My favorite actor was Preston Foster. Smiley gave me the Preston to use as my last name and I became Terry Preston.

Tracy: You started working for Bill McCall at Four Star Records.

Ferlin: That is right. Four Star had a great stable of talent including Webb Pierce, Maddox Brothers and Rose, Hank Locklin, Patsy Cline and Jimmy Dean. Bill helped more people than nearly anyone that I know of. Everyone called him a crook. It wasn't until I worked for Capitol and some of the other big outfits that I found out who a crook was!

Tracy: You had an incredible run with Capitol Records.

Ferlin: Yes sir, it sure was but they had changed a lot of the personnel like they do on all of them. Then they changed different A&R men, different people. Then one thing lead to another and then when you are with a company so long you think you can do better somewhere else. It was our arrangement and agreement when I left Capitol to leave on good terms. I still get royalties, but they were the main one for me and helped me to build and become an entertainer. Different people and different types of songs came in and it was a mutual agreement that I left Capitol and moved on to ABC at the time. But I just thank the Lord I have been in the business as long as I have been.

Tracy: You helped start the career of many entertainers including Jean Shepard.

Ferlin: Yeah, the duet "Dear John Letter" was the first gold record I was on or lucky enough to be on. I was picking material for her and Fuzzy Owen was playing steel at the time. Bonnie Owens was Buck Owens' wife but they were no relation to Fuzzy. I think Fuzzy is still with Merle Haggard now and is his manager. But Fuzzy and Bonnie had a local record on it their fan club kept requesting the song and I was doing disc jockey work in Bakersfield at the time with Simon Crum. People would call and I thought, "son of a gun this song is getting a lot of action." At first I thought it was just their fan club or local people. But then Conway, Arkansas is where Fuzzy Owens was from and the stations down there played the fire out of it. I started getting requests from different places. I told Ken Nelson at Capitol that he should have Jean to do "Dear John." I wasn't even going to do any talking. I wasn't going to do anything. I was playing bass fiddle on the session. He said who is going to do the talking on it. I told him that he should do the recitation and he said "no you do the talking". I was lucky and it turned out ok. You never know what happens. It became a monster record for us.

Tracy: You also played a part in the career of Buck Owens, Tommy Collins and Dallas Frazier.

Ferlin: I always tried to help anyone that I could. At that time, no one was making the big money that they are in the business today. Dallas (Frazier) was like a son to me. He went on to write some great songs and even wrote for my company. I changed Leonard Sipes name to Tommy Collins – from the drink Tom Collins. I even bought Buck Owens some decent clothes and took him to Capitol and got him a deal with them. Even Elvis opened shows for me when he was starting out in the business. People helped me along the way and I didn't want to forget it.

Tracy: "Gone" was one of your biggest hits.

Ferlin: It was actually my biggest hit. I recorded it for Four Star and then cut it again in 1956 in Nashville. I talked them into putting more production on the song and we had the Jordanaires and Millie Kirkham as part of it. Ken Nelson with

Capitol wasn't thrilled with the arrangement, but after it became a hit he was proud of the song.

Tracy: "Wings of A Dove" is still your signature song.

Ferlin: "Wings of A Dove" has become a standard in the business. I tried to record it on several different occasions, but they didn't want me to record it because of the reference to God and baptism in the song. As a matter of fact, I had to change it up a bit just to get it cut. It has become a standard in the Country and gospel field and has been recorded by hundreds of entertainers.

Tracy: You are now performing in Branson, Missouri.

Ferlin: Yes, I am at the Boxcar Willie Theater here in Branson. I do a ten o'clock show five days a week. And then they have breakfast at the Plantation Restaurant.

Tracy: Do you enjoy being off the road after fifty years?

Ferlin: Yes, I do. I still like to go out once in a while. I love to see different areas of the country again. It is good to go back anywhere I have been. But there are so many places that are not there anymore. There are so many memories. Just like where I was raised back in Missourri. I have never been back to the home I was raised in because it was changed. It was changed while I was in the service. But it is just like where you work and you go back, time changes everything.

Tracy: What are your plans for the future, Ferlin?

Ferlin: Just try to hang in there like I am doing. If I quit I don't know what I would do. You know I would just walk the floor. No, as long as I can stay and enjoy it and the people seem to enjoy it I guess that I will continue to perform. I just thank the Lord I am still able to go on, to be able to walk out on the stage and have friends like you and fans like you bring up here to us. They still make me feel like I am just starting out. It makes me feel wonderful.

It is so ironic how time changes things for all of us. In the early days of my radio career, we took a couple of buses each year to Branson. We attended the Ferlin Husky Show on nearly every trip. He had a morning show there and all of my people loved to see and visit with him at the Boxcar Willie and Christy Lane Theaters. Ferlin was always very kind to me and even gave us a white tuxedo for our museum years before we broke ground on our building.

At that time, I never imagined that I would have the honor of working so many shows with Ferlin and that he would record for our Heart of Texas Records label. I have been with only a few entertainers that receive the respect immediately from the audience that

Ferlin does. I have seen him getting standing ovations time and time again for just walking out on stage.

One of Ferlin's former band members told me a very funny story last year. He told me that they were traveling down the road and Ferlin and Simon got into a horrible fight. They were fighting in the bus and Ferlin made him pull the bus over on the side of the road. He kicked Simon off the bus and told the driver to drive off. About thirty minutes later, Ferlin came to the front of the bus and told the driver that he was missing Simon and wanted to go back and get him. The driver couldn't believe it and thought that Ferlin was kidding. Ferlin insisted and they turned the bus around and drove back to pick poor Simon up. I've never asked Ferlin about it, but it would not have surprised me!

It is an honor to be able to work with Ferlin on a consistent basis not only on the road, but day by day. I hope that we have many more successful years together.

Tracy: How did you become involved in the music industry?

Floyd: There was nothing else I could do. I had to do something for a living. I went around to the beer joints and played for nickels and dimes and sometimes a dollar a night.

Tracy: Was it easy breaking in to Country Music?

Floyd: It is quite different now getting started than it used to be. I would hate to have to start out today. I didn't work too hard then. There wasn't much competition and you didn't make a lot of money, but it was a lot easier. There were only three or four songwriters in the whole state of Texas. I was told that you weren't supposed to write songs. They were supposed to come from Tin Pan Alley. I worked some shows in a pop band and that had a lot of influence on me and then I went back to Country Music. I couldn't play the songs that I wrote in the pop band, but the Country band could. And then after I went back to Country, Bing Crosby recorded one of my first songs. (It Makes No Difference Now) It was one of the first crossover songs from Hillbilly to pop music.

Tracy: Your song writing ability was what really made your career.

Floyd: I did better as a songwriter but I made a living playing the guitar. At first I did not do any singing I just played take off guitar. It was something new. In West Texas I played some dances before I went to big cities. I lived in Post, Texas, and we had a trumpet player who played take. I learned a few things from him. He was also a very good trumpet player. He was home from college. During the summers he would play with us in Post. I learned by listening to him. I use to play the mandolin but the take off guitar was unheard of then so people would crowd around and watch. It was different at that time to play lead on a guitar. Someone told me that you were supposed to use a guitar to play second with, nobody was supposed to play lead guitar.

Tracy: In 1949, you recorded your composition "Slipping Around".

Floyd: I overheard a telephone conversation while I was in a diner in West Texas. We had just finished a show. This woman was asking a man to call her, but to hang up the phone if her husband answered. I thought to myself-now that woman is slipping around. I wrote the song not really realizing that it was the first song to commercialize adultery. That was my biggest song as a singer but "I Love You So Much It Hurts", was my biggest song as a writer. I wrote that in 1948. I still make more money on that song than anything that I ever wrote.

Tracy: Did Ernest Tubb have the biggest hit on "Slipping Around"?

Floyd: No, the biggest hit was Margaret Whiting and Jimmy Wakely. Mine was second, I sold about two million and Ernest has about half a million.

Tracy: E.T. was a very good and close friend throughout the years.

Floyd: We were. I thought a lot of Ernest Tubb. He was one of my best friends. On one of my albums, I used ten of my best friends and he was one of them. It was called Floyd Tillman and Friends. It was on Mickey Gilley's label and Ernest and I recorded a song called "One Way Love." I recorded my part in Houston and Ernest added his vocals in Nashville at Pete Drake's place.

Tracy: After "Slipping Around", you wrote, "I'll Never Slip Around Again" and had a hit.

Floyd: It was about half as much. After "Slipping Around" was so big, I thought it needed an answer. At that time, answer songs were so popular and "I'll Never Slip Around Again" is the rest of that story.

Tracy: Your first major hit as an artist was "They Took The Stars Out of Heaven".

Floyd: That song came out about the time of WW II. It came out while I was in the Army. I recorded it in 1940. It was on the Hit Parade as number one for about six months. They called it hillbilly. It was my first hit song as a singer. My first hit as a writer was "It Makes No Difference Now". Mel Tillis did it the other day on Nashville Now. I actually sold it to Jimmie Davis for $300. I needed the money. Then twenty eight years later, I got the song back and made more money that year than I originally got from Jimmie.

Tracy: How many songs have you written?

Floyd: Nearly 1,000. I wrote about twenty a year for a total of 100 for the Gilley Organization. I am kind of slowing down now. I have a few pretty good ones now that I have been kind of saving up for the right time.

Tracy: How many records did you record in the course of your career?

Floyd: I have recorded about 200 records. Some of my songs keep coming back. When I do personal appearances, the fans want to hear the old songs. The songs that I wrote forty years ago are more popular with the audience than the more recent ones.

Tracy: Do you have someone in particular that you would like to record your songs?

Floyd: Nearly everyone in the business has recorded one of my songs unless they are real young.

Tracy: Do you have a favorite version of any songs?

Floyd: I like the way that Ella Fitzgerald did "I Gotta Have My Baby Back" with the Mills Brothers backing her up is one of my old favorites. Vic Damone did a good job on "I Love You So Much It Hurts". Perry Como also had a very good record of it. He did it with the Kraft Music Hall band. Lucky Strike Hit Parade did "Slippin Around." I had a wire from the publisher and had to change the line "though you're tied up with someone else and I'm all tied up to." I had to change that just for that show to "I guess I had it coming there's nothing I can do." That inspired me to go ahead and write an answer song. I still make more money from Patsy's (Cline) version of "I Love You So Much It Hurts." It is truly remarkable how many albums that she still sells to this day.

Tracy: Your song "All Because of You" also opened a lot of doors for you.

Floyd: I did that with Decca Records. It was in the late 30's. I actually got my foot in the door with Decca on a count of "It Makes No Difference Now." I was recording with the Blue Ridge Playboys and we were with Vocalian. They turned down "It Makes No Difference Now" because they said it was too sad. It wasn't a good dance song. Back then practically all of the records were bought by jukeboxes. People bought radios to hear music. They would then go out to the jukeboxes and dance and drink beer. There were very few record players. They had players back in the 20's. Jimmie Rodgers and Vernon Dalhart were very popular. Vernon was one of my favorites when I was a kid. Back then, they called them Victrolas and you could get one for $5.00, wind it up and play a record on it. Nearly everyone had one when I was a kid and then they went out of style when radio got so popular in the 30's.

Tracy: Is there anything in your career that you have not done?

Floyd: No, I think that I have done almost everything. I was elected into the Country Songwriters Hall of Fame in the 1960's and the Country Music Hall of Fame in 1984. I have done just about everything. I have never been a no show. I have always done my very best to be there anytime that I was scheduled to do a show. I will always make the job as long as my name is on the contract. I don't work as much as I used to. I work about once a week. I have also won some awards and am proud to still be in the business after all this time.

Tracy: How would you like to be remembered?

Floyd: Just as a songwriter. I think my songs will be around a lot longer than I will.

I was very fortunate to become friends with Floyd Tillman very early in my career. Floyd lived in Marble Falls, Texas, with his wife Francis. Floyd and I visited on many occasions. I started booking him at several smaller opry shows in the state. His fee was $500.00 and would always give the buyer their monies worth!

Even in his later years, Floyd still had the charisma. He would swing his head around with great emphasis on certain words and loved to play his old Gibson guitar. Floyd was working for us in Brady, Texas, one night and fell on stage. As he was falling, I tried to catch him to no avail. He fell on his back but held that Gibson guitar up so that it would never touch the ground! After that night, he gave me his boots-blaming the boots on his fall.

One night in Llano, Texas, a gentleman came to me and told me about buying Floyd's guitar at a pawn shop in Marble Falls. I was shocked and asked the man to let me know if he ever wanted to sell it. He replied that he planned on keeping it forever. I asked Floyd about it. He told me that the vintage guitar did not sound as good as it used to (I think it was Floyd's hearing instead of the guitar), so he took it down to a pawn shop. The owner told him to pick any guitar out in the shop and he would trade him even if Floyd would sign the old Gibson. Floyd traded that great instrument for a cheap guitar and was happy as he could be. A few months later, the guitar buyer called me and needed some money and was willing to sell the guitar for $1,500.00 firm. We had just made $900.00 off a Leon Rausch gig, so I added $600.00 to it and the guitar is now at the Heart of Texas Country Music Museum.

Justin Trevino and I talked about Floyd entering the studio one more time. We thought it would be neat to have a couple of his friends join him for some duets. At that time, we had no idea what would become of our little idea. I approached Floyd about the project and he was very excited at the thought of recording again-it had been twenty years. I called on several of the people that were influenced by Floyd-Johnny Bush, Willie Nelson, Hank Thompson, Frankie Miller, Ray Price, Merle Haggard, Connie Smith, Leona Williams, Johnny Gimble, George Jones, Lawton Williams, Mel Tillis and Justin all were so excited to record with this elder statesman of Country Music. I need one more artist to record "Slipping Around" with Floyd. I approached Loretta Lynn about the project and she was in negotiations with another album and then turned my attention to Kitty Wells. Kitty was having some vocal problem and just did not feel she had the ability to record again. I thought about Dolly Parton and simply sent her a letter about the project. She immediately replied and agreed to the session. It was incredible and "The Influence" would become Floyd's last album.

Unfortunately, Floyd would never get to enjoy the success and publicity that "The Influence" would attain. At that time in his life, Floyd's wife Frances had passed away and his former wife Marge and their son Larry moved in with him. Marge would soon become ill and pass away. Floyd had began to slip a little mentally as many older people do-he was in his late 80's. He received some bad advice from some people that were trying to control him and it caused problems with many people that had done business with Floyd in the past. Several people that booked and worked with Floyd in the past were literally cut out of his life.

It took us nearly two years dealing with lawyers and thousands of dollars to get "The Influence" commercially ready. In the end, the only problems that these people helped to create was to keep this great legend from hearing the final version of "The Influence" and enjoying a small resurgence in his career. Johnny Gimble and I talked extensively about this problem. The day after Floyd died, Larry did apologize to me for all the problems in the last couple of years. Larry then passed away in 2006.

When I think of Floyd now, I do not dwell on those last few months of his life. I concentrate on the vibrant life that he had and our friendship. He was a wonderful entertainer and friend.

JANUARY 27, 2007

Tracy: It is always good to visit with Frankie Miller. Tell me how you get started in the Country Music business.

Frankie: My home town is Victoria, Texas, down in South Texas. I really got started there with my brother Norman Miller. He taught me how to play the guitar and he was a great fan of Ernest Tubb. We formed a little band and started playing clubs down there and had a daily radio show on KNAL.

Tracy: You named your band the Drifting Texans.

Frankie: That is right. When I signed with Gilt Edge, I name the band the Drifting Texans. Gilt Edge was out of California. It was owned by Four Star records which was Bill McCall's record company. Hank Williams had the Drifting Cowboys and I had Drifting Texans.

Tracy: There was another Hank that helped you at that time.

Frankie: Hank Hocklin. Hank had a radio show in Houston on KLE in Houston. I would to appear occasionally because I had kinfolks in Houston. He had a daily 15 minute radio show at noon with just him and his guitar. He would always ask me to sing a song when I came by. He was going on vacation one year and asked me about filling in for him while he was gone. That really helped me in that area.

Tracy: I know you released several single records on Gilt edged.

Frankie: Yes, I recorded several 78 records until I went with Columbia.

Tracy: You served the country in Korea.

Frankie: I joined the army in 1951. When I got out, I ended up doing some demo sessions and got a deal with Columbia Records which was a major label at the time.

Tracy: That had to be a really important time in your career.

Frankie: It was like going to the moon to get a deal with a major record label and they were really a good label at that time. They had Carl Smith, Marty Robbins, Jimmy Dickens, George Morgan and a great stable of good artists.

Tracy: You began working at the Cowtown Hoedown at this time.

Frankie: Yes, I moved to Fort Worth and did a Saturday night show in Ft. Worth called the Cowtown Hoedown. It was a Grand Ole Opry type stage show. It was done in an old theater in downtown. I then signed with Starday Records in 1958 and had "Blackland Farmer." It came out in the last part of 1958. I was also working at that time on The Louisiana Hayride.

Tracy: "Blackland Farmer" became your signature song. Why did you decide to write the song?

Frankie: Being from South Texas, I had an uncle that had a farm down there and all of his life that's what he did. They have a tremendous amount of black land and one day I got the idea that I needed to write a song about him.

Tracy: It became one of Starday's most successful songs.

Frankie: Yes, and it was of course the biggest record that I had. I have eaten a lot of biscuits from the song.

Tracy: You also met a Starday label mate that would become a life long friend.

Frankie: I knew George (Jones) from Houston. He was on Starday and we got to be real good friends. I traveled a lot with George and we had some wonderful times together.

Tracy: How was working the road at that particular time in your career?

Frankie: Working the road was a tough deal. We did one-nighters. We would do a show in one town and the next night we would be three or four or five hundred miles down the road to another town. We traveled in cars back then. It was before the bus scene came on. It was a pretty tough life but that's what we wanted. That is what every artist worked for-to get a record that they could go out and book with.

Tracy: What kind of money were you making on personal appearances at time?

Frankie: When I started, I was making fifty dollars a night and later on I was making three hundred as a single. That was good money in those days. It's not anything like they're doing now. That was a different era in Country Music. I really had a lot of fun working the road with George Jones, Webb Pierce and almost all the guys on the Grand Ole Opry. We would do what we called package shows that would put five or six people on one show. We would work the big auditoriums.

Tracy: You also started having some success as a songwriter.

Frankie: I wrote some stuff that did pretty good. Webb Pierce had a big hit with the song I wrote called "If You Were Me" years ago. After over 30 years with it lying around, we got another cut on the song when Dwight Yoakum recorded it.

Tracy: "Blackland Farmer" was actually released again.

Frankie: It was released again in 1961. In 1958, it was in the Country charts for 26 weeks and started crossing over into the pop stations. It started doing very well in Houston and in Chicago and they decided to release it again. There was never a song that was as Country as "Blackland Farmer," but at one time there were three songs on the Pop charts in Billboard magazine. My song of "Blackland Famer," George Jones's "White Lightning" and Johnny Horton's "Battle of New Orleans" were all in the pop charts at the same time.

Tracy: Cashbox Magazine gave you a very nice award in 1960.

Frankie: I was given the award for Most Promising New Male Artist which was a very nice award at that time.

Tracy: You then started working the Grand Ole Opry.

Frankie: I was living in Nashville at that time and I wanted to get on the Grand Ole Opry. Don Pierce and Tommy Hill from Starday had been plugging for me to get on the Opry. I was doing a show down in Florida with Ferlin Husky and the manager of the Grand Ole Opry at that time was Ott Devine. He was at the show and saw me perform. I did well on the show and after the show was over he came and talked to me about the Opry. He told me he would like to sign me to the Grand Ole Opry but he could not sign any new acts for a certain period of time. He invited me to be on the Opry on any Saturday that I was not on the road. Every Saturday, they always had me a spot on the Opry.

Tracy: How did that make you feel?

Frankie: I never will forget the first night that I worked the Opry. It was like I was in Heaven. Ernest Tubb was the host that night and he introduced me for the first time. It was such a good show at that time. It was like you're walking on a cloud when standing in front of the mike on the same place that Hank Williams sang "Lovesick Blues." It makes you feel awful good.

Tracy: You also signed with United Artists in 1964 or 1965.

Frankie: George (Jones) was on United Artists and he told Pappy Daily to sign me with the United Artists. I think the next week we went to Nashville and recorded a session thanks to my friend George. I also recorded for Stop Records. Tommy Hill was a great friend of mine. He produced many of my sessions and Pete Drake played steel guitar.

Tracy: You were also a part of Bill Anderson's first major tour.

Frankie: We went to Canada and that was the first tour that Bill Anderson was ever own. Bill Anderson is a great friend of mine. He was just starting out and was opening the shows for me.

Tracy: Was it hard at that time to know who is going to have the next big record?

Frankie: We never even thought about that. We just got in there and tried to find some great songs and record.

Tracy: There are very few people still performing that worked with Patsy Cline.

Frankie: I toured with Patsy. I remember that she saved my life one night. She really didn't save my life, but I like to say that she did. We were traveling with Ernest Tubb on a package show with Hank Locklin, Patsy Cline and I. We were working in Colorado and my coat was locked up in the bus compartment. It was 2:00 AM in the morning and I was freezing to death. I got some of those head protectors off the back of the seats and I was trying to get them around to cover up. Patsy came walking in the back to go to the restroom and she saw me and she said "Frankie, are you cold?" I told Patsy that I was freezing to death. She went to the front and had a big coat and brought that big coat and covered me up with the coat. I always like to say that she saved my life. She was a very nice lady.

Tracy: You left the business at the height of your popularity.

Frankie: I really got tired of the road and all the traveling. I was gone most of the time and I had a wife and two little girls at home. I needed to be home more so I moved back to Texas and I never have regretted it.

Tracy: In the last few years, you started doing some more in the business.

Frankie: I met a guy by the name of Tracy Pitcox and he got me back in the business. I have really had a good time since I started playing some shows and I would thank you partly for that. I'm really having a good time with the music and I don't have to worry about trying to make a living.

Tracy: Does it amaze you that you have the fans all over the world?

Frankie: I can hardly get over. I hear from people all over the world that collect my old records and still enjoy my music. Everywhere we go, we always meet somebody that has seen me somewhere in the past.

Tracy: In the future, when people think about Frankie Miller how do you want to be remembered?

Frankie: The main thing that I would like to be remembered by is that I stayed a Country Music singer and that I've never tried to do anything else. Country Music is what I loved and what I still love today.

I met Frankie for the first time at Terry Beene's annual Terry Awards in Ft. Worth. I had often wondered what had happened to Frankie. Frankie was with Joe Paul Nichols, Lawton Williams and a few other people. I introduced myself to him and told him about being a fan. Frankie gave me a cassette that had just been released of four of his old songs from the Starday Records days. He was so friendly and even received an award that night.

Throughout the years, Frankie started working on several of our shows and was a frequent radio guest on KNEL's Hillbilly Hits radio show. Frankie lives about three and a half hours away. His many stories were so intriguing to me and I devoured as many as he wanted to share.

I was so proud when he agreed to record an album for our Heart of Texas Records label. His history in the business is so unique and he still sings great. I love watching him work for an audience. His great love is Country Music and he enjoys singing as much as anyone that I know.

Frankie and his wife Ann have truly treated Charla and I as a members of their family. I admire Frankie's singing and Ann's cooking. They both are a winning combination!

Heart of Texas Recording Artist Frankie Miller,
Buck Owens, Charlie Walker and George Kent.

1989

Tracy: I am speaking with Garth Brooks. Garth it seems like you have become an instant success. I know it may not seem that way to you, but to the Country Music community, that is the way it seems.

Garth: Being in Texas, you guys have a different view. Texas jumped on the product and has really supported us. I am not comparing myself to Strait (George), but it is like his success. He blew up in the Mid West and has worked his way out. That is what we are seeing with this. We do not draw near as well up in New York. We have not been up to the West Coast, so Texas and Oklahoma are definitely the reasons why I am having the success that I am.

Tracy: "If Tomorrow Never Comes" was number one for two weeks, how does that make you feel?

Garth: I was at the West Texas Boys Ranch and we were talking about that today. Number one has always been a place for George Strait and George Jones. Seeing my name up there as an artist and a writer really floored me. Seeing it up there two weeks in a row, it just does not get any better than this.

Tracy: George Jones is one of your biggest inspirations.

Garth: Sure, he is the king. He has always been George Jones, if you like him or hate him, he is who is he. He has never changed for anybody and I admire that because in this business it is easy to change and fit the needs of somebody else.

Tracy: Do you have any other inspirations?

Garth: George Strait, he held on the Country Music during the Urban Cowboy phase. (Reba) McEntire and (Ricky) Skaggs did too, it took a bold stand to do that and I admire them.

Tracy: Tell us about your new song, it is getting a lot of play all over.

Garth: "Not Counting You" is in a no win situation coming off of "If Tomorrow Never Comes". Hopefully it will show the diversity in Garth Brooks and the band. Really it is to setup what we hope will be the biggest single off this record and that is, "The Dance".

Tracy: Are you working on any other albums right now?

Garth: We are in the studio right now cutting an album. It will be out on August 1.

Tracy: What do you see Garth Brooks doing in the future?

Garth: More of the same. I want to see him having fun and doing the "number one" thing. I want to make sure he remains sincere and if he gets commercial we will have to have all seven of my guys beat the tar out of me.

Tracy: Earlier you said you wanted to donate the time after it all to your fans. That is not what many artists do.

Garth: The fans are the reason I get to do what I do. The great gift of radio allows me to go out and make a living doing this. I worked for a living before and I never want to do that again. This is fun! All the people around me work hard and I just have to show up and do what I do and that is sing.

Tracy: Do you stay after and sign autographs?

Garth: I think that it should be included in the price of the ticket. Admission is a lot of money and albums are a lot of money. It is quite a compliment for people to spend their money but mostly for them to spend their time because they can never get that back. You try to give them a good memory in return and I think signing autographs when you can and when the establishment lets you, and when your scheduling lets you, you should.

Tracy: There are not a lot of artists that do that anymore. Do you plan to continue doing that through out your career?

Garth: I hope so. I hope it never gets to the point to where I cannot sit and talk to my fans. If it does, I think that it will be over for me so I never hope it does.

Tracy: You met your wife Sandy at one of your former jobs.

Garth: My wife is a true representative of what I think a woman should be. She is very feminine and very graceful. I met her in her college years; she was 19. She was in a club called Tumbleweed in Stillwater and she had a little too much and I had to escort her out of the building and I kept thinking how cute she was so I asked her to go home with me and she told me to drop dead. I called her the next day and she reluctantly agreed to go out on a date. We went out and two and a half years later we got married.

Tracy: Is there anything you want to say to your fans?

Garth: I have to say thanks for my dream come true and I can't carry my Christian shoelaces but I am nothing without the Good Lord so keep Him in your heart.

I was very glad to have met Garth in the early days of his career. It is very interesting looking back at his place in the business at that time as compared to today. He was so excited about the industry and was just on the verge of great success.

Garth was working in San Angelo, Texas, on the evening of this interview. He had spent the day visiting and entertaining at a ranch for troubled and homeless young men. He was actually getting ready for the show that night and was running a few minutes behind schedule. As I entered the bus, he was actually still in his underwear! We had a great visit about what he anticipated for the future of his career and the industry.

He stayed that night and signed autographs until the last person left, but that would soon change. As he became a superstar, the luxury was taken away from him. It is impossible for him to sign for the thousands that attend his performances.

He did bring many into the Country Music fold. He changed the business and probably for the better. I was really turned off when he smashed the guitar into thousands of pieces on network television. I was even more offended when the Country Music Hall of Fame placed that guitar on display and continually replayed its destruction.

Garth Brooks on one of his early tours in San Angelo, Texas.

MAY 19, 1998

Tracy: You have a new album out that is doing very well.

Gene: I am not much of a watcher. I just keep stay busy out on the road and keep my fingers crossed and hope they do well.

Tracy: Within the last few years you signed with the largest independent record producers in the world, Step One Records.

Gene: Yes, I signed with Step One Records and Mr. Ray Pennington.

Tracy: You have already put out some successful albums on that label.

Gene: It has been good to us. In the music business you have some highs and lows but I have hooked up with Ray and we decided to make records. It is hard sometimes to get airplay when you are not on a major label. We started making what I thought were good records and apparently the radio and public did as well. We have been pretty successful with airplay and the people. We have been playing packed out places. I think that it has been a really good relationship with Step One and myself. We have been having a good time satisfying the people and playing what we think they want to hear.

Tracy: I have been listening to radio stations that I had not heard play Gene Watson in quite awhile but they were playing, "Change Her Mind". That was a single that did very well.

Gene: It is a great song. I still believe that if you have the right production and the right song and the people can hear it, then it has to be played. I was extremely fortunate to get the success out of it that I did. Several different artists had recorded the song but it did not do anything. "Love In A Hot Afternoon" was another song that got us back on the charts.

Tracy: You have had a lot of hit singles in your career. Do you have any idea how many?

Gene: I really do not know. I have people come up to me all the time giving me statistics so they know more than me.

Tracy: You are just providing great Country Music.

Gene: I try to. Instead of being a one hit wonder, I made up my mind that I would rather be consistent. Thanks to the people I have been fairly successful as far as consistency and that means a lot to me. I think it is more important to have several years worth of good records rather than just one monster hit.

Tracy: Has the music business always been a top priority for you growing up?

Gene: No, in fact, it was not a priority for me growing up at all. I always thought that I would work on cars. Singing was something that I was going to be doing anyway but I never dreamed that I would be making money much less a career out of it. Now, I make music as a living and play with cars on the sideline.

Tracy: Do you still have you paint and body shop?

Gene: That is where I am as we speak. It is a hobby as well as a way for me to relax.

Tracy: It is amazing that someone as successful as you are in the music business still loves to do something like that. It is not really work for you is it?

Gene: I used to work on cars to make a living but now I work on cars to get my mind off of the music business.

Tracy: You new project is called, "A Way To Survive".

Gene: It is titled after an old Ray Price song that I always thought so much of. I think that it is a good album. We included a few things that I had recorded before because some of the older stuff is getting hard to find. So we are putting some of the old with the new and making it versatile. It also contains our latest single "Someone's Child". I think that it is a great song. It has a powerful message. To anyone who has ever been to a large city, like myself, I live in Houston, and pulled up to a street corner and seen someone holding a sign or a cup, it will make you stop and think. I know everyone has their own opinion and the song is just one but you just never know who is standing at that corner.

Tracy: You are still playing for packed houses all over the country.

Gene: We are having really good luck. The fans are what it is all about. I have had so many fans that have stayed with me through the ups and downs.

Tracy: You have a lot of fun entertaining.

Gene: The fans have been really good to us and stand behind us. It seems like it does not make any difference. As long as you are trying your best and having a good time, they are going to be on your side.

Tracy: What are your future plans?

Gene: The way the music business is today, who knows. I am always trying to look for new material and looking for that song that will make people stop and think. I just hope to keep doing what my fans expect of me.

Gene Watson is one of our most consistent draws. He has a huge fan base in Texas and always does a great show. He always seems to pack out every show that we book him on.

Gene was battling cancer a few years ago. Some of his friends and fans decided to do a benefit to help offset his medical expenses. My friends Sharon Jackson and Rhonda Hull were helping to organize a benefit for him in Paris, Texas. They asked me to MC the benefit. It was so much fun to help organize the show. Everyone that we asked wanted to help in some way. Darrell McCall, Claude Gray, Jean Shepard, Justin Trevino, Lawton Williams, Leona Williams, Dave Kirby, Barbara Fairchild, Jimmy Eaves, Frankie Miller and several others joined in to help this Country Music great. Sonny Davenport, Gay Stevens and I drove up and made it just in time for the show. As soon as it was over, we headed back to Brady and got in just in time for me to do the morning show at 6:00 AM. It was a whirl-wind trip, but it was worth it.

I am happy to say that Gene is cancer free and doing great today. He is still on the road and recently toured Ireland. His is still one of the greatest voices in Country Music. Just listen to him sing "Farewell Party." No one can touch him on that song.

On stage while MCing a Gene Watson benefit concert in Paris, Texas. Gene was battling cancer and as of this writing is now cancer free.

George Hamilton IV

1998

Tracy: How did you become involved in Country Music?

George: I grew up in Winston-Salem, North Carolina. My granddaddy was a mountain man. He was a real hillbilly from Ash County North Carolina in Beaver Creek. He came down from the mountains to work on the railroads and that is how I became a city-billy instead of a hillbilly. Granddaddy loved Country Music. When I was a kid, he would put the 78's on the windup Victrola. He would play a lot of Jimmie Rodgers and Gene Autry. He was a railroad man and he loved Jimmie Rodgers singing "Brakeman's Blues." My early musical influences were thanks to my granddaddy.

Tracy: Ernest Tubb was also very influential in your career.

George: Very much so. Mr. Tubb would help me out as a kid and he would encourage me. He invited me to be on the Midnight Jamboree several times. One time, he took me up to the Princess Theater in Nashville for a March of Dimes Telethon and he got me on the show as part of his unit. I will never forget it because I forgot the words to the song half way through it. I was so embarrassed because Ernest stuck his neck out and got me on the show and I forgot the words. He was really good to me. There is a man in the Bible called Barnabas. I was told that his name meant the great encourager and Ernest was like the. He was always encouraging people. Justin Tubb told me that when Elvis did the Opry in the 1950's and it did not go over very well, Ernest invited him to the Midnight Jamboree and put him on the record shop and treated him really nice. Justin told me that when Elvis went back to Memphis, he wrote Ernest a hand written letter saying, "Dear Mr. Tubb, thank you for you kindness and hospitality. You were the only person in Nashville that was nice to me." Ernest had it framed. A lot of people did not realize what Elvis was all about until he became a superstar, and still some don't.

Tracy: You are known as the International Ambassador of Country Music. How did you get that title?

George: I went to the Soviet Union in March 1974. I was invited to do a lecture concert at Moscow University on the history of Country Music. We did some concert while we were there. In those days, the iron curtain was firmly in place and it was the first time that an American Country singer had performed in the eastern block. It was before Tennessee Ernie and the Opryland Group went over and before Roy Clark. This was a pioneering trip for us hillbillies and Billboard Magazine presented me with a memento when I came back to the United States. They referred to me as the International Ambassador of Country Music and I think that they were half kidding but I took it serious because I think that we should all be ambassadors for the music we love. Most of the folks here at the Grand Ole Opry are. They travel all over the world. I think that we should represent the music we love with dignity and present it to the best of our ability.

Tracy: You still do much of your performing overseas.

George: I am getting ready to leave Monday. I am doing a church tour. I have a church program about Fannie Crosby, the Hymn Writer from the 1800's. The tour is called "This Is My Story, This Is My Song, the Fannie Crosby Story".

Tracy: Do you have a lot of memories growing up in church?

George: I grew up in the Moravian church in North Carolina. It is a small denomination and a lot of people may not know what a Moravian is. A Moravian is a Protestant Church similar to the Methodist's and the Lutheran's. The Moravian has a very long history. It is the first organized international Protestant Church. They were the first to send missionaries to the new world. They were sent to minister to the Native Americans in Georgia in the early 1700's. The Moravian's celebrate Christmas Eve with what we call a love feast. It is a church service but unlike most churches, there is not a sermon. We all get together and sing Christmas Carols. The men of the church pass out coffee and hot chocolate to kids and we have sugar cake that the ladies bake. We have a simple meal and the minister talks about how Jesus spent a lot of time witnessing to people over simple meals. We sing carols, visit with each other and the minister reminds us all of the real reason for the season. We turn out the lights at church and we light our candles and the church lights up. The minister makes the point that Jesus came into the world on Christmas Eve almost 2000 years ago to bring light to the world and we should do the same. We should light a candle into our own world of darkness. He mentions how the church was dark until we each lit a candle. We then leave the church and go out into the night carrying our candles. It is a wonderful reminder of the real reason for the season. That is my fondest memories of church and Christmas, the love feast and the candle service.

Tracy: First Generation Records has just released a project that you recorded several years ago. 'The Man I Use To Be" is this album.

George: I love that song. It is a really good tune. I am so glad to see that it has been released. Pete Drake produced it. I was always real proud of the recordings. Melba Montgomery sang "Until I Gain Control Again" with me on the album. I really like Rodney Crowell's writing a lot. "The Man I Used To Be" is one of my favorite songs on the album. It tells a story. "Music Man's Dream" was also one that I really enjoyed doing. This album was a labor of love and getting to do it with Pete Drake was very important to me. I believe the first session that Pete played in Nashville was "Before This Day Ends". The next day he did something with Roy Drusky and Webb Pierce. It was such a thrill to get to work with Pete in the early days when he was still perfecting his style. Prior to that, we worked together on the Grand Ole Opry. When Pete and I got together to do the album, it was like a reunion. Pete called me up one day and told me that I had started him out so he is going to finish me up. He wanted to do an album together. He put a lot of heart and effort into the album as well. It did get out in the British Isles but I do not think that it has been in the States until now.

Tracy: Pete really loved the music business.

George: He sure did. He loved the business and he was a great man. He put so much into it. Before he had his own record publishing company and record company, he was an a-team steel player in all the big sessions right up until he passed away. I was thrilled that he remembered me after all these years and wanted to do an album with me. The project that he did with Ernest Tubb was phenomenal. It captured all of the greats in Country Music.

Tracy: "It Must Be Love" is a typical song for you.

George: There is not a single track on the album that is not important to me. Pete and I spent months selecting songs for the album. I was flying back and forth to Nashville to look for material and practice with Pete so I cannot think of any song that I don't love but, "It Must Be Love" is very special.

Tracy: What are your future plans?

George: The Duke and Dutchess of Hamilton from Scotland are going to be with us on the Opry. I am a little nervous but we owe allegiance to him. I am from the poor side of the family and there is a rumor that my ancestor Gavin Hamilton might have had to leave Scotland for sheep stealing. I am going to England to do the church tour and I am working on an album in Ireland with a lady that performs in Patsy Cline –The Musical. It is a play that has been touring in the British Isles for the past five years. I have been the narrator of that play. Sandy Kelly from the West Coast of Ireland plays Patsy and we are doing an album of Irish Folksongs. I also have a new gospel album out on Broadland International, a Canadian label called, "High Country". It is new Country gospel songs. They have done some great stuff. They did a Johnny Duncan album, Gene Watson and Billie Joe Spears as well. Broadland are good people but I feel especially loyal to First Generation Records because Pete Drake did not forget an old friend and if it is true that I started him out, I think that he has helped to finish me up in style with a wonderful album and I am very proud of it.

George Hamilton IV is one of the nicest entertainers in the business. He has an incredible speaking voice and is known all over the world. While on tour in Ireland with Leona Williams, I heard so many comments about George and his past appearances in that country.

At the 50th Anniversary dinner at the Ernest Tubb Record Shops, George was one of the speakers. He was the highlight of the evening honoring the memory of Ernest and promoting the future of the business. At that time, there was no tombstone on E.T.'s grave due to a family dispute. George called for the squabbling to end and to honor the man he loved so much. I had enjoyed his music for many years, but I gained so much more respect for him after that evening.

1990

Tracy: It is an honor to be visiting with one of Country Music's greatest legends George Jones. Your history in the business goes back many years.

George: Yes, it is a long story. We got out of the Marine Corp in 1953, and there was a new label forming in Beaumont, Texas, where I was from by the name of Starday Records. They were naturally looking for talent and it was fairly easy for me to get on with them. It took me until around 1955 or 1956, before we had a fairly good record with "Why Baby Why". We went from there to different labels such as Mercury and Musicor, United Artists and finally I went with Epic Records and I have been there for about 22 years. So that is just about the way it happened.

Tracy: Was "Why Baby Why" your first hit?

George: That was the first hit that we had. Red Sovine and Webb Pierce had the biggest record on it. They covered me on my label. It came out for me in the later part of '55 and it started hitting and reached in peak in '56. I got to about number four with it, but Webb and Red got to number one with it.

Tracy: How old were you when you recorded "Why Baby Why"?

George: I was about 23 years old.

Tracy: That is pretty young for someone to sky-rocket on the Country Music charts.

George: I was lucky to get started early but I had been playing at different places for quite a few years. I had been doing radio shows and things like that since I was about 16 or 17. I started on the radio show with a man and wife team, Eddie and Pearl, in Beaumont, Texas. I did the radio show and some gigs on the weekends in little taverns and what have you. I made $17.50 a week, room and board. I actually made $15 a week but they gave me $2.50 extra for doing the radio show.

Tracy: After your recording of "Why Baby Why", you recorded other big hits such as "White Lightening."

George: We started doing our best around 1959. We had "Window Up Above" and "White Lightening" that year. Following that, we changed from Mercury Records to United Artists and our first release with United Artists was "She Thinks I Still Care" which was around 1961. After that, things really started happening for us. Those were great years.

Tracy: Who were some of your idols growing up in Texas?

George: I would have to say that at first when I was very little when we didn't hear much Country Music except on the Grand Ole Opry, it was Roy Acuff and then as I grew up and when I started in the business, it was Hank Williams, Lefty Frizzell, Ray Price and one of my favorites today is still Merle Haggard. As for new talent, they have some fantastic new talent in Country Music today. It is good to see Country Music getting back to more of what it used to be-real Traditional Country Music. There for a while it really got wild and away from us. It broke my heart I'll tell you. Even though we are kind of coasting ourselves right now, it's good to see new artists and good material and good sing singers out there.

Tracy: You have had some great duet partners throughout your career.

George: The first was a girl named Jeanette Hicks on Starday Records. We sang a song called "Yearning". Then I had some duets with Margie Singleton. We did a thing called "Milwaukee, Here I Come" with Brenda Carter and also we did "Flame In My Heart" with Virginia Spurlock. I had a number one record with Melba Montgomery. I had a lot with Tammy Wynette. We did a lot together.

Tracy: You and Melba had some big chart records in the early days. How did you team up with Melba?

George: We just happened to meet in Nashville. We were on the same label. Her brother Peanut Montgomery was a songwriter. He did a lot of songwriting and he wrote the song "We Must Have Been Out Of Our Minds." The label started thinking about doing a duet together and they came up with that song. I thought it would be great and so we did it.

Tracy: When did you become a member of the Grand Ole Opry?

George: I first joined them in August of 1956. A lot of things happened to me in 1956. We got our first hit in '56 and I joined the union in'56. We sort of got an old saying now. If I don't feel good, I say "I've been sick since '56."

Tracy: After listening to that institution all of your life, how did you feel becoming a member?

George: I never dreamed that I would even so much as meet Roy Acuff in person much less sing on the Grand Ole Opry or even be in the business as far as that goes. I just loved to sing when I was little. That was a very, very meaningful day for me to come into that town and went on the Grand Ole Opry and to be able to meet back-stage Roy Acuff, Bill Monroe and other people.

Tracy: Who introduced you for the first time on the Opry?

George: My hero Roy Acuff introduced me.

Tracy: I am certain that made the event even more important for you.

George: It did. I was scared stiff. I went out there and didn't get a very big hand at all. I said OK, try it again later. I was scared to death and I am sure that I did not sound all that good, but it was still a big thrill but it was very scary.

Tracy: You made a big impact on the awards shows during this time. Do you know how many awards you have received?

George: I have never counted them up through the years. In the '50's, we had Most Promising Male Vocalist and several things like that. In '61 or '62, before the Country Music Association was formed, we won "Male Vocalist" several times through the trade magazines. That is how you won back then. When the CMA came along, we won again in 1981 with "He Stopped Loving Her Today." We went to New York and won a Grammy Award for that song. We have been very lucky. We also won an award for the video of "Who's Gonna Fill Their Shoes". We kindly coast a little bit and then we luck out and find that material. You know you have to have that material to make it in this business.

Tracy: One of my all time favorite George Jones songs is "Just A Girl I Used To Know."

George: That is one of my favorites too. I believe it was just right around that time that I had "She Thinks I Still Care" that I got that one. Jack Clement, the one that brought me "She Thinks I Still Care" from Dickey Lee, helped me find that song and "Not Exactly What I Had In Mind." It was a beautiful song.

Tracy: You have created so much great music throughout the years. You have spent a lot of time in studios recording many albums.

George: Tracy, I really could not count them up. I have some real good fanatic fans that have 125 or 140 albums and I am sure that some of them have been rehashed albums with a new picture on the front. You know how they do when you leave one label and go to another. We have spent a big part of our career in the recording studio.

Tracy: The 1970's were not a good time for George Jones.

George: Well, you have got to remember that this was back in the time when Country Music went to "pot" so to speak. They were bringing in middle of the road Pop music in and calling it Country Music. They still play a lot of it now. Praise the Lord for people like Clint Black, George Strait, Alan Jackson and Garth Brooks for getting Country back to where it should be. When you look at it and think about it, all of our veterans like Ernest Tubb and Roy Acuff and people like that have made

Country Music what it is supposed to be. When you see it go to "pot" like that the way it did, there were a lot of us hurting in the '70's. I had a rough start in the '50's because I was getting into the business and I had to compete with rock and roll when it was getting so hot. We were really fortunate to be as lucky as we were.

Tracy: George Jones fans have to be the most loyal fans in Country Music.

George: I have got to admit that and praise them. They are the greatest fans that anyone in the world could have. I have done so many wrong things in my life and I have tried to do some good things and they have stood by me between the right and the wrongs. They never gave up on me. I am proud of them.

Tracy: It was not too long ago that you met someone who had turned your career around.

George: I sure did. I have to praise Nancy. I was really needing help bad and she came around at the right time. I was divorced at the time and had been for quite a while. You miss that love in your life. You can have everything in the world and all the money and it don't make any difference. She came along and gave me piece of mind. She is quite a woman. I call her Skinny Legs. All of my fans know about Nancy and they all love her as much as they love me. She is quite a woman.

Tracy: Your Country Music Park, Jones Country has enjoyed a really big success.

George: Yes. We had to close down one year, last year in fact because Nancy was really sick with her spastic stomach and nerves. She was trying to do too much. Nancy was trying to do all this phone and road work for me and try to take care of that too and it was just too much for her. The only thing that we could do was close it down one year and try to get her health straightened out. She got my health back on track, so we needed to work on hers. We are starting back on this Memorial Day Weekend and we will be there for July 4th weekend and Labor Day Weekend. It looks like all the camper spaces are full and all the motels are sold out, so it will be another big success.

Tracy: You have a new single on the market now titled "Hell Stays Open All Night Long."

George: Yes, but we are having a little problem that I cannot discuss right now. Sometimes there is a problem with the artist and some companies, but we are in the process of either trying to get it straightened out or changing labels.

Tracy: What do you want to be doing for the next few years?

George: The main thing right now is for me to be happy with my recording and the people that I work with and try to get that straightened out like we were just talking about. I want to get on with finding some good material and try to keep putting out some good records.

Tracy: Is there anything that you have not done but would like to do?

George: I think I have pretty much done it all. I am not interested in going to California and becoming a movie star like some of the others have done. I don't care about things like that. I just want to sing. I love Country Music. I love it religiously. I always have and always will. As long as I can keep making music and making fans happy, I will be happy.

Tracy: In the future, how do you want to be remembered?

George: I know that I had some great fans and still have and I know that they loved me very much. I just wish that I could express how much I love them. I love Country Music and I love to sing it as long as there is someone out there that loves it as much as I do. I would like to be remembered by the songs that I have had and the enjoyment they got out of it. Tell your listeners that in case they forgot, I am still a Texas boy. I've got Texas in my heart and I want to tell them all hi and come and see us if they can and thank you Tracy for all the support throughout the years.

George Jones may be the greatest Country Music singer ever to live. During my interviews, George is always named as one of the most influential singers in the business. He has been dedicated and true to the Country Music industry and it is a shame that they have not honored him in the way that he deserves.

This interview was done prior to a George Jones personal appearance at the Abilene Civic Center in Abilene, Texas. I brought a large group of twenty or thirty people with me that night to the auditorium. Nancy Jones told me to make sure and come backstage and visit with them and that I could bring my friends with me. I think we wound up with about fifteen or so backstage and we had a wonderful time. George and Nancy took photos with every one. He did tell me that he should kill me for bringing all of those people backstage with me!

I have been honored to spend time with George and Nancy on several occasions since then-at more concerts in Texas, Loretta Lynn's museum opening, Golden Voice Awards and even at a recording session for Heart of Texas Records.

I sent George a note about the Floyd Tillman duet album and asked him to be a part of it. Nancy called me one afternoon at the radio station. She was telling me that George told her the other day that he did not want to do any more duets. She asked me to play along with her as she walked into the den where George was relaxing. She said, "Tracy, we got your letter about Floyd Tillman wanting George to do a duet with him. We are just so sorry, but George is just so busy that he doesn't have time to do anything like that with Mr. Tillman." I heard George say, "Just wait a minute. I never said that." Nancy then handed George the phone and she was laughing hysterically. George told me that he would love to record with Floyd and wanted to sing on "Driving Nail In My Coffin." I flew to Nashville for the session and it was one of the best afternoons that I have ever spent. George asked me to get him a Coke. After the session was over, I saw his Coke can on the counter. I picked it up and brought it back home!

George Jones deserves every good thing that has come to his career. And thanks to Nancy, he finally has been getting some of that much deserved attention.

Goldie Hill

MARCH 1988

Tracy: Can you tell us how you started in the Country Music business?

Goldie: Do I have to go back and say how far it was? It was actually 1952, and my brother Tommy Hill was working with Webb Pierce. Kitty Wells came out with her records and had something pretty good and Webb decided he needed a girl singer in the band. My brother said, 'I got a little sister at home.' He gave me a call and said 'do you want to sing?' and I said 'why not.' That was in April and I came to Nashville with Tommy and Webb in I think June. In July, I had a record in the Top 10.

Tracy: At that time, Webb was one of the hottest acts in the Country Music business.

Goldie: He had "Wondering" and he had a couple more records. It was just before he was getting really kind of hot. I worked the road with him for about eight months and he moved to Nashville. We were on the Louisiana Hayride at that time and I continued to stay on the Hayride until the last of '53. Then I came to Nashville in about September of '53.

Tracy: You recorded several sides for Decca. How did you come to the attention of Decca?

Goldie: Webb was on Decca and when I came to Nashville with him and my brother, they were doing sessions for Decca. They were doing all of their recording here in Nashville. Webb asked Paul Cohen if he would listen to me sing and Paul said yes. So, I got up and sang about a verse and Paul said we will record tomorrow night! It happened to me just all real fast. I was working for the government. I was working on IBM machines at the time my brother wanted to know if I wanted to sing. I was nineteen years old and single. I didn't have no obligations and I thought that might be fun because he had enjoyed it. I had never done anything professional before like that. I had just been home with the family.

Tracy: Both of your brothers were very musical.

Goldie: Yes, I had another brother named Kenny, we lost him about a year ago. They had a band and they played on the weekends in the clubs around San Antonio and Bandera and around a hundred miles of San Antonio, where I was raised. Once in a while I would get up and try to sing, so that is how I got started in the business. I was in it from '52 until Carl (Smith) and I got married. When we got married, I quit. So,

I had about five and a half years of the music business and it was fantastic to me and I loved every minute of it and I still enjoy it.

Tracy: What was your first hit record?

Goldie: It was an answer to a Ray Price song. Ray had a song out titled "Talk To Your Heart." I came out with "Why Talk To My Heart?" because that was the thing at that time-answer songs. That was the first one and a little bit later on I did "I Let The Stars Get In My Eyes." That was I guess the second release that I had.

Tracy: I also remember a song titled "Lonely Heartaches."

Goldie: It was good. I think I averaged a couple of albums a year and that was a lot of albums then. I think about four singles a year and I had quite a few songs out for not being in the business any longer than I was. "Lonely Heartaches" and "I'm The Loneliest Girl In Town" and "Say, Big Boy" got a lot of play.

Tracy: You also became a member of the Grand Ole Opry during that time.

Goldie: I came to Nashville the last of '53 and I appeared on the Opry and became a member not too long after I got up here. I was on the Opry regular from the latter part of '53 to the first of '57. Philip Morris cigarettes started a tour, so Carl and I left the Opry and went on this tour for Philip Morris cigarettes. It was a thirteen week contract like they did with all the radio stars. There was not much television then, but that was kind of a standard contract. That thirteen weeks ended up lasting seventeen months.

Tracy: How did you meet Carl Smith?

Goldie: I met Carl in New Orleans the first time. He was on the same package show and we said hello. I saw him again at another performance and we said hello. Then I moved to Nashville and we said hello. Then four years later we didn't have to say hello any longer. We were married thirty one years last September. It was my first marriage and his second and we have three grown beautiful children and they have children. We have a real nice family.

Tracy: One of your biggest hits came as a duet with Justin Tubb.

Goldie: "Looking Back To See" was a great record for us. Justin was on Decca Records also and after the answer thing, here come the duet thing. For some reason or another, Paul Cohen with Decca asked if Justin and I could sing together. I knew Justin from Texas, when he was going to college in Austin. I met him and his cousins, Doug and X Lincoln. I knew Justin and them when I was on the Hayride and become friends. When we were both in Nashville then and they wanted to know if we could do a duet together, we tried and it didn't seem like we had any problems singing together at all. I had some other records that got up in the charts as far as it did, but the charts were so much different then than they are now. We had a category for just radio, for jukebox and for selling. So if you made all three charts you really had a good record. Now there is just one chart, but then there were three. We had two or three songs that made all three charts at the same time. But I guess "Looking Back To See" got more play and is still getting play. I think the reason that people think it was the biggest, because it has gotten so much play throughout the years. As a matter of fact, I think that is the only one that WSM even has of me. I guess that I will have to look into that!

Tracy: Would you ever consider going back into the music industry?

Goldie: No, no. I had that opportunity to do it because of Carl. I wasn't taken away from the music business, it was my idea. I was much happier staying at home and we were married for a year and our first child came. I just didn't want to be in another place and that baby being somewhere else. Carl is a homebody and he worked mostly on the weekends.

Tracy: How is Carl doing and what are your future plans together?

Goldie: He is doing fantastic. Our future plans are strictly with cutting horses. He has had horses ever since he came to Nashville and he got into quarter horses and was raising quarter horses. He had an AQHA champion and good blood lined mares. Then he somehow or another got acquainted with cutting horses which is a quarter horse but their trained to work cattle. He started that about twenty years ago and I guess that we are on the road more now than we were in the music business. We go to a horse show every weekend. We go within a two hundred mile area. Our future is going to cutting horse shows and entertaining grandchildren.

Tracy: Do you still enjoy Country Music?

Goldie: We still listen to the radio and that sort of thing, but our desires are somewhere else. Carl had thirty years of the music business and it was really good to him and he just decided it was time for some of the younger people to go ahead and do their thing. I just hope the fans still have as much fun listening to the records as we did when we were making them. We still enjoy listening to everybody sing. We are just full of fun and I hope that everybody will just continue to appreciate life because we enjoy it very much.

Frankie Miller told me that the first time Goldie appeared on the Grand Ole Opry that all the men on the show fell in love with her. She was a beautiful lady and had the talent to back her great looks.

Goldie and her brothers started their careers in Texas. Big Bill Lister was responsible for starting Tommy Hill's musical career. Several years ago, he joined me on the Hillbilly Hits radio show and gave Bill credit for the start of all the good things that happened in his career. He became a successful producer, musician and even a writer. He penned "Slowly" for

Webb Pierce and "Teddy Bear" for Red Sovine, among a hundred others. Kenny was a part of the family band and it was just natural that Goldie would follow the brothers.

I only had a chance to meet Goldie once in Nashville a couple of years before her death. It was such a thrill to meet her and I even got Carl Smith to snap a photo of us! We corresponded for several years by email and she would help keep me up on the latest especially after her brother Tommy became ill. I remember her emailing me one night about midnight after Tommy passed away with the sad news.

My favorite memory of Goldie was at the Golden Voice Awards in Nashville. Jan Howard was given the Female Vocalist Award that year. During her acceptance speech, she gave the award to Goldie to the delight of the audience. It was a moment of extreme generosity on Jan's part and humble appreciation on Goldies'. It just proved to me that the "Grand Ladies" of Country Music still stuck together throughout the years.

Goldie passed away February 24, 2005.

JULY 1990

Tracy: How long have you been in the Country Music business?

Grandpa: Sixty-two years.

Tracy: When did you start and how did you start?

Grandpa: I am from Kentucky and the whole family of us moved to Akron, Ohio in 1928, in order to get work. While I was there, I was going to school and in 1929, the fellar who made "Ain't Gonna Rain No More" famous, Wendell Hall, the Red Headed Music Maker was playing in the theater in Akron for a whole week. He put on a week long amateur show. There were 450 contestants and out of that, and I don't know how, but I won first prize. The last night, there were four groups left and I won first place, which was $50 in $10 gold pieces. I wish I had them now! That is how I got started and I was on the air the next day and have been on ever since. I finally got a little commercial for $16 a week and I have been on ever since. When I was in the Army, I was on American AFM, and American Forces Network. I would get off for an hour in the morning and do the show. Then I was an MP over there.

Tracy: How did you get the name "Grandpa"?

Grandpa: Harmonica Joe and I had a little act together and Bradley Kincaid came to Akron and saw our act. He asked if we would like to go to New England. We had never been nowhere so we said that we had to ask our folks. They let us go so we got on WBZ in Boston and it was connected with Springfield, Massachusetts. They covered the entire New England. We played in Maine and had to drive back to Boston to get a few hours sleep because we had to be on the air in the morning. Me and this boy and I sat around like dead lice were dropping off of us; we were so tired. Bradley would tell me to get up to the microphone and that I was just like an old Grandpa. People would write in and ask how old I was because I sounded like I was eighty. So that is how I got started with Grandpa. There were a couple of black-faced comedians that took me down and got me a false mustache and a pencil to make wrinkles you know.

Tracy: How old were you?

Grandpa: That was 1935 so I was about 22. I have been Grandpa ever since and I am still not a real one.

Tracy: How does it feel to be a member of the Country Music Hall of Fame?

Grandpa: That was a nervous deal. It really made me nervous. I had a speech in my pocket and when I got up there to accept, I forgot about my speech. I don't know what kind of speech I made but I got by with it.

Tracy: Do you think that Country Music has changed from the time you got started to today?

Grandpa: No, not Country Music. Roy Acuff does the same thing so does Bill Monroe, Bill Carlisle and myself. What they call Country Music now is the modern kind. The real Country Music has not changed. They have just added drums and things like though. More of a rock beat in some of it. The true Country is still the same as it was when I started.

Tracy: What are some of you most requested songs?

Grandpa: "Mountain Dew" and "Old Rattler" are two that I get the most requests for.

Tracy: Is there anything in Country Music that you would still like to do?

Grandpa: No, I don't reckon. I would like to do a film and be a character in a western movie. I would love to try that.

Tracy: So you would like to do some acting?

Grandpa: Of course we already do a little bit of that on Hee Haw. I would love to act. We have a few guys who really know their business.

Tracy: How long have you been associated with Hee Haw?

Grandpa: Ever since it started. We are on our 23rd season. We just finished yesterday. We film in June and October.

Tracy: It is just as successful today as it has ever been.

Grandpa: I guess so. Some say it is and others say it is not. Some towns have it while others drop it.

Tracy: Do you plan on staying at the Grand Ole Opry?

Grandpa: I reckon so. As long as they don't kick me out I guess I will be around here.

It was always an exciting time when Grandpa Jones hit the Grand Ole Opry stage. The camera flashes were everywhere as his banjo rang out throughout the auditorium. His long association with *Hee Haw* and his tenure with the *Grand Ole Opry* gave Grandpa instant celebrity status all over the world.

I was interviewing him one time backstage at the Opry House. The interview was going great and I was so proud to be talking to Grandpa. Of course, any person interviewing an artist wants you to believe they know each other well. The artist and disc jockey relationship is many times not as close as some will lead you to believe. Right in the middle of this ten minute conversation, Grandpa looks up at me and says "now who are you again?" right as the tape is running.

Dave Kirby told me one of my favorite Grandpa Jones' stories. Dave was just starting to work guitar sessions in Nashville. He had a session with Grandpa scheduled. Dave arrived at the studio and was ready to play. At that time, Dave had kind of long hair and tinted glasses. Grandpa arrived and walked in with his banjo. He sat the banjo down and looked around the room. His eyes caught Dave (whom he had not met before). Grandpa looked him up and down and said, "now son, don't go playing any of those hippy licks on a Grandpa Jones record!"

MARCH 9, 1990

Tracy: You had a big record in 1949 with "That Same Sweet Girl", was that your first big hit?

Hank: Yes, it was on Four Star. Pappy Daily in Houston was the one who got me started with Four Star Records.

Tracy: You spent a lot of time in Texas.

Hank: I lived in Houston for about ten years and had a radio program for KLEE sponsored by a car dealer. I was actually born about twenty miles from where I live here in Florida. I really enjoyed Texas. It has been so long since I was out in that part of the country. The last big trip that I made out there was with Red Foley. We went down to Midland and all in that country and all out through that country.

Tracy: How did you find the classic "Geisha Girl"?

Hank: Lawton Williams from Ft. Worth wrote that song. I guess he had me in mind when he wrote that and I am sure glad that he did. He also wrote "Fraulein". It was a big hit all over the world. Lawton was and still is a very dear friend of mine. I went to Japan and Germany on the strength of that song.

Tracy: "Send Me The Pillow That You Dream On" was also a big hit for you.

Hank: That was it. That was one great song. I wrote the song. I was in Houston the time I wrote it. It kept going. Almost everyone has recorded it. I am hoping that someone will record it as a single. I would like to see Ricky Van Shelton do it as a single. He is a good singer. Dwight Yoakum also put it in an album. He sells lost of records.

Tracy: When did you make your first appearance on the Grand Ole Opry?

Hank: In 1952, I made my debut on the Grand Ole Opry. I had a song called, "Let Me Be The One". That was a big record for me. With that song, it got me a guest appearance. In 1960, I had "Help Me I'm Falling" and that is the song that carried me to the Grand Ole Opry.

Tracy: How did it feel the first time you appeared on the Grand Ole Opry?

Hank: One night I was driving from Houston to Beaumont, Texas, and Red Foley was on the Prince Albert part of the Opry. Something spoke to me asking how I would like to be on the Grand Ole Opry. You know how a feeling will come on you starting from the top of your head? It was a great feeling and I never thought it could happen. At that time it was a great honor to get to come to the Opry.

Tracy: Who influenced you to make a career in the Country Music business?

Hank: Red Foley and Roy Acuff. I always tried to sing like Ernest Tubb but I guess there were a million people that tried to sing like him in the early part of my career. A guy told me that I needed to find my own style and so that is when I started to do. I was a picker. I never thought that I would become a singer. When I made my first record and they started selling, I quit trying to pick the guitar.

Tracy: You recorded a song in 1961 called "Happy Birthday To Me".

Hank: Whispering Bill Anderson wrote that. It came off real good. It is a bread and butter song. It has been going for a really long time. I still get many requests for that song out on personal appearances.

Tracy: Do you have any idea how many top ten songs you have had over the years or how many records?

Hank: "Please Help Me I'm Falling" was my first Country record to spill over into the Pop field. That is when you first heard Floyd Cramer. A boy by the named of Don Robertson and Hal Blair are the ones that wrote the song. Don is the one who wrote the lyrics with Floyd Cramer on there. I had the pleasure one night at the Opry of having Floyd play the piano as I was singing the song.

Tracy: Do you still play the Opry?

Hank: Yes sir. I got to get started back up there. It is about 385 miles for me but I will be going often. I have been a regular since 1960.

Tracy: Management required a certain number of appearances at one time for their members.

Hank: They have stopped requiring that. When more artists came available they loosened up on that. At one time, there were not many artists and they had to do something. Ray Price was hot at the time and he made about one appearance that year. Things were starting to slow down so that is why they did that.

Tracy: Do you still tour?

Hank: I have slowed down. I do not go to Europe anymore. There are a lot of good Country Music fans over there, but there is a lot of unrest over there. In the past

week, I have received two letters from East Germany since they opened up and started letting them write. It is great to hear from those people. A couple of years ago they
re-released my project of Irish songs Country style. They should re-release another LP
because there is a big market.

Tracy: "Country Music Hall of Fame" was a very unique song.

Hank: That was a good one. I recorded that song in 1968. Carl Davis wrote that. I
have not heard anything about Carl so I do not know if he is still alive or not. He
wrote "Alabama" as well.

Tracy: What are your plans for the future?

Hank: About seven years ago I committed my life to the Lord and I have written
about twelve songs of how he came into my life. I am planning to make a gospel
album. When a person gets the Lord in their life it really makes a difference. I dearly
do love the people in Texas, because they are such a different bread of people. I also
hope that you have a long very satisfied career in your life. God Bless you.

*I booked four dates on Hank Locklin in Texas in 2004. I was able to make three of those
with him. Hank brought his son Hank Adam with him. They spent one very entertaining
evening co-hosting my Hillbilly Hits radio show over KNEL. They even did a few live songs
over the air to the delight of the listening audience. Hank visited the Heart of Texas Country
Music Museum and even brought a shirt to donate to the museum.*

*The last time I saw Hank was in June of 2006. He was appearing at the ROPE Reunion
show during Fan Fair. Hank Adam was assisting him once again and he performed the
majority of his many hits throughout the evening. At the conclusion of his performance, he
sang "Danny Boy." Although he did not hit the notes as he once did, the audience gave him
a rousing applause and standing ovation.*

*As of this writing, Hank is not in the Country Music Hall of Fame. That alone is a crime
against Country Music.*

Hank Thompson

AUGUST 19, 1999

Tracy: I am talking today with one of the legends of Country Music, Mr. Hank Thompson. How did your great career begin?

Hank: When someone asks me when I got started in the business, I don't really know. When did I start walking or talking? It just seems like I have always been in the business. It is actually the only occupation that I have ever had except when I was in the Navy. As for as making a living, the only real occupation that I have ever had is the music business.

Tracy: Waco was an important city in your career.

Hank: I actually started on radio on WACO radio there. I had a morning program there and I was called "Hank, The Hired Hand." It was for a grocery store and flour company there in town. It was just me and my guitar. I would pick and sing and then go back on Saturday afternoons and sing for the folks down at the store. They had some pictures made up and I would sign autographs. I got in the professional part of the business at a rather young age.

Tracy: It was at that time that you began to develop your own style.

Hank: I think that everybody has someone that inspires them or they look up to in music, sports or acting. There is someone that gets you interested in that and you try to do things similar. I was influenced at a very early age listening to Jimmie Rodgers records. That was actually before I even started school. I would crank up that Victrola and play those Jimmie Rodgers records and those by the Carter Family and Vernon Dalhart. I would play them over and over until I learned them and then I would go around singing them. Later on, I was influenced by Gene Autry because I could actually see him in the movies. You could actually see Gene pick up that guitar and start singing and I was quite influenced by him and Ernest Tubb, Roy Acuff and several others that were popular at that time. They all influenced me and helped to develop the style that I still use today.

Tracy: Your band "The Brazos Valley Boys" have been a very important part of your career.

Hank: I formed the group after I got out of the Navy in 1946. It was mainly a group of some pickers around town there. We would go out and work some of the schoolhouse auditoriums and I had my broadcast there. I did not use the band on my radio broadcast, but we would go out and work some of the schoolhouses together. We would play those little towns within the listening area of the radio station. After I left Waco and moved to Dallas, I formed a more permanent group around 1950. I took on a full time band and really built a good organization. We then moved to Oklahoma in 1952, and from there we started with heavy emphasis with the Western Swing and what we kind of call the Honkytonk Swing. That was the music that we were playing in the dance halls. People liked that kind of music because they could dance to it. That was when I really started to develop the band and the sound, in the early '50's.

Tracy: Your album "Hank Thompson and Friends" was one of the most historic albums in the Country Music business.

Hank: We had a lot of snags along the way and had to overcome a lot of problems on that album. I guess that anything that is worthwhile, you have to work for. We had such fine competent help on this one musically, that it turned out above my expectations. I knew that it was going to turn out to be an excellent album, but after getting to listen to it, it excelled what I had hoped for.

Tracy: Was it your idea to bring other artists in for the project?

Hank: That was the concept for the thing way back there. About ten years ago, Mike Curb had mentioned to me about getting some artists and doing some duet things. He thought it would be a good concept for me. Ernest Tubb had done one of those. He said that a lot of people in the business would be happy to record with me. It just seemed like we couldn't get it together. The main problem was getting the people together from producing to financing to get it all rolling.

Tracy: My favorite cut is your duet with Kitty Wells and Tanya Tucker on "The Wild Side of Life/It Wasn't God Who Made Honkytonk Angels".

Hank: That was really a piece of history. To have Kitty and me in the studio and then add Tanya who wasn't even born when we recorded those songs, was very special. As a matter of fact, Tanya was one of the first that I talked to about the project. Tanya told me that she would love to record with me several years ago. We had contacted her office and she never seemed to be available. By accident, we ran into her in a restaurant in Nashville. She came up to me and said, "I want to be on that album!" We told her that we tried to contact her and she said, "well, nobody told me about it and I want to be on it." We asked when she could do it and she gave us a date. We then checked with Kitty and I flew in and we did it.

Tracy: When you recorded "The Wild Side of Life", did you ever imagine that it would not only be a monster hit for you but start the female revolution in Country Music?

Hank: I had absolutely no idea. I really wasn't that excited about the song. It actually came out as the B side of the record. We recorded it because it had been popular by Jimmie Heap and his Melodymasters in Taylor, Texas. They recorded it on Imperial Records. It was popular on the jukeboxes around Texas and Oklahoma. That was my first session with Ken Nelson at Capital. I had written a song called "Crying In The Deep Blue Sea." We thought that was the best song that we had in the bunch. I thought "Wild Side of Life" was an alright song, but I was not really impressed with it. We decided to put it on the back side of the song that I had written. After "Crying In The Deep Blue Sea" made a little spurge and was kind of popular, it started turning over and became a hit. It really surprised all of us. Answer songs were done quite a bit. I had a number one hit on "Wake Up Irene." That was an answer song to "Goodnight Irene." When you had a song that was real popular, it was not unusual for someone to come back with an answer to it. Of course, Kitty was relatively unknown at that time. She sang a few songs with the Johnny and Jack team. She was not the feature and just part of the family. "It Wasn't God Who Made Honkytonk Angels" started her career in a big way. All the female artists owe Kitty something because she brought the women to the forefront in the business.

Tracy: "Six Pack To Go" has been another staple in your shows throughout the years.

Hank: I actually came across that song by accident. I was out in Arizona, at a club out there one time. I was on the way to California to record and we had played a date there in Holbrook. I ran into an old friend of mine that had a bar there and was part of the rodeo circuit. He was in a little combo there and he was singing this song. I told him that I really like that song and after the club closed, his wife wrote the words out for me. I still have the original hanging on my wall. I did a little rewriting on it to adapt it to my style and try to polish it up some, but the song was good as it was. I told them that I would be recording it in the next few days. I knew right away that "Six Pack To Go" would be a good song for me. Vince Gill told me that was his brother's favorite song when they were kids.

Tracy: Your induction into the Country Music Hall of Fame has to be one of your biggest accomplishments.

Hank: I guess that is the single most important thing that has ever happened in my career. I don't think there is anything that actually epitomizes an industry any more than to be put into a very select group of your peers like the Hall of Fame. I think my plaque is hanging up there close to Vernon Dalhart and Jimmie Rodgers.

Tracy: You will soon be honored once again when you are inducted into the new Texas Country Music Hall of Fame.

Hank: That is a rare honor. I have had some other recognitions but this one is right there at the top.

Tracy: You are one of the entertainers that began having hits in the forties and have continued throughout your entire career.

Hank: I have been very fortunate because my very first record was a hit. We have gone right on down the line to each decade. Although, " Hank and Friends", did not make the Billboard Charts, it did chart into Gavin, and Americana. It would be difficult to do that today.

Tracy: I know that you credit your career to your many fans.

Hank: I really appreciate the fans. It is because of them that I have been able to make a career of this. They are the ones that make it possible for me. I certainly want them to know that I appreciate it and if they want me to sign autographs or sign pictures, I am delighted to do it. I thank the fans for listening to and buying my music throughout the years and I always look forward to seeing them.

I will be happy to admit that Hank Thompson was one of the few artists that intimidated me in my early days. OK, I was just scared of him. I guess it was his long standing career and my admiration for him that made me fearful of approaching him for any length of time.

His personal assistant at the time, D.D. Bray set up the first interview that I did with Hank in Mason, Texas. He was working an event and I was actually DJing a school dance in Rochelle, Texas, with my friend Randall King. I was so excited that Hank was coming to Mason that I left the dance and drove for forty minutes to do the interview and then drive back and finish the event up. I was sixteen years old and the interview was awful. I was just starting out in the business and Hank should have told me to go back home, but he didn't. He was kind to me and I was scared to death!

Since that time, I have probably interviewed him twenty times and each time I have left having even more admiration for him. Hank and his wife Ann conduct their career as a business. Hank is very sharp and well educated and has given me some great advice.

We were on a cruise together a few years ago. He called me aside and wanted to give me some advice concerning a certain aspect of running the show that day. He was exactly right and after implementing his advice, the show was even better.

I am happy to say that we have grown much closer in the last few years. I still have the utmost respect for the Country Music Hall of Famer, but I now really enjoy spending time with him whether at his home in Texas or on the road in Washington, D.C.

Hank Thompson is a living legend and a national treasure. It is great to be able to call up a national treasure and ask him how his day was. Hank is one of Country Music's last pioneers.

Jack Greene

JULY, 1990

Tracy: You are currently working on a gospel album.

Jack: We are doing five old songs and five new songs. We are looking for the five best old hymns that have not been done over and over. We are looking for some of the best new songs. We have a lot of new material picked. Gospel music has been an important part of my life for a long time. It is always good to give something back to the Lord. He has given so much to me.

Tracy: Have you written any of the songs?

Jack: No, I have not been a productive writer in a longtime. I always enjoyed writing and have written some pretty good songs. I have just been too busy with other business to find time to write. I cannot force myself to write. It has to come naturally.

Tracy: An Ernest Tubb live album was just released with you playing the drums. The version of "Do What You Do Well" is doing very well and you are the one playing the drums.

Jack: It is called "Ernest Tubb Live 1965." Cal Smith, Leon Rhodes, Buddy Charleton, Jack Drake, and myself are playing on the album. That was a great album and every time I hear it I can't help but remember the night we cut it in 1965 at the Spanish Castle in Seattle. We had a great time that night and I think you can hear that come through on the album.

Tracy: Touring with Ernest Tubb is what helped you get your start.

Jack: I spent five years traveling all over the world with Ernest. I would meet new fans, meet disc jockeys, play new places and at the same time I would help promote Ernest Tubb. We spent more time on the road than we did anywhere else. We traveled in that bus on every interstate and two way highway that we could find. Ernest loved to work. He would work the big concert halls and the small beer joints. We were a family. We had to be because we saw more of each other than our own family!

Tracy: The Rex Griffin song "The Last Letter" opened a lot of doors for you.

Jack: Yes. It was not a big hit but it was a door opener. It was a hit to me but the one that established my career and took us out of the Ernest Tubb Band was, "There Goes My Everything". We had many hits after that and we had Ernest's blessings and his support. I will always remember what he told me. He told me that I could go out and try to pay for my kid's education but if it did not work out, I could always come back and be a Troubadour.

Tracy: "There Goes My Everything" was a career song for you.

Jack: That is true. It was an answer to prayers. Dallas Frazier wrote the song and it was in Ferlin Husky's publishing company. In 1967, it was voted Song of The Year, Album of The Year and even earned a couple of Grammy nominations. Of course, I followed that with "All The Time" "You Are My Treasure" and the other big one "Statue of A Fool."

Tracy: When did you join the Grand Ole Opry?

Jack: I joined the Opry on December 23, 1967.

Tracy: What does the future hold for Jack Greene and the Jolly Green Giants?

Jack: We are looking into working overseas. I just talked to Ted and Tom LeGarde who are well known in Australia. They have a great television show in Australia that covers the entire continent. We are wanting to go places we have never been like Australia and going back to England and Germany. I have not had the pleasure of touring Denmark, Sweden or Ireland. I would like to go to Ireland. I would like to continue working the Grand Ole Opry and The Nashville Network as well as tour other countries. We do a little of everything just not to get bored and tired.

Jack Greene has been an integral part of the Grand Ole Opry and the Country Music scene for over thirty five years. He worked his way up the ranks of the business. He started out as a drummer and then became a vocalist. He moved to be half of one of the most popular duets in Country Music and now has become an elder statesman of Country Music. In that form, he is now working to help launch the career of new artist Candi Carpenter. Candi is booked on all of Jack's shows and is a great artist in her own right.

While working on this book, I recalled one of my "naive moments." On one of my first Nashville trips, I was backstage preparing to interview Jeannie Seely. Jeannie and Jack had a number of hit duets including "Wish I Didn't Have To Miss You." They also toured all over the country with a very successful road show.

Jack (and his then wife June) walked past us. I thought how wonderful it would be to interview them both at the same time. I asked, "Jack, would you join Jeannie and I in this interview?" Jack immediately past up the opportunity and continued walking away as June was mumbling something to him. Jeannie then relayed that June did not like Jack doing interviews or songs with her any longer. I was kind of shocked. It was one of the times that a little more knowledge of the industry would have helped me avoid an embarrassing situation. The ironic part of this story is that June would later run off with someone else leaving Jack in a bad situation.

At this writing, Jack is back out on the road and doing better than he has in years. He has a new manager, new show and a new lease on a happier and more productive life.

1998

Tracy: You recorded an album for First Generation Records and Pete Drake that has just been re-released. Pete was a longtime friend of yours. How did you meet Pete?

Jean: When I first came to Nashville, I met Pete through his brother Jack. Ernest Tubb worked with Jack for many years and Pete was on many sessions. Every time you turned a corner, there was Pete.

Tracy: Tell us the story of you and Skeeter Davis on Ernest Tubb's bus.

Jean: Skeeter was working with Ernest and Hawkshaw Hawkins and I were on the show and we were riding on Ernest's bus. Skeeter and I were sitting across the aisle from one another and Ernest was always taking pictures. He had his camera out and Skeeter and I were talking and he snapped a picture. When he got the picture back, both of us had our mouths open. He always put captions under the pictures and under this one he put "who's listening"?

Tracy: On the First Generation album, you recorded some of your older hits and added a few new songs. As a matter of fact, E.T.'s son Justin joined you on "A Dear John Letter."

Jean: Justin Tubb sang Ferlin Husky's part on it. I received a Grammy award for "Second Fiddle To An Old Guitar", "Seven Lonely Days", " He Touched Me" and "Slipping Away". Lorrie Morgan and Tommy Cash helped write "Leavin' Fever". "In The Palm Of You Hand" is a very fine ballad. Years ago Brenda Lee recorded a song called "Too Many Rivers" and she recorded it real slow. My husband, Benny Birchfield, told Pete that he and Buddy Spiker should do the song with a little western swing. Buddy is a great fiddle player. He kicked it off and it came out so good. We did, "Too Many Rivers" and it is one of my favorites on the album.

Tracy: "Dear John" is one of the first hits that you recorded.

Jean: That goes back a long time, back in 1953. We cut the song in California and Ferlin Husky did the talking part of the song. Back then, there were not many women in Country Music. Kitty Wells, Rose Maddox, and myself were about it. Ken Nelson, who is a wonderful man, did not believe in women singers. I had recorded one song before this and Hank Thompson put a little pressure on him to get me on the label. Ken told Hank that there is not any place for a female Country star but every band needs a girl singer. We got a hold of "Dear John Letter" and after it sold a million I went to Ken and asked him if he still thought that there was not any place for a girl singer. Ken was like a father to me. Justin did a great job filling in for Ferlin. Pete did a series of these albums. I have one called "Stars of the Grand Ole Opry". Stonewall Jackson did one, Ernest, The Wilburn Brothers, and a lot more of Opry members did these albums. Justin did "Dear John" with me and I did "Lookin' Back To See" on his album.

Tracy: "Second Fiddle To An Old Guitar" is one of your most popular songs.

Jean: I did that for Capitol originally. On the other side of that was "Two Little Boys". I had two little boys and Marty Robbins wanted to write me a song for me after I lost Hawkshaw. I told him he could not write a song because he did not know how I felt. I saw him after I recorded it and told him he did a pretty good job.

Tracy: In 1963, you lost your husband Hawkshaw Hawkins at the height of his popularity. His song "Lonesome 77203" was really moving up the charts.

Jean: I bring this up a lot because it is a very touchy subject for me. A lot of people forget that Hawkshaw Hawkins and Cowboy Copas were in that plane crash, not just Patsy Cline. Please don't misunderstand me, I loved Patsy Cline. She was great. My husband and Cowboy Copas meant a little bit more than "the two guys who were killed in the plane crash with Patsy Cline". I hope people will listen to me with an open mind and open heart. I am not being faceious about this at all. Let me tell you a little story. On the anniversary of the plane crash I went down to the site of the crash. TNN was going to do an interview with me and right before the interview, the guy who put the show together pulled me aside and asked if I could tell him something about Patsy Cline. It was like someone had thrown a bucket of ice water on me. I said no but I can tell you an awful lot about Hawkshaw Hawkins because I was married to him. It really set my day off. Our youngest son had his arm around me and I knew he was going to deck the guy. That was just one incident. It is nothing against Patsy. The guy probably was not thinking. Cowboy Copas and Hawkshaw were more than just the two guys who got killed in the plane crash with Patsy Cline. They had sold over a million records before Patsy was born. I have a problem with people not knowing that.

Tracy: After his death, you were forced to carry on with your career while raising a family.

Jean: I had been traveling with Hawkshaw for quite a number of years. I traveled with Ferlin after "Dear John". A lady wrote a letter asking if anyone realized that I was the first female artist who stepped out in front with a band. Most of the time females would go on the road with their husbands, Rose Maddox had her brothers, Kitty had her husband, Wilma Lee and Stoney were husband and wife. I never gave it any thought. I looked back and realized she was right.

Tracy: You were also one of the first women to sell a million records.

Jean: Actually, Patsy Montana sold a million on "I Wanna Be A Cowboys Sweetheart" but back then, everything was categorized and she was looked upon as a western cowgirl singer. "Dear John" was actually the first. I am very grateful for that, it has been with me all these years. Actually the fans have been with me all these years. The longevity of the great Country Music friends of mine like Billy Walker and Skeeter Davis…these people can never be replaced. I thank God everyday that I grew up in the era that I did and that I knew these great people like Webb Pierce, Faron Young, Ernest Tubb and Red Foley. No one realizes what a wonderful era that was. These people made Country Music what it is. I got meet Hank Williams. The first time I met him, we just shook hands and the second time, someone told him that I wanted to be a Country Music singer and Hank looked at me and said, "young lady, I hear you want to be a Country Music singer". I said yes sir. He said, "there ain't many woman in Country Music". I said that I was about to change that and he said, "well good luck to you sweetheart". I love the old Hank Williams songs, that was the real deal. I also loved Jimmie Rodgers. I learned every yodel that he ever did. Then one day I heard Elton Britt sing "Chime Bells" and I went down to the record shop and I put it in the sun and it melted. The next week I bought another one and laid it in the seat and my brother sat on it. I went back and got another one and the record store worker wanted to know if I was eating them! I held the record on my lap all the way home. Anyway, I learned to do the Swiss yodel off Elton Britt's records. I still yodel sometimes. I am not real fancy at it. I do not do the tricks with the voice like Margo Smith can. I really enjoy it and so do the people. It is a lost art.

Tracy: What would you like to be doing in the future?

Jean: Grow old gracefully. I sing better now then I ever did. I guess I am like wine; I get better with age. I am worried about the Grand Ole Opry because it is going through some trying times. I really hurts to see something that I have put 43 years into have trouble. We really need to help John Q Public. I encourage anyone who had never been to the Grand Ole Opry to come and let us entertain them. Some might say that they don't want to see the old guys singing but you have never seen Country Music until you have seen some of these guys sing. Don't misunderstand, I love Vince Gill and I love Patty Loveless. Vince comes to the Opry quite often but there is one of the big females who joined about eight years ago and she has been one time since she joined and I resent that. If you think enough of the Grand Ole Opry to be a member, come see us every couple of months and you will find out just what it is like to be part of this wonderful family and we really are a family.

Tracy: When you joined, you were required to be there a certain amount of time.

Jean: Yes, twenty-six Saturday nights out of the year. Bud Wendell took over the Grand Ole Opry and when he did, it was dropped down to twenty nights out of the year. It was a strict rule. That year, New Year's Day fell on the first Saturday and I had a $5000 show booked, that was three times more money than I had ever gotten. I had only done 19 Saturdays at the Grand Ole Opry. Bud approached me about it and I knew that I was going to get fired. He said that if I would come in January 1, he would call it even. I said yes sir and I cancelled my $5000 date and I made my Grand Ole Opry appearance. I was happy to do it because I loved the Grand Ole Opry that much.

Tracy: How much did you make that night?

Jean: I made $9.50

Tracy: What are some of your most memorable holiday memories?

Jean: I was born and raised in Oklahoma but my people lived in California and I had something that had been very trying in my life. I was about two inches from throwing it all away, my music career and everything. I went home for Christmas and had one gift under the tree, which that did not matter, that one gift was my white bible from my mother and daddy and inside was a message that gave me the strength to overcome the trials that I had and continue my music career. I will never forget it. I sat there and cried for about an hour. Another was at Easter. Between Hawkshaw Benny and I we had ten kids. We actually have nine but a boy lived with us from age seven until he was twenty-three so we count him in with the rest of them. Our oldest son got into a little bit of trouble. He got picked up from a DUI and I told him that if he ever went to jail not to call me because he was over twenty-one. This was on Easter Sunday and I did not go to church that morning. He called me and I told him to spend his forty-eight hours or what ever they had to spend in there. I did not go get him out. I did not go to church but my husband Benny did, and he told me that I would not believe who was in church. He said Donny, who is my oldest son, and he got saved. That was a great gift.

Tracy: In the future, how do you want fans to remember Jean Shepard?

Jean: Someone who loved what she did and was grateful that she could make a living for her family doing what she loved to do. Being a good gal and a good Country singer but most of all for being a good person. I am very plain spoken and it gets me in trouble a lot. Don't ask me any questions if you don't want me to tell you what I think. Sometimes that has been bad for me but I am a very truthful person. I have never tried to go above my raising. If we were not honest, we would have a double razor strap used across our rear end.

Jean Shepard is truly an amazing person. I also met her for the first time at the Grand Ole Opry. It is easy to become friends with Jean. She is so outgoing and has a wonderful personality. She will also tell you exactly how she feels about almost any topic.

I wanted Jean to work for me so bad. I would ask her every time that I was around her. She has been trying to "slow down" for many years. She finally agreed to come to Texas. I kept asking her what she was going to charge me and time after time she would put me off. I knew that she was booking many dates all over the country for $4,000 to $6,000 a show.

The Llano Country Opry was a smaller venue from many of the major auditoriums that she works. Finally, about a week before the show I told her that I had to know how much to pay her. I knew that she had to drive 800 miles to just work the appearance. She finally gave me a extremely generous (nearly unbelievable) answer just because as she said "she loved me." That made my year. If Jean is a friend, she is truly a friend. In a business where the ego drives so many artists and their show prices, it is great to work with someone like Jean Shepard.

This interview was conducted while Justin Trevino and I were in Nashville doing some work for Rose Drake. Rose owns First Generation Records and wanted to have several interviews in the can for future projects to promote her record label.

The reason that Jean Shepard is not in the Country Music Hall of Fame is simply those individuals that vote need an education in Country Music history. Jean deserves to be in the Hall with all the others that gave birth and raised our music industry into what it is today.

Jean Shepard should be in the Country Music Hall of Fame.

JULY 1990

Tracy: How did you get started in the Country Music business?

Jeannie: That is always a tough question to answer. I first went on radio when I was eleven years old in Pennsylvania. I started singing with the dance band when I was 13 and sang through my high school years. I did not start singing professionally until I moved to Los Angeles. That is where I really learned to write. I had already tried to write but it was not until I moved to Los Angeles that I actually learned how to do it. I had songs recorded by several artists before I ever recorded.

Tracy: So you were primarily a Country Music songwriter before becoming a recording artist?

Jeannie: The way I look at it is the entertainment business and the more ways that you can think of to entertain, the better that you are. I have been involved in the Country Music business in more ways than you can think of. I started recording in 1964. I had three releases on Challenge Records. The songs did well in different regions but never the national coverage. When I moved back to Nashville and recorded for Monument Records, I had the hit "Don't Touch Me". That was in 1966.

Tracy: You actually received a Grammy for that song.

Jeannie: That was a very proud moment for me. The Grammy was for Best Country Vocal Performance by a Female. A year later, I joined the cast of the Grand Ole Opry. The Opry has been a very important part of my career.

Tracy: "Don't Touch Me" would cement your position in Country Music.

Jeannie: Hank Cochran wrote the song. In fact, he wrote it in my dressing room. I was traveling with Porter Wagoner at the time. We were in Rochester, New York, and Hank was in Indianapolis when he got the idea for the song. He called me and asked me if I liked it and I did so he got on a plane and flew to where I was. He wrote the song in my dressing room.

Tracy: Why did you move to Decca Records?

Jeannie: We wanted to make a change from Monument Records. Monument was a great label but it was an independent label. It did not have the distribution world wide that we thought that we needed. We were looking for a place to move and we had three different offers from three different labels. I chose Decca because I wanted to work with Owen Bradley and I also wanted to record duets with Jack Greene. We were both on Ernest Tubb's television show. When you are doing a television show and your not doing your part on camera, there are hours of free time on your hands. Jack and I started singing just to entertain ourselves and we sounded really good together. That was at the time that the trend was to have a complete package show unit. We would travel together so the promoter and the fans got the full package of the male artist, female artist, duet team and the band. It was an organized show. Bill Anderson and Jan Howard were traveling at that time as well as Porter Wagoner and Dolly Parton. It was a trend and a thing to do at that time.

Tracy: The Ernest Tubb television show also gave you some added exposure.

Jeannie: It was a thrill to me to get to know Ernest and to get to know him as well as I did. I miss him very much. I learned so much from Ernest. When I do a show at the Grand Ole Opry, people ask me what I am going to sing and they are amazed when I tell them I do not know. I do not know until I check the line up. I learned that from Ernest. He always taught me to make the show the priority. If everyone is doing a ballad, do something else. Give the show some variety.

Tracy: What is in the future for you?

Jeannie: I would like to do some more writing. It is a new field. I am working on my book. The book is actually filled with thoughts that I have had throughout the years. I gathered them all up and weeded through them and put them in a book. I would like to do some more acting. I really like the theater. It gives good sense of discipline. You can get rusty and lazy, but you don't when you do theater. The last play I did was, "Everybody Loves Opal". I played Opal, an eccentric little bag lady. It was hard for me especially here because I worked at Chaffin's Barn Theater. One night was Grand Ole Opry night and everywhere I looked out there was somebody that I knew. It was hard when they were setting as close as you and I are to stay in character as Opal and not Jeannie. It was pure comedy, no music at all. I would like to do some more of that and I would like to try my hand at writing a script whether it be for a TV movie or a stage show. I am still just trying to learn. I just want to keep entertaining. It is really what I love.

Jeannie Seely is a great entertainer. I always enjoy her appearances on the Grand Ole Opry. She is an incredible MC as well. Jeannie's introductions of other artists are always so articulate and full of energy.

Jeannie has a great sense of humor. Sonny Davenport and I drove to Conroe, Texas, to be a part of a Grand Ole Opry package show a few years ago featuring Jeannie with Jack Greene, Bill Anderson, Johnny Rodriguez, Jim Ed Brown and Jan Howard. A couple of days before the show, Jeannie and I were talking on the phone. She was on the way to get a new shirt made for the trip. When we got to Conroe, Jeannie was wearing her new shirt.

Across the front of the shirt was "Jeannie Seely's" and then underneath "Greatesthits". I commented on her new shirt and even took a couple of pictures. In a few days, I received a package in the mail. It was Jeannie's new shirt and she autographed it to me.

She was married to songwriter Hank Cochran at one time. I think that the combination of Cochran's writing and Seely's singing was phenomenal. "Don't Touch Me" "Can I Sleep In Your Arms Tonight Mister" and "Tell Me Again" were just some of the songs that they collaborated on. Unfortunately, like so many relationships in the industry, their songs lasted longer than the marriage.

Jeannie Seely is a very special person in the Country Music business.

Jack Greene, Jeannie Seely and Jan Howard in Conroe, Texas.
Jeannie actually gave me the shirt off her back that day.

Jeannie Pruett

OCTOBER 27, 1990

Tracy: You had one of the biggest hits in the history of Country Music with "Satin Sheets". You have been busy ever since that recording.

Jeannie: This has been a busy time in my life and for every Country Music star who is involved the CMA Productions every year.

Tracy: You are wrapping up a big Country Music week.

Jeannie: Tonight is the big celebration at the Grand Ole Opry. It is our 65th birthday party, so we are excited about that.

Tracy: Will you be performing tonight?

Jeannie: Yes. I am going to be doing the 3:30 matinee and then the 10:30 show this evening.

Tracy: Tell us how you got started in the Country Music business.

Jeannie: It goes so far back that sometimes I have to shake my head to remember. It has been almost twenty years. I started out as an exclusive songwriter for Marty Robbins Publishing Company in Nashville. I continued to write songs for the first four or five years of my career. During that time, I established myself as one of the new up and coming female writers. To coin one of Marty phrases, "I can't tell the difference between your lyrics and mine". That has always made me feel special. Marty was also instrumental in helping me get my first recording contract with RCA Records many years ago.

Tracy: Were you living in Nashville at that time?

Jeannie: Yes, I was.

Tracy: You actually grew up in the Country Music business.

Jeannie: I stood back stage at the Grand Ole Opry for about ten years watching other people on there. I hoped that I was a quick study and learn a lot. I have been able to put to use a lot of things that I learned by other performers. It is just like stand up comedy, you learn a new joke and you try to apply it to your everyday way of doing

154

things and saying things. It works out good that way when you take the time to learn from other professionals that have been able to please audiences for a lot of years. It makes it a lot easier. I am always, "taking my hat off", on stage when I do a Hank Thompson or Kitty Wells song. They were the fore runners of it all. I never lose sight of the fact that there were a lot of great talents in the business before myself or Dwight Yoakum, Holly Dunn or any of the young people that have came along since then.

Tracy: Who was your biggest influence in the early days of your career.

Jeannie: Marty Robbins for one, he always was, even before I met him, I always thought that he had the most wonderful voice and could, "turn a phrase", as far as his writing better than anyone in show business at that time. To be honest I have not seen anybody come along the turnpike that had it all like Marty has. Marty had it all. He was a great writer and a wonderful performer and was just a super personality and talent. The fact that, "his army of fans", as he called it, still gets together and has parties for him and still gets involved in Nashville during the Fan Fare celebration in his honor is a great tribute to him as a talent. Not only did I like Marty, I always liked Ernest Tubb as a human being. He was one of the nicest people that I ever knew. The way he was with the fans, and the fact that he loved the people so much was what always endeared him to me. As for voices, Merle Haggard was one of my all time favorites along with Lefty Frizzell, Patsy Cline, I could go on forever and still miss somebody that was special to me.

Tracy: In order to find your own style, you have to combine all those talents together.

Jeannie: Yes, you do. You do not want to copy anybody. I have had people tell me through out the years that Pasty Cline's voice and mine are similar but that was never intentional. I always tried to sing my own song and write my own songs and perform it in my own manner.

Tracy: Your big song, you call it your "bread and butter song" is "Satin Sheets".

Jeannie: Yes it is. In fact, a lot of people tell me that I always sing that whenever I go on stage. Any time I go on stage, even if I only have one song to perform, it is going to be that one. It is not because I have not had any other big hit records, it is my signature song and it is the song that I think the fans are listening for me to sing.

Tracy: A few months ago I was at the Opry and you sang that song. I would have been disappointed if you had not performed that great song.

Jeannie: I think it is that way with everybody. People come so far to see their favorite singer and they want to hear the song that made that artist's career happen and they want it performed as close to the record and they possibly can. I take great pride over the years in my shows because I tell my boys in the band to play it exactly like the record and don't full around with because if there was a better way to record the song I would have found it when we went on the studio. It is really important to me that the music sounds like it does on the record. I have seen a lot of artists go on stage and jive it up or perform it in a different manner than what it was recorded in.

Tracy: How did you get "Satin Sheets" and did you think that it was going to be such a big success.

Jeannie: I knew that "Satin Sheets" had a different message to it than any Country song that I heard before or had written. I think the message that it gave at that particular time in life was, whether it be male of female, whoever happened to be the spouse that was out working and making money and not taking care of the love and the devotion that they had at home. It just pointed out the fact that you can fall out of love with love. A lot of people thought it was a cheating song but it wasn't. "Satin Sheets" was a song about life, it was a statement of fact.

Tracy: You have had a lot of other hits throughout the years. A couple of my favorites are "Back to Back" and "Temporarily Yours".

Jeannie: Those were two of my favorites too. One of those happened to belong to one of my songwriting friends, Sonny Throckmorton. He was my favorite writer all through the seventies. I recorded anywhere from two to six of his songs on every album for a long time.

Tracy: "Please Sing Satin Sheets For Me" is a song that is very personal for you.

Jeannie: That was a true story. I probably could re-release the song and it would be a hit all over again. It has been eight years since it has been out and it is a true story, every word of the song. It took me about three months to come to terms with that incident happening and to decide that I needed to put it on a record so the fans can hear that when they play a part in your life, it makes a lasting impression.

Tracy: Have you ever had the opportunity to see that gentleman again?

Jeannie: No, I do not even know his name. He never told me his name, he just told me his story that I put into the music. I never did divulge where the little club is because there are so many clubs in Alabama but this one is real close to my hometown.

Tracy: The song makes a complete circle in your career.

Jeannie: Yes it does. You make a full circle. I think about every fifteen years, an artist should go back to exactly where they started and where they have gone and if there is anything they can do to improve their career.

Tracy: Another big record for you was your duet with Marty Robbins "Love Me".

Jeannie: I recorded that song as a single and Marty Robbins recorded it and had a

156

number one million selling single. He cut that song four different ways, four different times and then he and I finally decided to do it as a duet on an album we had started before he died. Neither Marty nor myself recorded a duet with anybody else up to that point. I am so sorry and that we were never able to complete a full album before he died. We were able to do two songs before he died. He wrote one "Walking Piece of Heaven" and one that I wrote "Love Me". I think the two voices were a wonderful blend. I would be pleased if by someway of magic, we could go in a take some of Marty's music and add my vocals to it, it would be such an interesting album and a good combination.

Tracy: Your last album was on MCA Dot Records.

Jeannie: Yes, it is called Jeannie Pruett. It was a great album. Other artists have taken four or five hits out of that album. I had the first cut of "I Told You So" by Randy Travis. Randy wrote the song when he first came to Nashville but I cut the song first. That was his first recording by an artist. I think that my cut on that album was still a great cut. Randy gave it more of a Country beat on his cut. I think he waited four or five years after my recording before he put it out. He always thought that mine would be on a single also.

Tracy: Were there any singles released?

Jeannie: They did not release any singles from those albums. There were seven major artists on that first effort on MCA Dot and Jimmy Bowen decided he would put out all seven albums at the same time and he did. The sad thing was that there were a lot of wonderful artists who collected some wonderful material and went in and made those albums and no singles were ever taken from them. I do not think that they were pushed as hard as they could have been. I am sure the budget does not go as far today as it did in 1973 when I made the "Satin Sheets" album.

Tracy: Do you plan on recording anytime in the future?

Jeannie: I plan on doing a TV album later this year. Today when you called, I was feverishly into the third cookbook and sorting through recipes and material. I am trying to get it ready for the Fan Fare rush in June. I wanted to get it out for the Christmas holiday but I think that it is going to be impossible to do because I am going to be involved in some other areas. Sometimes you meet yourself coming and going when you don't set you priorities.

Tracy: You already have two cookbooks out so you are working on your third?

Jeannie: Feeding Friends is the name of it.

Tracy: Is there going to be I, II and III?

Jeannie: Yes, I imagine that is what it is going to be because Minnie Pearl always had the saying "If it ain't broke don't fix it". This title is not broke. It has been working for five years and we are probably going to continue because the third book is going to be in a similar format as the other. It is going to be simple and easy to understand and be relatively inexpensive in preparation. It is also going to have some serious information about diabetes, heart problems, low sodium and low calories. It will also have some of the "old time cookin" that I am noted for and also some of the, " I remembers", which has been a proven thing for me. We will continue with that format but with all new material. I do not ever repeat recipes in cookbooks because I think if fans are going to pay money, they do not need the same thing over and over.

Tracy: What do you see in your future?

Jeannie: Other then the television album, I am going to continue with Nashville Now and continue with the cooking segments and the music segment on the show and continue with the third cookbook. That is all that I can think of right now. I am going to take a little time and enjoy my fire around the Christmas holidays and just be lazy.

Jeannie Pruett is one of the nicest ladies in Country Music. She is one of the few entertainers that is completely retired as of now and donates most of her professional time MCing shows and charity events. She told me that after so many years of performing that it was time to pass the microphone to a younger generation. I do not necessarily agree with her and would love to turn on WSM and hear "Satin Sheets" blaring from the speakers once again.

Jeannie is a much loved cook in Nashville. She makes a great 'melt in your mouth' peach cobbler. Jeannie has a very successful line of cookbooks and her "Feedin' Friends" restaurant at Opryland was always a favorite stop for our bus groups. Jeannie was there very often to visit with the fans.

My late friend Peggy Jackson was such a fan of Jeannie's singing. Peggy made her a red shirt with some kind of boot design on the front. About six months later, Jeannie was on the Crook and Chase Show on TNN. She entered the studio and waved to the audience. I was so surprised that she was wearing Peggy's shirt on national TV! It was a very special occurrence for Peggy and one that I still have on video.

Little Jimmy Dickens

FEBRUARY 25, 1994

Tracy: We are at the legendary Farmer's Daughter in San Antonio with Little Jimmy Dickens.

Little Jimmy Dickens: Do you know that all the years that I have been doing what I do I have never been to the Farmer's Daughter.

Tracy: I can't imagine that. I thought that you have been everywhere in the world.

Little Jimmy Dickens: Me too. I have performed in the smallest dance halls and the largest concert halls entertaining my friends in the best way that I know how.

Tracy: I know that you are glad to be back in Texas.

Little Jimmy Dickens: It is always a joy to come to Texas. I feel that I have a lot of friends out here. I have worked so many shows in Texas throughout my career.

Tracy: Where are you going to be playing at next on this Texas tour?

Little Jimmy Dickens: We are going from here to Corpus Christi, and then we will be going on down to McAllen. I will be there with Johnny Wright and Kitty Wells. From there I will be going to Harlingen, way down in South Texas territory.

Tracy: Let go back a few years, I know that Mr. Roy Acuff was very instrumental in you career getting started, is that correct?

Little Jimmy Dickens: Fully, yes indeed. He is the one who brought me to the Opry. He got me my recording contract and I even lived in his home for a year when I first came to the Opry. I met Roy in 1945, when I was at WLW in Cincinnati. I was doing an early morning program and he was there in concert. He let me do a guest appearance on his show and he liked what I did. Three years later I met him again while in Saginaw, Michigan, and he invited me to come down to the Grand Ole Opry. I did a couple of guest appearances and then he arranged for me to stay. I was under his direction there for a long time and it worked for me

Tracy: I am sure that you learned so many of the talents of the Country Music business from Mr. Acuff.

Little Jimmy Dickens: Yes, indeed. I will never be able to say enough thanks for what he did for me. Mr. Acuff will always be missed at the Grand Ole Opry.

Tracy: In return, you are responsible for much of Marty Robbins success.

Little Jimmy Dickens: I don't like to take that kind of credit. I was just the one to tell them about him. I heard him sing on his fifteen minute radio show in Phoenix while I was on tour. He really knocked me out the way that he sang. When I got to Los Angeles, I mentioned that someone should really go down to Phoenix and listen to him. He was quick to give me credit throughout the years. We were really good close friends.

Tracy: Going over you recording career you have had a lot of hit novelty records, but there is also a serious side to Little Jimmie Dickens.

Little Jimmy Dickens: Thank you very much. I have recorded a lot of ballads that I love to do and people request them and that makes me happy.

Tracy: One of your most requested ballads is "Raggedy Ann." It is an incredible story about a man, his daughter and a little doll.

Little Jimmy Dickens: My friend Red Lane is a great writer. He wrote some things for Tanya Tucker. We were watching a ball game one night and after the game was over and in the hotel he said I got something that I want you to have and if you don't record it nobody ever will. He told me that he wrote it for me and he handed me Raggedy Ann and I knew right away I wanted to do it.

Tracy: What is the biggest song you have had over your career?

Little Jimmy Dickens: The biggest selling record was "May The Bird of Paradise Fly Up You Nose" in 1965.

Tracy: Not one of the earlier hits that you recorded?

Little Jimmy Dickens: Oh no. The earlier songs "Take An Old Cold Tatar And Wait" played first and "Country Boy" second, "Sleeping at the Foot of The Bed," "Out Behind the Barn" .....a lot of them did very well. The novelty songs were good to Little Jimmy Dickens. "May The Bird of Paradise Fly Up Your Nose" was a song that became a hit not only in the Country field, but was also a good Pop hit as well.

Tracy: Whenever Barbara Mandrell came on stage and introduced you the latest inductee into the Country Music Hall of Fame, how did that make you feel?

Little Jimmy Dickens: Oh what a night!

Tracy: I remember that night. I also remember a couple of tears coming down your cheeks.

Little Jimmy Dickens: Absolutely. I had been nominated for four years. That was the fourth year and each time you sit there with the anticipation of them calling your name and you always have something planned that you are going to say. I was sitting there and they called my name and on the way to the stage I forgot it all. So I was babbling I guess, I just tried to express my appreciation.

Tracy: The Grand Ole' Opry is very important to you, how long have you been on the Opry?

Little Jimmy Dickens: I came in 1948. It is a very important part of my career.

Tracy: You play there nearly every weekend when you were not on tour.

Little Jimmy Dickens: When I am not on the road, I am on the Opry. In winter months, I am on there a lot and in the summer months I still go out on the road. Although now it is a little different, I don't work the road as I have in the past because I have a commitment to Opryland and I go up there the days I am not on the road.

Tracy: And you sell those taters at Opryland don't you?

Little Jimmy Dickens: Yeah we have a little restaurant called Tater Patch Café.

Tracy: Not too far from Jeannie Pruett. Are you in competition with each other?

Little Jimmy Dickens: No, no, not at all! Jeannie serves those full course meals and all we serve is taters in the amazing ways that we fix them.

Tracy: We have eaten lunch at the Tater Patch and really enjoyed it. Tell me about your future plans.

Little Jimmy Dickens: My plans are laid out for me by the folks at Opryland. There is so much happening and they have added so many shows now with George Jones doing 108 days and Alabama doing about 100 the Oakridge Boys doing 80. Now they have opened up the Ryman and they built a saloon downtown called the Crazy Horse and its going to be great. Music Valley Drive is expanding, there is so much going on that I don't know the future but I am going to be there if they need to call on me for anything.

Tracy: Is there anything that you would like to say to all of our listeners?

Little Jimmy Dickens: Nothing more than a sincere thanks for their kindness to Little Jimmy Dickens throughout all these many years and all the best.

This was the first interview that I ever conducted with Little Jimmy Dickens. My long time friend Darrell Cowen and I drove to San Antonio to see the Jimmy Dickens show.

Jimmy had just bought a new van and they were enjoying a five day trip in Texas. Ironically, Billy Deaton (talent agent) had called me and wanted me to book Jimmy in Brady. He told me that I could have a tie in date for $2,500.00, which included Jimmy and the Country Boys. At that time, I was in college and that seemed like a substantial amount of money. I turned it down and I regret it to this day. Jimmy only works a very limited amount of dates and his single price is more than double that!

Jimmy and his wife Mona have been great to me throughout the years. I even took some KNEL Nashville trip winners to his home a few years ago. I believe that he may be the finest entertainer that I have ever had the opportunity to see perform. Jimmy can make you laugh till it hurts and then make you cry with the very next song. Seeing Jimmy at the Opry is not enough. If you have not caught his show, you need to!

Jimmy is currently the elder statesman at the Grand Ole Opry. He worked with Hank Williams, Cowboy Copas, Patsy and all the pioneers and is still performing today. He is one of the the last links to the Golden Age of Country Music and still is a great entertainer to this very day.

A few years ago, I was backstage at the opry talking with Jimmy. Me cell phone rang and it was my darling wife Charla. After talking to her for a minute, I handed to phone to Jimmy to say hello. After a few minutes, he hung up and kind of looked at me funny. He said, "Tracy, I don't know where your wife was but there was sure a lot of loud music in the background." The ironic part was that Charla was working the Llano Country Opry show while I was in Nashville. Jimmy was just looking out for my interests!

Little Jimmy Dickens is the today's Country Music link to Hank, Lefty and Patsy.

February 5, 2007

Tracy: Joe Paul, you actually started your career at a very early age.

Joe Paul: That's right. Actually, my father played the guitar and sang and had a little Country band. I got to singing with him and we didn't have a lot of entertainment at the house except for the radio when I was growing up. I listened to the radio and heard that good old Country Music and my dad sang some of it. He taught me to play the guitar and it just grew from that.

Tracy: At that time, where were you performing with your dad?

Joe Paul: My dad played a lot of the school houses and community centers for different celebrations, fire departments and other functions. They played a lot of dances at people's houses. They would move the furniture out of one room and the band would set up and play. This would be out in the country, and people would gather to have a dance at individual's houses.

Tracy: Your dad started taking you to the Cowtown Hoedown in Ft. Worth soon after this time.

Joe Paul: I got to listening to the Cowtown Hoedown on Saturday nights on KCUL radio. I used to listen to the Grand Ole Opry, the Louisiana Hayride and the Big D Jamboree. I then got to listening to the Cowtown Hoedown and it was just sixty miles from home. My dad took me down and I auditioned for the show. At the time I was there, Boxcar Willie was there using his name Marty Martin. Tony Douglas, Frankie Miller and Howard Crocket, who wrote "Ole Slewfoot" and "Honky Tonk Man", were all on the show at that time. They had a Grand Ole Opry star there every Saturday night.

Tracy: It had to be amazing for you to be working with all of your heroes when you were so young. How old were you when you joined the Cowtown Hoedown?

Joe Paul: I think I was about fifteen years old. I admired those guys so much when they came out with those fine guitars and those rhinestone suits. I had heard their records on the radio and for a youngster who lived out in the country and hadn't been anywhere, that was really something. We were raised pretty poor. We always had something to eat, but really never had any extras.

Tracy: Your first record was "Shy Young Sue." How did that session happen?

Joe Paul: Lawton Williams, who was a DJ and also did some MC work on the Cowtown Hoedown, had mentioned to me that he had some songs that he thought I could sing. I went over to his house one day and he played several of them for me. I picked out "Shy Young Sue" and another one and we went to the studio and Lawton produced my first single in January of 1963. I was twenty one.

Tracy: How did you make the transition from the Cowtown Hoedown to the Big D Jamboree?

Joe Paul: Lawton moved over to the Big D Jamboree and became their MC. Ed McLemore decided that Lawton needed to be the MC of his show. Lawton talked me into the notion of leaving the Cowtown Hoedown and going to the Big D Jamboree. It was a good step for my career.

Tracy: At this time, Country Music was really happening in the Dallas/Ft. Worth area.

Joe Paul: We had KCUL in Ft. Worth and another great station in Grand Prarie. They both were listened to all over the area and the club business was really hot. We had the Cowtown Hoedown in Ft. Worth, the Big D Jamboree in Dallas at the Sportatorium and I am here to tell you that there were a lot of entertainers coming into the Dallas/Ft. Worth area in the 1960's and 1970's.

Tracy: Tell me about forming the Five Pennies Band.

Joe Paul: That was in 1970. Actually, in 1969, I tried to work with another fellow. I was going to let him handle the band and I was going to do the booking and recording. It just didn't work out, so in 1970 I started the Pennies. It was one of the better things that I did at the time. I was working quite a few stage shows including school houses and community centers. I was also working a lot of dance halls and night clubs. We had a circuit throughout Texas that I worked and three or four in Oklahoma. We would go to these every three months and some as often as two months. You covered quite a bit of area that way.

Tracy: During this time, you were also working a day job as well as your music career.

Joe Paul: I was an inspector for Texas Department of Transportation. Most people didn't realize that I even had a day job other than the local people. I would get off work many times on a Tuesday night and go work 150 miles away and work a school. Then on Friday night, we would take off another 150 miles another direction and work another stage show. Then on Saturday night, we mostly played the dances.

Tracy: You have enjoyed a long prolific recording career and now even record for your own label.

Joe Paul: Actually, I started out recording for Lawton and then went to Tyler and started recording for Curtis Kirk who owned Custom Records. When he died, I started doing things on my own. I found out when you have three or four people involved that it is hard to please everybody. It has worked out reasonably well. I need to hire someone all the time to be out on the road promoting me. If I ever get in that financial position, I am going to do it!

Tracy: The Country gospel scene opened up for you in a big way during the last few years. It has always been an important part of your career, but it has become more important lately

Joe Paul: It really has. I am very heavy on the "Country" part of Country gospel. I use the fiddle and guitar and so much of my gospel that it has kind of become a signature thing. Even overseas, I get really good airplay in countries like New Zealand, Ireland, Denmark, Australia and the many European Countries. A lot of the different countries don't buy the Country gospel as well as they buy the Country, but they play it on the radio stations over there. They really love the gospel with the fiddles and the steel guitar. "Route Three Gloryland" and "Jesus Is The Same In California" really opened a lot of doors for me.

Tracy: You have witnessed so many changes in Country Music throughout your career. What do you think are some of the biggest changes?

Joe Paul: In the early days, I saw the shows were big. The concerts and Saturday night shows were everywhere and then in the 1970's and 1980's, the club scene really took over. The show business kind of faltered a little. In the 1990's, I saw people returning to the concerts more once again. I also noticed that the club business faltered quite a bit. Shows have come back in again. I have also seen Traditional Country Music take a backseat to Modern Country or Country pop in the 1980's. Starting in 1988 or 1989, I saw the tide begin to change to Traditional Country and Western Swing. It seems to still be going in that direction and I hope it continues for a long, long time.

Tracy: In the future, how do you want to be remembered?

Joe Paul: I think that I would like to be remembered as someone who loves what they did and didn't do it so much for the monetary reasons, but for the love of the music. I just hope that maybe some of my music will move on and touch the hearts of the folks in the future.

Joe Paul Nichols and His Five Pennies were constant performers throughout the Central Texas area while I was growing up. My parents and grandparents enjoyed the musical sounds that Joe Paul provided to countless audiences on countless nights. During the 1970's, Joe Paul and his great band were playing many of the dances that my family enjoyed attending.

I would hear about Joe Paul from many people. I played Joe Paul's songs throughout

my entire radio career. Joe Paul always provided a guaranteed Country sound for the listening audience.

I will never forget the first time that I contacted Joe Paul about working many years ago at one of the dances that I was promoting at the Brady Civic Center. I was still such a fan and was a little worried about asking Joe Paul to work for me. I was still niave about booking and really didn't know what I was doing. I also had no idea what he would charge me. I called him and told him all about what I was trying to do-promote Traditional Country music in this area and build up something that we could all be proud of. Joe Paul said, "We'll now Tracy, it is a long way to Brady from Jacksboro and I would have to charge you $150.00." I immediately told him that I would give him $200.00. I did not realize what he was doing at that time, but I do now. He was trying to help me build something because he believed in what we were trying to do.

Joe Paul has proven to be a great friend and a wonderful entertainer. He told me the other day that he was definitely not the greatest singer in Country Music, but that no one worked any harder at it that he did. He is exactly right and that is why he is one of my heroes.

JOE PAUL NICHOLS MUSIC COMPANY

COUNTRY & GOSPEL

ROUTE 1, BOX 224-A, JACKSBORO, TX 76458
(940) 567-2779   FAX (940) 567-3008

3-12-98

Tracy Pitcox
KNEL Radio
Brady, Tx.

Tracy,
   I Just Returned From FT Worth And on the Trip I Listen Again To Two Cassettes of your show Back in Sept. of 1994 when you interview me over the Phone. I Enjoyed Listening To your show Again. I am Always Impressed With your Knowledge of Country Music Considering How young you Are,
   I Rounded up some of My old Singles From years Past And I'm Sending Them To you To Add To your Collection of Country Music.
   Hope To See you Soon.

Keep up The Good Work
Joe Paul Nichols

Johnny Bush

FEBRUARY 8, 2007

Tracy: You were born and raised around Houston, Texas.

Johnny: I was born in an obscure part of Houston called Kashmere Gardens. I even wrote a song called "Kashmere Garden Mud" because of the old grey sticky gumbo mud. Nothing was paved out there and you would get that all over the heels and souls of your shoes and the bottom of your pants. It was always embarrassing to me and I never could get used to that. We have titled my new album "Kashmere Garden Mud" and it will be released with my autobiography "Whiskey River Take My Mind-The True Story of the Texas Honky Tonk."

Tracy: You have been working on your book for a number of years.

Johnny: We have been working on it for about seven years. It took six years to write and another year because of a publishing company that held it up for year and then decided to pass on it. University of Texas Press published it and I am excited about the release.

Tracy: I saw the mock up of the book and it really looks great.

Johnny: A guitar player that used to work for me, Waylon McBride was working with me at one of the Willie Nelson Picnics. His wife was about a quarter of a mile away with a telescopic lens and she took the cover that we used on the cover. I like it because it shows the reflection of the crowd in my glasses. The photo on the back was taken a few years later at another picnic when Willie and Ray Price were singing a song with me.

Tracy: Was it hard for you to write the book, John?

Johnny: It was in this respect. You know, but maybe some people don't, but I've got a neurological speaking disorder called Spasmodic Dysphomia. It disables my speech flow where my vocal cords just slams shut. It took a long time for me to choke these lines out into a tape recorder. Rick Mitchell would then transfer the tape into a word processor. That took a long time and then I had to proof read. It took a lot of time for me to keep my vocal cords going and then my thought process would skip. I would then find out that I left something out or determine that I needed to move something to another place.

Tracy: You were very open and honest in the book. Why did you decide to write a book?

Johnny: I guess that everybody wants their life to be told. I have had second thoughts about it after I have seen it in print. I don't know if it was a good idea or not. In order to do it, you have to be completely honest and put everything in there. It has a redeeming factor. I am not the same guy that I was when I started out in this business. I talk about bad choices and mistakes and things that happened to me because of making bad choices. The choices that I made actually hurt other people by being self-ish and controlling. Maybe it will help someone else to not fall in this trap. When I joined the church in 1986 and got married again, my life begin to change. I told my family that I know that God has forgiven me and I hope that they will too. One of the best books that I have ever read was Jan Howard's "Sunshine and Shadow." After I read it, I called Jan and asked her if she had any regrets. She told me that she had a thousand regrets. I know what she is talking about now. Once it is out there, it can't be taken back.

Tracy: I know that your uncle Jerry Jericho was one of your first inspirations.

Johnny: My brother and I were on a radio show when I was thirteen and he was eleven. It was called the Blue Jean Jamboree on KTHT. After I got into junior high school, some of the kids started to pick on me and I just kind of gave it up. When I was about sixteen, my uncle called me and asked me if I wanted to drive him to San Antonio. During that trip, he asked me what ever happened to my aspirations of becoming an entertainer. I told him that I still had them, but I just kid of put them on the back burner. He told me that I should sing one on his radio show that day. The place that he was working had bought a radio spot and he was going to the station with his guitar to sing a few songs and advertise the dance that night. It was on KMAC and I just knew that every person in San Antonio was listening to the radio that day. I was scared to death and he strapped that guitar on me and then walked out of the room. It was amazing because the next week when we went back, one card poured into the station. That got me back into the grove again and I started singing around San Antonio. I got my first professional job at the Texas Star Inn on December of 1952.

Tracy: While in San Antonio, you changed your name from John Bush Shinn III to Johnny Bush. How did that come about?

Johnny: When I got my first professional job at the Texas Star Inn, I had a belt that my uncle had given me that belonged to Johnny Sapp who used to play for Ernest Tubb. He later played for my uncle and his band. It had "Johnny" on the back of the belt and I needed a belt, so I thought that Johnny was close enough to John. Everybody all of my life had called me Bush by my middle name. Frank Cline heard people calling me Bush and saw Johnny on my belt and started me introducing me that way. When I went down to the union to get my card, I talked to Eddy Brazel. He had my union card all typed out. I picked it up and it said "Johnny Bush." I threw it back down and told him that my name was John Bush Shinn III. He told me that was not a very good professional name and that Johnny Bush sounded a lot better. He just didn't want to type out another card. In 1968, when I started recording and getting checks, it was going to start getting confusing. I went to a lawyer in Fayette County and had the Shinn dropped from my name.

Tracy: When did you meet Willie for the first time?

Johnny: I met Willie Nelson at a south side joint, skull orchard called Al's Country Club. We had to do a matinee on Sunday and it was customary in those days to allow people to sit in with you. I was working with the Mission City Playboys. This fiddle player and this little red headed guitar player walked in and set in with us that day. They actually came as a pair and they were both hired to join the band in 1953. We hit if off and he was married at the time and had a little girl. We had been great friends ever since.

Tracy: Willie actually even helped to finance your first album.

Johnny: I had been in Nashville for a while and had been working for Ray Price. I woke up one morning and I was thirty years old and I had two pair of Levis, a couple of shirts and a jacket and a set of drums and a mortgaged ten year old car. I knew the party was over and had to do something with my life. It was an awakening. I knew that I could write songs and we had been booking these guys on these package shows. I also knew that I could sing just as good as or better than they could. I was sitting back there making $25.00 a night and they were making three hundred singing three or four songs. I turned my notice in after Ray recorded my song "An Eye For An Eye" for Columbia Records. I knew that would open some doors for me. Tommy Hill was helping to keep me alive by throwing demo sessions that paid $10.00 a side. The only problem was that everything went through the union, so it would be thirty to sixty days before I would get my money. It was hard for a cowboy to live on that. I was going to be thrown out of my apartment, so I went by Willie's house to see if I could store some things out at his farm. He asked me why I left Price and I told him that I wanted to do what he did. I wanted to record my songs and get something started. He told me that he had been working Texas with Wade Ray and he said that the drummers were killing him. He asked me to make ten days with him through Texas and that we would talk about it. He paid me $35.00 a day and it was on that little ten day tour that he told me he would do a session on me if I would stay with him and work the road. He kept his word.

Tracy: Did Willie produce the first project for you?

Johnny: He let me pick my own material and musicians and let me have control of the session. He didn't tell me who to hire or what songs to do, but at the last minute instead of doing four songs on a session he asked me to split the session with Jimmy Day. That actually cut my songs from four to two and Jimmy didn't have any aspirations to become a recording artist. I really never found out what that was all about, but anyway I went for it. I had hired the guys that I had been working these demo sessions with including Jerry Reed on guitar, Jerry Smith on piano, Junior Huskey on upright bass and Buddy Emmons on steel guitar. We recorded "Sound of A Heartache" and "A Moment Isn't Very Long." All publishing companies had something called a utility label. They would find a young artist and put a record out on them and if they got any attention they would lease it to a major. My first record was on Ray Price's publishing company's label Allstar. We started getting radio action and nobody could buy the record because it wasn't distributed. Pete Drake and Stop Records leased those two and we recorded eight more to make a full album.

Tracy: You started having some hits soon after that on Stop Records.

Johnny: We had "Undo The Right", "What A Way To Live", "You Gave Me A Mountain", "Jim, Jack And Rose" and the first thing you know it was a dream come true for me. The offers started coming in and when that contract was up, RCA had called. It was a big step and really opened up my career.

Tracy: Everybody recognizes you as the writer and performer of "Whiskey River." That song has to be something that you are very proud of-a true success story.

Johnny: When I signed with RCA, Jerry Bradley was my producer. He looked at me and said, "All you have to do now is right a song." I thought, "We got Willie Nelson, Harlan Howard, Hank Cochran, Mel Tillis and all these great writers and you want me to write a song?" That put the ball in my court. I really believe that all these songs are being transmitted and all you have to do is be aware of that and have your mind become a receiver. You have to learn to tune in to that and you do that when there is a need. The deal was hinging on me writing a song. By the time I got to Texarkana from Nashville, I had the idea of "bathing my memored mind in the wetness of its soul." I thought that it sounded like a Willie Nelson song. By the time I got to San Antonio, I had written it.

Tracy: Did you ever imagine the magnitude of "Whiskey River"?

Johnny: In fact, I am always more critical of my songs than anyone else's. If you got a better song written than I do, I am going to record your song. I live for the music. I didn't think it was a bad song. Willie was living in Bandera and I called and sang it to him on the phone. He told me what he thought of it. After we recorded it, Bradley put the ball back in my corner again and asked me what I wanted to release first. I found out later that producers put it off on the artist, so if it flops the producer can blame it on the artist. I had been doing "Whiskey River" in Texas and I knew that the crowds had liked the song. I knew that if you had Texas that you could always work, so I told him to release "Whiskey River."

Tracy: Of course, Willie has recorded the song on many occasions. Many other artists have added it to their live shows and even albums.

Johnny: The song has become bigger than me and that is alright. Willie recorded it first for Atlantic Records and for the second time in 1978 for a live album on Columbia. From that time until now, he has recorded it over twenty times. In 2003, I had five different cuts including Willie's box set, the duet with Sheryl Crow, Trick Pony, Tommy Alverson and Cross Canadian Ragweed. Every ninety days, it makes the trip to the post office that much nicer getting a check from BMI.

Tracy: I appreciate your long time friendship and your association with KNEL.

Johnny: I was certainly glad to do it as it is always a pleasure for me to visit with your listeners. They are the finest people in the world.

Johnny Bush surprised me one night many years ago. He was driving through Brady and happened to catch my radio program. I was playing Classic Country and asked the listeners to call with their requests. John thought he would test me and called in a Roy Acuff request which I played a short time later. He called back and was impressed that we were really playing "real" Country Music on a small AM station in Central Texas. He wanted to come and set in with me at the radio station. Of course, I was elated and honored that John wanted to come to KNEL. He spent the entire night with me and we had callers from all over our area requesting John's songs and stories about his classic recordings.

That night would start a long friendship that I am still very proud of today. We had worked dozens of shows together and it is always an honor to share the stage with Johnny Bush.

I was at a recording session with Johnny, Leona Williams and Dave Kirby in San Antonio a few years ago. I spent the night at Johnny and Lynda's home. It was great to see all his awards and musical mementos in his music room. I was most intrigued with a bounced check under a glass top table. I believe the check was in the amount of $100.00 and it was returned for insufficient funds. It was from Willie Nelson. Of course, this was well before Willie became a household name. John told me it was worth more to him now than the face value of the check.

In 2007, Heart of Texas Records released "Texas On A Saturday Night" as a duet album by Johnny Bush and Justin Trevino. The project is one that I am extremely proud of and I know that Justin and Johnny had both wanted to do a duet album for many years. "Texas On A Saturday Night" is pure Texas Country Music in its finest.

Johnny Bush has made his mark on the industry and would have even if he never wrote or recorded "Whiskey River."

Tracy: How did you become involved in the music business?

Johnny: Someone told me they were looking for a drummer. I told them that I was playing the drums in high school so they told me when I was ready they wanted me. I asked my mother and she said it was fine. I sold ice cream and newspapers and saved up my money and my mom bought me a drum. She paid $14 for the set. My mother told me I had to be a good student so I studied hard and that is what I did. We went to California to pick grapes, figs and other fruits but my mother did not want me to go. She sent my brother and I stayed home and practiced the drums. I heard that there was a band coming up in the studio. I went to the studio and I was setting up the instruments. I went up to the drummer of they band and I told him that I was a drummer as well. He asked me to tune his drum so I did not realizing that it was Billy Wills. I finished and I was getting up but he told me to sit down. Billy was playing the bass, but Bob put him on the drums because they had a drummer to disappear. Bob Wills and Tommy Duncan walked up and Bob took his hat off, grabbed his fiddle and started singing. He was producing Kaleidoscope Records.

Tracy: When did you go to work for Bob?

Johnny: It was that day. He asked if I wanted to work for him when he was done. I did not know who he was but I said sure. Later on, I went outside and one of the guys told me who he was and I could not believe it. I did not even realize that it was Bob Wills after I agreed to work for him! I was not nervous at all because I did not know who he was. Bob hired me and I told him that I did not have any hats or boots and he told me not to worry about that because he was going to have all of that for me.

Tracy: How long did you work for Bob Wills?

Johnny: I started working for him in 1946 and I worked with in for almost two years.

Tracy: That had to have been a really exciting time in your career.

Johnny: It was. Tommy and Bob were wonderful people. It was also a very important time in Bob's career. We were playing a lot in those days. You never really thought that you were actually making history back then. We were just having fun and it was a job.

Tracy: There are not many Texas Playboys around.

Johnny: No, there are not. There are maybe fourteen or fifteen around.

Tracy: What did you do after you left Bob Wills?

Johnny: I went to college and then I finally got a job with another band. When I was about 25, I saw a young boy who was about 18 and I saw the way that he was practicing. He told me that he would go to Los Angeles and his teacher would have him put a glass on his hand to see if he was nervous. If he was not, he could play the drums. I learned to play the drums by using my wrists. I would practice with one hand at a time and then I worked up to two hands.

Tracy: At 91 years old, do you still drum?

Johnny: Yes, I come out at the end of the show. The crowds are wonderful. I usually do "Drummer Boy." I was even a part of a recording a couple of years ago. It kind of told my life story with Rod Moag, who is a disc jockey in Austin.

Tracy: What are your future plans?

Johnny: To keep serving up music. I have been retired for 25 years. I still drum and practice everyday.

I was working at KNEL, when my friends Billy Jackson called to inform me that Texas Playboy Johnny Cuviele was at the Heart of Texas Country Music Museum taking a tour. Johnny soon then came down to the KNEL Studios. It is very difficult to believe that he is 91! He is very spry and can still do a great job drumming with the best of them.

Johnny had just enjoyed a trip to Ruidoso, New Mexico, and the Lincoln County Cowboy Symposium. Johnny had performed on that show and was headed to Austin to be a part of a couple of other gigs-at 91!

His love and appreciation of Bob Wills is still very strong today. You can immediately understand his admiration for Bob by just listening to him tell the stories from so many decades ago. Johnny was proud to be a part of something very special and unique.

Johnny Duncan

NOVEMBER 11, 1995

Tracy: How did you get started in the music business?

Johnny: My mother is a picker. She plays rhythm guitar in De Leon, Texas. She is 80 years old. There is a lot of musicians on my mom's side of the family. There are the Seals Brothers, Danny and Jimmy. That is how it started. When I was growing up, I knew that I wanted to be in the music business. I went to Nashville in the 1960's. I was introduced to Ralph Emery. I was put on TV and the Don Law of Columbia Records saw me and signed me.

Tracy: Was it easy to get your first recording contract?

Johnny: I was there two and a half years. I was carrying concrete blocks and bricks for $1.25 per hour. I was a common laborer when I went to Nashville. I got involved in radio in Franklin, Tennessee. That is what I was doing when I started singing. I was actually in Bowling Green, Kentucky, which is about an hour and a half north of Nashville.

Tracy: Where were you born?

Johnny: I was born in Dublin, Texas, in the old Rex-All Drugstore. Dublin is where they have the real Dr. Pepper store. They make it with real pure cane sugar.

Tracy: What was your first hit in the business?

Johnny: "Sweet Country Woman". I had several good records. "Hard Luck Joe" was released in the late 1960's, and did well in radio. "Sweet Country Woman" brings back a lot of memories for me. It was my first time in the studios with producer Billy Sherrill. Billy produced David Houston, Charlie Rich, Tammy Wynette, George Jones and many more. When I first went into the studio, Billy asked if we could cut hits together and I told him that if there was anyone in town who could make hits out of me it would be him. We got off to a really good start.

Tracy: Larry Gatlin also produced you at one time?

Johnny: At the time "Sweet Country Woman" was released, Charlie Rich released "Behind Closed Doors" that Billy recorded. That song became a great hit around the world so Billy was busier with Charlie. At the same time, my divorce finalized and I brought my girls back to Texas. I was out of the music business for a few months and then Larry called me and said he would like to go into the studios with me. I knew he was a great singer and songwriter but did not know he was a producer. He got permission from CBS to record me and that is how I got introduced to Janie Frickie.

Tracy: You really established her career.

Johnny: Yes, it was the first time she had been heard and given credit to a national audience. Someone with her kind of talent is going to do it anyway, I just happen to be there when she first started.

Tracy: What was the first song you recorded together?

Johnny: The first song that Janie really got her recognition from was "Stranger". It was such a great song. I do not think I have ever heard her sing a bad note.

Tracy: Do the two of you still keep in contact with each other?

Johnny: Yes, Janie went through a bitter divorce a few years ago but she is now married to a great man. I wish her the best. She went through a lot during her previous marriage, it really harmed her career. She is now in Branson and seems very happy.

Tracy: "She Can Put Her Shoes Under My Bed Anytime" is your biggest hit.

Johnny: A man out of California wrote it. The demo record that came to us was so bad that Billy Sherrill told me to take it home and listen to it. I did but I could barely understand what the man was saying. He told me to listen to it again and a few months later he asked me about it. I could tell by the tone in his voice that I was going to miss something if I did not listen to it. He really wanted me to listen to it. He has a rare talent of finding hits.

Tracy: Who wrote the hit?

Johnny: A gentleman named Aaron Schroeder. He wrote a lot Elvis' hits.

Tracy: Most of your recordings were on Columbia.

Johnny: Yes, I was with CBS almost 14 years. That ended in the early 1980's. They wanted me to go to Hollywood. I did go out there and looked the situation over and realized that I did not fit the life style. I had three half grown daughters to think about and if I got involved in the Hollywood lifestyle, I might neglect to help my daughters grow up. That is when we parted ways.

Tracy: For quite a while no one heard from you.

Johnny: Between raising my daughters and the politics of the music business, I knew that the most important of the two were raising my daughters. I do not have any regrets about the direction I took.

Tracy: You have remarried.

Johnny: Yes, her name is Connie Smith. She is from Georgia, and we have a little boy.

Tracy: You have a new CD out with some great new songs as well as some of your classics.

Johnny: I am very proud of it. Canadian producer Gary Buck came in and was excited about working with us in Nashville.

Tracy: What do you do during a typical Johnny Duncan Show?

Johnny: I will do some songs that I have written and I will so some other great things that might surprise even me.

Johnny lived only a couple of hours from me between Stephenville and Dublin, Texas. I booked Johnny on several occasions in Brady, for some dances. He always did a great job and worked very reasonable for me. When I asked him about doing the first gigs, he only charged me $500.00 per show. I did pay him $750.00 a few times, but he always wanted me to make money. I appreciated the fact that he was concerned about my financial well being. It was early in my career, and I was learning how to promote and "get the word out" concerning shows.

Johnny and his wife Connie always paid me 10% for every job that I found for them. A few days after every show, I could expect to get a check. I never asked for it, but they always paid me commission. I just wanted Johnny to be out there working. He had so many hits and needed to be out entertaining. I think maybe I wanted him out there working more than he did.

For the last few years of his life, Johnny had to fight some personal demons. He missed a show for me in Llano, and I did not stay in touch with him as much as I should have. Connie sent me a note and told me that Johnny was finishing a new album. She sent it to me a short time later and I heard that Johnny was doing much better. I told my wife Charla that I was going to book him again in our 2007 season in Llano. I did not get the chance. Johnny died of a heart attack on August 14, 2006.

At the Johnny's memorial service, Charla and I sat with Frankie and Ann Miller, Curtis and Pat Potter, Sharon Jackson and Joe Paul and Carolyn Nichols. I was most impressed to see his former singing partner Janie Fricke in attendance. Janie owed a lot to Johnny and I think that she realizes that today. The First Baptist Church in Stephenville was packed as we all said goodbye to a friend and a legend.

MAC WISEMAN ENTERPRISES
P.O. Box 17028   Nashville, Tn. 37217
Phone: (615) 361-0861

May 17, 1993

Mr. Tracy Pitcox
"Hillbilly Hits"
KNEL/KIXV
1308 South Bridge #7
Brady, TX 76825

Dear Mr. Pitcox:

First, allow us to apologize for the great delay in
replying to you. We just recently rediscovered your
letter in a bundle of mislaid mail.

Per your request for a cassette to use on your
"Hillbilly Hits" program, find enclosed "20 Greatest
Hits." This tape includes my most requested and
popular numbers, and suit your show's strictly
traditional format.

I appreciate your time and interest, and your efforts
to answer the need for "traditional" programming. I
meet many fans and radio listeners on the road, and
know first hand there is a demand for it.

Again, our apologies for the delay. Wishing you the
best,

Sincerely,

Mac Wiseman

/mmw

Letter from
Mac Wiseman.

Whisperin' Bill Anderson and Brad Paisley
backstage at the Grand Ole Opry.

Country Music Hall of
Famer Charlie Louvin.

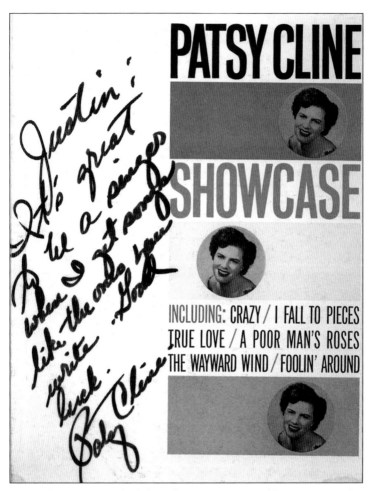

Pasty Cline autographed this album to Justin Tubb. We acquired
it in our Museum Collection.

Working a package show with Ron Williams, Leona Williams, Tony
Douglas, Ferlin Husky and Freddie Hart in Vernon, Texas.

Hank Locklin joins me at the
KNEL studios.

Johnny Rodriguez while on tour
in Conroe, Texas.

George Jones demon-
strates his Floyd Tillman
impersonation for his
wife Nancy and Johnny
Moore as he records his
duet for "The Influence"
on Heart of Texas
Records.

Hanging onto two
of my favorite
ladies, Wanda
Jackson and Pretty
Miss Norm Jean at
the Florida State
Fair.

Curtis Potter presents the Will Rogers Disc Jockey of the Year Award to me in 2005.

Hank Thompson, Hank Snow and Hank Williams or otherwise known as "The Three Hanks" in one of my favorite and most rare photos that Hank Thompson gave me.

Johnny Moore, Sonny Davenport, Frankie Miller, Bobbie Stokes, Jimmy Eaves, myself and Gay Stevens at George Jones' gate in Franklin, Tennessee. He never let us in.

Whispering

Bill Anderson

July 26, 2002

Hi Tracy:

I'm sorry to have taken so long to thank you for the pictures
you sent me from the Hall of Fame ceremony.

It was a very special day for me, and I'm so glad you could
be there to share it with me.

I'm sure I've got some ole song lying around that Frankie Miller
could probably sing the heck out of, but what type thing is
he looking for? Up tempo, ballad? I know he's probably not
looking for a crossover pop type song...at least I hope he's
not! Give me a bit of direction and I'll send some things down.

Take care, and thanks again for the pictures. All my best,

[signature]

Bill Anderson

Letter from Bill Anderson

One of my heroes, Johnnie High and I at his Country Music Review in Ft. Worth.

MCing "The Tony Douglas Story" in Tyler, Texas, with Tony and Disc Jockey Hall of Famer Tom Perryman.

Roy Acuff always called Connie Smith "The Sweetheart of the Grand Ole Opry".

"The Happiest Girl In the Whole USA" Donna Fargo. Our first visit was at the Golden Nugget in Las Vegas.

Tommy Cash, Ferlin Husky and Leona Williams help me celebrate winning the Wylie Award. The award was named after long time San Antonio Express News critic Wylie Alexander.

Austin radio personality (and half of the Geezinslaws) Sammy Allred with Charla and I at the Llano Country Opry in Llano, Texas.

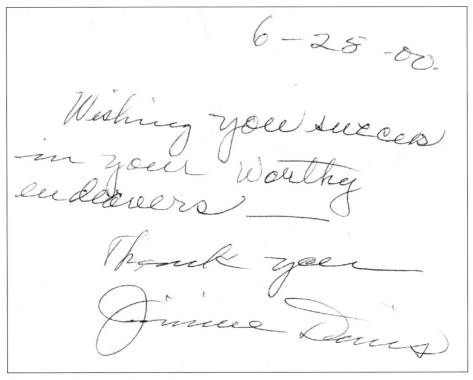

Letter from Governor Jimmie Davis.

Fiddlin' Frenchie Burke and Jim Ed Brown in San Antonio.

On my 35th birthday, my darling wife Charla organized a day of Country Music visiting with my radio hero Larry Scott, Joe Paul Nichols and Frankie Miller.

FLOYD TILLMAN
PO BOX 53
MARBLE FALLS TX   78654-0053

9-1-99

TO TRACY PITCOX

DEAR FRIEND:

Thanks for the "nice note" I think I'll keep it.

ENCLOSED IS TWO "C D"s for whatever use you may have of them.

                          BEST WISHES,
P S KEEP UP THE GOOD WORK ALL OF US OLE FOKS THINK YOUR GREAT.
                          FLOYD TILLMAN

OH YES ANOTHER PS

THE CRAZY CAJUN ALBUM WAS RECORDED IN THE MIDDLE 1960's and
added on to sometimes later.

THE HERB REMINGTON ALBUM WAS RECORDED AS AN INSTRUMENTAL IN
1999

This is one of my favorite letters from Floyd Tillman.

I was honored to MC the Missouri Country Music Hall of Fame and have a chance to honor Ferlin Husky.

A very early photo of (then married) Ralph Emery and Skeeter Davis. I picked up this photo and the dress at Skeeter's estate sale.

Letter from Country Music Hall of Famer Pee Wee King.

Ernest Tubb wearing a
suit that is now on display
at the Heart of Texas
Country Music Museum.

While on tour with Ferlin,
Leona and Hank, Charla
and I enjoyed touring
Washington, D.C.

Frankie Miller, Ferlin
Husky, Leona Williams
and I attend the
Academy of Western
Artists Awards in
Richardson, Texas.

Eddy Arnold

June 30, 2005

My dear people:

I have autographed the pictures. They bring back a
lot of fond memories when I was a young man.

My best wishes.

Yours sincerely,

Eddy Arnold

EA/re

Letter from Eddy Arnold.

Cheryl Crabtree,
Wanda Jackson, Mona
McCall, Johnny Cox,
Don Tharratt, Shane
Lively, Lonnie
Atkinson, Cody
McCall, Justin
Trevino, Tony
Pickens, Darrell
McCall and I on our
2006 Country
Cruisin' to Cozumel,
Grand Cayman and
Key West. We usually
take 150-200 fans
with us each year.

1990

Tracy: How did you get involved with Country Music?

Johnny: We had a band in East Texas. I grew up around Tyler and my brothers and I had a band and that was our life. We listened to the Light Crust Dough Boys and that was what we wanted to do when we grew up. When I was thirteen years, my brothers and I had a radio show and as soon as I got out of high school, I went over to Shreveport and went to work with the Shelton Brothers on KWKH. From there, I went to Jimmie Davis' band and then I went into the army. It was all I ever wanted to do. Of course there are times throughout the years that you have to do other things to support you music habits. The music business is unpredictable and it goes up and down. All in all it has been a good trip.

Tracy: You are called the Master of the Fiddle. When did you first pick up the fiddle?

Johnny: When I was about nine. My brothers and I started playing. We learned together. We would go to musical parties that they had back then and watch and learn. I never did take formal lessons on the fiddle but everyone was nice to help me learn.

Tracy: Growing up, who were some of your musical influences?

Johnny: The Light Crust Dough Boys and Cecil Brower. Cecil was a studied musician. He was a good enough reader to play with the Fort Worth Symphony. He was the type of musician that I listened to and Cliff Brewer on Decca Records who had been with Milton Brown. The Shelton Brothers had several good fiddlers. We would listen to them on records when we had a record player. Around 1939, when I was 13, we began to listen to Bob Wills records.

Tracy: Who was the first person you recorded with?

Johnny: In 1948, I was with a band in Corpus Christi called Roberts Brothers Rhythmairs. Buck Carton and Curly Roberts had a little band and we made a record for a small label in Austin.

Tracy: You made many recordings for a variety of entertainers as a session musician.

Johnny: Back then, the record company would record the entire band. Not like it is now with the studio musicians. They would record Ernest Tubb and they would record his whole band, Red Foley and Lefty Frizzell were also using their own band. When I was in Dallas in the early 50's, I was getting calls to record for different artists. I had a Columbia Records account and Lefty Frizzell was the first one I worked with in 1952. Lefty Frizzell, Ray Price, Marty Robbins and Billy Walker, who were all on Columbia, would record in Dallas so I got to play on their records. Through the years, as I did other things, I played with different groups like Chet Atkins, Merle Haggard, Connie Smith, George Jones, Loretta Lynn and Conway Twitty. When you are doing studio work for a living and they like what you do, you get their account. Every time they record, they will call you. I did that for ten years. I recorded with a lot of different people.

Tracy: You did a couple of volumes of "Dance Hall Favorites" as a solo artist.

Johnny: Yes, and I got a contract with Capitol and did an album in 1974 called "Fiddlin' Around" and I did "Texas Dance Party" with Columbia in 1975. I have also done a couple of albums with a CMH label in California. The last one was with MCA Records called "Still Fiddlin'Around". I still go to Nashville when they call. The last few years I have done all of George Strait albums. I feel that it is more of a freelance job. I do everything. I take a band when they need something like a dance. Tomorrow night I am going to Fort Worth and play Johnnie High's Country Music Review. I am already getting bookings into 1991. I am playing in San Angelo for the Concho Festival in June. I don't have an agent. I just take what comes along. I also play the Nashville Now show when they call.

Tracy: Has the Country Music business changed since you started in the business?

Johnny: I do not think so. When you go to a record session, the song and the rhythm dictates what you play. I play whatever fits. George Strait has been good to play a variety. You just do what ever fits the tune. That is why I love this business.

Johnny Gimble is a name that virtually every true Country Music fan knows. Johnny has played with all of the greats in the studio or on the road. He is the most recognized fiddle player in the industry.

I became acquainted with Johnny primarily through Floyd Tillman. Floyd and Johnny were long time friends and always enjoyed working together. Johnny was always great about servicing KNEL with his latest projects. He has joined me on several occasions live on the air and I have even booked him a few times at various shows.

When I was planning Floyd Tillman's 85th Birthday party, I contacted Johnny and he readily agreed to attend the show in Llano, Texas. Johnny brought his fiddle and played with Floyd, Willie Nelson, Johnny Bush and all the other acts. It was quite a show and Johnny refused any pay. He did it for his love and admiration for Floyd.

We also hired Johnny to play on Floyd's last recording session for Heart of Texas Records. He did a great job and it was a fitting end to a fifty year friendship.

February 9, 2001

Tracy: How did you get started in the Country Music business?

Johnny: Tom T. Hall heard me singing at a place called Alamo Village in Bracketville, Texas. I was working and Tom T. Hall and Bobby Bare came down on vacation. That was around 1970. I worked there for two summers and the last summer I was working construction with my brother and Bobby Bare had just been down doing a concert. Bobby Bare and Tom T. Hall told me to look them up sometime. I called Bobby but he was doing a West Coast tour so I called Tom T. Hall at his office. When I got to Nashville, I did not have a job or anything so Tom T. gave me a job playing guitar in his band. He had just lost his guitar player so I got lucky. After I had been there a while he took me to Mercury Records to meet with Jerry Kennedy who is head of the A&R department. Roy Day was in the next office and Tom T told me to sing a couple of songs for Roy so I sang, "If I Left It Up To You", a Merle Haggard song and I sang, "I Can't Stop Loving You", in English and Spanish. He went next door and told Jerry he wanted to sign me.

Tracy: Tom T. Hall also helped you with your songwriting skills.

Johnny: While traveling, he was always so busy so I was like his traveling secretary and co-writer. We wrote the first album together. He was writing songs like "Old Dogs and Children and Watermelon Wine". He needed someone to write what he was thinking so that is what I would do so I learned a lot about writing that way. It was the same way with Willie Nelson and Roger Miller.

Tracy: You have had a lot of great songs in your career including "You Always Come Back To Hurting Me".

Johnny: That was one of the songs that Tom T. and I wrote on the bus. It was a very special song to me and one that did a lot for my career.

Tracy: "Riding My Thumb To Mexico" was a big hit for you.

Johnny: That was the first song that I wrote that was a number one record. It followed "You Always Come Back To Hurt Me". It is great to have a song become a hit, but it is even better when it is a song that you wrote. It is definitely one of those signature songs.

Tracy: How did you come up with "Riding My Thumb To Mexico"?

Johnny: I was raised ninety mile from the Mexican border so as a kid I would hitch-hike and go to Mexico. That is what got me thinking about the song. It was from personal experiences. I think that songs are much better when they come from personal experiences. Sometimes I experience a little too much!

Tracy: You have done many of your songs in English and Spanish. Many people became acquainted with you because of that.

Johnny: I did not even realize what was going on, I just did it. It was just something that I always did. Many people thought it was unique because I was singing Country Music.

Tracy: Was that something that you did earlier in your career?

Johnny: Yes, I would sing in Spanish. I still do.

Tracy: Another big hit of yours was "Pass Me By If You Are Only Passing Through".

Johnny: That was written by Tom T. Hall's brother, Hillman Hall. It is also one of my favorite songs and one that I always do on my shows. Hillman was a great writer but never achieved the success or fame that Tom T. did.

Tracy: What is your favorite song that you have recorded?

Johnny: I go from one to another. It is hard to decide. Dolly Parton explains it perfectly. She says they are like her children and how can you pick out your best child?

I believe that everyone really loves Johnny Rodriguez. He has a great soul. I know that he has been in so much trouble and has demons that cause him continual problems, but he loves people and they certainly return the favor to him.

The first time that I booked Johnny, we had to turn people away at the theater. We had about 900 come out to see him. This was back in 2000, and Johnny had gone through some more personal problems. For the majority of people, that bad publicity would actually harm their following. Johnny always seemed to come out on top.

I also believe that with the right people behind him, Johnny could once again have a hit on the market. He is truly his worst enemy. He still sings well and has fans all over the country.

Leona Williams is very fond of Johnny. She related a story to me one time about a luncheon they were having in Nashville. Leona, Johnny and a couple of others were having lunch in Nashville. Johnny was having a lot of problems within the industry at that time. He did not want to discuss the business and even made some off hand comment about "killing anyone" who discussed the industry. As you can imagine, when you have two or three singers or songwriters gathered together, the subject of music would eventually come up. When something was mentioned, Johnny jumped up with a gun in his hand. Leona talked him down and made him put the gun up. She told me that it was one of the scariest times that she had ever encountered.

Johnny is still out on the road today performing in front of his countless fans. He still has a lot of music to give to his many fans. He is the first major Mexican American Country star. His star is still shining bright today.

JUNE 8, 2000

Tracy: Tell us how you became involved in the Country Music business. Did you start out as a songwriter?

Johnny: No, I started out as a singer and then realized that you had to have songs if you wanted to make records so that is when I started to write songs. That was back when I was twelve or thirteen years old. The first song that I wrote was about my baby brother, it was called, "My Little Baby Brother".

Tracy: Did anyone ever cut the song?

Johnny: No, I do not even remember how it goes.

Tracy: When did you move to Nashville?

Johnny: I first moved here in 1959.

Tracy: Did you move there as a recording artist?

Johnny: I had made a record for Fabor Robison on Radio Records in California. It was a song called, "In A Mansion Stands My Love". Jim Reeves later recorded it. It is also on my new CD.

Tracy: In your career, you have has so many great people cut your songs. I love to hear the story of, "Act Naturally". That was a song that you had trouble cutting originally.

Johnny: I had it for two years and no one wanted to cut it. I played it for everybody in the world. We did not play it for Buck (Owens), we give him an acetate that had five songs on it because he was going to record a ballad that was on the dub. Don Rich kept playing the tape and he learned, "Act Naturally", so Buck suggested that they cut that one instead.

Tracy: Other than Buck Owens, you have had others cut, "Act Naturally".

Johnny: Yes, we did. The other night Ringo Starr was in town and my son, his wife, my granddaughter and I went to see him and we were backstage talking to him and my son thanked him for his college education and his first car. I was thinking the other day when they called and told me they had passes for us if we wanted to come down and see Ringo, how in just a few minutes he had changed my life and my kids life. It was just something in passing to him, he did not even realize it. We sat and talked about it for a little bit the other night. He is still changing my life. Blockbuster is using it for a commercial and it is in the new Denzel Washington movie. The song keeps having things happen to it and I get paid for it.

Tracy: One of my favorite songs is, "Got No Reason Now For Going Home", Gene Watson was the one who had the major hit on that song.

Johnny: Yes, he did. I love to hear Gene Watson sing. I think that he is one of finest singers that there it. I was very proud that it was such a great song for him.

Tracy: You have a brand new album out that you are really proud of.

Johnny: I am because it is the first thing that I have done in at least fifteen years. I was talked into the album, I turned them down the first two or three times that they called. They kept calling my secretary Pasty, and she would keep telling them no. Finally, she called me and said for me to tell them no because she was tired of telling them. So I called them and agreed to do it. And we have been very surprised by the success that we have had.

Tracy: This is your first "new" CD that you have put out.

Johnny: We had a couple of things that RCA Records and London Records put out. I also did some things for Ktell Records and they sold it to somebody and they put out a CD. I own all my hits from RCA Records, I bought all those so we put out a CD with those on it.

Tracy: This is your first brand new project and it is called, "Acting Naturally". You went back and recorded some of those greatest hits with your friends in the music business.

Johnny: That just happened. We did not plan it. Earl Scruggs and I had been at a party at Grandpa Jones' house a few years back. He told me that he wanted to record, "Act Naturally", and I told him to go ahead but he never did. When Hugh was talking to me about doing the album, I suggested that we get Grandpa Jones to play the banjo. We asked him and he agreed. Hugh was involved in discussing a project with Crystal Gayle and her husband Bill and one time they were talking and he said he was fixing to do a project with Johnny Russell and did she want to sing on it, it just happened. After we did that, the Osbourne's and Dolly Parton had just finished, "Making Plans", so I called Bobby Osbourne to do "Making Plans" with me and he agreed so I called Dolly and she said she would do it also. She came out and did it and Bobby Bare came by the studio one day to pick me up for lunch and I told him I had a recitation that I wanted him to do. He went in the studio and in about five minutes he had it done.

Tracy: This is a landmark album for Johnny Russell. It is an acoustic album.

Johnny: It is all acoustic, no electricity at all except the machine.

Tracy: Bill Anderson's album is the same way.

Johnny: Oh, he always copies me (jokingly).

Tracy: I think that it is a great sound for Country Music.

Johnny: It is the true sound of Country Music. I had several Bluegrass Festivals to do last year and I was using a bluegrass band and a couple of my musicians we would go do them and it all just came together. I used Larry Stephenson's band. He is also on the album. I also got Dale McCurry's two boys Ron and Robbie, Josh Graves, and Benny Martin.

Tracy: The project is getting some great review and you sound great vocally.

Johnny: I am very proud of it and I appreciate you saying that. And I appreciate you playing it. I did not know if anyone would be interested in playing a record by me because it has been such a long time since I have done anything. I still work a lot but I have not recorded anything.

Tracy: The most requested song for KNEL is "Ain't You Even Gonna Cry", a duet you did with Crystal. That is a tough version of that song.

Johnny: The week that we cut it, there were three other people that did that song for projects. It is great that songs like that live on. When you look at song like, "Act Naturally" and see what they have done, it goes beyond the money. Financially it has been very good but it is amazing to see everything that the song has done. I was in London, England, and I was sitting in the dining room at the hotel that we were staying at and Mick Jagger came in and I had a cap on that said Nashville and Mick sat at the table next to me and asked me if I was from Nashville. I said yes and he said that it was a big music city and wanted to know if I was in the music business. I said yes. He asked what I did. I told him I was a songwriter and he wanted to know if I had written anything that he might know (*talking in a English accent*). I told him I was a Country songwriter and that I did write a song that Ringo did and he wanted to know what it was. I told him that I wrote, "Act Naturally", and he said you mean the one that goes, "they're going to put me in the movies". I said yes and he said oh yes, I am familiar with that tune. Later that night, I was at the Wimberley Festival and another pop musician there and the promoter of the festival took me over to him and told him about "Act Naturally" and he said you mean the one that goes "there gonna put me in the movies". I realized then that people from all walks of life had heard the song.

Tracy: Johnny we would love to get you down to Central Texas.

Johnny: Brady, Texas, the hometown of Dave Kirby.

Tracy: You are right! In fact, Dave and Leona Williams played your homecoming a few years ago.

Johnny: Yes. They came down there and did the Dave Kirby Day a couple of years ago.

Tracy: Yes, they come every year.

Johnny: Do they still do that?

Tracy: Yes and we will have to get them to bring you down one of these years.

Johnny: I love Dave Kirby. He is a great guy and a great talent and a lot of fun to be around. Leona is kind of cute too. I recorded her the first time she was ever put on tape. Her and her first husband, Ron, worked for Loretta Lynn. I helped her get that job. It was when I was working for the Wilburn Brothers. I played the tape for Loretta (Lynn). It was the first that she had heard of Leona .

Tracy: So she owes you a little credit.

Johnny: Yes, but she has more than paid it back. For two years we worked in the Troubadour Theater three nights a week. We had a lot of fun. There is nothing like Country Music entertainers and our friends-that's the reason we keep going.

Johnny Russell was one of the biggest men in Country Music. He would actually tell you that himself! Johnny and I were never very close. I did a few interviews and caught his show several times in Nashville and even Pigeon Forge, Tennessee, one night. He had a great sense of humor and was a much loved entertainer.

Johnny enjoyed being a comedian in the later years more than singing. He really enjoyed hearing people laugh. His songs were recorded by hundreds of entertainers. Johnny suffered from diabetes and his last few years were plagued with some major health problems.

Johnny was in the hospital for a long time and according to a nurse that I talked to one time, held "court in his room" with many of his fans and fellow Opry stars. In the end, many of those fellow entertainers came to his rescue with a couple of much needed benefit shows. Friends included countless celebrities including Garth Brooks. That is the biggest legacy that anyone can achieve in this business.

Justin Trevino

OCTOBER 16, 2006

Tracy: How did you become involved in the Country Music business?

Justin: My dad was a big Country Music fan and a record collector. As early as I can remember, he had me listening to the Ernest Tubb, Johnny Cash, Hank Snow, Tex Ritter, Kitty Wells and a lot of other Grand Ole Opry singers. I always tried to sing with them. When I was seven years old I told my parents that I wanted a guitar for my birthday. I had an aunt who went to Mexico and she bought me a guitar for $25. It was not a great guitar but it served its purpose in helping me learn to play. I started taking guitar lessons and learned to pick. The singing just came along with the guitar lessons. I was always singing around the house anyway. My guitar instructors would teach me a song and it made no sense to just sit there and strum the guitar so I would sing and play at the same time.

Tracy: Would they teach you songs that you liked?

Justin: Yes, because they would always let me pick. They would tell me to bring the tape of a song that I wanted to learn so I got to choose. The instructors would ask me what kind of music I liked and I told them Country so they would get a Hank Williams song book and that is what I would learn.

Tracy: Did the lessons come easy for you?

Justin: Fairly easy but I did not practice. I would be a better guitar player today if I practiced. I would go from one week to the next without practicing. The only practicing that I would ever do is when I was singing. Back then, they were trying to teach me lead guitar but I really wanted to sing. I got to the point where I could play rhythm and sing but I never worked hard on the lead guitar. In retrospect, I wish that I had. Now I am working on becoming a better guitar player.

Tracy: When you were learning the guitar, you were also singing in honkytonks and bars.

Justin: Yes, by the time I was twelve or thirteen, I had my first paying job in a honkytonk. As far back as I can remember, I would go to the honkytonks with my dad and all I wanted to do was play the jukebox. Once I was at the age where I was picking and singing, we would go to the same bars and I would pull up a stool and play for the old men. I was only nine, ten or eleven. By the time I was twelve, I would start getting paid for it.

Tracy: How much did you get paid on your first paying job?

Justin: I am not really sure. I know that it was for tips only and it was me only. I was using my guitar only at first but then I got a solo drum machine. My very first job was at a place called The Red Onion in Menchaca, Texas but it is no longer there. About that same time there was a place on William Cannon called the Longhorn Barbecue, it is gone as well. I would play there every Saturday just me, my guitar and my drum machine.

Tracy: You were also involved with a band in high school.

Justin: It was not a high school band, but I was in high school. It was my first band and the band was called, Sunset Country. I was the singer and the band leader. All the guys that were in it were in their forties and fifties. I was the only kid in it. We would play local bars and dance halls.

Tracy: You were also involved in the FFA Talent Contest.

Justin: My Ag teacher encouraged me to do that. I had done competitive singing but he saw it as something that I could do and represent our chapter. We went to state one year and it was I and a girl that I sang with named Marcy but we were beat by a bluegrass band.

Tracy: When did you make your first initial recording?

Justin: My first recording was in 1990. It was released in 1990 or 1991. It was recorded in the Bob Angelo recording studio in Nashville, Tennessee. It was released on the Misty Country Label. The song on side A was a song that I wrote called, "Get A Bottle Turn A Cap", and side B was, "If Teardrops Were Pennies". We also recorded a cassette and there were five original songs and five other songs.

Tracy: Did you do the album before you did the single?

Justin: Yes, the cassette was called, "King of Clubs: Texas Justin Trevino Texas Honkytonk King". Don Jones was the record label guy and he came up with that. I did all the recordings at Bob Angelo's Recording Studio. Joe Paul Nichols does his records there as well. It is not at the same place but the same engineer.

Tracy: You had the opportunity to meet Bill Phillips during this session.

Justin: I met him and he was supposed to sing harmony on one of my recordings but when it came down to the wire the timing was not right. I hope I can get him to sing with me one of these days.

Tracy: You also had the opportunity to meet Johnny Bush around this time.

Justin: I met Johnny at the Eisenhower Flea Market in San Antonio. Johnny would play there once a month. I went there one time and saw Johnny Bush and the Bandeleros. I had always been a Johnny Bush fan. I thought that it was really neat to see Johnny Bush and in the background there was a huge sign that said, "Official Home of Johnny Bush". Two weeks later I went back and he was gone. I asked around and I was told that they quit going. They were having a jam session so I figured since I was already there I figured I would stay so I signed up to sing. I got up there and sang, "Whiskey River", and the guy who owned the flea market, Harry Wise, came over to me and told me that I sing just like Johnny Bush. I told him that it was not an accident because Johnny was one of my heroes and someone whom I patterned my singing after. Harry told me that Johnny and he were best friends and that he would like to introduce me sometime. I told him that I would love to meet him. I had met Johnny casually. As a fan, I stood in autograph lines and had my record signed but he would have never known who I was. Harry said he was going to call Johnny and have him come back to the flea market the following weekend. He asked if I would also come back and of course I said I would. I knew the guy was telling the truth because I knew that Johnny and him had a relationship but there was still apart of me that was skeptical and thought he was blowing smoke. That week I received a phone call from Harry Wise and he asked if I could be at the flea market the following Sunday afternoon. I went and we actually spoke right outside of the men's room. One of us was coming in and the other was going out. He did not ever say it, but I think that he knew that it was me that he was supposed to be meeting. When Johnny would play at these things he would set up his guitar and his amp. He really did not like to sing, but he did like to play lead guitar. He was playing guitar with the guys and they introduced me and told me to sing a Johnny Bush song. I sang, "Undo The Right", and a gentleman named Brent Horton, who eventually worked for me, was playing bass and if he ever played the right cord change in that song, it was an accident because he did not know the song at all. I was trying to sing a Johnny Bush song while Johnny was picking and this bass player was lost as a goose. We got to the end of the song and Johnny said, "well, that was close". I asked Brent if I could play bass and he said sure so I played the bass and Johnny got on the microphone and Johnny said, "ladies and gentleman, I am kind of hoarse today, that is why I sound like Kermit the Frog and from what I understand, this guy knows all of my songs so I am going to let him sing all of my songs so y'all can listen to him and look at me." I stood up there for forty-five minutes and I was very nervous. I sang all the songs that I thought the band would know. That day I did not know it was going to happen but sometimes it is good to be under the gun. I had recorded a Johnny Bush song on my "King of Clubs" album so I gave Johnny a copy. I don't recall meeting Lynda until our next meeting and they were very cordial. Every time I would go to a Johnny Bush show, he would call me up on stage with him on the last set. I would intentionally sing songs that he had written and make myself nervous in the process. I was still very much in awe of him. I wanted to know that there was someone out there that really loved his music and wanted to keep his songs out there. Johnny was a heck of a writer. His songs go beyond, "Whiskey River". He recorded an album with Darrell McCall and we would do a couple of those duets. We would usually do "There Will Always Be Honkytonks In Texas" and "The 24th Hour" and then he would have me pick a song and I would play one of his and my knees would be knocking but I would make myself sing it and if I was lucky he would sing harmony with me.

Tracy: Johnny must have been very impressed with you because soon after that time, he asked you to tour with him.

Justin: It was not too long after that. The first time I worked for Johnny was when he asked me to fill in for his front man Slim Roberts. Slim was a fiddle player. Slim had to do something that night so they called me. It was at the old Ramblin Rose in Llano. I was asked to do the opening set so I did. This was during a course of about three years. I was about twenty years old. I had known Johnny since I was seventeen. We had some other opportunities to work together. I was working a club in Canyon Lake that Johnny had played through the seventies and he would pack the house. The same club owner still owned the place but he had a guy named Roy running his club for him. The owner for some reason was not very excited about having Johnny Bush play. Roy, who I knew pretty well was all for it. So Johnny played and Harry had to eat crow because that place was packed. The people came to see Johnny Bush because I had worked that place several times and I never had a crowd like Johnny Bush did. That was the first night that I played bass for Johnny but it was with my band. He complimented me at the end of the night. It was not too long after that I became Johnny Bush's bass player in the Bandelero's for a longtime. Dwayne, his bass player at the time had just gotten married and he was not able to work Fridays and Johnny knew I was sitting on ready.

Tracy: Don Walser was another gentleman who was instrumental in the early stages of your career.

Justin: Don was trying to do what Johnny Bush ultimately did. He tried to get me signed to a record deal with Watermelon Records. At the time, Hines did not think I was ready so Don was never able to pull that off but he really did try. Don's health was not very well so he was missing many dates so I would fill in for him. Don told me one time that if he could not play anymore that he wanted me to take the Pure Texas band and keep playing. The fact that he felt that way was really something to be proud of but without Don, there was not a Pure Texas Band. When he retired from playing, the band went their separate ways.

Tracy: "Texas Honkytonk" was your first independent project on your very own label.

Justin: It is hard for me to listen to it because of the Pure Texas Band players. That album started out as demo to get me a recording contract with, what use to be, Watermelon Records. We put the demo together and still could not get Hines to listen to it. When we finished the demo we realized that it was pretty good and we need to get it out there and then came along Johnny Bush. I was with Johnny Bush and I played him the tape and asked what he thought of it. He said well, you need to get rid of the electric drummer and let me play drums. I had mixed feelings because I was excited that Johnny wanted to be part of the project but any recording engineer will tell you that the hardest thing to do in the studio is to get a good drum sound and I had never recorded live drums. I was terrified that I could not do it and at the same time I was not about to look a gift horse in the mouth and turn it down. Johnny came over and played drums on the record. I wish that I had more recording hours under my belt because I know that I could have gotten a better quality sound than I did.

Tracy: You have come a long way since that first project and you also have your own recording studio.

Justin: Yes I do. We have also managed to make some upgrades a little at a time. We went from an 8-track analog recorder to an adat. I now have a 24 track hard disc recorder.

Tracy: How did you learn to record?

Justin: All my life growing up I was always messing with gadgets like recorders, radios and electronics. The first multi track recorder I had was an eight track reel to reel that was not all that different from a four track reel to reel. All the machines still have the same buttons. Stop, rewind, fast forward, and play.

Tracy: You have received a lot of success as a songwriter, bass player, singer and an engineer. Which one of these do you enjoy the most?

Justin: I like it all. I love playing and singing. I love the end results of producing records. I do not really enjoy the in between stuff like mixing records. I do love the hands on approach. I would not trust it to anyone else. It is just tedious.

Tracy: You have had your success without the gift of sight.

Justin: It is hard for me to comment on it because that is the only way that I have ever done it. If I had ever had sight, I could tell you what was different about doing it without sight.

Tracy: How did you lose your sight?

Justin: I was born three months prematurely. I was blinded in the incubator. My understanding is that there is a special light that the doctors have to expose the premature babies to in order for the babies to absorb the oxygen that they need. They told my mom to go home, you are young, you can have another one. I was not supposed to live. I did not die soon enough for them. They told my mom that if I were to live that I would suffer blindness or brain damage. I tell people that I went the whole nine yards. I got the brain damage and the blindness!

Tracy: I admire you for what you have done. I wish I was as talented as you are. What do you consider the highlight of your career?

Justin: I really enjoy the people that I have meet in this business. There are a lot of highlights and many of them I owe to you. A lot has been in the record producing end of it. Who would have ever thought that we would have been producing Leona Williams, Darrell McCall, Johnny Bush, Ferlin Husky, and Norma Jean records? Every one of them has been a highlight in my career. The fact that we keep doing them over and over again is amazing. It is the magnitude of the people that I am the proudest of. Along with that, I am very proud to be working at this time with Johnny Bush. We are working on an album together. As a kid I really looked up to Darrell McCall. I am currently playing most of his dates. I really enjoy playing with him. We just finished a Darrell McCall record and we are fixing to be doing a Mona McCall record. They are two of my favorite people. A couple of other people are the people at the Midnight Jamboree. Having Connie Smith come out and sing with me was great. Becky Hobbs and Dawn Sears are two other people that I really enjoy working with.

Tracy: What do you see in the future for our kind of Traditional Music?

Justin: The future looks brighter right now than it ever has. XM radio has really made a difference. Specifically Willie's Place and Eddie Kilroy have done wonders for us. They are exposing the kind of music that we really love. These guys are playing Johnny Bush. Curtis Potter, Amber Digby. They are playing dance hall music.

Tracy: Whenever someone thinks about Justin Trevino, what do you want them to know you for?

Justin: When it is all said and done, I want them to be proud of what we left behind. All that is left of us when we are gone is the records we made and the way we treated the people around us. I know that there are people out there that like my music but the legacy is more important to me. I want to make as many solid Country records we can make. Not just of me but of Johnny, Leona, Curtis and Norma Jean. I want to contribute as much as I can to making good quality records.

Justin was actually named after Justin Tubb. Justin Tubb was Justin's dads favorite songwriter. Justin Trevino still has an album that Ernest Tubb autographed to him before he was even born. Justin's parents went to an Ernest Tubb show and told E.T. that their son would be named after his son.

Justin Trevino and I crossed paths many times before actually getting to know each other. During the late 1980's, I was a frequent listener to the Ernest Tubb Midnight Jamboree on WSM in Nashville. Justin Tubb and I became very good friends and he would dedicate the Ernest Tubb record that was played each Saturday night to me and a few other E.T. fans on a regular basis. I was listening to the show in Brady, and Justin was listening to the show near Austin. In 1989, I was elected State FFA (Future Farmers of America) Vice President. At the time, I was also the Area VII FFA President. Justin and his group won the Area VII Talent contest and was then eligible compete at the state level.

Truthfully, I do not remember hearing or seeing Justin at those events. I now wish that I had paid more attention.

Justin remembers me being introduced and giving a speech. He told me years later that he thought I must be Tracy Pitcox Jr. He could not believe that someone could love the same kind of Traditional Country Music that he cherished.

Several years later, I was introducing Johnny Bush at London Dance Hall. Justin asked Johnny to introduce us. We became fast friends. I not only consider Justin one of my best friends, but a part of the family.

Justin and I have worked hundreds of shows together, traveled thousands of miles and discussed every Country singer and the majority of Country songs. He is a walking encyclopedia and I enjoy our working relationship. I feel that we have been mutually beneficial to each other with each of our careers. Heart of Texas Records posted over $60,000.00 in sales in 2006. The majority of that can be attributed to the great production ability of Justin.

Justin's future is very bright. I am proud to be just a small part of that future with him.

Ann and Hank Thompson and Justin Trevino in the studio for Heart of Texas Records. I think that Ann is telling the boys what to do.

Justin Tubb

July 1990

Tracy: You are the youngest male singer to ever join the Grand Ole Opry.

Justin: Yes, I was about twenty and I have just celebrated 34 years on the Grand Ole Opry. Before I joined, Hank Williams was the youngest male singer to join the Grand Ole Opry at the age of twenty five. Until someone joins younger that twenty, I guess that I will hold that distinction.

Tracy: You roots began in San Antonio, Texas.

Justin: Yes, my dad got his start in San Antonio, right around the time that I was born and we then moved to Corpus Christi, San Angelo and then to Fort Worth. During this time was when he got his start recording with first Blue Bird Records, which was RCA and then Decca Records. He started recording for Decca Records in Houston in 1940. The next session was in Dallas. "Walking The Floor" was cut in Dallas and "Blue Eyed Elaine" was cut in Houston. We are Texans from the word go.

Tracy: You are a songwriter and the first song you wrote was for your dad.

Justin: Yes, it was called, "My Mother Must Have Been A Girl Like You", it was released in about 1951. I was still in high school. It was actually the B side of dad's hit "Somebody's Stolen My Honey." Charlie Walker was a disc jockey in San Antonio and "My Mother Must Have Been A Girl Like You", was a top ten because of Charlie Walker. I really got excited about the business at that time. I had a period of about five years where I was trying to prove that I could do something else. I had heard it so much that I kind of rebelled against 'well, your going to grow up to be just like your daddy.' I went to the University of Texas for a year studying journalism and radio and had every intention of becoming a sports writer or sports announcer. That was my other great love. When he cut my song and then Hank Williams died, it made up my mind for me. My first love was songwriting. Hank Williams was, and still is, the greatest Country songwriter ever. His passing really hit me hard and I made up my mind that I was going to be another Hank Williams as a writer. I moved to Nashville and got started in the business and as they say, the rest is history.

Tracy: You have had a lot of hit songs in your career.

Justin: I have been very lucky. Songwriting is a God given talent. It is amazing that you can make a living doing something that you love to do. It is creative and you can write something that might help other people or make them happy or whatever. I thank God that I have this talent and I hate to work.

Tracy: When did you start recording?

Justin: In 1953. I had been in Nashville for about 6 months and my dad took a tape of some of the songs that I had written. I was doing a disc jockey show and he took a tape to Paul Cowen who was the A&R man for Decca Records. He said the songs were pretty good but he wanted to record me. Paul decided that instead of pitching my songs to the other artists on Decca that he would just record me. As far as I know, I was the first, second generation artist to be signed to a major label. It was a lot different back then compared to today. It was harder for the people and the disc jockeys and the fans to accept me because I was Ernest Tubb's little boy. You really have to live up to a certain level of expectations because they have a lot of expectations because of who my father was. It is a little bit different now because there are a lot of second generation artists now. It is a little easier to get accepted. Shortly after I started, Betty Foley made a couple of records for Decca and we were the first couple of second generation people to do that.

Tracy: At this time, you did not want your dad to help you did you?

Justin: No, I did not. We talked a lot about it, even changing my name but I did not want to do that. Outside of giving me some great advice and being my mentor or advisor, he agreed to stay out of my career and let me go my separate way and that is the way that I wanted it. For years the Grand Ole Opry would not even put me on the same show with him because they did not want him to have to introduce me as his little boy. I did not want anyone think that the only way that I could get on the Grand Ole Opry was because of my father. However, he was responsible for getting many people on the Opry. He helped Hank Williams, Hank Snow and Stonewall Jackson and a lot of other people on the show. He did not have anything to do with my getting on the show. I had three top ten records in a period of about a year and Gabe Tucker, who was managing me and my dad at that time, went to the Opry people and arranged for me to become a member. I am kind of proud of the fact that up until Lorrie Morgan joined the Opry three or four years ago, that I was the only second generation artists to be made a member of the Opry. It has been a lot of fun. I am getting back into the writing and it is a lot of fun. I think that writing is what I do best. I love to sing and I love to perform but I get more pleasure in sitting down and creating some new piece of material that I think the people are going to enjoy. Your creative juices dry up if you don't use them. I have not been using my writing skills lately so I if I do not use them, I may lose them.

Tracy: When Highway 101 released the song that you and Roger Miller wrote "Walkin' Talkin' Cryin' Barely Beaten Broken Heart" you did not get the same recognition that Roger received.

Justin: That is just one of those things. More people that are not familiar with

Country Music know Roger Miller than Justin Tubb because of his success on Broadway with "Big River". He had his own TV show and had some pop songs as well. He was even in the Highway 101 video. I did not get recognized as one who co-wrote the song but Roger and I both know. As a matter of fact, I wrote 75% of the song and Roger will tell you that as well.

Tracy: You and Roger co-wrote several songs together.

Justin: I wrote the answer to "Dang Me". I wrote the lyrics to "Dern Ya" with Teresa Brewer. Ruby Wright recorded it. Archie Campbell recorded a song that Roger and I wrote called "Don't Jump From The Bridge" or something like that. We had a few others that were cut in albums. Roger and I ran together a lot in the early sixties. When he called me to tell me that Highway 101 cut our song, he said he wanted to get together again and write some new material. He comes to town every once in a while. Our minds are a lot a like and it would be fun to write together again. I am going to get me a T-shirt that says "Paulette Carlson For Queen or President." I just love them for bringing the song back. It has gotten my creative juices flowing. Johnny Wright recorded it first in 1964. It was one of the first things that he recorded on his own after Jack died. It was a chart record for Johnny on Decca Records. I recorded the song on an album for RCA. That was the only two cuts on it until Highway 101 cut it.

Tracy: Do you have any idea how many songs you have written?

Justin: I have many that I have never put on tape. I guess I have a couple hundred recorded. We have been lucky in having "Lonesome 77203", which has been cut maybe a hundred times. "As Long As There's A Sunday" is a favorite song of mine. I re-wrote it for Sammi Smith. She did the song from her view point. I like to write and I re-signed with Tree Records. I am going through old material and I have people wanting to hear my songs again.

Tracy: Do you still have your publishing company?

Justin: No, I am getting out of that. I found that you cannot do anything right if you are doing too much. We have the Ernest Tubb Record Shops now and I leave that up to David McCormick. I do the Midnight Show and front the operation but he does all the work. I do not know anything about running the record shop and my dad did not either. David has always taken care of that. I got out of the publishing business. I sold my two publishing companies to Tree Records. I am devoting my time to working the Opry, doing some television work, some personal appearances and mainly writing. That would be an ideal situation for me is to work the road when I wanted to get out of town for a few days and visit the fans and spend some time writing and making records when possible.

Tracy: You have a re-issued album out on Starday Records.

Justin: Yes, the first album I did with Starday Records in 1961. The album still sounds good after 30 years. There is some good material on the album. Some of the best material that I ever did was when I was at Starday Records. I re-recorded a couple of songs on the album that I did with Cutlass Records in 1972. It had "Traveling Singing Man" and Texas Dance Hall Girl" in it, and I rerecorded some of my Starday stuff on that album as well. I may even do it again. That is the kind of stuff that people are asking for now.

Tracy: Do you have any regrets in your career?

Justin: I don't know. That is something you think about a lot. If you go back and change something that you would have done differently, you may not be as happy as you are. There are a few things that I could have done differently but nothing major. I wish that I had not partied as much as I did. I learned my lesson there. I think we all go through that and in show business, it is awful hard not to do that. I never did drugs or anything like that. I did have a drink or two but I have not done that in over three years now and I am very proud of that. In show business, it is especially difficult because of the type of life that you are required to lead and the hours and the travel. It is just awful easy to look for that crutch. It never was a big serious problem for me. I never got to be a No Show Jones or missed a bunch of shows because of it. That is the only thing that I wished that I could have done a little easier on. I enjoyed everything that I have done. I don't know how I could have changed it. I am just happy that I got the chance and I hope that I can keep going. We have some expansion plans.

Tracy: Is there an Ernest Tubb Record Shop in the plans for Fiesta Texas in San Antonio, Texas?

Justin: It is being discussed. It is an ideal place to have an Ernest Tubb Record Shop there because that is where he got his start as well as myself. I would love to have one there. We have had some inquiries about a record shop in some other areas as well.

Tracy: And on top of all of that, you are keeping your father's memory alive.

Justin: I try very hard to. It is not very hard to do because so many people loved him and know him. He gave a lot back. Mrs. Rogers helped him get started and that is why he helped so many people. He promised her that he would do the same thing for other young people and he did. He kept Jimmie's name alive and if it ever gets to the point where we feel that they are forgetting who Ernest Tubb was, I will take care of that or try to any way. I don't think it will be as big a problem as it was with Jimmie because Country Music is a lot more important now than it was in Jimmie's day. Jimmie was one of the very few Country artists during his time. The tradition goes on and as long as I'm around it will.

Tracy: There seems to be some new Traditional trend in the music right now.

Justin: I am so excited about Country Music now. As a matter of fact, somebody told me that I should rewrite "What's Wrong With the Way That Were Doing It Now" and I think I am. I have been playing with the lyrics. But make it from the standpoint that there's nothing wrong with the way that we're doing it now as a way of thanking Ricky and Randy and Ricky and Alan Jackson and Doug Stone and Garth Brooks and Clint Black and all these new young Traditional Country singers because this is what I have been screaming about for thirteen years. It has all come about and I feel so much better now than I did when I wrote that song about what is happening in Country Music. I am just glad to see it get back to basics so to speak. All these Traditional Country singers are winning these awards and it really makes me feel good.

In the beginning of my Country Music career, Justin Tubb did more for me than any other person. He was the first "friend" that I had in the industry. I had long been a fan of Ernest Tubb. I was in Junior High school when E.T. passed away on September 6, 1984. I remember hearing about E.T.'s death on the radio and then going the next day to the library to read the obituary that was covered in all the major Texas newspapers. In the article, it reference the Ernest Tubb Midnight Jamboree and mentioned that Justin was now the predominate host of the radio show on WSM in Nashville. Three weeks later, I tuned in and heard Justin host the show for the first time. Nearly every Saturday night after that time, I tuned in to AM 650 to hear Justin and started corresponding with him.

I met Justin for the first time during this interview. David McCormick had set up the interview at 1:40 AM on that early Sunday morning after the Midnight show. The interview was conducted in David's office at the Ernest Tubb Record Shop on Music Valley Drive in Nashville. It was a great day for me.

The friendship that Justin and I enjoyed would soon turn into a business relationship as well. I began booking dates for him primarily in Texas. He was the most agreeable artist that I have ever booked. He virtually took anything that I brought to him-from $250.00 to $1,000.00 a night, Justin worked it all. When he was in Texas, he generally stayed in Brady and we would work dates and then return back to my hometown. He loved being in Texas and the small town atmosphere. He hosted our "Hillbilly Hits Radio Show" a total of eight times. Each time, he would be with us for the full six hours and loved being a "disc jockey" for a day again.

He made sure that I had backstage Grand Ole Opry clearance and introduced me to so many people in the industry.

Justin fought many demons in his life. He discussed his problems many times with our listeners and then while he and I were just driving from one gig to another. Justin was an alcoholic and he had continual financial problems and even filed bankruptcy. He would wind up losing his part of the Ernest Tubb Record Shops and even many of the classic songs that he wrote throughout the years in the mid 1990's. He had a major misunderstanding with the Grand Ole Opry management. His time slots on that great show were cut back.

Then it seemed that everything was getting better. He headlined the first benefit show for our Heart of Texas Country Music Museum. He was planning on going into the studio for a project titled "Heart of Texas Country" that we were putting together and rerecording

"What's Wrong With The Way We're Doing It Now." I had a string of dates booked for him and he was scheduled to be on the television portion of the Grand Ole Opry on January 24, 1998. That all changed. Justin was forced to have surgery to repair a stomach aneurism. He did not survive the operation and passed away early on that Saturday morning. David McCormick called me with the tragic news very early that morning.

We had Justin's funeral at the Ryman Auditorium in Nashville. There was not a dry eye in the house as Connie Smith sang "How Great Thou Art." Many of Justin's friends were in attendance including Marty Stuart, Ricky Skaggs, Eddie Stubbs and other members of the Grand Ole Opry. He was laid to rest near his father.

Justin followed a large and ever present shadow. His father was such a huge star in the industry. He also cast a large shadow himself. I just wished that he would have realized that more in his life. I still miss him every day.

Season's Greetings

Tracy –
Sorry this is late – but this is as close to "caught up" as I've been in three years.
Give my best to all your members and listeners, and I'm sorry I missed your tour when you were here. Had a spastic-colon attack right about that time. Even missed a couple o' spots. (As had as I need them)
Carroll Parham called yesterday. Will let you know as soon as I talk to him. Thanks for everything.
Justin

Keith Whitley

NOVEMBER 5, 1988

Tracy: Keith will you tell us a little bit about your Country Music background. You started out in Country Music and then you progressed into bluegrass

Keith: I am glad to hear you get it right. Most people get it wrong. They think that I started out in bluegrass. I started out playing what I play now which is Traditional Country Music. When I was 14 or 15 years old, as a way to get into a band, I become interested in bluegrass music and so I spent the next few years in a couple of bluegrass bands. Ricky Skaggs and I worked with Ralph Stanley and JD Crowe. But my heart kept telling me that I needed to be doing what I started out doing. In 1984, I moved to Nashville and was lucky enough to sign with RCA in 1985.

Tracy: What was your first hit song?

Keith: My first hit record was "Miami, My Amy", which happened in 1986. "Love Ten Feet Away", "Homecoming '63"and "Hard Living" were also top ten records. "Don't Close Your Eyes" was our first number one record and our new record is looking really strong. Last week it went from nineteen to twelve and now it is at number nine.

Tracy: Tell us about your new album. Is it a more traditional sound?

Keith: Definitely. The reason for that is because I co-produced this album. This is the first time that I was allowed to do that. I took a very healthy step backwards to the direction of my roots and the music that I grew up listening too. I grew up listening to real traditional styles of Country Music. The single most influential person for me was Lefty Frizzell. In addition to Lefty, I also liked George Jones, Merle Haggard, and Buck Owens. Those were the guys that I grew up listening to and they influence what I do now.

Tracy: I recently heard you on the Ernest Tubb Midnight Jamboree in Nashville.

Keith: You were lucky enough to hear one of the very few things that we do in Nashville. I actually live in Goodlettsville, a suburb of Nashville, but with the exception of some of the TV shows that we do or when we happen to do the Grand Ole Opry, we very seldom entertain in Nashville. People are always asking when we are performing in Nashville but in the past three years, we have done maybe two concerts in Nashville. We just usually work on the road. I think the same is true for most artists. We very seldom work at home. It is always on the road.

198

Tracy: You are married to Grand Ole Opry star Lorrie Morgan?

Keith: She is with RCA records herself and we have a 16-month-old boy named Jesse Keith. We also have a daughter, Morgan, who is seven years old. I am getting to go home tonight for the first time in about two weeks and spend a couple of days at home so I am really excited about that.

Tracy: What are your future plans?

Keith: My future plans are to just keep doing the same thing. We are looking for songs right now. I am trying to write as much as possible and we hope to get back in the studio as early as December to do a few new things. The majority of the album will be cut in March or April. We are looking at about three more singles from the "Don't Close Your Eyes" album. That album will run us through the big part of next year. We just want to keep doing the same thing. We have worked about 15 years to get things to where they are now and we want to keep progressing with each record and I hope to be in this business for a long time.

Unfortunately, the time was not very long for Keith. He passed away six months after this interview from alcohol poisoning at his home. When I was called about his death, I was immediately reminded about this interview and visit with Keith. At the time of our conversation, Keith looked very healthy and was excited about the business. He was straight and gave no indication of the demons that were plaguing his personal life.

Keith would enjoy his greatest success as a performer after his untimely death. His songs would be released and his fan base would grow. It is very unfortunate that he could not enjoy what he worked so hard to accomplish. His influence is still heard today on many of the current artists in the business. His life was a testament that the business and personal pressures are sometimes greater than the enjoyment of fame and fortune.

1994

Tracy: How did Kitty Wells, get started in Country Music?

Kitty: I started out right here in Nashville singing gospel songs at church meetings. My cousin and I got on a program here at WSIX called, The Old Country Store, which was an amateur show on Saturday afternoons. We started singing on that. We then got an early morning program. We sang on that for a long time. When Johnny (Wright) and I got married, we were still singing on the radio station. We would work around here on nights and weekends at the schools or theaters of something like that. That led from Nashville to North Carolina, West Virginia and other places.

Tracy: Johnny was the one who changed your name. Your real name is Muriel Deason.

Kitty: We were working in Knoxville and the radio station announcer and program director did not really like my name. We were on a program called, The Midday Merry Go Round. I was working with Johnny and Eddie Hill because Jack was in the service. The announcer said people like to hear that girl sing and if she had an easier name to remember, she might go far in this business. Johnny thought about it and he came up with Kitty Wells. It is the name of an old folk song. That is where I got the name. I have been using it ever since. It has been very good to me.

Tracy: "It Wasn't God Who Made Honkytonk Angels" was a really big hit for you.

Kitty: I recorded it in May 1952. It was the very first song that I recorded on Decca Records, which is now MCA Records. I was surprised that I made a hit because I had recorded about eight songs on RCA prior to that. They were mostly religious songs and they did not do anything. I left that label and sent Paul Cohen, who was the A & R man for Decca, a record to see if he would be interested in recording me. In the meantime, we moved from Shreveport back to Knoxville. Johnny saw Paul one night at the Ernest Tubb Record Shop and asked him if he was interested in recording me. He said yes and he had a song that he would like us to listen to and if we liked it, we could record it. He told me the name of it but I did not think anything would come of it, but at least it would get some station play. I also thought that that we would at least get session pay.

Tracy: You once told me that you were ready to retire before recording "It Wasn't God Who Made Honky Tonk Angels."

Kitty: That is right. I had worked in radio for several years. Johnny was having a very successful career and I had decided to stay at home with the children and raise the family. After recording "It Wasn't God Who Made Honky Tonk Angels", I went back out on the road and have been there since.

Tracy: Do you know how many copies of, "It Wasn't God Who Made Honky-tonks Angels" were sold?

Kitty: I have a gold record for a million and I know it sold many over that.

Tracy: It was the first of many hits for you. You even started recording with Red Foley a couple of years later.

Kitty: Red also recorded for Decca Records. During that time, Decca was pairing up several of their artists to record duets. I recorded with several artists including Webb Pierce, Roy Drusky and of course Johnny. Red and I recorded several hits including "You and Me" and "As Long As I Live". They were big records.

Tracy: Did Paul (Cowen) decide on your duet partners or did you choose?

Kitty: I do not remember if it was Paul or Owen Bradley. They worked together. Owen was on all the sessions that I did for Decca.

Tracy: The two of you were a good combination.

Kitty: It turned out to be really good. We had a song that Pee Wee King and Redd Stewart had written. It had a recitation in it and Red Foley was really good at doing those. Johnny came up with the idea of Red doing the recitation on it. Red said that we needed a song to go on the other side so we did, "One By One". That happened to be the "A" side, we just happen to put it on the "B" side.

Tracy: You also recorded, "Make Believe", and later on you recorded, "Making Believe". What is your favorite song of all that you recorded?

Kitty: That is hard for me to pick just one favorite. I suppose "Making Believe", "Searching" and "How Far Is Heaven" would have to be my favorites of the songs that I recorded.

Tracy: Are you still touring?

Kitty: Oh yes. We just finished a twenty-day tour in Canada.

Tracy: Are you still touring as a family act with Johnny and Bobby?

Kitty: Oh yes. We are billed as the Kitty Wells/Johnny Wright Family Show. After Jack died in 1963, Johnny had to decide on his career. Johnny and Jack had so many great hits. He was trying to decide on a new duet partner or have a solo career. After taking some advice from several in the industry, Johnny decided not to get another duet partner. Every one would always compare the new partner to Jack. We have been on the road with our family show ever since. Our grandson is traveling with us as well

Tracy: What is the biggest change you have seen in Country Music since you started?

Kitty: I think that there are more modern changes to the lyrics. They try to go in the middle of the road and be more modern. I am thankful for people like Clint Black, Randy Travis and George Strait that are coming back with the Traditional Country Music.

Tracy: You have a cookbook out. You are known all around Nashville for your good cooking. How did you get the idea to do a cookbook?

Kitty: There were a lot of people coming out with a cookbook so I thought that it would be a good idea for me to put one out. I have published a couple of cookbooks in the past, but this is the first one that we have released in a long time. We sell them on the road and at our museum here in Madison (Tennessee).

Tracy: When they write the big history book of Country Music and they come to the page that has Kitty Wells on it, what would you like that page to say?

Kitty: Being down-to-earth and a good person. One who cares about people and likes to entertain. I think that is the way I want people to remember me.

Kitty Wells is still the greatest female vocalist in the Country Music business. Today's female vocalists do not appreciate what Kitty did for the industry. Kitty broke down barriers making it easier for every future female vocalist to make it in the industry.

In 1989, my family took a trip to Branson for the first time. My aunts, uncles, grandmother, parents, brother and sister all traveled to the "new" Music City for the very first time. When we checked in, I immediately asked the attendant who was in town. She mentioned all the regulars and then casually mentioned the Kitty Wells, Johnny Wright and Little Jimmy Dickens were filling in for Mel Tillis this week. I could not believe it!

The following day, I called for a ticket and we were in bumper to bumper traffic trying to get to the Mel Tillis theater. The traffic was so bad and the time was getting so short. I got out of the car and walked down 76 Boulevard for a mile to the Mel Tillis theater. I was placed on the front row and sat there spell bound. Little Jimmy Dickens came out first and did a wonderful show. Bobby Wright then entered the stage followed by Kitty. When Kitty hit the microphone with "I Can't Help Wondering Who's Holding You Tight", a tear came to my eye. I was listening and watching the greatest female vocalist right before my eyes. Johnny Wright came out after Kitty and did a fantastic job as well. I thought it was the greatest show that I had ever seen!

After the show, Kitty and Johnny granted me thirty minutes for an interview. It would be the start of a long friendship. I asked Johnny about working in Brady, Texas, in the future.

A couple of weeks later, Johnny called and we sat up a date at the Brady High School auditorium. I had never booked a date in my life and really did not know how to promote anything. I did a bad job promoting and we ended up loosing about $500.00 that night. We would have lost another $250.00, but Johnny refused to take my check and gave it back to me that night. He knew that I was green and did not know what I was doing. He also knew that being kind to me that night would possibly be an investment in the future. It was. I would go on to book many successful dates on Kitty, Johnny and Bobby. As a matter of fact during their "Farewell Tour", I made over $6,000.00 in profits and commissions from the tour of Texas dates alone.

Kitty and Johnny broke ground at the Heart of Texas Country Music Museum in Brady, Texas, for us. They would also come back a couple of times during the museum's construction.

I asked Johnny for one of his suits to display at the museum. We went in the backyard and crawled on the bus. He opened up his closet and told me to pick anyone that I wanted. I loved one of his Nudie designed green, flower encrusted rhinestone suits. I asked him for that suit and he took it out and handed it to me. It is still one of my favorite museum pieces.

Today, they tour only very infrequently. We worked a date with them in 2006 in Lancaster, Pennsylvania. I stood backstage watching and listening to every word. Seeing these great legends work is something that I never want to forget.

I never go to Nashville without visiting Kitty and Johnny's house in Madison. They are Country Music royalty and two of the greatest people in the business.

Johnny Wright and Kitty Wells with a rhinestone encrusted Nudie suit that they presented to the museum.

Tracy: Kris, you were born in Texas.

Kris: I was born in Brownsville, Texas. I left there when I was young.

Tracy: When did you write your first song?

Kris: I started writing when I was eleven. I have been writing for as long as I can remember. I seem to be writing all the time in my mind. I don't always write the songs down, but I am forever writing.

Tracy: You were actually attending Oxford University in England when you got your first break.

Kris: I met a promoter named Paul Lincoln in England. He ran an ad in a newspaper that said "Just dial FAME". I called him and we had a meeting. I was signed to Top Rank Records. We recorded some songs that were never released. I had another contract back in the States and the guy read about the session and threatened to sue if the records were released. It was probably a good thing, because the songs were not very good anyway.

Tracy: Who were some of your influences growing up?

Kris: As a kid, I was first impressed with Hank Williams. I listened to Hank on the Grand Ole Opry and owned ever record that he released. I was in high school when Hank died and I thought my world was ending. He was my hero. I also listened to Johnny Cash, Elvis and a lot of folk music.

Tracy: When you moved to Nashville, you had to take a job before your songwriting became known.

Kris: I was working in several different fields. It was a tough six years and I nearly starved to death in Nashville. I was working as a bartender, in the construction field and even a janitor at Columbia Records. I was also pitching songs to everyone who would listen to me. That is also when I met Johnny Cash for the first time.

Tracy: You have enjoyed a close relationship with Johnny throughout the years.

Kris: Johnny and June both have been like a part of my family. I have worked with them all over the world and John has recorded several of my songs. He is such an icon in this business and one of the nicest guys in the world. We really had a great time during the Highwaymen years.

Tracy: Grand Ole Opry Star Roy Drusky was one of the first to cut one of your songs. Of course, many others would follow.

Kris: He recorded "Jody and The Kid." I started to have some success after that including Faron Young with "Your Time's A Coming" and Waylon's "Take Her." Of course, John recorded "Sunday Morning Coming Down" and Sammi (Smith) did "Help Me Make It Through The Night." My luck began to change during that time.

Tracy: What about "Me and Bobby McGee"?

Kris: Everybody has recorded that song. Janis Joplin had such a great record. It was also recorded by Roger (Miller) and even the Grateful Dead. It seems like every year or so that someone else puts it on an album and I am grateful.

Tracy: You were very close to Janis Joplin.

Kris: Janis was a wonderful person. She was so flambouant with all the feathers and her heart tattoo and those high heels. She was a happy person and loved to make you laugh.

Tracy: Do you enjoying performing?

Kris: I haven't ever really thought of myself as a performer or an actor either. I did my first movie "Cisco Pike" and really did not know what I was doing. I don't believe that Nashville ever really accepted me. I never became an Opry act or worked the road with those guys. I never considered myself a good enough singer to be considered a Country Music entertainer. Many considered me more of a folk singer.

Tracy: Tonight you are being inducted into the Texas Country Music Hall of Fame. How does that make you feel?

Kris: You know, I appreciate every award and honor that comes my way. I have enjoyed this business and the opportunity to have friends all over the world. The business has been good to me and I hope that I have given something back to it.

I met Kris for the first time at his induction into the Texas Country Music Hall of Fame. He and Johnny Bush were being inducted into the Hall of Fame that night and Willie Nelson was there to do "a guitar pull" with Kris during the ceremony that night.

The ceremony was being held at a Carthage, Texas, school auditorium. Justin Trevino and I were backstage and Kris came in and was ushered into a classroom. He was visiting with Johnny when we entered the room and met and visited with Kris for a few minutes. He was kind enough to grant an interview that night.

I remember him discussing some political event with someone and enjoyed listening to him debate the issue with evident vast knowledge about the subject.

It would be impossible to recognize just one song as Kris' greatest composition. One song that will surely go down in history is his "One Day At A Time". He wrote the classic with fellow Texan Marijohn Wilkin-an interesting fact since he prefers to write solo. That song has not only become a prayer for millions of Country and gospel fans, but is truly the prayer of the writer.

Kris may not be the best singer in Country Music, but he can rest assured that he has enabled some of the better singers to enjoy a bigger career because of his incredible writing.

Kris Kristofferson and Johnny Bush at their Texas Country Music Hall of Fame induction in Carthage, Texas.

November 9, 2006

Tracy: You grew up with a big musical family is that correct?

Leona: Yes I did. I have seven brothers and four sisters. My dad played fiddle and mom played banjo. She also played the piano or organ in church. I remember waking up lots of times with my mom and dad singing.

Tracy: Your husband Ron was very instrumental in your early career. How did you meet him?

Leona: I met Ron when I had a radio show when I was 15. I told them I was 16 because I thought that you had to be 16 to be on the radio. Ron was stationed in the Philippines, in the Navy. He wrote me a letter and told me that he thought that I sounded like Wanda Jackson. That was a big compliment to me because I love Wanda, and I still do. He wrote me a letter and asked me to sing a song and send it over to him and he would sing with it and send it back to me so I could hear what we sounded like as a duet. I told my mom about it and she told me that I could not be writing to the soldiers. Later on when I was working at a shoe factory in Missouri, Wayne, one of my brothers, was playing with a band and he gave his full name and a guy asked if he was my brother and Wayne said yes, he was my brother, so that is how we met up with each other again. We were married for about 14 years.

Tracy: Around this same time is when Loretta Lynn entered the picture.

Leona: Ron and I started a band and we moved to St. Louis and I was a beauty operator during the day and at night we played dances. We got to back Loretta Lynn, The Wilburn Brothers, and Granpa Jones. I met Loretta in Missouri. She was with The Wilburn Brothers and I was with Wayne, my brother and his wife. I thought that it was the finest that I had ever seen Loretta. After the show, we all went out to eat and Loretta said that if she ever made it she was going to help us kids. Whenever she put her first band together, we backed her some more. Loretta was really good to us. I played upright bass and I sang harmony with her. We sang songs like "The Home Your Tearing Down". I loved that.

Tracy: Loretta was one of the first major artists to record one of your songs.

Leona: She recorded a song that Ron and I wrote called, "Get Whatcha Got And Go". She took it to Nashville and she changed some of the lyrics, but we are all three credited for the song. She was the first to record any of my songs.

Tracy: Do you remember the first time that you appeared on the Grand Ole Opry?

Leona: Roy Acuff introduced me and I sang, "Once More", which was a song that I had out on Hickory Records. I can see Roy to this day with his hands behind his back listening to me and I was so nervous that it was like I was blind. I do not remember seeing a thing. In 1968, was when I first started recording for Hickory Records. Lonzo and Oscar were the ones who got me a record contract. I went to a studio in Goodlettsville, Tennessee, and my back up singers were the Four Guys from the Grand Ole Opry. They took my demo to Hickory Records and played it for Wesley Rose. Wesley slowed the record down and said that they had to sign me because I sounded like Roy Acuff. I was with Hickory Records for six years.

Tracy: You toured Vietnam with Lonzo and Oscar at a very critical time.

Leona: We went to Japan and Korea. I spent ten days in Vietnam and Okanawa was beautiful. Korea was having a lot of trouble at the time so it was just as scary as being in Vietnam. In Korea we were in the big motel and we were in about the fifth floor. You could see out the window and could see the bicycles with heavy things on their heads. We got a call and were told not to be looking out the windows because it was too dangerous. Every night when we would work, we would drive from Soul Korea and we would get stopped almost every night. Vietnam was kind of scary. That was the first time that I met Linda K. Lance. We went to a club in Taiwan and they had a jukebox and I heard my first record on the jukebox in Taiwan in a club.

Tracy: You have mentioned to me that the service men were some of your most appreciative audience.

Leona: Oh they were. If I had been a boy, I would have been over there anyway. It is really neat that I was able to be there. Some of the soldiers and I exchanged addresses. They gave us some advice about where to go. We were going to go down the Delta but the boys begged us not to go because some of the convoys were being blown up everyday. I told Oscar that he was the boss and that he did not have to pay me for the whole trip if he did not want to, but I was not going to go. At the time, I was barely pregnant with Ron. Oscar told me that if I did not want to go then he was not going either.

Tracy: Ernest Tubb was also someone who was influential in your career.

Leona: I loved Ernest Tubb. He was the best person in the world. We did a lot of shows together. Sometimes we would work twenty to twenty-eight days a month. I was young then. It was about 1968 or 1969.

Tracy: When did you and Ron get divorced?

Leona: We started having problems in the music business. I do not believe in getting divorced but sometimes it just works out that way. Ron was a good singer and a really good person, just like my son Ron. They are so much a like. Ron is a good songwriter too. Ron and I got to where we were irritated with each other. Ron and I seperated in early 1974. In 1975, Ronnie Reno called and he was working with Merle Haggard. We had just finished a bunch of shows with Ernest Tubb and The Wilburn Brothers. I was good friends with Ronnie and he was working with Merle. Merle had always been a fan of mine. Ronnie told me that Merle wanted me to go to the studio so he could talk to me. I got ready and went to the studio and that is how I met Merle. Merle pitched me some songs and I was recording a few days after that. I started working with Merle. I opened a show for him in 1975. The first trip we went on was in Cincinatti, Ohio. I was on my way to California to work with Merle and The Strangers. I worked in Ohio with Ferlin Husky on the way. Ferlin had his fiddle player, Willis Wade on the show with us. Someone took me to the airport and Lewis Talley, who was like Merle's road manager, drove the bus. I told Merle to have him pick me up because I liked him. We went to Merle & Bonnie's house. We worked at a place called Hag's Place in Los Angeles and a few days later we all went to Hawaii. I would go out every night and it was the best you had heard Merle. He would do imitations of Johnny Cash, Hank Snow, and other people and he would sound just like them. I thought he was really cool. It was one of those things where he and Bonnie had more of a business relationship than husband and wife. I knew they were not together but yet they were married. Lewis called Bonnie and told her that that Merle really liked me and Bonnie said that she knew that and she wished us the very best. Bonnie was the best person there ever was. Bonnie was even my matron of honor at our wedding

Tracy: Who decide that Bonnie would stand up for you?

Leona: That was actually Merle's choice. I really did not want people to gossip. When we were going out, Bonnie was with Merle's bus driver so that made Bonnie be there all the time. I went on the road and when I got back, which was around six in the morning, my daughter Cathy told me that Merle had been calling me every hour all night long. I called Merle and he told me that we were going to get married. I told him I couldn't because I was going to Florida. He said that I had to fly into Reno and that he and Bonnie had been planning this all night. They actually had the entire wedding planned. We were married in 1978 and we divorced in 1984.

Tracy: That was a good time for you, but it was also one of the worst times in your life.

Leona: It was because we made really good music together and a duet album. We even had a top ten record called, "The Bull and The Beaver". We may have sung it on stage once or twice. It is a shame to have a top ten record with someone and they don't want to sing it with you. That is just how it was. He said that he was not going to be Johnny Cash and June Carter. I was good enough to sing harmony on his records and not get any recognition. I sang a lot of harmony for him. I really enjoyed it because Merle is a great singer and songwriter. We had a lot going for us but things just happen. He had a lot of girlfriends, ex-wives and he even had another wife named Leona before me.

Tracy: It is hard to be in a marriage with someone of Merle's popularity and try to have a career yourself.

Leona: Yes it is. I think I was just in the way at times. Merle would say some really hurtful things to me. He would tell me that he wished I would just disappear and one time he told me that I was getting too old and that I needed to quit singing. I thought that I was still young. I told him that Janie Frickie was older than me. He said that at least Janie could sing. It was just very hurtful. Sometimes he was just really hard to deal with. He would start smoking marijuana with my kids in the house. I told this woman in our house that she better not be hiding drugs in the house because I have two little kids in the house. I told her that I would throw her through the door if I ever find out she did. It just got so bad that I had to leave. I did not want to wait until someone got hurt and I did not want my kids around it.

Tracy: After your divorce, you concentrated on your career. You formed a band and went on a cruise and someone else entered your life that you had known for a while.

Leona: George and Nancy Jones were going on a cruise and they wanted me to go with them. This girl named Susie Perkins, who worked with me at my publishing company, went with me and I had a baby Martin guitar that I took with me. We had a great time. John and Jamie Anderson also went with us. I told George and Nancy that we should get someone to book us on a cruise so that we did not have to pay for it and we could sing. The next year we did just that. I called Dave Kirby and I told him that I wanted to get a band together, but I never heard back from him. So I called Joe and told him that I had not heard from Dave so they helped me get a band together. Dave and I had the best time together. We even went to Miami and wrote a song together. Dave and I stayed together after that cruise for about 19 years until he developed throat cancer and passed away.

Tracy: He told me one time that not only were you his wife but you were also his very best friend.

Leona: That is the truth. He was a great guy.

Tracy: Was it easier to have someone who was involved in the music business as a spouse?

Leona: All the men I had been involved with were in the music business. We just have a lot in common. If I were married to a doctor, I do not think that it would work because I would not have anything to say to them. Maybe if I had a cowboy who had a farm that might be a little different. Dave really liked the farm. We bought a farm in Missouri. Dave always wanted a big farm and John Deere tractors so we got brand new tractors. We got all the things that he wanted. Right before he got really sick we sold some of the property and I still have quite a bit left.

Tracy: After he passed away you went right back to work. It was like therapy for you.

Leona: It was. My friend started a show and he told me that he did not have much money to advertise it. I told him that he needed to put my name up there and I did not care if I did not make any money. I just wanted something to do.

Tracy: You are back in the recording part of this industry.

Leona: Yes. We came to Texas and got started with you on Heart of Texas Records. It is the best thing that could have happened. You give us a chance to keep things going.

Tracy: I have often given you credit for Heart of Texas Records. You were the first major artist to agree to do a project with us. Your name and talent is the backbone of our record label.

Leona: When you get to choose, you get the best. You have some the best. You have Curtis Potter, Darrell and Mona McCall, Frankie Miller, Justin Trevino, Ferlin Husky and of course Amber Digby. I have known Ferlin for a long, long time. We have done a few shows together. The first BMI award show that I went to, I sat next to Ferlin and his daughter and Hank Thompson. I was going through a divorce and he had been through a divorce and we laughed and laughed and he said that we should get a rumor started about us. That scared me to death.

Tracy: The story of you and Ferlin is rather unique. You contacted him about an award.

Leona: Yes. In Missouri, they started a Country Music Hall of Fame and they want to build a museum some day. I was really excited to have something like this in my state. The first year they put me and Leroy Van Dyke and some other people in there. They asked me my opinion of different artists and I thought it would be great to have Jan Howard. They really wanted Ferlin but I did not know how to reach him anymore. Jean Sheppard said that he moved to Florida. They kept after me to find Ferlin. One day I called Jean and asked if she knew Ferlin's phone number, because we wanted to put him in the Hall of Fame in Missouri. She called him and laid the ground work. She called me back and said it was a good time to call Ferlin. I called Ferlin and I really did not know what to say, but he knew why I was calling. He told me that no one would be able to come and accept the award. He asked me if I would accept it for him. I told him I would and the next time I made a trip to Florida I would take it to him. Ferlin was going to have surgery and he did not think he was going to be able to make it. After his surgery, he talked as if he would be able. I told him that if he could get to Nashville that I would take him to the awards show in Missouri. He had some neighbors bring him to Nashville. He got his award and he and I have been best friends ever since.

Tracy: I think you enjoy the music business more now than you ever have.

Leona: I do. I am at the age where I do what I want to do. There are so many people that like the Traditional Country Music so that makes me not worry about anything else. I remember one time Bill Mack, who was a good friend of mine in Texas, told me that one of the best compliments someone could give you is to tell you that you are "Too Country." I had someone in Arkansas tell me that one time.

Tracy: There have been many new artists that credit you with being an influence on their career.

Leona: Yes. I am so thankful. Rhonda Vincent is one. I think Rhonda Vincent is fabulous. I think it is a compliment to have people say that we sound alike. I really like her and Amber Digby. I am really glad that she is on Heart of Texas Records with us.

Tracy: You have been in the business for about 45 years, the biggest part of you life. How do you want people to remember you?

Tracy: I want to be remembered as a really good person and a good Country singer. I do not care what they think about my life. I have been divorced and some people do not like that, but sometimes you cannot help those kinds of things. I have to move on. I have three fine kids and my son Ron is a good singer. He will take my place one day. He is as Country as me. My daughter Cathy is also a great singer and my son Brady has a great job. He is smart enough to make a living with out singing at all! I have had a wonderful life and a great career. I love Country Music and I love the fans that have enabled me to have that wonderful life. They are simply the best.

Leona Williams is the best friend that I have in Country Music. As a matter of fact, I consider her a part of my family. We have shared some of the happiest times of our lives together and some of the saddest.

Leona and I corresponded with each other for years. I met her the first time at the opening of the Ernest Tubb Record Shop in Ft. Worth. She was working the Cross Timbers Opry in Stephenville a few months later and I took a group with me to see her show. We were in our fifteen passenger van. After the show, Leona and Dave came out to tell us goodbye. Leona crawled up in the van and told me that she was going home with us! My friends became Leona Williams fans in a hurry!

Dave Kirby, Leona's husband, was born in Brady, Texas. She and Dave became regulars with us and we hosted some very successful Dave Kirby Days celebration honoring Dave with many guests including Johnny Bush, Darrell McCall, Gene Watson and many others.

I started booking show dates for Leona and started handling some of her business during this time. She had been very generous to me throughout the years with her time and talents.

I have had a chance to travel to many places that I would have never seen without her help. My darling wife Charla and I spent ten wonderful days in Ireland with Leona. As a matter of fact, this interview was conducted in West Virginia while we were on the road working a PBS show with Ferlin Husky.

Leona has given me more than even she realizes. She is responsible even indirectly for much of the success in Country Music that I have enjoyed. She is also responsible for much of my happiness and I love her for it.

Tracy: How did you get started in the Country Music business?

Leroy: I got into it just like everybody else. I wrote a song that caught on. I wrote a song called, "Auctioneer". As the result of a talent contest, I got it on a record and sold a million records. "Auctioneer" and "Walk On By" became my biggest hits in the business and started the long career that I have enjoyed.

Tracy: How did you get "Walk On By"?

Leroy: It was time to record again and I was making my rounds to publishing companies in Nashville and checking with my friends and I ran across this song in Nashville. I liked it so I took it home and touched it up a little bit and it has done really well for me.

Tracy: When did you get introduced to the Grand Ole Opry?

Leroy: I joined the Grand Ole Opry in 1962. I was there a couple of years and then they made the requirement that we needed to be there for 26 Saturday nights but I could not make that commitment so I took an indefinite leave of absence.

Tracy: Are you still touring?

Leroy: Yes, we are staying very bust. We are traveling about 100,000 miles a years, not including the miles that we fly.

Tracy: What projects are you working on now?

Leroy: I have a couple of albums already cut on Sun Records. I do not have any release times on them yet. I have done an album of traditional western songs and the other is a pop style album. We also have an album in the planning but it has not taken shape at this point.

Tracy: Some of your hits have been, "Dim Dark Corner", "Wake Up Little Suzie" and "Go Away Little Girl". What was your favorite?

Leroy: I like "Wake Up Little Suzie". But some of my favorite songs and not necessarily the ones that sold the most records. My very favorite song is, "All Other Boys Are Talking", and "Just A State Of Mind". That song is on my twentieth greatest hit album. Many of the songs that I really like were never hits.

Tracy: Is the number of hit songs that you have enjoyed important to you?

Leroy: It means nothing. I have recorded about 400 songs but I think that the most important thing is to be a good entertainer and to keep your nose clean. Try to provide a good example for other people and not show up drunk or do drugs.

Tracy: You recorded a song called, "Big Wide World Of Country Music". How did you get that song?

Leroy: Before the CMA Awards became televised, I had the entire Country Music Association Award Banquet Show. I had some guests but my band and I had most of the show and that song was made for the show as the theme song.

Tracy: That was a big hit for you

Leroy: Yes. It had a lot of chart action.

Tracy: The, "Auctioneer", is the song that everyone thinks about when they hear Leroy Van Dyke. I know you wrote it but how did you come up with the idea?

Leroy: Many people do not know this but I was actually an auctioneer before I became a professional entertainer. As a matter of fact, I went to auctioneer school during the summer of my junior and senior year of college. I was then drafted into the army and I went to Korea. While I was over there I had a lot of time on my hands so I wrote the song about a second cousin of mine named Ray Sims. He is one of the best, if not the best, livestock auctioneer. That is where the song came from. It is a true story except for one word. Ray is from Missouri but the song says that he is from Arkansas. I could not think of anything to rhyme with Missouri so I put down Arkansas.

Tracy: Who were your influences in the Country Music business?

Leroy: Well I got into it on my own. I do not know of anyone who really went to bat for me. It was a combination of circumstances. I got in on my own song. I then joined the ABC television Ozark Jubilee and had it not been for that fact that I had a hit record, I would not have been able to go there. Later one, "Walk On By", was a 3 million hit record. After that I was asked to join the Grand Ole Opry. I just did it on my own.

Tracy: You have been very lucky because the fans have loved you.

Leroy: Yes. We cannot do it without the fans. I have had a very loyal group of fans that I could not get a long with out.

Tracy: Many of the older Country Music songs are coming back. Asleep At The Wheel released "Walk on By". How do you feel about that?

Leroy: Once a song becomes a standard and everyone knows the song, it is pretty much fair game. Their version did not really do anything for their career. I guess they liked my version the best. I do not take exception to that. We all cut other peoples songs. We have too. There is not enough great ones to go around. When we go in to record a new album we all go back and get some old standards and put in there. One of my favorite writers is a fellow from Texas called Floyd Tillman. I have recorded some of his songs. Almost every time that I do a show, I sing some of his.

Tracy: What do you want to be remembered by?

Leroy: I want them to remember that every time I went on stage I was prepared, I was never late and I never missed a show and I was always a professional.

Leroy always impressed me with his professionalism. He always looks great and does a great job on stage. He understands that this is a business and treats Country Music in that fashion. He enjoyed a great amount of publicity a few years ago when Country America magazine voted his song "Walk On By" as the number one Country song of all time.

I worked with Leroy in 2006, at a benefit show for Hank Thompson's long time assistant D. D. Bray. Leroy had worked with D.D. booking various shows. He came all the way from Missouri to be a part of the benefit. After I introduced him, the crowd gathered around the stage for his show. His ability as a showman is incredible and he still delivers what the audience wants.

Loretta Lynn

APRIL 2002

Tracy: One of my favorite people is with me, Loretta Lynn. You have just released a new book, "Still Woman Enough". Why did you decide to do another book?

Loretta: I may even write another one! I didn't have sense enough to tell all the things in the first one. After I read this last book, it didn't even have half of what I wanted to say in this one. The best thing that I wanted to put in there was not in there.

Tracy: Your daughters Peggy and Patsy were not very supportive of this project at first.

Loretta: No, they were not. They were worried that I may say something that would hurt their daddy. I told them that their daddy hurt himself and to not blame it on me. The movie had already shown it. Everybody knows that he drank.

Tracy: You started the book with your first memory at eleven months old. It is hard for me to believe that you could recall that moment.

Loretta: I could not either. When mommy told me how old I was, I asked her to figure that up again. It was when my grandmother died. I remember my daddy was wearing a white shirt and he was crying. He was holding me and I was crying too. My mom asked if someone had told me and I told her that she was the only one still alive that could have told me.

Tracy: In your new book, you talk about, "Coal Miner's Daughter". You mentioned that it made $64 million dollars but you did not get much of that money.

Loretta: No. I didn't get nothing. They still show it all over and sell it today. If I could tell you all about it I would, but I would get sued.

Tracy: Universal was hesitant about the project at first.

Loretta: They wanted to do it on TV and I said no. I'm not going to do a TV movie. I'm going to do a movie. So they come back to me after I said this and about ten minutes later, they said guess what we got the movie! I already knew it was going to be one because I was talking to the movie people. Universal was MCA and that is who I was recording for, so they had already been talking to me about it. I wasn't going to settle for a TV thing.

Tracy: The movie bolstered a couple of careers especially Tommy Lee Jones.

Loretta: Doo kinda got a little jealous of Tommy Lee. Poor little Tommy Lee bought him a green sweater and had his hair dyed red. He came into Vegas to meet Doo Little. Tommy walked in and he said to Doo "how do I look?" Doo kind of brushed him off. He said "how do you like my hair?" Doo said "ok". I didn't think he was ever going to talk to him. Finally, when the movie started and the kid got onto the bull-dozer and had to drive the truck and the jeep, Doo had to help him. He got over being jealous of him. That was really funny.

Tracy: It is incredible that it made that much money.

Loretta: There were too many hands in the pot.

Tracy: The movie was accurate but there were a couple things wrong that you point out including Patsy Cline's drinking.

Loretta: Patsy Cline may have had a drink or two but she did not bring beer into the hospital. Since Doo drank, I hated that stuff so I would have noticed.

Tracy: Your book also mentioned that Hollywood did not want you to use Ernest Tubb in your movie.

Loretta: They did not even want Sissy (Spacek) to do the movie. She would see me on the Tonight Show and Merv Griffith and I would tell everybody that Sissy was who I had picked out to play the part. I picked her out of a picture because I had not even seen any of her movies or anything else. She said that she got all of my eight track tapes. She said that she never had her radio on a Country station because she was a rock and roller. She was trying to decide to do the movie. She got in her car and turned on the switch. When she heard her rock station playing, "Coal Miner's Daughter", she knew that the Lord had answered her question. She fired her manager and told him she was going to play me.

Tracy: They did not want Ernest because they thought he was too Country.

Loretta: They did not want any of the Country people. They saw us as being a little too earthy. I am glad to be earthy.

Tracy: How did the movie change you?

Loretta: It didn't change me, Tracy. You know me better than that. The only way that it changed me was that it broadened my audience. I do not think that it changed me. It will take more than a movie to change me.

Tracy: Your book also talked a lot about Tammy Wynette.

Loretta: I talked to her the night before she died. She told me that she had gained a lot of weight. She was great. She was up having a good time. She told me that when she had a little more fat on her she was going to get a facelift. I told her to wait on me. The next day, Crystal Gayle called me and told me to turn on the television there are cops over at Tammy's house. I already knew that she died. I don't know what happened.

Tracy: You mentioned that she never found her true love.

Loretta: She loved George Jones always. I will believe that she always did. When they were first married it was really neat. She really loved him she just could not take the drinking.

Tracy: You wrote about Doo and his business ventures like the Loretta Lynn Longhorn Rodeo. Some of those ventures were not very successful.

Loretta: I was so happy going out making a little money and then I would come home and he would have spent three times more than what I had made. He had that rodeo for ten years and it was more of a heartache than anything I had ever done.

Tracy: You didn't even have a band at that time.

Loretta: No. In fact, I asked him if when he rides out on that arena if he has the best horse that money could buy. He said you bet I do and that is the way it is going stay. I told him that when I left that weekend, I was going to have a band. He said no your not and I said just watch and see. I got one too. It was not a very good band but I got one. Doyle and Teddy quit the road and I took their band on the road for about six months and then I got a band called, "The Coal Miners".

Tracy: You include the Wilburn Brothers in "Still Woman Enough" although you left them out of "Coal Miners Daughter."

Loretta: I have always loved them.

Tracy: They were good to your career and you were good to theirs.

Loretta: Doyle was a good manager besides just being a singer. Teddy looked over the music more. Doyle was the one who really put the business together.

Tracy: Teddy had a small part in your great classic "Don't Come Home A Drinking."

Loretta: My little sister Peggy Sue was a writing on this song and it didn't make too much sense the way that she had it. She had something like "You Come Home Last Night As Drunk As You Could Be" or something like that. Anyway, me and her took whatever she wrote and got with Teddy Wilburn and he helped us with the song. I think Peggy had a little bit of trouble with her husband drinking and I did too, so we didn't have too much trouble with it, but Teddy did help us a little.

Tracy: You actually started before there were many females in the business.

Loretta: There was a lot of females in the business, but I was the first to step out and say hey its going to be like this and I think the others kind of fell in line. They were all in Nashville when I got there, but they didn't work clubs. I worked all the club dates. I had to or me and my kids would of starved.

Tracy: Texas was important to your early career.

Loretta: Texas is actually what fed me. They played "Don't Come Home A Drinkin'" and "You Ain't Woman Enough" on their pop stations. They sent me from one club to the other one and they didn't pay me a lot of money, but they fed me. So I lay it all on to Texas. Any time Texas needs me, they can holler for me.

Tracy: There was a lot of forgiveness in your book. You talk a lot about Doo and his drinking and womanizing but you always forgave him.

Loretta: Now that he has passed away, none of that means anything to me. I cannot remember anything that bothered me that much.

Tracy: It was hard on you but it was also hard on him

Loretta: He really seemed to enjoy it then!

Tracy: I meant not having you around (Tracy and Loretta chuckle). The 1990's brought you a lot of heartache as Doo became ill.

Loretta: That was the worst time of my life. I do not ever want to go through that again.

Tracy: After Doo passed away and you were deciding what to do for the rest of your career, the Opry was a big help for you.

Loretta: I knew that I had to do something. I was losing it. I was running is what I was doing. I thought that I had just been a way for a few weeks and my friend Rosie said that I hadn't worked in nearly a year. I was so confused. It was time for me to get back to work and I started back at the Opry.

Tracy: Being a member of the Opry has to be a highlight of your career.

Loretta: That has been so many years ago. Naturally, it's a big thing for me. Knowing its there and everything, but it don't seem like it used to be since they left the old Grand Ole Opry. To me that is where it should be now.

Tracy: You are now working a lot out on the road.

Loretta: This year is really going to be rough. Next year I am going to pick what I want to do and not be gone from my ranch as much. I want to do a lot of stuff

Tracy: Your new Coal Miners Daughter Museum is fabulous.

Loretta: It really is. I kept everything. We have put a lot more stuff in it since you were here last. You will have to come back.

Tracy: You have so much more to do in your career but are you satisfied with your position in Country Music today?

Loretta: I am. I am not worried about what the rest of them are doing. I am just doing what I want to do. That is what I have always done so I do not have to worry about it. People spend too much time worrying about it and don't spend anytime working on their career.

Loretta Lynn is one of my favorite people. When I started working at KNEL in 1986, I started ending every one of my shows with a Loretta Lynn song. I still do that to this day as I sign off.

I first met Loretta in Branson. She was working the Lowe Theater on the 76 Strip. I was given a backstage pass through her management. I waited in the small backstage area of the theater while Loretta was preparing for the show in her bus. It seems like I was there for an hour and I was so nervous! Peggy Lynn was backstage as well as a couple of others. We all exchanged small talk and then the back door opened. I looked up as Loretta appeared in a beautiful green dress. She looked like an angel. The road manager directed her to where I was sitting on the old couch. She came over and introduced herself as I struggled to rise up to meet one of my all time idols. She smiled and stuck out her hand and said "I'm Loretta." Before I even thought, I said "you don't have to tell me who you are." She was gracious and I was on Cloud Nine.

Since that time, I have attended dozens of shows and have enjoyed nearly that many visits with her in Texas, Tennessee, Nevada and Oklahoma. Loretta's assistants Tim Cobb and Rosie Hamilton have always been extremely kind to me as well.

Loretta actually lives in Hurricane Mills, Tennessee, near her old plantation home. She owns the entire town. Loretta gave me an awesome tour of her home a couple of years ago. I was in Nashville for Fan Fair and decided to drive out to her museum. While visiting the museum, Rosie approached me and told me that Loretta wanted me to come to the house. She was going through her Indian Arrowhead collection and several unique rocks that she had found on the property. Loretta was doing this while cooking a large pot of beans and homemade bread. She has an incredible home and gave me the grand tour. I was amazed that the only item relating to music was a red, white and blue guitar that Buck Owens gave to her sitting next to her bed in her bedroom. I relayed the story to my wife and she replied that everyone didn't need to have posters and music items scattered throughout their home-especially if you had a huge museum like Loretta does just across her creek. I really enjoyed the afternoon and Loretta was a gracious host.

Loretta was one of the first artists to donate something to the Heart of Texas Country Music Museum. As a matter of fact, she was the first artist to record a promotional announcement for the museum. She has been very gracious with her time and talents towards our cause.

There are very few icons in the business. Loretta has become an icon and deserves all the accolades and recognition that she receives in this industry. It is truly an honor to consider her a friend.

May 18, 1999

Tracy: I am talking with one of the greats in Country Music, Lynn Anderson. How are you Lynn?

Lynn: I am doing great, I just got back in town from doing a few shows.

Tracy: Your career started quite a few years ago at a disc jockey convention didn't it?

Lynn: I was a mere baby. My mom Liz Anderson got a recording contract. Her vocal performances and her song writing talent came to the attention of Chet Atkins so she got a record contract with RCA and I went a long just to see the sites and sing harmony. I had been singing harmony with mom all my life. Nothing sounds better. We were the Judd's before the Judd's. So they heard me sing and asked if I wanted to make a record too. I was just 16. I literally had to call to see if I could get a couple days off of high school.

Tracy: That was for Chart Records right?

Lynn: Yes, it was, very good. I am glad you have been doing your homework.

Tracy: Your parents were very influential in your early stages of your career.

Lynn: Mother wrote quite a few of the songs on Chart Records. Oh, I have good news and I bet you do not even know this unless mommy told you but CBS/Columbia called me just a few days ago about putting a package together of some old stuff of mine and I said why don't you put "Rocky Top" in there. "Rocky Top" has not been re-released for about thirty years and they said they did not own it and I said, yes you do because I sold it to you! So the guy called me real excited last week and they are not only putting one, but three new Lynn Anderson CD's. Two of them will be CBS and the other one will be just Chart Records and that is the old stuff like, "Rocky Top". "Rocky Top" has not been available to buy for at least 25 years. They asked my mother to write the liner notes because she wrote half the song.

Tracy: Was "Mother May I" a Chart Records song?

Lynn: I cannot remember if that was Chart or Columbia but I need to find out because it would be a great song to put in there. It was a neat record to do.

Tracy: You also worked for Lawrence Welk. That had to be very interesting.

Lynn: It was. At that time, my one song a week was the only Country Western Music on television. We were Country when Country wasn't cool. Mr. Welk was trying to do something for everybody and he saw the rising popularity of Country Music and his son had a crush on me. Lawrence's son and a couple of other business people went to Nashville to scout out somebody Country to use on the show. They invited Charley Pride, another artist and myself to try out for the show. My mom and dad, Lawrence Welk and his wife were determined that Larry Jr., and I were a pair and that we should run off together.

Tracy: It just didn't work out

Lynn: To this day he still races cutting horses and every time I go to Fort Worth, and race in the National Champion Races in December I get to see Larry Jr., once a year.

Tracy: 1971 had to be one of the highlights of your career when "Rose Garden" was released. It was a song that is still played all over today. It was one of those career records for you.

Lynn: Absolutely. It is one of those songs that come along once in a lifetime. No one could have predicted just how popular that song was going to become. It changed my life.

Tracy: Did you know that it was going to be such a hit when you recorded it?

Lynn: We had a real good idea that we had a number one Country hit. It was one of those special evenings when music and everyone clicked. When the recording session was done, nobody went home. They called all their buddies and told them to come over and hear the recording. We stayed for hours and listened to it over and over. I have never seen that happen before or since. Nobody could imagine what the song would do. It was and still is such a monster! I feel fortunate to have recorded "Rose Garden".

Tracy: Are you working on any new recordings?

Lynn: We are actually working on a new project. We are going to do one on songs about roses in conjunction with the American Rose Society. There are a lot of songs about roses. They will all sound Country by the time I get through with them

Tracy: You have had a phenomenal career and it is something to be proud of and I know that you are. You career has been great and you always seem like such a happy person and I admire that about you.

Lynn: I try to have a good time. I have been real lucky in my life and I really think it would be dumb of me to act like I am not a lucky kid.

Lynn Anderson enjoyed much attention in 2006, as Martina McBride hit with "I Never Promised You A Rose Garden." The song was played on radio all over the Country and it brought attention to the songs original singer Lynn Anderson. In a few interviews, Lynn acknowledged Martina's recording and seemed to be happy that the song had gained another life with a new generation of Country Music fans.

Unfortunately, the last few years have not been very kind to Lynn. She has been arrested for drunken driving and even shoplifting. It does surprise me, because every time that I have been with Lynn has been very joyful and happy times.

I also understand that everybody has their own demons that others may never see. My favorite recordings that Lynn made were her Chart recordings. I have long appreciated Liz Anderson's records and she was a great influence on her daughter.

Lynn's mom actually set this interview up for me. Liz and Casey Anderson are two wonderful people who we have enjoyed spending time with on various occasions-including eating a delicious ham meal and pecan pie at their Nashville home! They have both enjoyed a good recording career. Liz and Casey were even on our very first album project "Heart of Texas Country" that was created to help raise money for the Heart of Texas Country Music Museum.

Mark Chestnut

September 27, 1990

Tracy: Mark Chestnut is working Texas The Club tonight in San Angelo, Texas. The club scene is nothing new to you.

Mark: I have been playing in clubs and beer joints around Southeast Texas for about 12 years. I had put out eight independent singles that I recorded in San Antonio and Houston. We did the best we could with the singles and eventually a friend of mine knew a promoter with MCA Records in Houston so he sent him one of my records. He brought it to Tony Brown in MCA Nashville and sent a bunch of people to see me. This took about a year for it to happen.

Tracy: Was it always your dream to become a Country Music singer?

Mark: Yes, that is all I have ever wanted to do. I have been singing for the biggest part of my life. Country Music has always been a part of my life.

Tracy: George Jones is a big fan of yours. Tell us about that relationship.

Mark: I do not know if he is a big fan of mine but he is a good friend. We have been friends for about six or eight months now and I am a fan of his. I have always listened to his music and have tried to sing just like him my whole life. To be able to hang out with him and talk with him and sing with him is just great. We have some shows booked with him and Conway Twitty that we are going to do in December.

Tracy: He is from the same area that you are.

Mark: He is from Beaumont, Texas. We have even played in some of the same places just 30 years apart. It is ironic that we both started out in some of the same clubs and honkytonks.

Tracy: I understand that you were also influenced by the music of Hank Williams.

Mark: Hank Williams was one of the first singers that I have ever heard. He had such a great style and his writing is still so powerful today.

Tracy: You have a new album coming out next week

Mark: It will be out October 2. I am really happy with it. It has ten really good songs on it. We recorded the album in March and at first MCA wanted to wait until January to put it out and I was unhappy about that but the single has done so well so fast so they decided they would go a head and put it out because the retailers were screaming. People were coming in wanting the album. They purchased the single but they wanted the whole album.

Tracy: I love the song, "Too Cold At Home". How did you come up with that song?

Mark: A friend of mine named Bobby Harden wrote that song. I met him about four years in Nashville. I was going back and forth to Nashville quite a bit trying to work out a deal. I was doing demos, trying to put my foot in the door. I met Bobby and he played that song for me one night and he said that he would hold it for me and it would be my first hit. He was right. That is the song that got me the record and it is the song that became the first hit. I am going to listen to him real close from now on.

Tracy: Do you have any other songs on the project that you are extremely fond of?

Mark: I have a new single that will be out before too long. It will be called, "Your Love Is A Miracle". It is an up-tempo song and I believe that people will like it. We have a lot of good songs on the album and I am anxious for people to pick one up and let us know what they like.

Tracy: The city of Beaumont is very proud of you. They gave you a key to the city not too long ago.

Mark: Yes they did. I do have a key to the city. I don't know what you do with it!

Tracy: What are you looking forward to in the future?

Mark: I want to keep putting out good records, keep doing good shows and make some good money. I want to keep playing Country Music the best I can. I do not want to get off into the weird stuff. I love traditional Country Music and hope that I can make a complete career out of performing it for my friends and fans.

I really enjoyed hanging out with Mark Chestnut on that cool September evening in San Angelo, Texas. He was in the very beginning of his career and was working on his direction in the industry. The crowd was there on the strength of his first single "Too Cold At Home." The song was one of the highlights of his career and promised to give us another true traditionalist.

Mark was great about delivering some hard Country songs, but it was unfortunate that his biggest traditional album was not released until he no longer had a recording contract in 2006. The major labels do not want to hear Traditional Country and the majority of the artists can not force steel guitar and fiddles on the executives.

Looking back, it was great to hang out with and see Mark in the beginning of his career. The cold beer was not bad either!

Tracy: I am visiting with Mary Reeves, wife of the legendary late Jim Reeves. How are you doing tonight?

Mary: I am doing fine.

Tracy: Jim started out in radio at the age of 10.

Mary: Yes. That was in Panola County, Texas. He knew how to play guitar so he played lead guitar with a band. They had their first radio debut on KRMD in Shreveport, Louisiana. He did not even know that he could sing at that time.

Tracy: He also worked as a Disc Jockey.

Mary: Yes, but he was a baseball player in high school and college before that. He had a baseball scholarship to the University of Texas. He only went for six weeks because he felt that he should do something more positive for the war effort during that time. It was 1942. He went to Houston and worked in the shipyards and also played semi pro ball while he was there. While he was playing, the St. Louis Cardinal team scout saw him and signed him to the St. Louis Cardinal's farm team in Lynchburg, Virginia. Jim got hurt playing baseball. We married in September 1947, and he did not have a job. He decided he would try out for an announcer's job. He got the job at KGRI in Henderson, Texas.

Tracy: How did a lady from Tenaha, Texas, meet Jim Reeves?

Mary: We moved to Marshall, Texas, when I was ten. We had to go somewhere that we could make a living. All of us kids had to go to work. My father died when I was nine years old. I went to a Country Music dance in my hometown and I had a date with a guy that had gone to school with Jim. Jim was also at the dance and he was by himself. He saw this guy that he knew and he came over and I was introduced to Jim.

Tracy: How did Jim get his start with the Louisiana Hayride?

Mary: He went to KWKH in Shreveport, and the Louisiana Hayride as an announcer. First he was a disc jockey and had a show in the evenings. He then was an announcer for the Louisiana Hayride. They never would let him sing, but one night someone did not show up for the show so Jim was able to sing. "Mexican Joe" had already been released and was the number one Country record at that time. This happened in 1953. Billy Walker was already a star on the Louisiana Hayride and Columbia Records and he had recorded "Mexican Joe" too. Jim was introducing Billy

Walker singing, "Mexican Joe". Jim finally got to sing himself and people recognized that, this is who they were hearing and they wanted to hear more of him. He encored six times that night. After that night, he went on the road and two years later, in 1955, he joined the Opry.

Tracy: How many hit records did Jim have?

Mary: He had, "Mexican Joe, "Billy Bayou", "Bimbo", "Home", "My Lips Are Sealed", among others and then he had the blockbuster hit, "Four Walls". He recorded, "Four Walls" in 1957, which was his first really big hit on a major label.

Tracy: What was his biggest hit?

Mary: "He'll Have To Go", was his biggest hit in the States. He sold three million records. The biggest record that he had overseas was, "I Love You Because".

Tracy: I read that Jim Reeves is still extremely popular in South America.

Mary: He is. In Columbia he is popular and in a lot of other countries in South America. His origin is from Holland, Norway, Belgian and Europe. He is extremely popular there as well.

Tracy: Jim was also featured in a movie titled "Kimberly Jim". When did he do that?

Mary: He did that in 1963 in South Africa. Chet Atkins, Bobby Bare, and Floyd Cramer did a very extensive tour of South Africa in 1962. He had 22 of the top 50 records while he was there. He was extremely popular and still is. They wanted him to do a movie so we went over and did it. It was an instant success. He was killed before the movie was released here in the States.

Tracy: I am sure that you remember July 31, 1964 very well. That is the day we lost your husband in a plane wreck.

Mary: Yes, it was near the airport here in Nashville. His piano player Dean Manual was with him. They had been to Arkansas to look at some real estate that Jim had thought about investing in. He was almost to the airport, it was raining and the plane went down. Nobody knows why or what happened. It was declared as a pilot error and Jim was the pilot. They were the only two in that accident. A lot of people think that Patsy Cline and Hawkshaw Hawkins were in there too but that was at another time.

Tracy: Right after that, they had one of the biggest searches in Nashville ever. Marty Robbins, Chet Atkins, Eddie Arnold, Ernest Tubb and about 700 volunteers helped search for him. I have heard a lot of people comment that if it was not for you, and your love and support through this, Jim Reeves might not be as big a star as he is today. You helped to keep his music alive.

Mary: That is true. He was just beginning to peak. He had not reached his height yet. I suppose looking back, I knew that. Jim did a lot of recording and we were fortunate to be able to salvage so much of that.

Tracy: You continued to release electric transcripts that Jim recorded as demos.

Mary: Yes and we still have some more. They are really good and I am going to try to get them out sometime this year.

Tracy: Jim had over 45 top ten songs.

Mary: I think so but I am not too sure of that. I really never worried too much about that and kept up with figures. I just know the great songs that Jim had.

Tracy: How did you get Deborah Allen and Jim together? Did you have anything to do with that or was that RCA?

Mary: That was my idea. We needed something now, something living that disc jockeys could play and talk about. All along I knew certain songs would make good duets. She was very good and good and Country and that is what I wanted her to be. I had not even met Deborah before we decided to do it. I told the guy who worked for me to find me somebody and he did. Deborah did a wonderful job.

Tracy: What about the Patsy Cline and Jim Reeves Remembering Album?

Mary: We did two of those. That was my idea as well. All the time, I knew that he recorded five songs that she had recorded. I thought to myself that at the right time, I would suggest to them that we should consider putting them together. You had to do it at the right time because you are fooling around with talent. A lot of people have different ideas and you do not want to offend anyone. I talked to RCA and they thought that I was nuts at first but they did think that it was a great idea and it worked beautifully. Only two of the songs would work putting them together. We split a deal with MCA and RCA so there were two LP's that came about because of those two songs. We have them in CD's now at the museum.

Tracy: You are running a museum in memory of Jim Reeves. Please tell us about that and what you have.

Mary: I always wanted to do it. I bought the piece of property that I always wanted in 1981 and we have been there since. We have our bedroom furniture from our house and the original radio station equipment from Henderson, Texas. We have his old records, guitars, costumes, Big Blue-his touring bus, his Eldorado Cadillac and a lot of pictures. We are very happy to have people from all over the world come and visit. I am there most every day because I enjoy it so much.

Tracy: You opened a mail order department for Jim Reeves Records.

Mary: I am glad you mentioned that. We do have mail order service. They do not make anymore of the LP's but they do make them in CD's and cassettes. I have some LP's, eight tracks, CD's, and cassettes because I have been buying them throughout the years and putting them in my warehouse.

Tracy: What do you think Jim Reeves would like to be known for?

Mary: I think that he would like to be known as a Country entertainer even though some of his records did go pop. In England they do not make any distinction between Country and pop. Over there it is all one music. He was one of the great there as well. I think that he would want to me known as someone who brought great pleasure to people.

Mary Reeves devoted her life to promoting her late husband. I can not recall any one person that dedicated as much time and effort to their spouse's career. Mary remarried but because of her devotion to Jim, many did not even realize that she was another man's wife.

On one of our bus tours to Nashville, I presented Mary an award from the Country Music Association of Texas. Bud Fisher asked me to present it to Mary on behalf of his organization. Although her walls were lined with awards, she was very appreciative of the gesture.

I remember looking at Big Blue, the Jim Reeves tour bus that day. I could have never imagined that one day the bus (and several other items in the museum) would be a part of our Heart of Texas Country Music Museum.

After Mary became unable to make her own decisions, the Jim Reeves estate was sold to Ed Gregory. Gregory was the owner of United Shows of America. I could write a book about this situation alone. He purchased the estate, which included virtually everything including the rights to Jim's songs, for a $7.3 million unsecured promissory note. The only problem seemed to be that he still owed $6.5 million to the estate at the time he filed for bankruptcy protection. Gregory then passed away on April 11, 2004. There are still lawsuits over the Reeves estate.

I attended one of the bankruptcy auctions on June 16, 2001, with express interest in brining Big Blue back to Texas. After a bidding battle (that I still believe was a little shady at best), we became the owner of the bus for $3,000.00. Big Blue did not have a transmission or motor, so after another $3,100.00 towing bill, it arrived in Brady and its new home.

Jim Reeves is making more money today than at any time when he was alive. His song royalties bring in over $400,000.00 per year. It is unfortunate that he did not live to see the vast impact that he would have on Country Music. I even question if his impact would have been as large if he did not perish in the plane crash. On many occasions, death makes a star even bigger than they were in life.

Mel Tillis

JANUARY 9, 1998

Tracy: I am visiting with Mr. Mel Tillis at Billy Bob's. Mel, tell us how you got interested in Country Music.

Mel: I remember when I was a kid, we got an old radio and this was in the late 30's. It was an old Magestic radio and we would get a Philco battery and I would pick up the Grand Old Opry. I use to listen to Roy Acuff, Bill Monroe, Bob Wills and all those guys and I was real interested in that kind of music and I have been interested every since.

Tracy: Webb Pierce was instrumental in you career also.

Mel: I went to Nashville in 1956 and they told me that they did not want any stuttering singers so I became a songwriter. Webb was one of the first ones to record my songs. The first one he recorded was "I'm Tired". It went #2 in the charts and then he recorded, "I Ain't Never' "Honkytonk Song" and "Tupelo County Jail". I was in Eureka Springs, Arkansas, visiting an antique store today and I found some old albums that I had some songs on. Kenny Rogers', "Ruby (Don't Take Your Love To Town)". I found some albums from Webb. For the first ten years of my career, I mainly did songwriting.

Tracy: You also give Red Foley credit for much of your career.

Mel: He was something else. He was my inspiration. He was my mentor. I loved his style.

Tracy: Branson has really been a big part of your life during the last few years.

Mel: It took me off the road for a while. It was incredible for not only me, but for so many of our fellow artists in the business. Now, I will go out from January through March. I have a pretty full schedule. We go to Reno, Connecticut.

Tracy: I know that you enjoy going out on the road to break from your regular routine.

Mel: I have always done a lot of touring in Texas. We play a lot of music and do not have to do much talking. When I do a show, they want to hear me talk, tell some stories, anecdotes, and that sort of thing. But at Billy Bob's and clubs like this, they want to dance. That is the reason I like coming to Texas is because Texans like to dance.

Tracy: You have been to many dance halls in Texas.

Mel: I have been to them all, several times over.

Tracy: One of my favorite songs, is "Burning Memories"

Mel: That is a good one. That one was recorded by Ray Price.

Tracy: There is a little story behind that song.

Mel: I was out one day rabbit hunting with Ray and I was humming the song and he wanted to know what it was. I told him that I was working on the song and he said that he liked it. He was going to the studio the next day and he asked me to bring it to the studio. I went home and finished the song and then I went to the Columbia studio. Ray was recording and asked me if I brought the song. At the time, Ray was rehearsing a song by my buddy Wayne Walker. Wayne was a great writer and was Ernest Tubb's son in law. Ray wanted to hear the song so I sang it for him and he said, "man I like that". He quit rehearsing my buddy's song and he recorded my song which was "Burning Memories". I felt badly because I had knocked my buddy's song out of the session. I said Wayne, I tell you what I am going to do, I am going to give you half of that song since I knocked yours out of the session. He said no, I am not going to do that, I am going to give you half of mine. I asked which one and he said I just had it recorded by Ernest Tubb, it is called, "Thought's Of A Fool". So I put his name on, "Burning Memories", and he put my name on, "Thoughts Of A Fool". A few years ago "Thoughts Of A Fool" was recorded by George Strait and it sold 8 or 9 million copies. It all evened out.

Tracy: It is amazing that a song that you did not even write gained you a substantial amount.

Mel: Wayne did pretty good on "Burning Memories", too.

Tracy: You are very busy with your theater in Branson, Missouri. What made you chose to have a theater?

Mel: I have been around for a while, 41 years and as you know, every little doggie has his day. Radio was getting stale so they changed it up and every generation has its input and I could see the writing on the wall and I did not want to go out to pasture so I moved to Branson and opened me a theater. My fans that I have been able to attract over the years come to Branson to see me now. My season in Branson is about 9 months and I take off for three months but I do not actually take off, I go and spend about 20 days on the road, January, February and March. That is what brings me to Fort Worth tonight.

Tracy: Your daughter Pam is going to be doing some shows with you this year.

Mel: Pam is going to be with us every Tuesday starting in April and my son is coming over from Nashville. He is a songwriter for Madonna for her Country division in Nashville. He will be coming to Branson one week out of the month. My daughter

Carrie April just finished her schooling down in Birmingham, Alabama, at Stamford University She sings opera. She sings on the show and gets standing ovations every time she sings. All the kids will be performing at the Mel Tillis Theater and we are going to have a big time next year.

Tracy: What does the future hold for Mel Tillis?

Mel: It looks like I am going to be at the Mel Tillis Theater for a while but I enjoy working and I will probably doing some television shows and maybe some movies. I got a new gospel album that I am working on called, "A Father's Son". I am working on that one and just a lot of things are happening. I also have a new album that is coming out, it is called, "Old Dogs'. It is with Bobby Bear, Waylon Jennings and Jerry Reed. There are twenty songs on the album. You will have to listen to it before you play it on KNEL because some of the songs are risqué. There are some really good songs on it. Next year at the Mel Tillis Theater, we will be doing the first half of our show with my small band and then we will have an upright bass and will be doing some old Country songs the way we use to do them. The last half of the show, we will be doing, "Rowing on the River". We are going to have an old paddle boat on stage with banjos, dancer and singers. I am going to be the captain. The music industry has been good to me.

Mel Tillis is a true icon in the Country Music business. He was actually the first major entertainer that I ever had the opportunity to meet and interview. I was serving in the capacity as Area VII FFA President at the San Antonio Livestock Show and doing some reporting for KNEL Radio in 1988. I was seventeen years old and Mel was headlining the Livestock Show and Radio that night.

With recorder in hand, I approached the bus and asked one of the musicians about interviewing Mel-never even thinking about scheduling such an event in advance. They realized that I was a very inexperienced interviewer, but I was very persistent. They told me to wait around the bus. If Mel had time, he would grant me the interview after the show. I waited for about three hours and they knew that I was not going to leave until the bus left, so I was ushered in for a "quick interview." Mel was extremely gracious to me. The first thing that he did was offer me a Miller Light beer. Already nervous, I immediately told him that I was too young. I was then so upset with myself for making such a statement. I wanted him to think I was so mature and serious about the interview.

I brought hundreds of fans to the Mel Tillis Theater in Branson since that first interview and always spent a few minutes backstage with him. He even gave us a great pair of boots for the museum. I loved the early days stories of his career. He told me one time that one of his first major tours was with Kitty Wells and Johnny Wright. It was a percentage date and they worked a string of one nighters. It was a hard tour and at the end of the shows, the money was to be divided. When Johnny came to Mel, he handed Mel a bill instead of the cash. Mel said that was the last time he worked any of those percentage shows!

Mel is still one of the greatest acts in the business and a perfect person for my first interview opportunity.

JUNE 1998

Tracy: When did your career begin?

Mickey: It began in Texas in 1971. I opened a nightclub in Pasadena, Texas. I struggled in the music industry for many years before opening Gilley's.

Tracy: Gilley's started out as a small establishment.

Mickey: It seated about 750 people. With all the success I was having and with the television show, the recordings and traveling with Conway Twitty and Loretta Lynn, the club began to grow. We then installed a mechanical bull. According to Guiness's Book of World Record's, it became the worlds largest honky-tonk.

Tracy: "Room Full of Roses" really helped your career as well as your success at Gilley's.

Mickey: Absolutely. I recorded it in 1973, but it did not become number one until 1974. It was released in the local markets in 1973 and then I leased it to Playboy Record Division in 1974. They are the ones who helped make it number one across the nation.

Tracy: You were actually recording before "Room Full of Roses."

Mickey: I had a local hit in the Houston market called, "Is It Wrong For Loving You". I also had a song called, "Lonely Wine", in 1963-1964. It was ten years until I had a hit nationally, and that was "Room Full of Roses".

Tracy: You received many awards for "Room Full of Roses."

Mickey: I received five awards. I received every kind of award you can think of. It was the beginning of a lot of recognition for Mickey Gilley.

Tracy: You helped to start the Urban Cowboy age of Country Music.

Mickey: Actually, my business partner installed a mechanical bull at Gilley's and it was a rodeo-training device. It was never meant to be in an entertainment establishment. After he installed it, things really began to turn around. We could have never imagined what was to become of the nightclub and the industry as a whole.

Tracy: Do you think it had an impact on your recordings?

Mickey: I think that the fact that John Travolta came down and danced on the dance floor at Gilley's changed things into a different direction. I met producer Jim Ed Norman who recorded "Stand By Me". After that happened, I had nine number one songs. That was quite a string of hits in the 1980's. The movie happened and nearly overnight things began to change for myself and Johnny Lee and the Country Music business.

Tracy: Why did you decide to move to Branson, Missouri?

Mickey: My recordings started slowing down and my business partner and I got into a squabble over Gilley's and how dirty it was. I asked him to fix the club. My goal was to fix it up and play Gilley's on the weekends and stay home. Things did not work out that way. Branson has been a blessing in disguise because I have my own theater. We have been doing about 700-900 seats a night and I cannot complain about it. The main thing is being able to entertain a smaller crowd. My steel guitar player Joey Riley is great to work with. He is also from Texas. We have a really good time together. The people really seem to like it when he slams me. I am starting to promote him a little bit. I am putting him on the billboards with me. A lot of people do not know that we have comedy.

Tracy: You still fly home to Texas nearly every week.

Mickey: I only do six shows a week. I work Thursday afternoons and then I get on my plane and fly to Texas. I am home Thursday and Friday nights and work Saturday's. I really enjoy aviation so for me it works.

Tracy: You have had a couple of troubling aviation experiences lately.

Mickey: Yes, I broke an oil line. Oil started spewing out of my left engine so I had to make a landing. I made an announcement over the radio and the guy on the other end thought I was practicing. I told him it was real. It was a scary time, but I pulled through and even got a little publicity out of it!

Tracy: What does the future hold for you?

Mickey: I am just enjoying what I am doing. I have a great time doing it. I love the fans. I sign autographs at every show except Thursday afternoons. The only downfall is that I am not at home in Texas. I work out in the mornings and play golf everyday. Mickey Gilley is truly enjoying a great life.

Mickey and his former partner Sherwood Cryer had a very successful relationship for many years at Gilley's in Pasadena. They made a lot of money and all the greats played the historic club. In the end, there were several lawsuits and a fire or two to destroy their part-

nership and friendship as well. In this business, the dissolution of friendships and business relationships is often a very common occurrence.

Mickey is one of the few acts that has remained a constant in Branson. He told me one time that he did not want the biggest theater in Branson. It was too difficult to try and keep a huge theater operating. He has been very successful in his theater and has one of the best shows in Branson.

Mickey understands that he has to do more than stand on the stage and sing the hits. He uses Joey Riley in a major way at the theater. They work off of each other and tell the same jokes over and over again. The way that the audience sees them is fresh every night. They have a winning combination.

Interviewing Mickey Gilley backstage at his Branson theater.

Moe Bandy

JANUARY 24, 1998

Tracy: I am visiting with Moe Bandy. Moe how are you doing?

Moe: I am doing great and looking forward to a great show tonight.

Tracy: It is good to see you back in Texas.

Moe: I was actually raised in San Antonio, Texas. I am away from my other stomping grounds but I am close to home.

Tracy: How did you get involved in the Country Music business?

Moe: I was actually born in Meridian, Mississippi-the home of Jimmie Rodgers. My dad plays guitar and sings and my mother plays piano and sings so I was raised around it. My dad had a band called "The Mission City Playboys" and they played for dances all over the area. I would do some work with them and by the time I was a teenager, I formed my own band. My parents love Country Music and played around this part of the country for years.

Tracy: You also had some other jobs during this time.

Moe: The band was primarily working on the weekends and we weren't making much money. I had to have a regular job as well. I was a sheet metal worker for over ten years while trying to break into the business.

Tracy: When did you start your recording career?

Moe: I met up with Ray Baker when he was hunting in Texas. I went up to his motel room and handed him a tape of some demos that I had made. I was recording some through out the 1960's but in 1973, I cut, "I Just Started Hating Cheating Songs Today". We had pitched our music to every label in Nashville and had been turned down. So, we decided to finance the record ourselves. It hit and it just went from there. It was on GRC which was a small label in Atlanta and then Columbia picked it up. I then signed a recording contract with Columbia.

Tracy: How do you explain your style of Country Music? Is it more traditional?

Moe: Yes, I have always done more of the traditional kind of Country Music. That is how I was raised living in Texas. In fact, when my first record hit, it was a time when

Country Music was going into strings and all that. I featured twin fiddles and steel guitars on my records. I wanted my music to sound like the music that I grew up with down in Texas. It kind of brought it back to a bigger audience, at least for me it did.

Tracy: You have has so many hits but one of my favorite songs is, "Someday Soon".

Moe: Ian Tyson wrote that song and Judy Collins recorded it many years ago. I was the first guy to cut it and then Suzy Bogus cut it. It is a song that really fit my style. That song has been really good to me.

Tracy: The 1980's were a very good time for your career.

Moe: It was a good time. So much of Country Music coming out of Nashville at that time was more of the pop kind of Country. We hit with some of those hard driving cheating and drinking songs like "Honky Tonk Amnesia" "It Was Always So Easy To Find An Unhappy Woman" and "Hank Williams, You Wrote My Life."

Tracy: You also teamed up with Joe Stampley for some hits.

Moe: Joe and I had a good run as well. We cut quite a few novelty songs like "Just Good Old Boys" "Boys Night Out" "Daddy's Honky Tonk" "Holding The Bag" and of course "Where's The Dress" which got us into quite a bit of trouble with a guy in England. It was good combination and we had some great times on the road working together. We still get together from time to time and it is like a family reunion on stage.

Tracy: What is the difference between your stage shows and the dance hall shows.

Moe: We do the records and I have a really good band so I like to show them off. We just like to put on a show. We like to keep it where they can dance if they want to. The concert shows usually feature more comedy and maybe even the band more. At the dances, I usually try to keep them on the dance floor.

Tracy: Why did you choose to move to Branson, Missouri?

Moe: It was an opportunity for me to do what I do every single day in one place. I did not have to travel so I could finally have a life and be able to put my stuff in a drawer. For so long, I carried it in a suitcase. Branson gives the entertainers a chance for people to travel and see us. It is a great family town.

Tracy: There are a lot of people continually coming to Branson. Do you feel that the town is going to continue to grow and prosper?

Moe: I think that Branson is going to get bigger and bigger. It is growing stronger every day. We got a bad rap a few years a go because of the traffic but now we have roads all over the place. We are trying to make it as easy as possible for people to come and see the shows and enjoy the great atmosphere of a beautiful part of our country.

Tracy: Do you have any recordings planned in the future?

Moe: I cut some things not too long ago in Nashville. It is looking good. We should be releasing sometime this spring.

Tracy: What does the future hold for Moe Bandy?

Moe: I want to stay in Branson. I have really had fun. This is our eighth year and I want to record and travel three months out of the year like we are doing. I was on the road for so long that it is still fun to get in the bus and travel somewhere. Working Branson gives me the opportunity to do both. I just want to keep entertaining as long as someone want to come and see me.

I have probably seen Moe Bandy twenty times and have enjoyed his show on each and every occasion. I always include him in our Branson packages. Our travelers enjoy his performances and Moe is gracious enough to spend a little "extra" time with our people.

I booked Moe for the first time in 2006, at the Llano Country Opry. We were not prepared for the response that we received. He sold out both shows three weeks before his scheduled appearance. We turned away a couple of hundred people. He was immediately booked for 2007, and sold out two more shows when the weather was awful in Texas.

During his 2006 performance for us, I brought an old stage suit for him to autograph. It was a bright red suit with lots of embeleshments all over the suit and large horse heads. The suit was worn on one of his album covers. I found it on the internet auction site ebay and continually bid until I bought it. Ironically, Moe did not tell me until a year later that he was the other guy bidding on the suit against me. I just outbid him! He had loaned the suit to someone down in Texas and they never returned it. They then sold it without him knowing anything about it until a fan brought it to his attention after seeing it on ebay. He told me that he was proud that I outbid him and had the suit. He is pleased that it is now on display at the Heart of Texas Country Music Museum.

I think that part of Moe's success is his accessibility to the fans. He loves to spend time with those people that have made his career. He never leaves until the last fan walks away.

1993

Tracy: I am speaking today with one of the great legends of Country Music. She had her first hit song in 1936, Patsy Montana. How are you Patsy?

Patsy: I am just fine.

Tracy: You were telling me that you just completed a long tour.

Patsy: Yes, it has only been about ten days but it was ten days before that and ten days before that. All together it is a long tour.

Tracy: You were in Canada.

Patsy: Canada and Montana. I am sure glad I call myself Montana because it is such a beautiful state. I would hate to call myself Patsy Dakota or something like that. Montana is celebrating their 100th year and I was on a concert out there. It really was great.

Tracy: Patsy tell us how you got started in the Country Music business.

Patsy: I grew up in a large family, ten brother and no sisters, there was music all around and there was fighting along with it. That comes with a big family. My first musical instrument was an old Victrola. Someone left it in the house that we moved into it. It had cylinder records and that was my first introduction to music. Later, I fell in love with the violin, notice that I did not say fiddle. A good violinist can send me to cloud nine; I love the violin.

Tracy: You were a big fan of Jimmie Rodgers.

Patsy: I owe a lot to Jimmie Rodgers but I never got to meet him. My career just started when he died. I did all of his songs. I will be in Texas next month for the Jimmie Rodgers Festival.

Tracy: You will be doing that with Big Bill Lister and some other entertainers.

Patsy: Yes, there will be quite a few others there. I am really looking forward to it.

Tracy: How did you begin your recording career?

Patsy: My first recording was with Jimmie Davis. A collector sent me some just yesterday. I thought they were all destroyed. At the time, I was home seeing my mom and dad. They live in a little town called Hope, Arkansas. They wanted to hear their daughter on the radio. I had been on the radio in California but I was just getting started, my learning years. Anyway, I went to Shreveport, Louisiana, and walked into KWKH and told them I wanted to be on the air. I blush now at the nerve that I had. I was on the air for two weeks. When I was there, a fellow called me and said he liked my voice and wanted to take me to New York. I said yeah, yeah, it sounded interesting so I got my brother who lived in Shreveport and we went out there. He took me to New York to play the violin and yodel and sing harmony with him on some records. I was under age so I had to get permission from my dad and I made those records. That was my first recording. I was singing with Jimmie. I remember that I had broken a string on my violin so I was sitting on the floor fixing it and someone said lets hear how Pasty sounds so I got up and sang an old song about Montana. They played it back for me and the only way to describe it was that I wanted to go out and eat worms. You never like your own voice. They released that record along with, "Don't Ya Love Your Daddy", that was with RCA.

Tracy: Was it hard for you to get started Patsy?

Patsy: A lot of these books print that there were no girls around which is true. It definitely was a man's world. It still is-we just don't let you guys know it. They told me I had to break the ice for the Tammy Wynettes, the Dolly Partons and to tell you the truth, I was not aware of breaking the ice for anybody but me. I learned to write songs because there were not any songs for women. I learned real early in the game to take boy songs and make girl songs out of them.

Tracy: How did you learn to yodel?

Patsy: I was so young I do not remember. I must have been four or five years old. I remember climbing up on a box and winding up a big Victrola and we had a Jimmie Rodgers record and I could always yodel but I did not know what a yodel was. For years I thought that it was hollering. My mom would tell me get out of the house with the hollering.

(Tracy asks Patsy to yodel and she complies)

Tracy: Tell us a little bit about the song that was a hit for you, "I Wanna Be A Cowboy's Sweetheart".

Patsy: I was so sick of singing, "Texas Plains". That is the first song that I sang in a barn dance and that set my style. That is why, "I Wanna Be A Cowboy's Sweetheart", is a lot like, "Texas Plains". Sometimes I started with one and ended up with the other. Who knows why a song clicks. It could be just the right timing. The singing cowboy came on scene at that same time. It was introduced in New York but it came back to Chicago right after that and got its big start. WLS Chicago Barn Dance was a very popular program. It was around before the Grand Ole Opry, a lot of people do not know that. I was not there then but it actually started before the Grand Ole Opry. Back then making records was sort of a sideline. We did not live the rating system like they do in Nashville. It just did not mean that much to us back then even though we enjoyed making records.

Tracy: What kind of record did that version create?

Patsy: I was the first Country and Western girl singer to have a record of a million sold. A few years later, Kitty Wells came along and was definitely Country. I guess they called me Country and Western. Will Rogers which is my angel because he discovered the song and discovered Gene Autry. He introduced me one night in Hollywood at a party as the first girl to sell a million records and so I got on stage and wanted to know where the money was. The phenomenal thing about the song is that it did not die. The last few months it has a big release by Suzy Bogus on Capitol Records it is going really well and I am riding on her coat tails.

Tracy: When did you record that song?

Patsy: I believe I recorded it in 1936. Up until recently I thought I had recorded it the day that Will Rogers was killed. But according to fact and figures it was a month or two later.

Tracy: How many copies has that particular record sold?

Patsy: I do not know. Back when it was recorded, the Prairie Ramblers and I were with ARC (American Record Company) they had seven labels and then Columbia bought out them all. I have recorded for every company I have been with so I have no idea how to find out.

Tracy: You have re-released that on your new album.

Patsy: I recorded that album in Washington D.C. I wanted to put songs on it that people remember and do no hear anymore because the DJ's do not play them. Somebody suggested "I Wanna Be A Cowboy's Sweetheart". At first I said no way but then I thought about it for about ten seconds and I wrote a new verse to it. That is what you will hear on the new record. I have milked it as far as I can go.

Tracy: You are with Flying Fish Records and the new record is out called, "The Cowboy's Sweetheart". Are you planning on recording any others in your future?

Patsy: I would like too but Frank Fisher is getting albums back; things that did not sell so it may wreck his company. I like him and I like his company so I am just waiting to see how things go. I do not want to think my recording days are over although I do not sing as well as I did. I do not have the strength in my vocal cords like I did. I really never practice anymore; it would help if I did.

Tracy: I know you tour a lot because I had a hard time catching you.

Patsy: I don't tour that much in the winter. Last year I was in Portland, Maine, on New Year's Night because I approved the date in July and forgot about it. It was 40 below and the wind factor was 70 below.

Tracy: What are your plans for the future? Are you going to continue your touring?

Patsy: I have to finish out this year. I am going to Europe in October. I am going to do about six shows. I would like to go back in April for personal reasons. I have made about nine tours over there. They told me that I was the first County and Western girl in Austria.

Tracy: You have toured several countries and nearly every state.

Patsy: I have not toured Hawaii and I almost toured Australia but they were a little slow in getting me what I needed.

Tracy: Patsy I want to speak on behalf of myself and everyone else. We appreciate so much the dedication that you have given to the Country Music industry.

Patsy: I don't think that I deserve that. I am doing what I love to do. I am not doing it for anybody. However, I did feel a little pride walking up to the Country Music Hall of Fame in Nashville knowing that I helped build it.

Tracy: When they write the history book of Country Music and they come to the page that has, "Patsy Montana", written on it, what do you want you countless number of fans to remember you as?

Patsy: Just as a friendly person. Snooty people do not belong in Country Music.

Patsy was a ball of fire. I conducted this interview just a short time of meeting her for the first time. She worked the Jimmie Rodgers Festival in Kerrville, Texas, with Big Bill Lister. Adeline Goldman and I attended the show and it was incredible to see the performance. Patsy was definitely passed her prime, but she sang for about an hour and yodeled her way into the hearts of those attending.

She was dressed in full western clothing that night including a straw hat and I was surprised at her short height. Patsy still loved to entertain and it was like watching a living piece of history appear on that small outdoor stage in the Kerrville hills.

SEPTEMBER 19, 2000

Tracy: It is an honor to be talking to one of the most recognizable Country Music entertainers, Porter Wagoner. Porter how are you?

Porter: Hey Tracy I am doing great buddy, how are things in big Texas? I am really delighted to be with you on the radio. Thanks for letting me spend a little time with you.

Tracy: Let's go back a few years and find out how Porter Wagoner got started in Country Music.

Porter: I guess I am a little unique in that I was a butcher when I first got started on the radio. I am still a butcher, I am just butchering songs now....(Porter and Tracy share a laugh). I was in my hometown of West Plains and I had a job at a meat market and the guy there got an idea to go on the radio three days out of the week and advertise our specials and stuff. He had heard me sing some and that is actually how I got started.

Tracy: When did you move to Nashville?

Porter: I moved to Nashville in 1957.

Tracy: How did that come about?

Porter: I was on the Ozark Jubilee which was out of Springfield, Missouri, it was a television show, The Red Foley Show. They had seen me and invited me to the Grand Ole Opry as a guest and I believe that was in 1956. They kind of liked what I did and liked me as a person so they invited me to come back in 1957 and asked me to become a member and so I did.

Tracy: Had you already been recording for RCA at the time?

Porter: Yes, I had out a couple of records, "A Satisfied Mind", of course was a big hit in late '55-'56 and I had a couple of other songs, "Eat Drink and Be Merry". I also had out a gospel song, "What Would You Do If Jesus Came To Your House?" Those were my claim to fame songs.

Tracy: Speaking of the song, "What Would You Do If Jesus Came To Your House?" you did a lot of recitations throughout your career. You were always so great with those.

Porter: Thank you a lot Tracy. I appreciate that. I really learned what I know about recitations from Red Foley. He was a great teacher and I admired him a lot. He was a great reciter as well. He taught me so much about how to recite and when to pause during the song. He was truly the master.

Tracy: For some many years you have been the ambassador for the Grand Ole Opry. What does the Grand Ole Opry mean to Country Music?

Porter: Tracy, I honestly believe that the Grand Ole Opry is the cornerstone for the whole industry of Country Music. From the biggest stars all the way through…. I cannot imagine what Country Music would be like without the Grand Ole Opry. I really think it is a very important cog in the whole Country Music industry. I have seen you there a lot of times too buddy and I appreciate you coming.

Tracy: An entertainer like you could be making a substantial amount more money at other places out on the road but the Opry is so important that you are there nearly every weekend.

Porter: I am yeah. This is part of my life and my career that I feel like I need to put something back. It is like I have taken so much from the industry for years so it is time I put something back. I think it is time for me to settle back and help the Grand Ole Opry everywhere I can and try to say thanks to the fans that have made my wonderful career possible. The fans are what it really boils down too. They are the bottom line of the whole thing. If they like you, they will buy you records. They will buy tickets to your concerts and they will request your records to be played. I just think that they are so important and so responsible for you success.

Tracy: Nearly as important as the Grand Ole Opry was the Porter Wagoner television show. How many years did you have the television show?

Porter: It ran almost 21 years. It ran a little over 20 years. That was of course probably my biggest accomplishment in Country Music. It ran all over the country, it was a syndicated show. I always get letters from people saying they loved to watch me and that always means a great deal.

Tracy: And you really found two of the greatest female artists, Norma Jean and Dolly Parton and you put them on that television show.

Porter: I think that the television exposure on my show really helped Dolly's career as much as the hit records she recorded. She gained a lot of exposure from the television show.

Tracy: You have a brand new album Porter and I am so excited. It has been a few years.

Porter: It has been a little over 20 years. I had not really planned on making another album and these songs that the guy from Missouri wrote were so good that I could not say no. I just wanted to record them whether or not they had any success or not I just felt they were great songs.

Tracy: It is called, "The Best I Have Ever Been".

Porter: I got that title from Dolly. I sent her a copy of the CD when I finished it and asked her to write me a note and let me know what she thought of it. Actually, I told her to write me if she liked it and to forget it if she didn't. She wrote me a really nice letter and said "Porter, no question about it, this is the best you've ever been in your whole career. The performance of the songs is just the best it's ever been and I had a problem thinking you could ever do anything greater then what you did with me and with the duets we did." So I took from the letter, the title and thanked Dolly for that. She is a very honest person and her and I are really close friends still even through our careers. I felt she would give me an honest answer and I believe she did

Tracy: Considering the many hit records and great albums you had, that is a great compliment coming from her.

Porter: I think it is too. Dolly is truly an honest person and that is why I wanted her to listen too it and give her honest opinion. She would have told me if she didn't like it.

Tracy: My favorite song and most requested song on the album is "I'd Like To Make That Mistake Again". That is a powerful song.

Porter: You know what, that is my favorite too. That one and, "I Knew This Day Would Come", those are my favorites.

Tracy: "I Knew This Day Would Come', is a very interesting song, it talks about a......

Porter: Older guy and younger girl?

Tracy: Yes.

Porter: That song really is a brilliant written song and very unique in the subject matter and of course I can relate to that song. I think I performed on that as well as the other too.

Tracy: What are your plans in the future Porter?

Porter: I want to work a few more concerts than I have been. I have not played a lot of concerts lately. I only work about 6 or 8 a year and I want to try to double that next year. Of course I love that, it is just hard going out and meeting the people face to face and seeing the excitement of being there. I feel like I owe a lot to the fans so that is really what I plan on doing.

Tracy: At one time, you spent the majority of your time on the road.

Porter: I worked over 200 days one year doing one nighters. That is a lot. I feel obligated to the fans. I think you need to always be honest and they will love you your whole life. They don't care if you are 18 or 70 years old the fans love you. I think that is a big misconception. The guys who are only playing the young artists, I think that they are making a big mistake. For fans, there is really not an age barrier there. They love you for what you do and how you perform.

Tracy: This is a question and I am sure you have thought of it before, but what do you want Porter Wagoner to be remembered as in future generations to come?

Porter: I don't think people honestly remember people very long but I hope that they will remember me as an honest person and a talented person and a guy with lots of respect not only for the music but for the people that make it all happen.

Tracy: You are one of a kind Porter, a real legend.

Porter Wagoner is one of the most recognizable entertainers in the Country Music business. His thousands of television hours and his rhinestone encrusted suits have guaranteed his place in Country Music.

The longest time that I ever spent with Porter was backstage at the Grand Ole Opry one night. I was with Ferlin Husky and Leona Williams. Porter found out that Ferlin and Leona were visiting backstage and wanted to see them. We spent a very enjoyable evening in Porter's dressing room visiting while they relived old road stories-some that I can't repeat here!

While looking at the hundreds of photos lining the walls of Porter's backstage dressing room, I could not find a photo of Pretty Miss Norma Jean. I was so surprised because they shared so many years and even a daughter together. I mentioned this to Norma later. Norma told me that she noticed it as well and brought it up to Porter herself during her last visit to the Grand Ole Opry. I haven't been back to see if Norma graces Porter's wall yet. I wouldn't want to face Norma if her smiling face is not on Porter's wall now.

MAY 10, 2002

Tracy: One of the finest ladies in Country Music, Pretty Miss Norma Jean. Norma how are you?

Norma Jean: What a nice thing to say.

Tracy: Do you get tired of people calling you Pretty Miss?

Norma Jean: Nope, never have. A lot of my friends have called me Pretty Miss for years.

Tracy: Where did you get the title?

Norma Jean: It came from Porter Wagoner. He started introducing me as Pretty Miss Norma Jean and it has stuck.

Tracy: You actually had a career before joining Porter Wagoner.

Norma Jean: I had been singing for quite a while. I had been on the Ozark Jubilee before Porter. I was there for a couple of years. Before I graduated from high school I worked with western swing bands on the weekends. I have done quite a bit. I worked with Red Foley for two years before joining the Porter Wagoner show.

Tracy: You also went to school with a great legend in the business.

Norma Jean: Wanda Jackson and I went to school together while living in Oklahoma City. Wanda and I have remained very close throughout the years. As a matter of fact, it is kind of rare for the two of us to kind of grow up together and then be involved in the entertainment business. We even dated the same guy-she just wound up with him!

Tracy: Working with Red had to be phenomenal for a young lady.

Norma Jean: He was such a wonderful person. He was a great guy. Actually he was the one that shortened my name. My name was Norma Jean Beasler. It was a hard name to remember so they wanted to change it. I did not want to change my name, so Red Foley suggested that we just use Norma Jean. He was actually the one that started that.

Tracy: When did you decide to make the move to Nashville?

Norma Jean: When I found out that the Ozark Jubilee was not going to be on much longer, I started thinking about going to Nashville. In the latter part of 1959 or 1960, is when I decided to go to Nashville. I worked some road dates with Porter and he had a chance to audition for the television show and he chose me to audition with him as part of the show. I was thrilled and of course we got it.

Tracy: Were you a part of the first show?

Norma Jean: Yes, from the very beginning. I actually went with Porter to get the show. It was a very good part of my career. All these many years later, I still have people come up nearly every day and tell me that they watched me on television.

Tracy: How many years were you on the Porter Wagoner Show?

Norma Jean: It was over seven years. I left in the later part of 1967.

Tracy: You were also recording for RCA Records during this time.

Norma Jean: I started recording for RCA Records soon after I joined The Porter Wagoner Show. I had been with Columbia Records and I didn't have much success. I had enough singles to do an album, which they later released. Porter was on RCA so when I started singing with his group he wanted to sing some duets together. He took me to RCA and Chet Atkins signed me and Columbia was glad to let me go. We were all happy.

Tracy: They regretted it later since you were having those big hits.

Norma Jean: My first RCA Record was, "Let's Go All The Way", so it started off good. We followed that with some other very good records. I was very fortunate to get some very good material. The television exposure together with all the road dates that we were doing at that time helped my recording career.

Tracy: "Let's Go All The Way" was a cutting edge song.

Norma Jean: It was. It actually says nothing but let's get married and spend the rest of our lives together. Back then, we were so careful… "Let's Go All The Way", sounded suggestive. A lot of stations did not play it but it was out for quite a while and people were still asking for it. They were forced to play it. By the time they did, we had to re-release the album because it had been so long in between. They re-released it so they had two backsides. There are now two recordings of the song with different backsides.

Tracy: At about this time, you had, "Go Cat Go", "I'm A Walking Advertisement For The Blues", "The Shirt" and so many others.

Norma Jean: Yes, they followed one another through out the years. It is easy to get those good songs when you have had a hit or two!

Tracy: But then you decided to leave the business for a while.

Norma Jean: I had been in the business for twenty years. I married a man from Oklahoma and moved back and I decided that I had enough for a while. We tried to go back and forth but we lived so far away. I formed my own band for a while and we did travel up until 1973 or 1974. I then decided to stay home for a while because I wanted to be with kids. We had three between us. Anyway, I felt obligated to do that so I ended up quitting a lot of things.

Tracy: Do you have any regret of doing that?

Norma Jean: I do, but I did not have much choice. I guess I was the only person that quit the Grand Ole Opry, the only lady anyway. It was the right decision at the time. It certainly did not help my career. But there are some things more important than one's career.

Tracy: Giving up your Grand Ole Opry membership had to be very hard for you.

Norma Jean: It was at the time, but it was something that had to be done. I had a daughter that I had not spent any time with and then the man that I married had two kids so I decided to be mother. We were traveling a lot. It was a time that the Grand Ole Opry demanded that we do twenty-six Saturdays a year

Tracy: That was every other weekend.

Norma Jean: Yes, and it was 700 miles away and plus I was in the height of my popularity and if I worked the Opry which did not pay much in those days, I could not do anything else.

Tracy: You are back on the road a little bit.

Norma Jean: I have been in Branson for two or three years and I have worked with the Grand Ladies for two years. I like it here. Branson is a great place to live and work. I really do not want to work much, but it is good for me to be with the fans that I have made throughout the years. Branson has given me the opportunity to do that and I still do a few road dates. I just get to be more selective now.

I have to admit that I am in love with Norma Jean. She has a great charisma and a wonderful heart and soul. Norma's records in the 1960's and 1970's were some of the finest ever produced. I believe that if she had not decided to leave the industry, she would have truly been a superstar.

When Dolly joined us in the studio to record her duet with Floyd Tillman, we started talking about Norma Jean. Dolly told me that it was so hard for her to try and replace Norma Jean on the Porter Wagoner show.

"I would be with Porter on personal appearances," Dolly remembered. "Porter would introduce me and people would call out for Norma Jean. It was very hard trying to be the 'girl' on the Porter Wagoner show and try to take the place of Norma. She was so popular."

I begged Norma Jean to work for us for years. At that time, she was living on a farm near Nashville. She always made an excuse. After she moved to Branson, I told her that Missouri was closer to Texas and she had to come down now. She finally did and it was one of my favorite shows. She has made several trips to Texas since that time and it is always a pleasure to spend time with Norma.

Norma Jean even joined Leona Williams, Johnny Bush, Curtis Potter, Tony Douglas, Joe Paul Nichols, Dave Kirby, Claude Gray and Bill Lister to sing for Charla and I at our wedding on September 7, 2002. It was a special day for me in several ways.

One of my favorite photos of two of my favorite people-Kitty Wells and Norma Jean.

AUGUST 1995

Tracy: How did you get started in the Country Music business?

Ralph: I started out in radio in the summer of 1951, as a young disc jockey. I was 18 years old. I was working at WGPR in Paris, Tennessee. In those days, there were not any formatted stations. We tried to be all things to all people. I played Country, Pop, Hawaiian music and Marching tunes. It was before the days of specialized broadcasting. I was a morning man for about six years. I played Country Music at about every station I worked at. In 1957, I came to WSM, which was the Grand Ole Opry station. Along the way, I met a number of stars at the other Country radio stations. I met some stars at Franklin, Tennessee and I met Fred Rose. Fred would listen to me on the radio and he took a liking to me. With his clout, he sent Webb Pierce down to us when he was the biggest act in the business. Webb had Doyle Wilburn with him. Teddy was still in the service. He also sent Marty Robbins down to us. At that time, Marty was a little shy. That summer I really got a lot of experience. I then came up to WSIX in Nashville and had a mid-morning Country Music show and that is where I met Ferlin Husky. Marty came back and he and I became really good friends. A short time later, I came to WSM and Marty would come up and bring his guitar and play tunes that were applicable to a piano. He would sit with me all night until we got tired. He would sing anything, but in most cases he would sing his songs. We did that for hours. He would sit with me at night a lot.

Tracy: How long were you on the midnight show?

Ralph: I was on there from 1957-1964. I got a divorce and I was not in the mood to stay up all night and play records. I was off for about a year and went back in January 1966 and stayed until 1972. When I went back in 1966, I shared the radio with Tex Ritter, a wonderful co-host. Tex and I were disc jockeys together for about a year and a half.

Tracy: During that time, you were also married to Skeeter Davis.

Ralph: That was the divorce that I mentioned.

Tracy: There was a lot of publicity about that when you came out with your book.

Ralph: I told the writer of the book that I did not want to talk about it and he said that I would be less than honest if I didn't. I was honest about everything else so I told him what I remembered. I related that time in my life just like I remembered it.

Tracy: You were in television with Country Music before TNN came along.

Ralph: There is a man who has played a very instrumental role in my career, Elmer Alley. Elmer was the program manager for WSM Television. Elmer heard me on the all night record show interviewing people. He thought that I might work on television so he game me my early morning television show in Nashville in which I did for a long time. Later on, he gave me a show called, Nashville Alive, which we did for two years for WTBS. Elmer then gave me Nashville Now. Elmer retired but did give me a lot of breaks. I owe a lot of my career to him. I went on television full time in 1963.

Tracy: I would think that Nashville Now and the Nashville Network have done more for you than anything else.

Ralph: I would agree. Nashville Now has been very good to me and I am very proud of that show. We did it for ten and a half years and I had a good time. We were good for Country Music and it was certainly good for us. We were able to introduce a lot of major artists like Randy Travis and Clint Black. Many of the major artists that came along between 1965-1970, made their debut with us.

Tracy: You now have a new show on TNN.

Ralph: We have been working on the idea for over a year. I had been watching some Arthur Godfrey tapes. He is one of my heroes, and as I was watching his shows. I got an idea to do a variation of the show in the Opryland Hotel. I talked to the Opryland hotel management and told him my idea and they loved it. We put together a staff and got American General Life and Accident Insurance to sponsor it. We finally got on the air in a restaurant in an atrium. We are on every morning from 8-9 CST Monday through Friday. It has been a long time since I have been on in the morning hours.

Tracy: Your program is the only program on TNN that is done live, other than the Grand Ole Opry.

Ralph: Yes, we are live. Crook & Chase is recorded. We are live in the morning and then they repeat it at noon. We do it in front of a live audience. I sat down one morning and I looked at everything on cable and I did not see anything like our program. We have a live band and a live audience. I love the spontaneity of it.

Tracy: What do you feel is your greatest accomplishment throughout your career?

Ralph: When I came to WSM, I was also offered a job in Tulsa and Buffalo, New York. I chose WSM because that is where I lived and because I grew up listening to the WSM so I knew that it was where I wanted to go. Being associated with WSM has been the beginning of everything that I accomplished.

Ralph Emery is probably the most successful and recognized disc jockey/masters of ceremony in the Country Music business. He had a multitude of fans during his radio days. That base grew substantially as Ralph entered into the homes of millions of Country Music fans each night with his Nashville Now program.

For the last several years, Ralph journeyed to Texas to MC the Texas Country Music Hall of Fame Awards in Carthage, Texas. I will never forget driving out to the Jim Reeves Memorial a few years ago. Ralph was there with Jimmy Dickens paying their respects to Jim Reeves. I watched both of them as five or six fans were walking around trying to decide if they were actually watching Ralph Emery and Jimmy Dickens. It was a very interesting afternoon.

I most recently visited with Ralph at a big package show in Lancaster, Pennsylvania. It was a great package with Kitty Wells, Johnny and Bobby Wright, Ferlin Husky, Hank Thompson, Jean Shepard, Jimmy Dickens and Leona Williams. The huge theater was sold out for two shows with hundreds waiting to get in just in case someone cancelled. Ralph did a great job keeping the show flowing. It takes someone with a lot of talent to pull off a show like that and he did-just as he has done hundreds of times.

One of Country Music's best loved personalities Ralph Emery.

1998

Tracy: How did you get started in the music business?

Ray: I started playing guitar at a young age. I was about eleven years old and I do not play much better now as I did then. When I got out of the service in 1958, I had an uncle who had a band. His name was Rod Pillow and he lived in Spouts Spring, Virginia. He came by my house one day and he had taught me some chords on the guitar. He told me that he needed a singer because for some reason his singer was not available. I was sitting on the back porch. I was very bashful and could not sing in front of anyone so I knew that he had the wrong guy. He talked to me for a while and finally talked me into singing. I went down to the American Legion Hall and I sang one song and the people started applauding and I became hooked. After that, there was a talent contest like the True Value Contest but Pet Milk sponsored it so I entered the contest and I won locally out of about 7,000 people. I went to Nashville and played with the finals but I did not win. Faron Young told me that I missed by one point. That was my first trip to Nashville and at the time I was still going to college and trying to raise a family. I did not have much time to devote to a music career. I continued to work dance halls around my hometown. I worked some square dancing shows in Virginia, and in 1963, I decided that I was going to try singing. I sold everything I had and I moved my wife and my kids in with my mom and dad for three weeks and I moved to Nashville and tried to put something together. I did not accomplish that much but I did get me an apartment so I went back home and got my family. I only had $100 and the apartment was $75 so I went to get my family on the remaining $25 and I figured I would borrow $100 from somebody and them go back to Nashville and find me a job in the music business. After about six or eight months, I got a recording contract so that is how it started for me. I got a recording contract with Capitol Records and everything I had on Capital was a chart record.

Tracy: How long were you with Capitol Records?

Ray: I was with them for about four years.

Tracy: You recorded a great duet album with Jean Shepard.

Ray: That album had some great songs and it is still great today. We had a hit on that song called, "I'll Take The Dog". I hated that song.

Tracy: Whose idea was it for the two of you to team up?

Ray: I really do not know how that happened. It was probably the record company.

Tracy: The Grand Ole Opry had been a big part of your career. How long has it been since you joined the Grand Ole Opry?

Ray: It has been 32 years. I love the Grand Ole Opry. I love everything that it stands for and I have always tried to represent the Grand Ole Opry in a good way by talking about it as I travel across the country.

Tracy: Other than singing, you have been a successful businessman in Nashville. You actually gave Lee Greenwood his start in the business.

Ray: I have had some success in different things. Back in 1979, I had a farm that I bought. I remember it was a cold winters day and I was sitting in my music room and I knew that I needed to find something else to do. I was becoming weary of the road and I knew that I needed a change. I had been traveling for about 15 years and I knew that I could not be traveling for the rest of my life. I loved the music business and I loved the traveling part but it was not fun anymore so I knew I had to find something else. I went over to Larry McFadden's house. Larry worked for Mel Tillis as a bandleader for many years and he and I came from the same town as me and we became really good friends. I call him my cousin even though we are not. Anyway, I drove over to his house and I suggested that we start a publishing company because I knew that he did not want to be a bass player the rest of his life and I did not want to be a traveler the rest of my life so we started writing and started the publishing company. Larry was still with Mel at the time but he found a guy name Lee Greenwood. Larry called me and he was very excited. He told me that he had a guy and that I was not going to believe how good he was. He had been playing in Vegas and I told Larry that if he was that good and he was from Vegas then he must have papers on him, meaning that he must be on a contract. Larry had not thought about that so he said okay, let me go check it out. Larry had been stalking this guy. Lee at the time had been playing at one of the casinos in Vegas and he was playing the piano bar and Larry was going between shows watching him. Larry called me back later and told me that there were not any papers on this guy and we had to sign him. I sent him the money and he got on a plane and came to Nashville. This was all over a matter of weeks. He got to Nashville and we recorded a demo tape and I took it around and gave it to a great producer, Jerry Crutchfield, who has since become a very good friend of mine. Jerry really liked Lee but at the time we were having a problem because Kenny Rogers was so hot in those days and Lee did sound a bit like Kenny, of course that would not matter today. In those days it did matter and that was one of the negatives. Crutchfield did have the vision and talent to come up with some great songs for Lee and the rest is history. We had some great songs in our publishing company, one of which was, "God Bless the USA". We sold the publishing company in 1985 to the Lawrence Welk Company. When Desert Storm happened, it became popular once again. They played the song for all the troops before they went to war. When I read the book on General Schwartzcoff, my hairs stood up because I owned the song. I don't regret selling it because it was a great success story in finding Lee and getting him a recording contract even though I sold it. It was a real fun time in my life.

Tracy: I know that your family is so important to you. You told me a great Christmas story one time about a Santa Claus.

Ray: This goes back to the late 1960's. I had a really good friend that I met around Orlando, Florida. His name was Gordon Baker. He worked for a car dealership so that must be where I met him. One of the things that they were giving away that year was a big Santa Claus. They were like five feet high and back in those days, that was a huge Santa Claus. I got them to give me one. The whole way home, he sat with me in the front seat and his feet were propped up on the dashboard. I am sure this was in the middle in the summer. All the way home people were staring at me. I took the Santa Claus home with me and I hid him. On Christmas Eve, my children were very small at this time, I pulled the Santa Claus out and sat the Santa Claus at the hallway where the kids would see it when they came out. I sat it in chair. This Santa Claus was as big as some people, bigger than Little Jimmie Dickens that's for sure. The next morning, we went into the room where the Christmas tree was. I got a camera and my wife got the kids up. Of course she shut the door so the kids would be surprised. They got up and my intentions were to take of picture of their eyes as they saw the Santa Claus. They were all three together and before I could take a picture, they opened the door, saw the Santa Claus and shut the door and went back to bed. They thought they had gotten up too early! That is just one of those precious moments.

Tracy: One of my favorite songs of yours is, "One Too Many Memories".

Ray: Kent Westbury wrote that song. Kent, Charlie Walker and I were out of tour in the 1970, and Kent tried to get Charlie to record it but for some reason he did not do it. I loved that tune and I recorded it. It was good for me. It was not a top ten record but it was a chart record. That is kind of my theme song. I still do it today. First Generation Records has just re-released a project on me. This album brings back a lot of memories. There are some great songs like, "Julie Loved Boston More Than Me", and "Wasted Again". The tenth song on the album is called, "Salinas", a song that I wrote for my daughters wedding. In fact as we speak, Charlie Walker has two daughters getting married and his daughters wanted him to speak and he wanted the read the lyrics. I told him that the song would not work because it was specifically written for one person. It had dates, names and stuff like that. I tried to re-work if for him but there was no way.

Tracy: Another interesting song that you included on this project was, "Thank God and Greyhound".

Ray: I hated that song. Pete Drake was such a wonderful guy and he played on all of my first albums. He really wanted me to do the song but I told him that I hated the song. He said let's just try it and if it does not work out we will not put it on the album. That was the only song in my career that I did on one take. It came out really good

Tracy: Did you like the song after it came out?

Ray: I liked it a little better

Tracy: What are your plans for the future?

Ray: That is a tough question. I am gradually easing my way out of the music business. I still perform at the Grand Ole Opry. It is a great experience not only to walk out of stage but the camaraderie that we have with the members and the guests. When you run into guests, you can catch up on things and get to know them. You would normally not get the chance to do that outside of the Opry, so that is one of the best parts. I just want to keep performing on the Opry for a few more years.

I love Texas swing shuffle songs. Ray Pillow is one of the masters of that type of music. I always enjoyed seeing him on the Grand Ole Opry, because he always reminded me of Texas with his music.

I spent a great morning with him in Tampa, Florida. I had flown out to be a part of a Grand Ole Opry package show featuring forty great acts at the Florida State Fair. My friend Gay Stevens went with me. We enjoyed breakfast the following morning with Ray Pillow, Darrell and Mona McCall and Jan Howard. It was a great morning and I should have had my tape recorder there! The stories were incredible.

Ray has made more money in the business end of the industry rather than actually performing. In my opinion, his talent has actually been overlooked to some extent. He is a professional all the way.

Ray Price

July 11, 1998

Tracy: I am visiting with the great Ray Price. Ray how are you tonight?

Ray: Pretty good but I am about to burn up.

Tracy: It is a little hot in Texas.

Ray: A little bit. I was born in Texas along time ago so I have seen hot before.

Tracy: Tell me a little bit about how you got into the Country Music business.

Ray: Accidentally Tracy. I was going to college in North Texas Agriculture College in Arlington, and we had a little band that were all veterans in WW II and the government was putting us through college and we were staying in the barracks and this little group played and this one boy wanted me to go down to a music publisher and demonstrate some of his songs and I did and I wound up with a recording contract. So that is how it started.

Tracy: I believe you started out with Bullet Record.

Ray: Jim Bullet in Nashville had a big hit called "Near You", with one of the Craig Boys but that was a long time ago.

Tracy: I know that you really changed Country Music. You perfected the hard core honkytonk sound of Country Music.

Ray: That was the only way that you could get a crowd in Texas. You needed to play dances and the only place to play was in the honkytonks. That is how it started. I got away with it and was working more than anybody before they wised up and realized what I was doing.

Tracy: How did you form the Cherokee Cowboy band?

Ray: It was a band that I played with in Poth, Texas, as the Western Cherokees and Blackie Crawford who use to be here in San Angelo. He had a band called the Western Cherokees. He backed Lefty Frizzell and myself and then when I went to Nashville, I was friends with Hank Williams. We lived together. When Hank died, I used his band until people began to think that I sounded like Hank and then I let them go and hired the Western Cherokees and changed their name to Cherokee Cowboys.

Tracy: Didn't you use Hank's band before he died?

Ray: Yes, some of the people because they had let Hank go because of drinking. He had gone back to Shrevport and the steel player Donnie Helms and the fiddle player Jerry Rivers had their families in Nashville and their homes so they could not go so they came to work for me.

Tracy: You also had one of the most recognizable styles of clothing during that time. Nudie designed some incredible suits for you.

Ray: Absolutely. I wasn't the first. Lefty Frizzell did that big time. The Wilburn Brothers and I had been on some shows and they would come out in those flashy clothes and the crowds would go wild. So Nudie and I sat down and I designed some things that I wanted him to do and he did them for me and the first night I wore them on stage. I got a full color picture in Life Magazine. Nudie really used the Indian style with my suits. I wore those gaudy things for about ten or twelve years. I still have a barn full of them.

Tracy: You are also very influenced by Bob Wills' style of music.

Ray: Bob was good to me. When I was in Dallas and I decided to me a musician he had the Bob Will's Ranch House which later became the Longhorn Ranch and when he would go on the road with his band, he would let me and my group play which was really a great compliment. I love Bob. I did not appreciate Bob for a longtime until I really sat down long enough to smell the roses a little bit and just listen and then I heard what everybody loved.

Tracy: You also had one of the first Bill Anderson cuts.

Ray: Bill was a DJ when I hit "City Lights". Bill and I have been friends for a long time. I have done a lot of songs and I have been real fortunate to have some good songs, good friends and I have found some good songwriters and good musicians and I am proud of that.

Tracy: "City Lights" is one of those great classic songs with that good ole honkytonk sound that you helped to create.

Ray: That was the only sound at the time and I was real happy that I came up with it. The shuffle beat came out of that era.

Tracy: You kind of changed that sound in later years didn't you?

Ray: A little bit. I sweetened it up a little bit. I went to the strings because I wanted more and more people to listen to Country Music and I knew certain sections of fans did not like the honkytonk sound so we dressed it up a little bit and it worked.

Tracy: You had some criticism for that but you also had a lot of people join your bandwagon after you became so successful.

Ray: Yes but somebody has to take the beating and who ever is in front is going to get the beating. It just turned out that way but I was fortunate that it worked out all right. Everything is just great.

Tracy: You have had a lot of people that came out of your group that have become big stars including Johnny Bush and Darrell McCall.

Ray: Johnny was on drums and of course Roger Miller fronted the band, Willie played bass, Buddy Emmons on steel, Darrell…it was a good band.

Tracy: Looking back at your career, one of the greatest accomplishments has to be your induction into the Country Music Hall of Fame, although it took a while to get there.

Ray: I didn't think I was going to make it. I made them mad you might say. Willie rode them pretty hard on TV and some of the other guys so I think they said let's just forget it and do it and so they did and I appreciate it.

Tracy: You have been traveling so long and you are still out there hitting the road probably as hard as you ever have.

Ray: Maybe a little harder. Everything just blew wide open in the last year and now that I am on a new record label. Everything looks great for the future as long as I can keep my health. That is the main thing now.

Tracy: What about you new record?

Ray: I think that it is going to be a gas. I can't tell you what it is but I think that it is going to be a gas!

Tracy: Ray thank you for the time you have spent with me. Do you want to tell the listeners in Texas anything?

Ray: I want to tell them to hold their head up. They are in the best state in the world. It might be a little dry but that will end. It always does.

Ray Price is one of the most recognizable legends in the business. He is still out on the road today commanding $15,000 per night. Unlike many of his contemporaries, Ray's vocals are still as strong as they were twenty years ago. He is in high demand all over the country and I even get to book a few dates on him from time to time!

My favorite time with Ray was one evening in Weatherford, Texas. Frankie Miller, Justin Trevino and I brought the Floyd Tillman album "The Influence" for Ray to hear for the first time. The first track played and then his recording with Floyd on "Gotta Have My Baby Back" came on the bus sound system.

Ray listened to the track and asked the driver to back it up again and then again. For a man that shows little emotion, his slight smile while listening to he and Floyd sing was a big sign of approval to me.

Ray promised me one of his Nudie suits to display at the museum some day. I am still waiting, so maybe he will read this and remember! Ray will long be remembered as one of the greatest in the business.

Ray Price and I backstage in San Angelo, Texas.

November 11, 1990

Tracy: We're speaking now with one of the early pioneers when it comes to Country Music Rose Maddox. How are you Rose?

Rose: I am happy everyday I live but these nights are about to kill me though.

Tracy: We want to look back into your career and see how you got started in the Country Music. How did that start so many years ago?

Rose: You mean you don't know?

Tracy: I would rather have you tell me

Rose: I started in it when I was a kid and I have been in it all my life. My brothers and I started when I was 11 years old. We started in radio and from then it just went on and on and on.

Tracy: I know you started recording with you brothers.

Rose: After my brothers got drafted during WW II and they came back, we picked up where we left off before. We got us a radio job and worked in dance halls in California. We are from California. I am originally from Alabama but we were raised in California.

Tracy: Was it hard getting started in the early days of Country Music?

Rose: Not like it is now. It is completely different then in the early days, there is no comparison. We just became so popular and we decided we wanted to record so we went down and got us a job recording in 1946.

Tracy: What label did you sing with?

Rose: Four Star Records. We went down, my mother and I did with these big acetate tapes and transcription of songs that we were doing. We went to RCA, Victor, Decca and Capitol. Capitol wanted us real bad. Cliffie Stone did but Lee Gillette who owned Capitol was home sick in bed and Cliffie could not get in touch with Lee so we had only three days to get accomplished what we needed to accomplish. I said lets go over to Four Star. They had T Texas Tyler and he is doing real good. We talked to them and they listened to the transcription and they said we want her (Rose) and not the boys. So we told my brother Fred and he said they don't get her without us. So that is the way it went, they took the whole group in order to get me.

Tracy: For so many years you recorded as The Maddox Brothers and Rose.

Rose: Yes, The Maddox Brother and Rose, the most colorful hillbilly band in America.

Tracy: When did you first perform on the Grand Ole Opry?

Rose: You are asking me in years. That is something that I cannot come up with….lets see, the Maddox Brothers and Rose split in about 1956 and it was before that, so it was about 1948 or 1949.

Tracy: After you split you went on the have a very successful solo career. Was it difficult for the fans to distinguish between the sounds?

Rose: Not to distinguish the sound. It was difficult for them to accept me. My brother Cal stayed with me but my other brothers got another girl to replace me but the public would not accept her. It was hard for me to book jobs because everyone was saying that I could not do anything without my brothers. So they would not give me an opportunity, but finally Cliffie Stone hired me for his Hometown Jamboree television show. He hired Cal and I. From that we started getting bookings and the work started coming in and I finally went with Capitol Records in I believe 1958.

Tracy: What was the reason behind the split?

Rose: Just like any family, everybody goes their own way at one time or another. It is just what happens to families.

Tracy: The song "Philadelphia Lawyer" has become a true standard.

Rose: That is everyone's favorite. It has been a wonderful song for my career. I wouldn't think of doing a show without it.

Tracy: What do you get most requests for when ever you go out on the stages?

Rose: I get most requests for the older stuff like, "Philadelphia Lawyer", "Sally Let Your Bangs Hang Down", "Chocolate Ice Cream Cone" and things like that. The older stuff that I did with my brothers are the most requested songs even today.

Tracy: Do you see that the fans have changed that much over the years?

Rose: Yes, they have but they still want to hear the stuff that I did with my brothers.

Tracy: We were talking a couple of days ago about you recently having another recording project going on.

Rose: I have a project going on with Merle Haggard. As of right now nothing has come of it but we are working on it.

Tracy: Are you going to try to record an album together?

Rose: No, I am recording at his studio in California. He is giving me studio time and we are doing it there and he is going to see if he can get it out for me. He has connections that I don't.

Tracy: I can understand that.

Rose: I only got friends in low places.

Tracy: What is the latest thing that our listeners can get by Rose Maddox?

Rose: Queen of the West, also Arhoolie stuff. The stuff they put out on the Maddox Brother and Rose 1946-1951. There has been some of my Capitol and Columbia material, mostly from over seas reissued. They have released the Stetson Records and a couple of other outfits from out of London.

Tracy: You recently went through quite a few health problems.

Rose: I was headed to Los Angeles to do an engagement and something went wrong and I knew it was wrong and I got as far as Bakersfield and I called my doctor. He told me to check into the nearest emergency room. I did and they said I would never make it back home because my heart was acting up. They did open heart surgery on me and did seven bypasses. I had every complication in the book and I almost did not make it through it. I was unconsceince for three months. But I am still living so everything went all right.

Tracy: I know that a lot of Country Music singers came to your aid during that time.

Rose: Yes they did.

Tracy: Are you still staying busy, touring and such?

Rose: Not as much as I did. It has taken me almost three years to recuperate and to have the wind to sing. Of course, I just kept plugging away at it because that is my life, singing. I am finally getting where I do not hurt through the chest when I breathe in. It was a long hard pull and I still have a ways to go but I am basically only working weekends. Social Security just don't get it. The hospitals and doctors just put me under. I will probably never get them paid off.

Tracy: Who were your influences and who did you listen to while growing up? I know you have your own style but you had to have an influence in the early days

Rose: My idol in the early days was Sons of the Pioneers. I seen them this year for the first time in years. I had always said that the first time I ever seen them was when I was 10 years old and I paid 10 cents to go to a movie and they were on stage performing. I said that if I could sing like that I would never quit. And so I kept on plugging at it. That is what tooled me to be what I wanted to be, a singer, an entertainer. I seen them this year in Reno, Nevada, and they are still the greatest group I've ever seen. They are still my idols. After all these years and all the changes in the group they still sound the same.

They still have an influence on me. I was absolutely petrified when they got me up on stage and I am not afraid to follow anybody. But I was scared to death to follow them.

Tracy: How do you feel about the new Country musicians and the new Country Music on the horizon?

Rose: They are going back, more or less to the Country Music from what they were. I love the Desert Rose Band and I think an awful lot of Highway 101. Merle Haggard, Willie Nelson, Waylon and Cash are still my idols. As for the women groups, none of them ever influenced me. I love Loretta Lynn, and people like that. I like the ones who worked there way to where they got.

Tracy: Like you did.

Rose: Yes.....they paid their dues. Dolly Parton, I love her.

Tracy: Rose we certainly do appreciate you talking with us. If they ever write a book of descriptions of all the Country Music singers there ever was, and they come to the page that has "Rose Maddox" on it what would you like your countless number of fans to remember you by?

Rose: As just plain ol Rose Maddox who got out there and did it. Even with all the trials and tribulations I would not change anything at all.

I credit this interview and Rose Maddox with the very start of my Country Music collection and the Heart of Texas Country Music Museum. Rose and I were talking after this interview about Marty Stuart visiting her recently. Marty visited Rose and purchased her vintage stage costumes.

Rose told me that he bought everything except for one dress that she had just found in the back of a closet. It was a gold rhinestone dress that Nathan Turk created for her. I asked her if she wanted to sell it. She said that she might as well and needed $100.00 to pay a bill that she could not pay. I told her that I would send her the money if she would sell me the dress. She sent the dress to me a week later all folded up in a shoe box.

This beautiful forty year old dress was a piece of Country Music history and worth much more than the $100.00 that I spent on it. That dress started a near obsession with collecting Country Music memorabilia. It also started the Heart of Texas Country Music Museum in Brady, Texas. Over fifteen years later, that dress and the memory of Rose Maddox still lives in the museum and in my memories.

Tracy: We want to get some background on how you came into the industry of Country Music. How did you start out?

Roy I started out while I was in the Navy. I played the guitar while in the Navy and we had a western band on the ship that I listened to. I became interested then.

Back in those days there was not a lot of Country that you heard. Eddy Arnold, George Morgan, Bob Wills predominately, Kitty Wells and that was about it. I got out of the Navy and formed a little band in Atlanta and that is where my singing career started.

Tracy: You scored your first hit with Decca although you recorded a few sides before then.

Roy: I had a record on Four Star called "Such a Fool" that was a regional hit, a record that we cut in Houston and it got me a contract with Columbia but nothing happened with it. I went to Decca and had some success

Tracy: You recorded "Three Hearts and a Tangle" in 1961.

Roy: That is right. That was a good record for us. It was a Decca record and it started in Cleveland, Ohio, and spread. That got up to something like 30 something in the Pop charts.

Tracy: "Peel Me A Nanner" was a song that became another hit, but I understand that you were not positive about recording the song.

Roy: That was a record. That was a strange one. I really did not believe they were serious about me recording it but they said it was a hit record but I didn't think so but I would do it. So I did and it really turned out to be a good record.

Tracy: But that was not exactly the kind of style you were use to?

Roy: No. It was definitely different and I guess you would have to say it was a novelty love song. It really had a cute story once you get past the title. When I heard Bill Anderson wrote that, I said that he could not have written that but I am glad I did it and it turned out to be a good record

Tracy: I know that you are very proud of your association with the Grand Ole Opry.

Roy: I will be 30 years this June. I kid people that I am still one of the kids there. You are not an ol' timer until you have been there at least 40 years. I was here about a year in Nashville and I moved here as a songwriter and I went to work for Hubert Long who at the time managed Faron Young and Ferlin Husky. I wrote songs and ran promotions on the road for Ferlin and Faron. One day, Del Wood was sick. She was starting a Michigan Tour with Jim Reeves and I do not remember who else, but they called and Hubert talked them into taking me. That was my first tour. It turned out nicely. Then I wrote a song called, "Another", and Faron wanted to cut that song but Hubert said I should do that one myself and I did and it turned out to be a #1 hit for us.

Tracy: Did you have any friends in the industry that helped you out? I know it is not really easy to break into the Country Music industry.

Roy: No, it is not. I tell people that as hard as it was when I broke in, it must be harder today. The competition today is just tremendous. I say that in a good way. There is so much good talent out there today, there are many great songs out there being written. It would really be tough to break through today. Of course radio has changed also.

Tracy: The entire industry at one time was virtually controlled by radio.

Roy: It makes it a little harder for an unknown to get a record played today. I did have some help. I had written, "Alone With You", while in Minnesota. I was born in Georgia and then moved to Minnesota for about 18 months and I worked in a radio station, I had written "Alone with You", while I was up there and a gentleman named Lester Vandor who was up there with Webb Pierce premiered in a movie called "Buffalo Guns" that Webb was in. They came to the station and we got to talking, the Louvin Brothers were on that show and several others and they were asking me what I was doing and so forth and I told them that I was working on a song and working in a club. Lester said he could get me someone to record it and I said yeah I bet (laughing) but I did & sure enough Faron recorded it. Then they said that I should move to Nashville and we were ready to go. We moved here with $300, a 1950 Buick, and two dogs. But it was a good move. Faron talked to Hubert, who was one of the greatest men of this business, into hiring me. I worked for a year and after "Another" became a hit song, Art Devine signed me into the Grand Ole Opry. That was just a dream because I had made my mind up that it was what I wanted. It made me realize that there is a way if you really want something. It may take time but it can happen if you really want it.

Tracy: In 1966, you recorded my favorite song "If the Whole World Stopped Loving".

Roy: I always liked it too. It always had a message. I don't remember who wrote that song at this time but it was one of my favorite songs as far as one that I enjoyed. I think that was one of the first songs that had a love sound. It had such a message. I still do that one on the Opry.

Tracy: What has been your biggest song?

Roy: In regard to sales, probably "Three Hearts in a Tangle" or "Mr. Peters".

Tracy: You recorded several duets in your career including a series with Kitty Wells. "Mr. Peters", was probably your biggest duet song.

Roy: Yeah, with Priscilla Mitchell, Jerry Reed's wife. Probably one of those two sales wise has been the biggest. Truthfully it was because both of them sold pop. I say that because back in those days if you sold 10-15,000 records you had a pretty good Country record. There are a lot of top 10 that sold 20,000 records and these were well over 100-200,000, then they sold pop so they were the biggest selling records for me. "Jody and the Kid", was another one that did well for me. Kris Kristoffenson wrote that for me and that was the first award song that Kris wrote. I thought that it was a super song.

Tracy: Sure, he is a great songwriter.

Roy: So your question of who helped me get here, truthfully, I would have to say Ferlin (Husky), Faron (Young), Lester for getting me to move here and Hubert (Long) definitely did by guiding my career. Art Devine who signed me to the Opry. A combination of all these people gave me a growing experience and helped my direction.

Tracy: Whenever they write the history of Country Music and they come to the page that has Roy Drusky's name on it, want do you want your fans all over this great country to remember you as?

Roy: That is a very good question. It is a question that you need to think about. I would like them to know that I appreciated Country Music and it was very good to me. I was never a super star, I do not even think that I was a star but I put God and my family above my work, I put my work third. That is probably how I would like to have folks remember me. I am grateful for what Country Music has done for us. The people are the best fans in the world, they hang with you and they don't drop you, they are dedicated people. There are some tours that we did over seas and they knew the back of the albums better then I did. They could tell you things about you that you did not even know were written. That shows an interest. When I was in radio, fun radio, when we could do 10-15 interviews then make up the spots............it's hard to do that now

Tracy: I still do it!

Roy: That's great. Well it is getting a lot of good feed back because this type of radio is what Country fans really want to hear. They really want to hear the dialogue they want you to do what you want to do as a DJ and if you want to go back and play a record that was hot in 1950, they want to have the ability to do that. I think that it is wonderful and I admire and applaud you for that. Whether I am played or not played I think you are doing the right thing and I hope you just keep doing great.

I met Roy Drusky on my very first trip to Nashville in 1990. At that time, he was still very active with the Grand Ole Opry show. He appeared on most weekends and still toured on occasion. He was referred to as the "Perry Como" of Country Music. His smooth vocals became very popular with his many fans. After the hits, he turned to writing more and even producing a few acts. His songs were recorded by many artists including Faron Young, Carl Smith and Webb Pierce.

Roy soon turned to the gospel music and worked extensively with several missionaries at revivals and stadium shows. He worked the Opry less frequently and passed away in 2004.

OCTOBER 29, 1996

Tracy: My special guest tonight is none other than Sammi Smith. How are you Sammi?

Sammi: I am good, how are you?

Tracy: Will you tell the listeners where you got started in the music business?

Sammi: Oklahoma and California. Music was always a big part of my life. We always had music around us while growing up. I always enjoyed it. My mother sang and so did my dad, but not professionally.

Tracy: You moved to Nashville in the late 1960's and obtained a recording contract.

Sammi: I sure did. It was through Johnny Cash. Marshall Grant was Johnny Cash's bass player and he played a tape for John. John was impressed enough with me to go to bat for me. He talked to some people and I got a contract on Columbia Records.

Tracy: It is a very big step for a singer to get to Nashville and join a record company like Columbia. You had a few singles on Columbia but they did not seem to work you.

Sammi: No, they did not do anything really. I did have a good song with "So Long, Charlie Brown, Don't Look For Me Around." Columbia had promotion people and money to put behind projects, but evidentially something did not click so I left Columbia. It was not until I went with Mega Records that we had the hit, "Help Me Make It Through The Night". That song did so much for me and for Mega. It was a huge record-a kind of career record for me without any question. Actually, it was not the first release. They released a song called, "He's Every Where", but the DJ's received so many requests for, "Help Me Make It Through The Night", that they recalled the album and released "Help Me Make It Though The Night" as a single.

Tracy: "Help Me Make It Through The Night" was written by Kris Kristofferson.

Sammi: Kris and I were friends and I wanted to do something that he had written so he and I went to the old Monument studios and put down four or five songs and that was the one that the producers let me do.

Tracy: That was one of Kris' first big hits.

Sammi: He had actually recorded it himself, but it didn't do anything. Johnny Cash had done "Sunday Morning Coming Down" that had done pretty well and he had a few others but, "Help Me Make It Through The Night" was a once in a lifetime song.

Tracy: Do you know how many records of, "Help Me Make It Through The Night", that you sold?

Sammi: We sold millions. The last count I had was about 17 million but I do not have any idea. It was released and put in so many compilation albums. I actually got paid for some of them, but of course not most of them! It did give me a chance to entertain thousands of people throughout the years.

Tracy: You have had some other great songs as well. One of my favorite songs is, "When Michael Calls".

Sammi: Thank you, I wrote that. I was in Arizona sitting around and I wrote it in about five minutes. There is really not much of a story. The line just came into my head and it seemed to fall naturally after that.

Tracy: Sammi are you still touring?

Sammi: I do a few select dates. I can't stay out on the road and work like I used to. During the seventies, we were out on the road all of the time. I just can't do it like that any more.

Tracy: You were living and working in Arizona at one time.

Sammi: I did a lot of work for Native American causes. I worked with the Apaches and even had my own band "Apache Spirit" which was made up of Native Americans. It was a very wonderful time in my career.

Tracy: Where do you currently live?

Sammi: We live on a ranch in Oklahoma about 40 miles south of Tulsa. My husband manages the ranch and trains cutting horses. I spend a lot of time at home but I do go out and do the dates that I want to.

Tracy: There is a new project that has been released of your classic works.

Sammi: Right, it is on Varese Records and titled "The Very Best of Sammi Smith". It is like an anthology of the older song and it gives a little bit of history. The put it together and did a great job. Most of the hits are included and it is a great compilation.

Tracy: Do you want to say anything to your fans?

Sammi: I appreciate the support of everyone over the years, it is wonderful to go to a club and have so many people show up. I appreciate them and love them all.

In the last couple of years in her life, someone talked Sammi into moving to Texas. Sammi was having financial problems primarily due to her failing health. She moved to Texas in promise of more work in the clubs. Unfortunately, there are hundreds of clubs in our great state, but sometimes the money is not that great. Sammi soon moved back to her beloved Oklahoma.

After so many years of corresponding, Sammi finally came to Brady and worked a show for us just months before she passed away. She was still living in Oklahoma at that time. She arrived a day early with her friends. I went out to the hotel and visited with her. It was early in the evening, but she was already in bed resting from the trip. I knew that she was ill, but did not actually realize that she only had a short time left. The thing that I remember was the hotel room filled with smoke. I think there were four in the room and everyone was smoking. I remember thinking that it could not be good for Sammi's health.

Sammi did a great fifty minute show for us that night and even did a duet with Justin Trevino during the performance. She was great and her live version of "Help Me Make It Through The Night" was very special to everyone that night. After the show, she had used all of her energy and her lungs were completely exhausted. She came out front and sat in one of the auditorium seats and visited with the audience. It was the last time that I ever got a chance to see Sammi.

Sammi passed away on February 12, 2005, at the age of 61 at her home in Oklahoma City. Sammi's son Waylon Payne would go on to portray Jerry Lee Lewis in "Walk The Line"-the story of Johnny Cash shortly after her death.

Tracy: How did you first become involved in the Country Music business?

Skeeter: I started singing with another girl during my school years. We were the Davis Sisters. We recorded our first record with RCA in 1953, "I Forgot More Than You Will Ever Know About Him". It turned into a wonderful record but we had a tragedy, she lost her life. I continued singing after getting over the shock of her death. It has really affected my life. I do not think that I am completely over it. I went on singing as a solo artist with RCA for many years. People ask me all the time how many records I have and I have lost count, the last time I counted, it was over forty.

Tracy: How many records did you have as the Davis Sisters?

Skeeter: We recorded one session, which was four sides. I started singing with her sister and carried on with the Davis Sisters for a few more years. We stopped because she had a family. I think I made my first solo record in 1958. Chet Atkins had been the guitar player for all the sessions and later on, Don Gibson and I were the first ones that he recorded as a producer. He is a major person in my career. We did a lot of good records together.

Tracy: You recorded, "Home Breaker", in 1959.

Skeeter: I had a record called, "Set Him Free". It was a top ten record. In fact, it got me signed to the Grand Ole Opry. I had been given the award for most promising girl singer so the record came out and it was a top ten.

Tracy: I know that you wrote several of your early recordings.

Skeeter: I wrote some. I never did pitch the writing. I really never had a lot of confidence in my writing. Chet tried to encourage me in that area but I just never really had a lot of confidence. When I think back I think I was foolish because I wrote the words to, "My Last Date", which was a hit as well as, "I'm Falling Too". My writing has been out there some. In fact, in England, they released an album of all the songs that I have written. Bob Powell, a British music guy went to RCA and made mention of all the songs that I have written. I was shocked because I did not realize that I had written as much as I did. I probably could be a really good writer if I tried.

Tracy: How did you find the song "Am I That Easy To Forget"?

Skeeter: I was working with Ernest Tubb and traveling on the road right after I joined the Opry. I took my first big tour with Ernest. That record was out by Carl Belew. Every time we stopped to eat, I would put a nickel in the jukebox and I would play that song. I fell in love with it. Later on, I had a dream that I was singing it and doing harmony. I had already overdubbed to carry on the Davis Sister sound but I had never done the three part but in my dream I was. I told Chet that I would like to record that song. I never told him about my dream. We recorded it and sent the master to New York. A couple days later, I started singing the third part harmony and he said that I had to put it on the tape. He called and asked them to send the master back so they did and we called the engineer and I put on the third part. I still sing it at all my concerts.

Tracy: Ernest Tubb and The Texas Troubadours were very influential in your life.

Skeeter: I do not know if that is the right word or not. He was more of a caretaker. He took me under his wing, brought me home to meet his family and I would go on tours with him. I was really naïve about the business and I was feeling really lonely and had that lost feeling about not having my singing sister beside me and it was wonderful having Ernest there. The Troubadours were all so wonderful. They were like big brothers. One time he told me that we was watching me and told me I was singing to nobody. He said I never looked at anybody. I did not even know he was watching me. I will never forget to this day what he told me. He said for me to look out in the audience and look in the eyes until I find somebody that loves me and then I sing to them. It helped me learn how to make eye contact. I was feeling very insecure and I was scared about singing by myself. He was a wonderful mentor. He was the daddy of us all.

Tracy: Tell me about, "It's The End of The World".

Skeeter: People talk about that song a lot and it has became more significant. Texas was a big place for me. That record did well in Texas. All of the sudden I was getting pop play by a lot of radio stations in Texas. The song came out around 1963 but a few disc jockeys were playing the other side, which was a pop song that Ernest Tubb had recorded. The "End of The World" had been out for about six months but they were only playing one side of it. I told Chet that if something did not happen with the records I was going to quit. I fell in love with the song. I had it recorded and my sister and me listened to it for a year and a half before it even came out. I never did that to any of my other songs. It was a special song. I also want to say that it is even more significant now because of the words. "I wake up in the morning and I wonder why everything is the same as it was. I can't understand. No I can't understand why life goes on the way it does". I did a concert in Carnegie Hall in the 70's with Eddy Arnold and I met the writer. I corresponded with her in writing but I never got to meet her. She came to the concert, brought me some roses and kept going on about how happy she was and how I had made her so happy. She was forty-four years old when I met her. I asked her why she wrote the song because it was so significant to me and expressed my feelings when I lost someone due to death. She said she started writing that when her father died. She was fourteen years old and she was expressing her feeling and how her mother would talk about missing her father. Most people thought that it was a love song. Most people would tell me stories about them breaking up with their boyfriend of girlfriend. I had one young man tell me that the song helped him get through the death of his father. He will never know how much that meant to me. I just worked my first concert since my daddy died so I have been a little sad these days. The last thing my daddy said to me before he died was, "sing pretty to the people and I love you hon". So I need everyone to say a special prayer for me.

Tracy: Out listeners will keep you in their prayers.

Skeeter: I like the idea that we are calling your radio show, "Hillbilly Hits", because I have an album called, "Skeeter Davis, The Hillbilly Singer." When I recorded that album, I got a lot of flack from a lot of my friends. They hurt my feelings bad. Now it just tickles me to death because that word is floating around the air all the time.

Tracy: What are you doing now?

Skeeter: I am traveling a lot. I have traveled overseas. In May, before my father's death, I was working in Jamaica. I worked a tour with The Drifters. I sang, "Under The Boardwalk" every night. By crossing over, it has let me have some wonderful experiences. I am a Country girl. I am Skeeter Davis, the Hillbilly Singer. I am really thankful that the records have done as well as they have in order to give me a long life in this business and cross paths with so many different people. I was in Jamaica a few years ago with Gladys Knight and the Pipps, The Beach Boys, The Grateful Dead and other people. The Jamaicans really love Jim Reeves and myself. I was in Norway in April. Most of my traveling has been over seas. I would love to do a Texas tour. It has been quite some time. I am planning on recording an album with a Norwegian artist. We were going to record that in August but with the death of my father, I just could not do it. That will probably happen in the future. I also want to mention that a lot of my fans that correspond with me know that I started a book in 1979. I thought that it was going to be out by last Christmas but because of my mother's death and my illness, I had to put some things on hold but it should be out by next Christmas.

Tracy: Is it an autobiography?

Skeeter: Yes. It is really exciting and interesting. I started it with my mother and father still alive and they went back through my childhood with me. I did a lot of exciting and interesting things. I went to see the man who murdered my grandfather. It is not something that I just threw together. I know that when it comes out, it will be worth the wait. I would have been sooner but because of my illness, it took a while. I am fine now. Whenever I needed an encouraging word, I would call Minnie Pearl because she had gone through the same thing.

Tracy: Whenever they write the history book of Country Music and they come to the page that has Skeeter Davis on it, what do you want that page to say?

Skeeter: First of all, I want them to know that I love Jesus and that did not just start yesterday. It has been since I was eighteen years old. I want people to know that I am a Christian. People have asked me what I wanted to put on my epitaph and I always tell them, "Will I see you later"?

I truly loved Skeeter Davis. She was always so full of energy-especially on stage. I met Skeeter for the first time in 1991. She gave me her telephone number and we started corresponding for the rest of her life. Skeeter battled cancer for the majority of that time. Even in the middle of her battle, she continued to correspond with her friends and sent cards just to let us know that she was still believing in the ultimate miracle. I feel that she finally found that miracle when she went to be home with Jesus.

At Fan Fair in 2004, they brought Skeeter out for what would be her final appearance. She came to the Golden Voice Awards show in Franklin, Tennessee. Ronnie Milsap, George Jones, Jimmy Dickens and a host of others were in attendance, but to me Skeeter was the star that day. She was helped to the stage that day and joined WSM disc jockey Eddie Stubbs. They talked about her battle with cancer and how hard the last several months of her life had been. After their ten minute conversation, Skeeter walked away to a standing ovation. She was led out by Eddie Fulton (Jeannie Pruett's husband) and Keith Adkinson (Jett Williams' husband). I was standing backstage and watched her slowly reach the waiting car to transport Skeeter back home.

A year later, I attended Skeeter's estate sale at her home in Brentwood. Many of her fans were there to purchase a little memento from Skeeter. It was strange going throughout her beautiful home where all of her belongings were being sold. I purchased several items for the Heart of Texas Country Music Museum including her outfit that was worn on her first album.

I had a few problems or maybe questions about the estate sale. I asked Jeanie Seeley about the sale and she said something that was so profound. She simply told me that "Skeeter didn't need any of those things any longer."

Skeeter was a great and unique person and one that will forever be missed by her many fans.

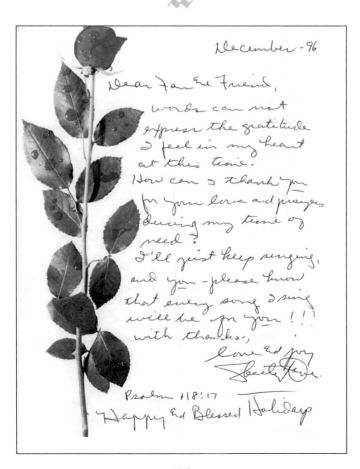

APRIL 25, 1997

Tracy: My very special guest today is Tammy Faye Messner. Tammy how are you?

Tammy: I am doing fine Tracy.

Tracy: You have a new book out titled, "Telling It My Way". Why did you decide to write a book at this time in your life?

Tammy: When Random House came to me I really did not want to write the book I felt that it was an old story. I thought it was like the O.J. Simpson trial; everybody was tired of it. But then I felt that there had been so much adverse press and there were some things that were made up. I felt that my children and grandchildren needed to know the truth plus the PTL partners that had faith in Jim and myself. So I wrote the book for my children, grandchildren and my PTL partners.

Tracy: Your life has been played out in newspapers, magazines and television for so many years. Was it hard for you to write this book?

Tammy: Yes, I would cry and then I write. I would cry and then I would write. I would then get to a place where I could not write anymore because it hurt too badly. I would leave it for a few weeks and then I would go back to it. I had a ghostwriter who would do the research for me. I knew that if I got one thing wrong with it, people would jump on it and say that if one thing was wrong, so was the rest of it. I wanted to make sure that I got everything correct. The young man that did the research would read the book and find out where I needed more or less of.

Tracy: The book does not just talk about PTL, but it goes back to the beginning.

Tammy: It goes back to when I grew up in International Falls, Minnesota. I was the oldest of eight kids and I grew up in a very poor family but I never felt poor. We were so happy that I never felt poor.

Tracy: Is it amazing for you to look back and see what you have accomplished through the ministry?

Tammy: Sometimes it is as if it never happened. But when people come up to me and tell me that they know the Lord because of the ministry, or their marriage was saved, or a baby was saved because of the ministry, it comes back to me that we really did do it and we really were there.

Tracy: Do you have any idea how many PTL viewers you had?

Tammy: All I know is the last year we were at PTL over six million came to see us. I am sure that there were many more than that. There were many that loved and supported PTL.

Tracy: Did you ever get tired?

Tammy: There were times that I did not think I could move (laughs). I was doing two television shows everyday. I was doing the PTL Show with Jim and then I had Tammy's House Party, which was syndicated. I loved it and every single day I thanked God that I was doing something that I loved to do so much. I think it is so hard for the people to have to get up and go to work everyday and they hate their jobs and I know many people do. I loved to tell people about God and tell people they can make it and never give up. That is still my message today. Don't ever give up no matter what happens in your life hang in there. There is nothing so tough that we can not handle it. I live, eat, sleep and talk Romans 8:28: "For all things work together for good for those that love God and to those that are called according to his purpose". If we love God, he is going to make everything turn out for our good and I believe that.

Tracy: Do you see yourself coming back into the ministry like you have done in the past?

Tammy: I am jumping in right now! I have had services for the last four weekends and I am getting ready to go out and do some traveling. I am real excited about that. It is fun doing talk shows like Roseanne, Drew Carey, and Larry King Live, but that does not bring fulfillment to me. The only thing that does is going out and telling people that Jesus loves them and he cares about them and their lives can be made better.

Tracy: You have a wonderful singing voice and we still use your material today. We are a Country Music radio station and you had a lot of Country artists on you program.

Tammy: Country is my favorite music. In fact, I did a new album about a year ago and I put the song, "Welcome To My World" on it. I sing it in every church service that I go too. I tell people that I appreciate them for letting me be a part of their world and I welcome them to be a part of mine. I think that it is a very neat song.

Tracy: I remember seeing Grandpa Jones and several other Country artists on your program.

Tammy: Lulu (Roman) was also on our program a lot. She and I are still good friends. We had a lot of Country artists on our program throughout the years.

Tracy: What is Tammy Faye doing now?

Tammy: I am preaching and singing.

Tracy: You are now married to Roe Messner.

Tammy: Yes and he is wonderful. I guess everyone thinks that they have the most wonderful husband but I think I do. I have been married for about four years now and he is the neatest man. He is a calm man. There is nothing you can do to get him upset. He keeps my feet on the ground

Tracy: Your book is called, "Telling It My Way", and I hope the listeners will pick up a copy. I really enjoyed reading it myself. Tammy you are such a cheerful person to talk to thank you so much for taking the time to talk to me.

Tammy: Thank you so much for being interested in me.

I had picked up a copy of Tammy Faye's book and read it. I was impressed with the book and her openness. It was very interesting. I dropped a note to her just to let her know that I appreciated it. It was sent on KNEL letterhead. About two weeks later, I got a telephone call from Roe Messner-Tammy's husband. He said that Tammy read my letter and appreciated it. He said that Tammy would love to do an interview with me if I wanted. I thought it would be neat, because I was still playing a few of Tammy's songs on my Sunday morning programming.

I remember telling KNEL radio station owner Lynn Farris about interviewing Tammy. At first, he was not too excited about using the Tammy interview. I gave him a copy and after listening to it, he told me to go ahead and play it. The only negative reaction that I received was from my friend Gene Tague. He did not think I should have aired it, but he eventually forgave me!

In the end, I was happy to have the opportunity to interview such an international figure. When they forget about me and some of the others in the book, many will still remember Tammy Faye Bakker Messner.

AUGUST 10, 1990

Tracy: Today I am visiting with the First Lady of Country Music, Tammy Wynette. How are you Tammy?

Tammy: I am doing fine Tracy how are you?

Tracy: I am doing great and I am so glad to be able to visit with you tonight.

Tammy: Well it's nice talking with you, thanks for taking your time to do it.

Tracy: How did the world discover Tammy Wynette?

Tammy: Well, I got started in Birmingham, Alabama. I had moved from my home in Mississippi to Birmingham to work in a beauty salon. When I got there, I had an uncle who was chief engineer at one of the television stations. There was a local Country show that came on every morning at six and I kept watching the show. It was called The Country Boy Eddie Show. I kept watching the show and there wasn't a girl on the show so I was just brass enough to ask my uncle why doesn't he have a female on there as its all guys. I asked him to get me an interview with Eddie and he said he would just take me with him in the morning when he goes to the station, so I kind of had an "in" there. He took me in and Eddie listened to me and told me that he would hire me to work and paid me the full amount of thirty dollars a week.

Tracy: Females were not very active in Country Music at this time.

Tammy: No, not at all. There wasn't many at all. I think there was Kitty Wells, Lois Johnson, Skeeter Davis, Loretta of course and Dottie West, but there wasn't a whole lot. Nothing compared to what there is now.

Tracy: So you kind of had to have some guts to get started I guess?

Tammy: Yeah, my mother called it determination. I said it was stupidity and igno-rance and I just did not know any better. I just thought that I could do it.

Tracy: How did you get your first recording contract Tammy?

Tammy: I went to Nashville for the first time with a disc jockey friend of mine that

I had been writing some songs with in Birmingham and got the bug to want to go more. I guess that is all it took was that one trip up there. It was during a disc jockey convention in October and when I saw so many artists it just made me want to go. So, I started going every weekend when I would get off of work at the beauty shop. I was told no, no, no. One told me they wanted a female Don Gibson, one said they wanted a female George Jones. I just kept on until another artist told me about a guy named Billy Sherill that had just recorded David Houston and I knew that I had heard, "Almost Persuaded", and it had been number one. He said that David Houston was his only artist and he might be interested in a female. So I went over and knocked on the door and I guess it was a thing of being at the right place at the right time. Billy's secretary had moved to the coast and I just walked in, nobody stopped me. I talked with Billy and he said he would record me.

Tracy: This was in the middle 1960's.

Tammy: It was 1966.

Tracy: I know that you had songs before then, but in 1967, "I Don't Wanna Play House", just sky rocketed onto the charts.

Tammy: It did. I had two records before that. I had "Apartment #9" and "Your Good Girls Gonna Go Bad" and then "I Don't Wanna Play House".

Tracy: That same year is when you teamed up with David.

Tammy: Yes, David and I did "My Elusive Dreams". That was a lot of fun. I enjoyed that.

Tracy: You have had lots of duet partners in your career.

Tammy: Yes, I have worked with David (Houston), George Jones, Mark Gray and on my "Higher Ground" album I did a lot of duets, if you can call them duets, actually it was just background vocals but I like to call them duets.

Tracy: I called your office a week or so ago and they said that you were recording with Randy Travis.

Tammy: Yes, I just did two duets with Randy. Randy is just finishing up an album called, "Heroes and Friends", and I did a duet with him on that album. I did two things with Michael Martin Murphy this past year and I did some background vocals with Matt McAnally. It has been a fun year.

Tracy: Do you have a favorite person that you have worked with in the recording studio?

Tammy: Oh gosh, I would have to say Jones in the studio. He would have to be my favorite person to have recorded with. There is no one quite like him when it comes to recording.

Tracy: We have had George on the program before and he said that there was such chemistry between the two of you.

Tammy: There really was. It was magic. I think to go back and try to recapture that would be a mistake. It happened then. It was wonderful and we had a great sound and we really enjoyed working together. It happened and its gone but that is all right.

Tracy: How many songs did you and George have out on the charts?

Tammy: Gosh, how many songs did we have? Lets see….. we probably had five or six albums. We had many number ones. We probably had five or six albums.

Tracy: I understand you had to put your solo career on the line during this because they were so use to hearing George Jones and Tammy Wynette as a duet.

Tammy: It really was. It was hard and Georgette was born in 1970, and we got married in 1968 so I kind of put things on hold for a while. I did not do a lot by myself. I turned down so many television shows because I did not want to do them solo. It's tough. You try to make a marriage work and you try to have a career at the same time and when you are working together 24 hours a day it really puts a strain on you.

Tracy: I know that you have been a member of the Grand Ole Opry.

Tammy: Yes I have. I was a member of the Opry for years. They require so many weekends a year for you to be a member and I just can't hardly do it. It is often hard to do, but I was a member for years.

Tracy: Do you get to go back and perform for the Opry?

Tammy: I don't go back often. I really don't. I am out almost every weekend and the weekends that I am home I just want to sit there and do nothing. I enjoyed the Opry. It is always fun to go backstage and see everybody.

Tracy: Going back and looking over all the songs that you have recorded, do you have any favorite song?

Tammy: I do. "Til I Can Make It On My Own" is my favorite of anything that I had part in writing. Richie and I wrote that together. The main reason it is my all time favorite is because the song said exactly what was happening in my life at the time and I think most people think almost all my songs do but that is not true. Some if it was just coincidence, it just happened that way. But that one did say exactly how I felt and was what was going on in my life at the time. It is very important to me and it is still my favorite.

281

Tracy: Of course for a signature song, the 1968 hit, "Stand By Your Man" has become one of Country's biggest standards. That is how a lot of people still remember Tammy Wynette.

Tammy: Absolutely. That song has done so much for my career. I could never say thank you enough to the people. I have people like Jack Nicholson who wanted it used in certain movies and things that really brought an audience to my music that I did not have before.

Tracy: What is Tammy Wynette doing now?

Tammy: Well I am working the road just as hard as ever. I also just finished a cookbook that is now in the bookstores. (Laughs)

Tracy: I saw that on the Ralph Emery Show not too long ago. Tell us a little about the cookbook. That is something different for Tammy Wynette.

Tammy: Well it is something different for me but I pride myself in being a good cook. I cooked all my life. I use to cook to stay out of the cotton fields and I learned to cook at a very early age. It's got a lot of old southern recipes that I have never heard of anybody ever fixing before. I knew that I had some very unusual things and I wanted to put it down so other people could find out what old southern cooking is like. I am very proud of it and I worked very hard on it. Most of the time I go into the kitchen and it is a pinch of this, a handful of that and a dash of this. So I had to sit down and work out every recipe but I finally got it down.

Tracy: How many recipes? I know that it is a large cookbook.

Tammy: How many recipes, lets see. I believe 200.

Tracy: I am sure that most of these recipes have been passed down from generation to generation, from your mom and grandma possibly.

Tammy: Yes. My grandmother and my great-grandmother have a couple of things in there. There are some recipes from my great-grandmother and we have no idea where they came from so I don't know of any family fixing the recipe besides us. In the cookbook I also gave credit to who taught me how to cook the dish. There are little stories of things that happened while I was growing up. For instance, there is one where my mother told me that I could cook for the field hands or go pick cotton. So I stayed home and tried to be creative so I put cake coloring in the cornbread. I made green cornbread! My dad said that he knew there was nothing wrong with it but it looked poisoned and he could not eat it. There are little tidbits like that throughout the book so I think that it is an interesting book.

Tracy: And you have a brand new album out with a single that is doing very well.

Tammy: I am excited about the single. It is doing just wonderful and I can't hardly wait for the album to be released. It will be released in September. The single is doing really wonderful and it feels really good to have a single that is creating much excitement again. It is called "Let's Call It A Day Today".

Tracy: How did you come up with that song?

Tammy: Bob Montgomery is responsible for that. He produced the album. I had never worked with Bob before. He is a tremendous producer and he went through, so I am told, and CBS says, over 2000 songs to find the songs that he really wanted for this album. He chose a lot of the songs and sent me home with about 40 and wanted me to pick out the ones that I liked best and so I did. I took them back in and together we decided on which ones for the album. That was Bob's idea to release that for the first single. I left it up to him. I know what I like to sing but he knows more commercially….what the average person likes to hear.

Tracy: Are these all news songs and do you have any favorites?

Tammy: Yes. "Heart Over Mind" is what the album is called. Tim Minsey wrote "Heart Over Mind" and I like it. There is a song that is called, "What Goes With Blue", that I like very much and one called "One Stone At A Time". My favorite of the entire album is, "Half The Way Home". It is just a tremendous song. It is written by a lady that has never written a song before. She is really coming on the scene and really writing a lot. I believe her name is Wanda Mollett.

Tracy: I believe you are in Branson?

Tammy: Yes, I am in Branson. I am working the Lowe Family Theater. I love the Branson area and the place is just busting at the seams now.

Tracy: You have won nearly every award that can be offered. Is there anything in the Country Music field that you have not done that you would like to?

Tammy: Well there is not really anything that I want to win now. I do regret not ever winning a duet award with George. That is the one regret that I have about the business, not winning anything after all the years together we were together. I would like to be on the very top as everyone else would, but you can't stay there. There is always going to be somebody to take your place and that's true in any business.

Tracy: Is there anything that you would have done differently?

Tammy: Yes and no. I am sure there are a lot of things that I should have done differently. But I think back and if I had done them differently, I would not have learned the lessons that I have learned from all the foolish mistakes I have made. So I guess that it is best that I not try to change anything.

Tracy: I was in Nashville three or four weeks ago and I heard about you being nominated for the Country Music Hall of Fame award.

Tammy: Oh….. maybe one of these days. There are a lot of artists that deserve to be there more than I do and have been in the business longer than I have. So I guess I will patiently wait.

Tracy: The Hall of Fame is the ultimate goal I guess.

Tammy: It is, yes. That would be the one thing that I would assume everybody would want to be nominated for and win. I don't know if Jones is up for that this year or not.

Tracy: I understand that he might be nominated as well.

Tammy: Oh, well I didn't know. I know that he should be after all the years he has been in the business and contributed. When you turn on the radio, about 8 out of 10 of the singers you can tell who there heroes are.

Tracy: Tammy, what do you want your fans all across that world to remember you as?.

Tammy: Just the average woman with a different job. I sing for a living and that makes me different from someone working at the bank, but I would like for them to remember me for good music and just an average woman. I just sang for a living where they didn't.

Tracy: That's great. Would you like to say anything to our listeners Tammy?

Tammy: Oh gosh, I would like to says thanks for being loyal and sticking with me after all this time. I am starting my 25th year this month so I owe it all to people like you. I just cannot say enough, thank you so very much. It was great to spend some time with you Tracy.

Tammy Wynette was truly an icon of Country Music. Tricia Black Lively and I attended a Tammy Wynette concert in Ft. Worth at Billy Bob's. Tammy was ill that night. She had to have help walking out on stage. She sat on a stool all night, but her performance was incredible. I sat there and soaked it all up like a sponge. She was too sick to do a backstage meet and greet, but her management told us to go backstage and Tammy would meet with us for a few minutes right after her show. She was so gracious and took a couple of photos.

A few months later, I was in Las Vegas with my friends Boyd and Maxine Turner and a couple other friends. As we arrived at the hotel, I picked up a newspaper. Tammy was finishing a week long show in Vegas. It was her final night. I called her office in Nashville. A few minutes later her tour manager phoned and we caught up a little. I told him to tell Tammy hello and we certainly enjoyed Billy Bob's. He asked if we were coming to the show. The tickets were $80.00 each and there were six of us, so we had already decided not to attend the show. About thirty minutes after our conversation, he called me back and said that Tammy wanted us to be her guests that night. We had fantastic seats and it would be the last time that I saw or talked to Tammy.

It was such a shock to pick up the paper the morning after Tammy died. She had her ups and downs, but always pulled through. There has been a lot of speculation about Tammy's death. It has been debated over and over again and one of her daughter's published a very damning book blaming the death on Tammy's husband and her doctor.

After the Billy Bob's show, Country Music Hall of Famer Charlie Louvin was visiting with me at the KNEL studios in Brady. Charlie saw the photos of Tammy from the performance. He looked up at me and said, "Who is that?" I told him it was Tammy. I will never forget what he said. He looked up and said, "He is going to kill her by keeping her out on the road."

I don't know if it was Tammy pushing herself, or someone else. Her loss was and still is a very big blow to Country Music.

Tricia Black Lively, Tammy Wynette and I after a performance at Billy Bob's in Ft. Worth.

Ted LeGarde

JULY 25, 2001

Tracy: How did the LeGarde Twins get started in the Country Music business?

Ted: My brother brought home some Gene Autry, Hank Williams, Jimmie Rodgers and Roy Rogers records. That was actually the first music our ears ever heard. We lived way out in the country. There was something in the music that attracted my twin brother and me. My mother took us to see our very first Hopalong Cassidy movie. We were about nine years old. We knew right then we wanted to be singing cowboys just like Gene Autry and Roy Rogers. We toured Australia in 1954 and then came to America in 1957 and worked with Gene Autry. We were on contract with Paramount. They owned KTLA and after a few years Gene Autry's production company, Flying A Productions, bought KTLA. We were then under contract with Gene Autry. Later we started rodeoing around Australia. We were in Victoria and we were thrown off everything, the bulls the broncs, you name it. Big Toby Jones was on the rodeo stands and asked if we did anything else but ride. We told him that we sang a little bit. He said he was going to introduce us and pass a hat around and collect some money for us. We sang and we collect 65 pounds. Back then, it was a lot of money, it was about $180 which was more than the first prize of the bull ride. We went back to the hotel and we realized that singing was a pretty good way to make a living. The next rodeo we went on we collected about 165 pounds. We faded out of the rodeo riding business and started recording.

Tracy: You had the first television show in Australia.

Ted: Yes, the very first one. We did the very first colored TV show as well. We only did one episode because it was very expensive to do back then. It was in 1964, and that is also when we brought Marty Robbins to Australia.

Tracy: What kind of show did you have?

Ted: It was like the Wilburn Brothers Variety Show, The Porter Wagoner Show, that kind of show. It was a classic show, we did 14 episodes and Marty is on two of them.

Tracy: Was it easier to be accepted in the United States than in Australia?

Ted: Not for a while. Back then it was not the bold thing to do. Throughout the TV show on KTLA, Dale Robinson who had the number one show with Wells Fargo happen to catch our show and he called and said he wanted to talk to one of the LeGarde

Twins. Dale had a number of rodeos lined up and he wanted some singers and musicians so he wanted the Holly Twins and the LeGarde Twins to be his backup band. We would open with a couple of songs and introduce Dale and then he would ride out on his horse Jubilee and do the show. That is how we were able to travel America. We went to Nashville and were under contract and we opened for more people than any other act in Nashville. We opened for Charley Pride, Willie Nelson, Johnny Cash and Barbara Mandrell. You name it and we opened for them. I will never forget the time we were opening a show in Kansas City and Jerry Van Dyke was headlining and told us he was going to go on for about ten minutes. He told us to come out and sing a couple of songs and to tell the audience that we are so happy to be on the Jerry Van Dyke Show and to tell them that it is so hard to come out and entertain someone who did not come to see them in the first place. My wife and I love America. We have been married for 39 years. We became citizens in 1976.

Tracy: Tell me about the song, "Tie Me Kangaroo Down Mate"

Ted: It was a big hit for us. Joe Allison was the producer. Joe was the one who wrote, "He'll Have To Go". Jim Reeves recorded "He'll Have To Go". We had a lot of chart records but we never had a really big hit. We had the song, "For The Good Times", "Sixteen Tons", "White Sports Coat", and "El Paso". "El Paso", was the very first Country song to win a Grammy.

Tracy: You are one of the few artists that have appeared on Star Trek.

Ted: That is my claim to fame. We are the only Country Stars in the world to appear on the original Star Trek. We were Androids in 1967.

Tracy: How did you get that role?

Ted: We were enrolled in a Columbia Workshop to try to develop our acting skills. Ed London was a New York director and he came up with the idea to present Tom and I and a Hollywood actress in a two act play called, "The World of Carl Samberg". It was a big hit on Broadway that starred Betty Davis, Gary Merrill and another actor performed. Opening night of the play, Leonard Nimoy, William Shatner, and Mr. Rodenberry, the producer of Star Trek Next Generation came to opening night. They had an episode called Planet Mud and they had already cast the set of girl twins but they needed a set of male twins. They came back stage and asked how we would like to be on Star Trek. We said great and asked what it paid. We asked what we had to do and they said not much, just stand there. William Shatner was a delight to work for.

Tracy: What are you doing now?

Ted: We are doing a lot of film festivals. We are semi-retired. The bad thing about being retired is that you cannot afford to take a day off. We just finished playing a film festival in Charlotte, North Carolina.

The LeGarde Twins have a great act. We had them at the Mason Country Opry and they did a wonderful show. I really enjoyed their bullwhip act. It was something to see.

The LeGardes had a long engagement at the Hall of Fame Lounge in Nashville. They appeared there for several years. After they discontinued the show, my darling wife Charla and I were walking past the hotel. Their sign was still wired to the fence. I asked the hotel attendant if I could have the sign. She told me that she could not give it to me, but she would turn her head if I wanted to take it. My wife nearly died as I took down the five foot sign and carried it back to lower Broadway. We flew it back with us in a ski box and it is now at the Heart of Texas Country Music Museum proclaiming "LeGarde Brothers Country Music Theater."

Ted told me that he was glad that we had the sign, so I guess that it is alright after all.

JANUARY 10, 1989

Tracy: Teddy, Country Music was always in your background wasn't it?

Teddy: Yes, we started out when I was barely six years old. I turned six on November 30, and we made our first public appearance the following Christmas Eve.

Tracy: You performed as a group?

Teddy: All the brothers and sisters were together. The four brothers were Lester, Leslie, Doyle and I and our sister Geraldine and of course dad and mother were in the background and you better believe that we could not make it with out them.

Tracy: When did you start professionally singing?

Teddy: That is a hard question because the first couple of years we traveled and sang on the street corners and things like that. Very soon after we started we were in radio. I suppose you would call that professional because we were on radio shows and work little schoolhouses, theaters and things like that.

Tracy: When did you decide to go on with Doyle and start the Wilburn Brothers?

Teddy: That happened when I was in Korea. I followed Doyle home eight months after he came home and in the same time he had started working with Webb Pierce while I was finishing up in Korea. We had worked with Webb down in the Louisiana Hayride. He had been fortunate enough while I was in the service to start out with, "Wondering", which was his first big hit record. By the time I got out of the Army, he was the biggest act in Country Music. He had about 12 number ones in a row. Doyle was already working with him and I went to work with Doyle as a duo on the Webb Pierce show when I got out of the Army.

Tracy: When did you start your own recording?

Teddy: About the same time because we had our first recordings out with Webb. We had, "Sparking Brown Eyes", and we ended up doing, "In the Jail House Now". Also, during that time we had, "If You Really Love Me", which was our first record and Webb's idea for us to record that. It was a big pop hit by Kay Starr. At that time, a few artists were doing covers in Country Music of pop recordings.

Tracy: One of your biggest recordings at that time was your duet with Ernest Tubb in 1958 with, "Hey, Mr. Bluebird".

Teddy: That was a very important record for us. We had a record prior to that with Ernest called "Mr. Love". It was a song that Rusty and Doug Kershaw had done on a smaller label. Later on we did another session with Ernest, which was "How Did We Know" and "Hey Mr. Bluebird"

Tracy: I know that you toured extensively with Ernest and also hosted his Midnight Jamboree show on a regular basis. How did the relationship with Ernest start?

Teddy: That started due to the fact that Doyle and I had been ex communicated from the Grand Ole Opry. Ernest Tubb always told us that if we needed any help to let him know. He had always shown an interest in Doyle's act and mine. When we found out that we were no longer members on the Opry, we called him to find out where he would go if he were us. He wanted to know why we were leaving and we told him and he said that there had been an injustice done and wanted to know what we were doing later that evening. So later that evening, we met him at his home in Nashville and he heard the whole story and did not feel that it was correct; before it was over with, we had been reinstated at the Grand Ole Opry and couple of people lost their jobs over it.

Tracy: So Ernest saved part of your career?

Teddy: I have always said that Ernest Tubb and Roy Acuff are the Wilburn Brothers' godfathers in Country Music. Ernest put us on his Midnight Jamboree when we were off the Grand Ole Opry. If he was working out on the road, we were the ones that handled his show for him, which was as heavily listened to as the Grand Ole Opry was. Roy brought us to the Opry in 1940 as just children. We enjoyed doing some over seas tours with Roy and the Smokey Mountain Boys and Girls. We went to the Caribbean, Panama Canal, Australia and Hawaii with Roy. We did not do any over sea tours with Ernest but we did go to Canada with The Ernest Tubb Show.

Tracy: In the late 1950's and especially during the 1960's, the Wilburn Brothers were definitely one of the top acts. You had, "Knoxville Girl" "Making Plans" and of course "Somebody's Back In Town". Was that your biggest?

Teddy: No it was not the biggest. It was probably one of the most consistent recordings. In fact, I understand that MCA records is just getting ready to bring out a new CD on the Wilburn Brothers that will be out before March. It is going to include some of those great old songs from yester year including, "Somebody's Back In Town". Doyle, Don Helms and I were writing in Pennsylvania and got the idea for, "Somebody's Back In Town". I know that we were on the road at the time because we were traveling in an automobile and the three of us got the idea while we were traveling together.

Tracy: Another big hit you had was, "Troubles Back In Town".

Teddy: Dick Floyd wrote that song. In fact, Dick was part of the Jimmie Dean show on CBS at the time. He wrote the song and then we came out with, "Somebody's Back In Town". So he said there goes my idea. He had planned to play the song for Doyle and I. Years later after he played the song for me I told him that I would really like to do that song because I could visualize the arrangement.

Tracy: About this time, you became very instrumental in Loretta Lynn's career.

Teddy: That is true. Loretta came by the office with a promotional man from I believe Vancouver, British Columbia. They came into Nashville and there were two artists that Loretta wanted to meet while she was here and one of them was Ernest and she wanted to meet us, The Wilburn Brothers. Ernest was out on the road and she was down at the record shop and they tried to get a hold of us and we happen to be around so Loretta and her promotion girl came up. That is when we were first introduced to her. She first came back to Nashville within the year. Meanwhile, I had sent her some demos of some songs including "Fool Number One" which Brenda Lee later did. That was on her first demo session and "This White Circle", that Kitty Wells did was also on her first demo session. A couple of things that she ended up recording later on like "World Forgotten People" was also on there.

Tracy: Later on, the Wilburn Brother's Show featured Loretta as part of the program as well as many of the Country artists including Ernest.

Teddy: Ernest was just a guest. We did an album called the Wilburn Brothers Show but Ernest was the guest of that show which was a live recording that was done at Bradley's Barn here. He was a special guest on the show occasionally and was a special guest on the long play album.

Tracy: How long did you have your television show?

Teddy: It ran from 1963-1974. There were some markets that carried it until 1976-1977.

Tracy: As everybody knows, you lost your brother not too long ago.

Teddy: It does not seem that long ago but it has been. We are going on the eighth year now. Doyle died in 1982 and he will soon be gone a decade

Tracy: What are you doing now?

Teddy: Right now I am on Nurti-System. I am trying to get off some of this body weight that I have put on my being a couch potato. I am not that active in the business anymore. I have done one show; I did the Patty Loveless Day show in her hometown of Kentucky.

Tracy: I understand the Patty is a big fan of the Wilburn Brothers.

Teddy: It is due to Roger, her manager that worked getting this album released on MCA. He was the force behind that. And Roger is determined that the Wilburn Brothers are going to become members of the Country Music Hall of Fame.

Tracy: When they write that history book of Country Music and they come to the page that has, "The Wilburn Brothers" name on it. What do you want all your countless numbers of fans all over the world to remember you by?

Teddy: I would say basically we could not have done it without the fans, we love you, and we thank you. Because of them, Country Music has been tremendously important in our lives. We owe it all to them. We love them and we thank them. No artist becomes what he or she becomes with out the support of the fans.

I was always intrigued by the great harmony that the Wilburn Brothers possessed. Their television show was such an important place for Country Music artists to promote their latest recording or bolster personal appearances. It is now featured on the RFD Television Network as part of Willie Nelson's video library.

A few years before Teddy's death, Justin Trevino and I were in Nashville. I called Sure Fire Music and asked about meeting Teddy. The secretary told me that he still came to the office every day for about thirty minutes and if we would be there at a certain time that we could meet him. Sure Fire Music was located on Music Row, so Justin and I actually walked about fifteen blocks in record pace to get to the office.

As we arrived, Teddy was there with his nephew. He was an ill man and was dressed in an untucked short sleeved shirt and a baseball cap. His thoughts were not good at that time, but it was such a thrill to get to meet this legend. Being a huge Loretta Lynn fan, I had to ask a few questions about Loretta and the early days. There had been some hard feelings between the Wilburns and Loretta and Teddy would not elaborate much on those days. They both certainly helped each other. The Wilburns in Loretta's early career, but also benefited financially in the millions by publishing so many of Loretta's compositions. Teddy passed away on November 24, 2003.

1996

Tracy: When did you come to Nashville?

Tom T: I arrived in Nashville on January 1, 1964. The reason that I arrived in Nashville on that day was because I hoped somebody someday would ask me that question. When I decided to moved to Nashville, I was in Roanoke, West Virginia, working at a radio station. I decided that I would go down there on January 1 so that I could remember when I went there.

Tracy: What does "T" stand for in Tom T. Hall?

Tom T: A lot of people ask me that question. When I made my first record for Mercury Records, my agent's name was Jimmy Key. He had a tendency to put initials on people's names such as Jeannie C. Riley and Jimmy C. Newman. He told me that I needed an initial. So I named myself after my son. His name is Dean T. His "T" stands for Tom but mine does not mean anything.

Tracy: When I think of Tom T. Hall, his writing and the person, I think about animals, nature, and children because that is what a lot of yours songs are about. Why did you write, "Old Dogs and Children"?

Tom T: I do have an affection for dogs and children and they depend on you. I have some donkeys and when I go down to the barn, they are standing there waiting for you he-hawing. They are glad to see me and how many people are really that glad to see you? I love animals, dogs, children, those things that cannot take care of themselves and I believe we have a moral obligation to take care of the things that cannot take care of themselves.

Tracy: I have heard you referred to as the flying fish by many entertainers. Where did that name come from?

Tom T: I do not know if I know the whole meaning of that but I think it is a person who does a lot of stuff. I have done a lot of things. I have written books, done television shows, wrote a lot of songs, been a spokesperson for different companies and I have owned restaurants, radio stations, been a Board of Directors for a bank. I play several musical instruments, been in the military so I have a lot of things to keep me busy so if that is what a flying fish is then I am one.

Tracy: Jeannie C. Riley recorded one of your greatest songwriting successes, "Harper Valley PTA". What inspired you to write that song?

Tom T: "Harper Valley PTA" was inspired by an incident that happened in my childhood. There was a lady in my hometown that went down and read to the PTA their indiscretions. I thought that she was a heroine. I thought that it was a brave thing to do and it stayed on my mind up until I wrote the song. There is no such place as Harper Valley by the way.

Tracy: You wrote a song called, "I Wash My Face In The Morning Dew" and it was a pretty big hit for you.

Tom T: That was the first song that I ever recorded and it was recorded at Mercury Records. Jerry Kennedy produced it. The Jordanaires were singing on that song. I was so pleased with the song. I got the idea from an old folk expression in West Virginia. It says that if you wash your face in the morning dew it will remove blemishes from your skin. I turned it around and made it a folk song.

Tracy: Was "Clayton Delaney" a real person?

Tom T: Yes he was. He died when I was about 7 or 8 years old. He died when he was 19 or 20. He was a neighbor and around the house a lot when I first started playing the guitar. He was a good picker. I was easily impressed by him and his death was a real shock to me. I remember him well.

Tracy: You wrote a song called, "I Like Beer". That is a song that the Country Music community can identify with.

Tom T: My wife, who we call Mrs. Dixie, and I were out having dinner one night and she ordered what I call a cheerleader drink. It is a drink with a lot of fruit in it. I wanted a beer. She told me to order a decent drink and I told him that I liked beer so she said that I ought to write a song about it so I did.

Tracy: The song, "Whose Gonna Feed Those Hogs" has to have some story behind it.

Tom T: The story behind that song is a favorite story of mine. I was visiting a friend in the hospital and there was a fellow in the back of the ward that was strapped up and was having a terrible time. My friend told me the story about how he was a hog farmer and his tractor turned over on him and beat him up pretty bad and he was worried about his hogs.

Tracy: You and George Jones both recorded, "Second Hand Flowers".

Tom T: That is a song I wrote that is a true story. The song is about something that happened to me in my life that has to be the saddest thing ever.

Tracy: You consider Ralph Emery a best friend. Tell me a story about Ralph Emery

Tom T: Ralph is one of my old time best pals. Ralph and I play golf together once in a while and Ralph is a fancy dresser. Ralph was all dressed up in his fine golf clothes and he was in a sand trap trying to hit a sand wedge out onto the green from a sand trap. He tried two or three times and did not make it so I finally turned around and told Ralph that if he did not get out of that sand trap pretty soon then his clothes were going to go out of style.

Tracy: Who are some of the people that influenced you?

Tom T: As far as the prose end of it, The Hemmingways and St. Clair Lewis. As far as the songwriting it has to be Willie Nelson, Harlan Howard, Hank Thompson, Bill Anderson, and Kris Kristofferson. These people through the years have written some great songs. Going back a little earlier, there is Hank Williams and some of those people.

Tracy: You are a health nut and you like to grow your own food.

Tom T: I am like everybody else; I want to stay around as long as I can. I live on a farm and I grew up on a farm. I love to dig in the dirt and grow stuff. I figured that while I was at it, I would grow me some vegetables. I enjoy it. I can go out to my garden, take a cracker and have lunch. Not many people can do that.

Tracy: What are some other hobbies that you enjoy?

Tom T: I like to play golf; I like to work with wood. I love carpentry. I like to do things you can do outside like digging in the garden, chopping down a tree or building something.

Tracy: What would you like to be doing in the future?

Tom T: Whatever the Lord is willing for me to do. I would like to give some of the young people coming along something to shoot for.

My parents recall that the first song that I fell in love with as a kid was "This Song Is Driving Me Crazy (I Gotta Hear It Again)" by Tom T. Mom says that I almost drove them crazy singing that song time and time again!

Tom T. is one of the most prolific songwriters in the business. He may not be the greatest vocalist in the business, but the style in which he delivers his songs has become legendary. In recent years, he has concentrated on bluegrass music. He has taken a "back to basics" approach to the business and enjoys working with several up and coming bluegrass musicians.

I met Tom T. for the first time in June of 2006. He was the host of a Reunion of Professional Entertainers banquet in Nashville. It was a great show and Tom T. did a wonderful job as the MC. Before the show, I approached him. I mentioned being friends with Frankie Miller. Tom T. lit up when I mentioned that Frankie had included a couple of Tom T. compositions on his latest album on Heart of Texas Records. Tom T. was most impressed that he recorded "Ruby," which was actually written by Hillman Hall, Tom T.'s brother. He asked for a copy and wanted Frankie to autograph it. Frankie sent the CD and then Tom T. sent back a very nice thank you letter.

I thought that it was kind of humorous that Tom T. seemed as proud of a Frankie Miller cut as he would have been one from George Strait. He is a true legendary writer, performer and human being.

Tommy Cash

DECEMBER 10, 1999

Tracy: I am visiting with Tommy Cash today, Tommy how are you?

Tommy: I am doing great Tracy.

Tracy: Tell me how you became involved in the Country Music business. I am sure your brother had something to do with it.

Tommy: Of course he did. It changed all of our lives when he became a star back in the 1950's. I wanted to be a basketball coach, which was my dream. But I picked up a guitar and it got in my blood. When I got out of the service at 24, I decided to come to Nashville and first I started managing a musical publishing company for my brother and then I got into the business of my own. The music bug is a powerful thing and once it bites you, you are destined to work within the industry.

Tracy: Did you start recording at that time?

Tommy: Yes, I started recording when I was 24. I had a radio background before I got into the music business. I was with the radio station in Memphis and when I was in the Army, I was with the American Forces Radio Network in Frankford, Germany. I worked at WFMC in North Carolina for a while and then I came to Nashville and got into the music business.

Tracy: I know that your most requested song is, "Six White Horses".

Tommy: That was a great record for me back in 1970. That was 30 years ago almost. It seems like it has only been about ten or twelve years. It was really hard to follow a record like that but we had some other hits of the 1970's like "Rise and Shine" "That Certain One" "Gypsy Woman" and a couple of other hits. I am grateful for that and I am also in the real estate business. I have been in real estate since 1984. When I am home I do real estate but I also do 60-70 dates a year. The real estate business has been very lucrative for me as well. I still get to work the show dates and perform for the people while staying active in the real estate business.

Tracy: "Six White Horses" made quite a statement in a turbulent time for our country.

Tommy: Yes, it did. When I first heard it, I thought that it was too sad. But people loved it and they liked to hear about John Kennedy, Bob Kennedy, and Martin Luther King. The way the song was written was so respectful to them. It brought back a lot of good memories. That record sold almost a million copies within six weeks after it was released. Eventually it did sell a million. I had an album with the same title that did real well.

Tracy: You have a brand new CD dealing with the millennium

Tommy: I do not pursue the music business like I use too but every now and then, I will find a song that I think needs to be heard. I found this song August of this year. A good friend of mine in Indiana, Lloyd Wood, wrote this song. I thought that it was a song that most people would like to hear. It is about Y2K. It is a funny song in some ways and serious in another. It is a song that I wanted to go in the studio and record and put out a single on. It is getting strong airplay all over the country and I certainly appreciate that.

Tracy: You also recorded a tribute to your brother Johnny Cash.

Tommy: Actually I cut that for an album in Denmark. That album has been released over there and I also received permission to put it on my album here. It is something that I always wanted to do. John has been so important to all of our family. He made a lot of our dreams possible. It is very hard to understand the important impact that he has made on the country. I was proud to record this album in his honor.

Tracy: I understand the you are also working on another project.

Tommy: I am actually planning on doing a Christmas album. I have done almost every kind of album that I can think of. I have done Country, gospel, a concept album, so now I am going to do a Christmas album.

Tracy: One of my favorite albums that you have done is your anniversary album. You had some high hitting friends on that on that album with you.

Tommy: Yes I did, I had George Jones, Connie Smith, my brother Johnny, Tom T. Hall and some others sang on that album with me. It was a very successful album for a guy who was near fifty at the time. I am going to try to do an album like that again in the future. We received a lot of attention on a song titled "Thoughts On The Flag." That was a very powerful song and it was an honor to have John, Tom T. and George sing on that song with me.

Tommy Cash had a very large shadow to overcome-throughout his entire life. It was a two edged sword. Johnny Cash gave Tommy (and everyone in the Cash family) opportunities that very few could enjoy. He was very generous to his family.

It was also difficult to try and have a Country Music career as the brother of Johnny Cash. There are very few exceptions of two or three in one family gaining equal success in the music business. Crystal Gayle and Loretta Lynn are probably the closest to achieving great fame in the industry with separate careers. Of course, their sister Peggy Sue and brother Jay Lee Webb also had chart records.

Since Johnny's death, Tommy has enjoyed a very busy touring schedule. His "Tribute To Johnny Cash" has played to packed houses all over the country. Johnny's career is probably bigger than ever and there is certainly a renewed interest in Tommy as well.

Tommy co-hosted my radio show a couple of years ago. I was intrigued with his stories about the early days growing up in near poverty. I will never forget him telling me how everything changed after Johnny started to achieve success. It just made me realize how important Country Music is to not only the fans, but also the families of the artists as well. It is up to those individuals how they handle those changes.

Tony Douglas

JULY 25, 2007

Tracy: It is always good to visit with Tony Douglas. Tony, you were born and raised in East Texas.

Tony: That is right. I was born in the Martins Mill community about fourteen miles north of Athens. At an early age, I started singing in church and then I would lead the singing in church some as well. I always loved to sing them old gospel songs about our Savior. They always meant a lot to me.

Tracy: When did you get the Country Music bug?

Tony: Country Music has always been a part of me all of my life. I never dreamed that I would be able to go into the music business the way that I did. While in the service, I was invited to sing with a band in Germany one evening. I sang a few songs with them and they talked me into going to the theater on Saturday night. It seated 1,100 people and I was supposed to sing two songs. I ended up singing five songs. They kept encoring me and I guess that is when the bug bit me.

Tracy: Do you remember what you sang that night?

Tony: The first song that I sang was "Slowly" which was a big hit for Webb Pierce in 1953. I came back and sang "Long, Gone Lonesome Blues" and "Walking the Dog." I also did one of Faron Young's songs too.

Tracy: You also wrote your first song while in Germany.

Tony: I was sitting on my foot locker in 1953 and thinking about Mimi (Tony's wife). I was thinking about how much I would like to see her and how much I loved her. I wrote "Echoes of You" and I will never forget one of my buddies over there. Neal said, "I'll bet you that when I get back to the United States that I will hear that some day on record." I didn't dream of that happening, but it did.

Tracy: The Cowtown Hoedown was important to your career.

Tony: I made five trips to the Cowtown Hoedown to get on the show. They kept telling me that they were filled up and that they were looking for professionals. The fifth Saturday night that I walked in up there, Jack Henderson said "not, you again." He told me that I could sing one song and that's it. I chose "Crazy Arms." It brought the house down and he came backstage and asked me to come back out again. I went back out there and sang "Singing The Blues" and then I left the stage. Then they would come back and get me until I sang five songs that night. It was a very heart-warming thing.

Tracy: How did you get the invitation to join the Louisiana Hayride?

Tony: Johnny Horton was the special guest one night at the Cowtown Hoedown. Columbia Records came in there. "Battle of New Orleans" had been number one for a good long while. It had sold 2,700,000. They presented him with his second platinum record that night. His manager Tillman Franks was there. I had a real good night that night and received several encores. I was sitting in the dressing room after we got through and Tillman came back there and sit down. He said "they sure did like you out there tonight." I told him that I was thankful for that. He asked me what I would charge him to make a guest appearance on the Louisiana Hayride. I said "what did you say?" He repeated himself. I said, "Mr. Franks, I will pay you to let me sing on the Hayride!" I was a guest on the Hayride a couple of weeks after that and they paid me $50.00. I went back the next week for my second appearance and they signed me to a three year contract.

Tracy: That was an important time for the Hayride.

Tony: It was right after Elvis had just left. You could sing a Hank Williams song and it would bring the house down. I was there six months. rock and roll had really took over the Hayride. Webb Pierce was there as the special guest one night and he even did some rock and roll and shook around out there. I would go out there and sing my three little old Country songs and get a handclap here and a handclap there. Mr. Frank Page, the announcer, came to me one night when I didn't get hardly any applause at all. That night I followed Bob Luman and he got eleven encores doing the rock and roll stuff. I was sitting there in the dressing room with my head down and Mr. Page came over and said "Tony, this is just tearing me up. Why don't you shake a little bit on your next show?" I said, "Mr. Page, if I got to shake to get in Country Music then I am never going to be in Country Music." I was there for six months nearly to the day. I had done my three songs on the first half and done my second song on the last half of the show. I did "Thy Burdens Are Greater Than Mine" for my last song. I got a standing ovation and I just left the stage. I really didn't pay any attention. Mr. Page asked me to come back out and do another song. He told me that he couldn't get those people quiet unless I came back out. I walked out there and I couldn't sing to save my life. I lost my composure and it just filled me up. I just left the stage bowing and thanking them. From then on, I was kind of accepted and it really helped my career there.

Tracy: When did you make your first recording?

Tony: I made my very first record "Old Blue Monday" and "Echoes of You" in January of 1956, on the Cowtown Hoedown label. KWKH got behind "Old Blue Monday" and got loads of requests for it.

Tracy: You started seeing some chart action in the 1960's.

Tony: The 1960's were really good to me. I recorded "Shrimpin'" in 1961 and "His and Hers" in 1962. Chuck Jennings and I were on our way back into Dallas from a show at the Tri State Jamboree. We had a wonderful night. We decided to drive on back home. Chuck had driven a long way and I had been asleep in the back. I raised up and asked Chuck if he was getting tired. He said he was and he pulled over and let me drive. I got under the wheel and started to drive. Back in those days, the cars had little song writing tables in the back seat. A light would come on and the little desk would fold out. I was driving along and kept hearing a little scratching sound. I finally asked Chuck what he was doing. He told me that he was writing a song. I asked him what the name of it was and he told me "His and Hers." That hit me. I didn't even know what the song was about, but it really hit me. We started working on that song for the rest of the night. We worked on it for seven months before I went to Nashville and recorded it.

Tracy: You were invited to join the Grand Ole Opry.

Tony: I was fixin to sign the contract when Mr. Denny told me that I had 120 days to move to Nashville or the suburbs of Nashville. I knew that, but the sheer excitement of getting to join the Opry made me forget about it. I told him that I was going to have to humbly decline the offer. He couldn't believe it. I told him that I wanted to live where I wanted to live and that I wanted to live in Athens, Texas. He said, "Who in the world knows where Athens, Texas is?" I told him that I did and I was hanging the first plane back home. I have never regretted it. I am happy here with Mim, my children and grandchildren.

Tracy: "Thank You For Touching My Life" really opened some doors for you.

Tony: I had recorded a song from Tommy Williamson called "State Trooper Sammy Young." He called me one day and told me that he had written a song and he didn't know what to do with it. I asked him what the name of it was. He told me "Thank You For Touching My Life" and it sent cold chills all over me. He sent me a cassette tape and I did not like the melody to the song when I first heard it. The message in the song just froze me to death. I knew that it was a hit song. I started working on it and it was released on September 18, 1972. That is the song that I opened my little independent record label with. Dot Records came along and picked that thing up and there we went with it.

Tracy: What it Tony Douglas doing now?

Tony: We have had Papa T's here for fourteen years. It is a produce and nursery place and we have expanded a couple of times. I sell my music at Papa T's and it amazes me when I answer the phone and here from so many of my fans. I am so thankful for it. It gives me great pleasure to talk and visit with those folks that enjoy my music.

Tracy: How do you want to be remembered?

Tony: Well, Tracy, I would like for people to know that I depended upon the Lord most times in my life. I would like for them to think that I kept my shows clean all down through the years and never did anything on them that people would be ashamed of. I have strived to have a show that anyone could bring their children out to. That has always been of up most importance to me.

My grandmother always said that Tony Douglas looked like he just walked out of powder box. She was always so impressed with the way he dressed and the way he looked on stage. I grew up listening to Tony's music while my grandparents and parents enjoyed his many personal appearances in our area.

While I was in high school, I attended a leadership training seminar in Trinidad, Texas. There were two places that I wanted to go while I was in East Texas. I wanted to visit Crisp, Texas, the birthplace of Ernest Tubb and Athens, Texas, to see Tony Douglas. At this time in my life, I was just a kid and never thought about calling ahead. I drove to Athens and found the Athens Chamber of Commerce and asked them where Tony Douglas lived. They told me just across the street. I marched my way to the house and knocked on the door. That visit would start a friendship that I cherish to this day.

Tony and his wife Mim helped to educate me about the Country Music business. I was so eager to learn about booking, shows and the history of the business. Without evening knowing most of the time, Tony taught me many things about the industry. He had enjoyed hit records and toured all over the country. He also had a very successful booking and promotions company.

When we first met, he was not very excited about Country Music. The business had changed so much. With the encouragement of his family, Tony started taking a few dates and even started doing some recording. He is now enjoying the business more than at any part of his career. His decision to decline membership in the Opry was probably hard on his career. The gold records and thousands attending shows are definitely important to many people. I know for a fact that Tony is very content with singing real Country Music to his true fans and spending time with his wife Mim. To Tony, that is worth more than all the gold records that could line his lovely home in Athens, Texas.

MAY 21, 1996

Tracy: How did you become involved in the Country Music business?

Wade: I started out as a child and then as time passed, I did anything to make a living. I played a little jazz. I played medicine shows, circuses, carnivals and anywhere else I could to make a living. In 1934, I came to St. Louis and joined a group called Pappy Cheshire's National Champion Hillbillies. That was my beginning into Country Music.

Tracy: How did you get to Nashville?

Wade: In 1964, I moved to Nashville after living in St. Louis, Chicago and the West Coast.

Tracy: You are a renowned fiddler and have done several recordings.

Wade: I was with RCA Victor for eleven years. We have a very successful run. We had some pretty successful records. We never had many major hits or what would be considered standards today, but it was a good run for both of us.

Tracy: How did you become involved with RCA?

Wade: Through a song writer from Texas named Cindy Walker. She wrote a song called, "I Was Just Walking Out The Door". Through that song, I got a contract with RCA. It was a great break for me. Cindy is an incredible writer and one of the most prolific writers in Country Music.

Tracy: You recorded a song with Webb Pierce, "It's My Way", that has been released on a new compilation CD along with another song, "Have Yourself A Party".

Wade: That was cut during a time that I was between contracts. We were able to do some freelance work from time to time when we were not under contract with any certain label. I have actually worked with many of the great legends in the business. Willie (Nelson) and I did a lot together and of course, I was featured on the Ernest Tubb television show.

Tracy: What is the difference in Country Music at that stage in your career and now?

Wade: Country Music in those days was more real. The words and the songs were written more about what was actually happening in life. The music was simple, it was not as complicated as it is today. The music was kept in a way that everyone knew what you were doing and saying. When you heard the Bob Wills Band or The Hank Thompson Band, you could tell the difference between the bands. Everybody loved to dance in those days. They played a beat to dance by.

I had a dance band, Leon McAuliffe had one of the best, Hank Thompson, Bob Wills, there were a lot of great swing bands. The guy who started the western swing was Milton Brown and His Brownies.

Tracy: Travel was so important in the early days of Country Music.

Wade: We traveled all over the country, wherever we could find a place to play. I went to Nashville to run Ferlin Husky's Band and I became a road manager for him. Willie Nelson and I traveled together for a few years as well. Willie and I had a ball together.

Tracy: The songs that you have recorded will be played for many years to come. How do you feel about that?

Wade: It thrills be beyond words. We moved from Spartan in 1945 and moved back in 1979, and people are still recognizing me. In the end, everyone wants to leave something in this old world. I guess that the greatest thing that I can leave is my music. It has been a great run and I was proud to be a small part of the great industry.

I never had the opportunity to meet "Pug Nose" Wade Ray. I watched him on the Ernest Tubb television show reruns. He was always so full of life and did a great job entertaining. After this phone interview, he sent me a stack of old autographed photos. Some from the early days of his career and some from a television program that he worked on called "Pappy's Place."

According to several of my friends, Wade was not only a great musician, but a comedian himself. There are many stories about his days with Willie that I should not pass along here. Evidentially, they had a great time while providing some great music.

Wanda Jackson

OCTOBER 13, 2000

Tracy: Wanda will you tell us how you became involved in the Country Music business.

Wanda: My dad gave me my first guitar. He was a professional musician until him and mother married. This was at the end of the depression. People did not have money to spend on entertainment so he gave that up after I came along. He got to live his dream through me. He traveled with me, he taught me to sing.

Tracy: You were still in high school when you got started in the business.

Wanda: I signed my first recording contract my junior year, I was 16. I graduated high school in 1955 and he gave up his job so that he could travel with me. I am an only child so my father was able do that. I would sing sometimes and I would forget to get paid so he thought that he should go with me. My mom stayed at home so somebody would get a paycheck.

Tracy: Hank Thompson had a lot to do with your early career.

Wanda: Yes, he heard the radio show that I had in high school and he invited me to sing with him and the Brazos Valley Boys. He called me one Saturday night after one of my shows and it was one of the biggest thrills of my life. That began a long time friendship he helped me get my first contract with Decca and two years later he got me my contract with Capitol. It was always my dream to record for the same company that he did.

Tracy: Your career really took off after you signed with Capitol Records.

Wanda: It did. I was already working with Elvis. I signed with Capitol in 1956, so I worked with Elvis quite a bit in 1955 and he encouraged me to try this kind of music and my daddy did too. That was about all that was being played. There was not any Country Western Music being played. If you wanted to stay in this business that is what you had to do.

Tracy: You even dated Elvis.

Wanda: We did date. Elvis and I were very close. As a matter of fact, one of my most prized possessions is his class ring. Elvis gave that to me and I still have it today. I still miss Elvis.

Tracy: A career in rockabilly was unheard of for a female entertainer.

Wanda: It was. I thought that it was very innovative for Elvis to even think of me singing this kind of music. I was the first other than Janis Martin who had a hit or two back in the 1950's. I recorded a lot of rockabilly, rock and roll songs that I did not use a lot in the beginning because people were not expecting me as a girl to do rock. I was recording it in hopes of getting another hit after, "Let's Have A Party". This was in 1960. I had some luck with "Fujiyama Mama" in 1959.

Tracy: That was also a big hit in Japan.

Wanda: Yes, it is still a standard song over there. Then I went back to Country Music.

Tracy: When did you make the change from rockabilly back to Country Music?

Wanda: It was in 1960. I recorded, "Right or Wrong" "In The Middle of a Heartache" and "Little Bitty Tear" all in one session. After "Let's Have a Party", we released "Mean Mean Man" but it did not get much noise so my producer had me go back to Country. It was Contemporary Country at the time with the strings and all the voices so I bounced around from Country to pop. I even tried my hand at calypso.

Tracy: Was Ken Nelson producing you at the time?

Wanda: Yes, he has been a great friend of mine. I see him about every year.

Tracy: One of my favorite songs is, "Tears Will Be The Chaser For The Wine".

Wanda: I really like that one too. It was also another song that did very well for me.

Tracy: Who helped you find material at the time.

Wanda: I was forced to begin writing in a more serious way. I had written a few rock and roll songs. I never considered myself a songwriter but I was not getting any material. I lived in Oklahoma City. I never moved to Nashville. There was just not any material available for a girl through rockabilly so that is why I started writing. I wrote a song for Brenda Lee but Ken Nelson heard me sing it and told me I was going to do it. The song was, "Right or Wrong". I was so glad he had me do it. From that time on, I wrote quite a few songs. Oklahoma City had quite a few musicians during that time, they probably still do. In fact, I was listening to some old stuff during my errands today and there were some really good songs. I got some songs there and then we would go to Nashville and they would have a stack of songs for me to listen too. Harlan Howard was always a friend of mine because I was the first artist to ever record a Harlan Howard song. He always came through with some good stuff.

Tracy: You had a lot of great musicians in your band like Roy Clark and Big Al Downing.

Wanda: I also had Rodney Lay and Vernon Sandusky who were on Hee Haw all those years. In fact, I am working with Rodney and Vernon in the next few weeks. I am happy to say that the Oklahoma Music Hall of Fame is inducting me October 24th along with Roy Clark and Jim Halsey who was my first manager. Roy was my protégé and I was Hank Thompson's protégé and he is going to be there to present my award to me.

Tracy: In 1971, something very special happened to you.

Wanda: My husband and I became Christians. In fact, we had a ministry. I did not want to get out of Country Music at the time but I was so excited about recording gospel music. Capitol recorded an album and when I was ready to record another one, they said no and that most artists just have one gospel album. I told them that I would not be happy with that so Ken Nelson understood and he got me out of my contract with Capitol, which was unbelievable. My husband and I did enjoy about 15 years of a wonderful ministry that God gave us.

Tracy: You have had such a great career in the rockabilly, Country Music and gospel music field. That is something that most people would never have an opportunity to do.

Wanda: Now I have come full circle. I am now doing so many rockabilly shows. The doors began to open in Europe and in America. I realized that God wanted me to be a voice for him wherever I sang so that gave me the freedom to do whatever came my way. I have been enjoying it thoroughly. All these young adults are enjoying the rockabilly music and it really knocks me out.

Tracy: I have got to get you to tell the story of your Opry appearance. You had a little problem with your wardrobe that night.

Wanda: I was invited to come sing so I was anxious to sing my recording at the time, which was with Decca. By that time, I was already designing my own clothes because I did not like cowboy boots and I did not like full skirts. My mother being a seamstress has always made my clothes and so we began designing and making my dress. I was getting ready to go on and Ernest Tubb said that I could not go on the Opry the way that I was dressed. I told him that I did not know what he meant. He told me that I could not show my shoulders and arms. It was not a revealing dress. It had a rhinestone spaghetti strap and a sweetheart neck and maybe a little bit of cleavage was showing and I wore high heels and earrings. He told me that I had to cover up so I ran and got my friends leather jacket and put it on. I was heart broken and that was the last time I ever did the Opry. Elvis and I had the same experience. It just was not for us. I also did not know the rules that the Grand Ole Opry had. I knew they did not use drums, which seemed real strange.

Tracy: If the Grand Ole Opry called you today and wanted you to do it, would you?

Wanda: Yes but on my terms.

Wanda Jackson has achieved a lot on her own terms. She was one of the earliest "sex symbols" in this business when gingham was more popular than short frilly dresses. Wanda exploded on the scene and forever changed the industry.

We booked Wanda for the first time in the middle 1990's. She was getting a lot of attention as rockabilly music was enjoying a resurgence in popularity. Rosie Flores had talked Wanda back into working many of the clubs where this music was once again gaining ground. Wanda had devoted much of the 1970's and 1980's to the gospel industry. She and her husband Wendell Goodman had a very successful ministry. Wanda would give her testimony and sing. Wendell would then deliver the message and literally thousands were brought into the fold during that time.

Wanda confessed to me that times were good and bad while working the gospel circuit. She said that many times they had to struggle to make it. That is the case with so many people who work solely in that industry.

Wanda said that she and Wendell were finally shown that they could share their testimony and love for God wherever they performed-even at a nightclub. To this day, Wanda gives a short testimony in her performance and then gives a rousing version of "I Saw The Light."

Wanda and Wendell spent seven days with us on a Caribbean Cruise in 2006. We had a wonderful time and I watched her on stage each day. I especially enjoyed her rockabilly selections and she enjoys performing them as well. She has a special charisma that is just as bright today as it was fifty years ago.

Willie Nelson

OCTOBER 6, 1995

Tracy: Visiting backstage with Willie Nelson at City Limits in Stephenville, Texas. Willie, weren't you born and raised in Abbott, Texas?

Willie: That is right. I was raised by my grandparents and my grandfather gave me a guitar when I was about six. I loved listening to the radio while growing up and hearing people like Ernest Tubb and Bob Wills and of course, the Grand Ole Opry. I listened to WLS in Chicago. I also was listening to some pop music and jazz and even some of the German polka music that was popular around our area of Texas. After leaving Abbott, I worked in radio before moving to Washington, where I made my first record.

Tracy: When did you start playing the guitar?

Willie: I started playing guitar when I was around six. I was already writing a little at that time and the guitar allowed me to put melodies with my poems and little songs.

Tracy: You worked as a disc jockey in Washington.

Willie: I was living in Portland and working at KVAN radio in Vancouver, Washington. I was also working some clubs in the area as well.

Tracy: You soon moved back to Texas and started concentrating on songwriting.

Willie: I wrote the song "Family Bible" and sold it to some friends that I had in the Houston area-Paul Buskirk, Walt Breeland and Claude Gray for fifty dollars. Claude recorded the song and it got into the Top 10. I moved to Nashville and met up with some other songwriters including Hank Cochran, Roger Miller and Harlan Howard and some of those guys. We were all just struggling to make a living.

Tracy: "Hello Walls" started to change things for you.

Willie: Faron (Young) recorded "Hello Walls" and then Billy Walker did "Funny How Time Slips Away". I then started recording for a couple of different labels as well.

Tracy: You never did really like Nashville.

Willie: I stayed in Nashville until my house burned down in 1970. I decided then that it was time to move back to Texas. It was the best move of my life. I decided to go back home and thought that I would work New Mexico, Oklahoma and Texas.

Tracy: Things really started to happen for you at that time.

Willie: The "Red Headed Stranger" album was released around 1975, and things began to happen for us in a big way. I used to sing "Red Headed Stranger" when I was a disc jockey. I had a radio show in Ft. Worth. Every afternoon, I would play fifteen minutes of children's songs. I'd get requests for "Red Headed Stranger" all the time. When CBS wanted me to put the project together, I decided to do a concept album around "Red Headed Stranger." It was a time of change for the music business. I was lucky to work with some great people and we had a lot of success. I have had a lot of failures too!

Tracy: Do you still enjoy going out on the road?

Willie: It is great therapy for me. The bus is just like my home. I am on it probably more than I am at home. I don't know what to do when I am not on the road. I do miss my family when I am on the road, but it is always good to see so many of the people that come out to the shows. I have my band with me and they are a part of my family as well.

Tracy: You have a brand new album titled "Just One Love" that is filled with some old style Country Music.

Willie: Grady Martin is responsible for this new project. Grady used to play guitar for me and we wanted to do something together, so we did. Grady was still working with me at the time. Whenever we recorded this new album, he brought a busload of the best musicians in the world including Buddy Emmons and all of those guys from Nashville. We even brought Granda Jones down to be a part of the project. I have done literally every kind of album that anyone could record, but Classic Country is among my favorite. It is essentially what I started with and it shines on this project.

Tracy: You also recorded some Floyd Tillman songs on this album.

Willie: I recorded a couple of Floyd Tillman songs on this project. I have done so many of Floyd's compositions down through the years. I am a songwriter so naturally I appreciate songwriters and great songs. You don't get any better than Floyd Tillman as a songwriter. His music was not the typical Country Music of the time.

Tracy: I remember you relaying a story about the song "I'll Keep On Loving You."

Willie: Yeah, that was always one of my favorite songs that Floyd wrote. I always thought it would take a very special woman to inspire such an incredible song. I asked Floyd about it one time and he told me that he wrote it about his car.

Tracy: Do you listen to the radio for new material?

Willie: I really have not heard much on the radio that would interest me in the recording end of the business. I will sometimes listen to the Classic Country stations and hear a song that interests me. Of course, I have heard most of them dozens and dozens of times, but sometimes you hear something that peaks your interest and you think that you might want to record it. That is what happened to me when I did "Blue Eyes Crying In The Rain."

Tracy: I know that your long time friend Johnny Bush wrote "Whiskey River" for you.

Willie: Yes. I have opened my shows with "Whiskey River" for a number of years. I opened with "Mr. Record Man" for a long time and then would end with "The Party's Over." I really liked "Whiskey River". It would always get the crowd energized, so it stayed on to open the show.

Tracy: What does Willie Nelson have planned for the future?

Willie: I have a new album that I'm writing that should be completed by the end of this year or the first of next year. There are a lot of new songs on this particular project.

Tracy: I was watching you at the bus tonight and was so impressed that you stayed back and visited with all of your fans tonight after your show.

Willie: Those are the guys that paid to come see us. They make it all possible.

Tracy: Is there anything you want to tell our listeners in Central Texas tonight?

Willie: I'm glad to be here in Stephenville and Brady and in this area. I always enjoy working this part of Texas. I hope to run into you down the road somewhere.

Willie Nelson has run into just about everybody down the road somewhere. I don't know of any entertainer that enjoys the road as much as Willie Nelson.

When I was working on Floyd Tillman's 85th Birthday celebration, I decided to invite some special guests to be a part of the show in Llano, Texas. I called Johnny Gimble, Al Dean, Frankie Miller, Jimmy Eaves and a few other people that knew and respected Floyd. I wanted to invite Willie, but I was not sure about how to ask him. I called Johnny Bush about the invitation. John told me that he would call Willie and run it past him. About ten minutes later, John called and said that Willie wanted to be a part of it. The week of the show, Willie called to check on the sales. He offered for us to use his name in case we needed help in drawing a crowd. Willie was commanding $50,000.00 a show and was coming to Llano, Texas, for free and he wanted us to use his name if we needed to fill the house. I always thought that was extremely generous of Willie. We did not need to use his name as the show was sold out. I still remember the smile on Floyd's face when Willie hit the stage.

Willie has been one of the most generous Country Music entertainers of all time. His legacy will be beyond the music. He is living his legacy every day.

Wilma Lee Cooper

1998

Tracy: You have had a long career in Country Music. How did you get started?

Wilma Lee: I got started with my mother, daddy and my two sisters. We were the Leary Family back in 1938. Before that, we sung in the churches in West Virginia where I was raised. From the time we were kids, we sang with my mother and father.

Tracy: You musical interest has been Country and gospel together.

Wilma Lee: That is right. My parents were gospel singers. My two sisters and I sang Country songs.

Tracy: How did you meet Stoney?

Wilma Lee: My mother and daddy hired him to play fiddle for us. They heard him on the radio in Fairmont, West Virginia, while he was working with Rusty Hisser and the Green Valley Boys. He was their fiddle player from Harmon, West Virginia. That was thirty miles over the mountain from where I was raised. I was raised on a farm six miles out of Elkins. The family was working at WSBA in Harrisonburg, Virginia, and my uncle Lanky Ware, who was my mother's brother, played fiddle for us. He was also a schoolteacher and so when it came time for school to start he would have to go back so that is when they hired Stoney.

Tracy: Was it love at first sight?

Wilma Lee: No it wasn't. I had a boyfriend and my sister had a boyfriend. We dated for two years before we got married.

Tracy: At that point the two of you were singing together.

Wilma Lee: We had a daily radio program out of the radio station in Harrisonburg and then we worked shows at night. Until we got Stoney, all we had was guitar and bass. With him, it made a good selection for the show.

Tracy: How did you get from West Virginia to The Grand Ole Opry in Nashville?

Wilma Lee: My family continued to perform and I got married and had Carol. Stoney said that we could not raise a family playing Country Music so he got a job driving a truck

311

for Vaughn Beverage. They sold soft drinks such as Squirt. He had to get up at 3:00 am and at times he would not get home until midnight. The man who owned the company would wait for him and help him load and unload he truck. After about six months of that, Stoney decided that maybe we could raise a family in the music business.

Tracy: How did you get on the Grand Ole Opry?

Wilma Lee: Stoney and I went to Nebraska and then to Indiana and Randy Blake, who was the program director of WJJD in Chicago heard us on the radio and offered us a job. We went to WJJD and worked the Breakfast Hour Folly. From there, the union called a strike and we had to get up every morning and get a program ready in case the strike was settled. They never did settle. They were trying to force the Atlas Brothers on WJJD to hire ten more entertainers. They already had twenty. They were all on a big salary so it cost everyone their jobs. From there, we went to Fairmont, West Virginia and formed our own band. We did that for two years and then went to Arkansas. We worked in Arkansas for 13 months and then to North Carolina. It was a great station with a big crowd. It was settled in the mountains so if you went over the mountain, you could not be heard. We found that out when we went to Boone, North Carolina to work and no one but the janitor showed up. Stoney asked the janitor what he thought happened and he told Stoney that they were unable to get the radio station in that area so the people did not know who we were. We were there for about four months and then went to Wheeling, West Virginia, and were there for ten years and then finally to the Grand Ole Opry.

Tracy: You have had a very busy career. Who is responsible for your early recordings?

Wilma Lee: My first recordings were done for Richtone in Ashville, North Carolina.

Tracy: "Walking My Lord Up Calvary Hill" is a very poplar song.

Wilma Lee: Ruby Moody wrote that song. She wrote several songs. Hank Snow recorded some of her songs as well. We were recording for Hickory Records at the time. First we were on Columbia Records and then we went to Hickory Records. Fred Rose was a great songwriter and he wanted to listen to what we were going to record. When we got to that one, he wanted to see the words. He said the first verse should be the chorus so he changed it around and made it the hit that it was. It was recorded three different times.

Tracy: When did Stoney pass away?

Wilma Lee: March 22, 1977.

Tracy: The two of you were well known as Wilma Lee and Stoney Cooper, I am sure that it was a hard decision as to what to do after his death.

Wilma Lee: Stoney had not been doing so well. He had several heart attacks and he told me that he was going to send me out with the band and he would book the shows for me. He really enjoyed show business and he never met a stranger. I can still see him standing and talking with the fiddle tucked under his arm. He got sick really easy. He was hurting across his shoulder and he went to the doctor and the doctor thought that it was just the flu so he gave him a shot of penicillin and a prescription. He got to where he did not want to get on the bus and ride, even though he had his own bunk. He sent me out to look at motor coaches. I did and brought it all to him. He found the one that he thought would be the best one so we watched them build it ground up. The day we bought it, he took me to the River Gate Shopping Mall at 11:00 pm and taught me how to drive it in the parking lot. The police came by to see what we were doing and realized Stoney was training me. I drove as long as 18 hours at a time. Stoney would always remind me that it was not a car, it was a truck and that I do not drive it by looking out of the rear view mirror. I had to learn to look at the side mirrors in order to read the traffic. Stony was preparing me for the future. He did not say so but that is exactly what he was doing.

Tracy: You had a very successful career on you own.

Wilma Lee: I have had many good things happen to me. In October, my home state of West Virginia named me Grand Marshall of the National Forest Festival Parade. There were over 200,000 people who paid $10 a ticket to get a seat on the parade route. I rode the parade with the Governor and was named a distinguished West Virginian. I was told that it was something that was given sparingly and only to people like Presidents. The Senators came up and they named a road after me and put up a big sign in the little town where I was born, Valley Head, West Virginia, and under the sign, there was another sign that said, "Home of Wilma Lee Cooper.

Tracy: How many years have you been on the Grand Ol Opry?

Wilma Lee: Forty-two.

Tracy: You are one of the pillars of the Grand Ole Opry.

Wilma Lee: Yes, I am. I am one of the oldest ladies here.

Tracy: What does the Grand Ole Opry mean to you?

Wilma Lee: The Grand Ole Opry was always the center of Country Music while I was growing up. That is what everyone worked for, to get to the Grande Ole Opry. It is like obtaining a goal but it is more than that. The Grand Ole Opry is the home of what we have left for homes for Country Music. We use to have a lot of shows throughout the country. But the Grand Ole Opry is the only one that I know of that is left so it is like a home for Country Music and it should be protected as such.

Tracy: What does the future hold for you?

Wilma Lee: I have thought a lot about retiring but I like to go too much. I am alone. I just lost my sister, Jerri Johnson, she worked 12 years with Roy Acuff and then she worked with my cousin Jody until he died. After I lost Stoney, she started traveling with me and worked on my shows. People really liked her. I lost her July 10. I tried to take care of her and work the Opry as well. She just got so bad. She had a doctor's appointment April 28 and I had to carry her out to the car. The doctor put her in the hospital and she never came home. It was really hard for me because she was all that was left. She was like a companion. Carol is still here but I live 130 miles from the Grande Ole Opry and she has her own family. The Good Lord has been good to me.

Tracy: Thank you Wilma for talking with me tonight.

Wilma Lee: I want to tell you that every time I go to Texas, I have a really great time. I always have big crowds. I worked Glen Rose and there was another group there and there were so many people that the police had to come and tell some people that they had to leave. . Also, there was a well-dressed gentleman who come by and told me that I had the best-presented show that he had ever seen. That was such a nice compliment.

Justin Trevino and I were together during this interview in Nashville. Wilma Lee was so open and ready for the interview. It is always so easy to conduct an interview when you have a receptive participant. It was great to hear the excitement in Wilma Lee's voice as she spoke of the radio days.

In the Golden Age, those radio programs were really the savior of entertainers of the day. Each major station had their own "superstars" and they could make a good living finding a sponsor and working show dates within the radio listening area.

Stoney and Wilma Lee were part of that pioneering era and she transcended into television and beyond. It amazed me that in her 70's, she would often get standing ovations at the Opry while competing with the likes of Vince Gill and Garth Brooks.

Justin and I were back in Nashville shortly after Wilma Lee's last major stroke. We visited the wheel chair bound legend. She was happy to visit with us and talk about the "great days." Unfortunately those days were over. She cried and I will have to admit that we did too.

HEART OF TEXAS RECORDS

1701 South Bridge Street
Brady, Texas 76825
(325) 597-1895
www.heartoftexascountry.com

JUSTIN TREVINO
"Too Many Heartaches"
"More Loud Music & Strong Wine"
"Before You Say Amen"
"Texas On A Saturday Night" With
Johnny Bush

LEONA WILLIAMS
"Honorary Texan"
"San Quentin's First Lady"
"I Love You Because"

FERLIN HUSKY
"The Way It Was"

FRANKIE MILLER
"Family Man"

CURTIS POTTER
"Down In Texas Today"
"Them Old Honky Tonks"
"Chicago Dancin' Girls"

BIG BILL LISTER
"Remembering Hank Williams"

DARRELL McCALL
"Old Memories and Wine"
"The Essential Darrell McCall"

AMBER DIGBY
"Music From The Honky Tonks"
"Here Come The Teardrops

PRETTY MISS NORMA JEAN
"Loneliest Star In Texas"

VARIOUS ARTISTS
"Heart of Texas Honky Tonk"

www.heartoftexascountry.com
All Full Length CD's Only $13.95
With Free Shipping